Cambodia
a country study

Federal Research Division
Library of Congress
Edited by Russell R. Ross
Research Completed
December 1987

On the cover: Detail from a tower of the Bayon Temple, circa A.D. 1200

Third Edition, First Printing, 1990.

Library of Congress Cataloging-in-Publication Data

Cambodia: A Country Study.

    Area handbook series, DA pam 550–50
    Research completed December 1987.
    Bibliography: pp. 323–44.
    Includes index.
    1. Cambodia. I. Ross, Russell R., 1935-   . II. Library of Congress. Federal Research Division. III. Series. IV. Series: Area handbook series.

DS554.3.C34   1989   959.6   89–600150

Headquarters, Department of the Army
DA Pam 550–50

For sale by the Superintendent of Documents, U.S. Government Printing Office
Washington, D.C. 20402

Foreword

This volume is one in a continuing series of books now being prepared by the Federal Research Division of the Library of Congress under the Country Studies—Area Handbook Program. The last page of this book lists the other published studies.

Most books in the series deal with a particular foreign country, describing and analyzing its political, economic, social, and national security systems and institutions, and examining the interrelationships of those systems and the ways they are shaped by cultural factors. Each study is written by a multidisciplinary team of social scientists. The authors seek to provide a basic understanding of the observed society, striving for a dynamic rather than a static portrayal. Particular attention is devoted to the people who make up the society, their origins, dominant beliefs and values, their common interests and the issues on which they are divided, the nature and extent of their involvement with national institutions, and their attitudes toward each other and toward their social system and political order.

The books represent the analysis of the authors and should not be construed as an expression of an official United States government position, policy, or decision. The authors have sought to adhere to accepted standards of scholarly objectivity. Corrections, additions, and suggestions for changes from readers will be welcomed for use in future editions.

Louis R. Mortimer
Acting Chief
Federal Research Division
Library of Congress
Washington, D.C. 20540

Acknowledgments

The authors are indebted to a number of individuals in government agencies and at private institutions who shared their time and specialized knowledge to provide research data and perspective to the production of this book. Among them were Bill Herod and Patricia D. Norland of the Indochina Project, Ok Soeum of the Cambodian Buddhist Association, and Rath Chhim of the MRM Language Research Center. Bill Herod, Frank Tatu, and Mr. and Mrs. Robert E. Hammerquist generously shared their personal and, in many cases, unique photographs of Cambodia for use in this book.

The authors also wish to express their appreciation to members of the Library of Congress staff who contributed to the preparation of this volume. These included Richard F. Nyrop who reviewed and coordinated all chapters; Robert L. Worden who reviewed all draft chapters; and Martha E. Hopkins, who, in addition to editing a chapter, managed editing and production of the entire book. Andrea Matles Savada was responsible for seeing the book through to its completion after the departure of the editor of the book. Other Library of Congress staff members who contributed substantial efforts were David P. Cabitto, Sandra K. Cotugno, and Kimberly A. Lord, who prepared and arranged all graphic material; Teresa E. Kamp, who drew the cover and chapter heading illustrations; Harriett R. Blood, who drew the topography map; Susan M. Lender, who reviewed the maps; Tracy Henry Coleman and Meridel Jackson, who performed word processing for all chapters; editorial assistants Barbara Edgerton, Izella Watson, and Monica Shimmin, who helped prepared the manuscript in final form; and Malinda B. Neale of the Library of Congress Composing Unit, who prepared the camera-ready copy under the supervision of Peggy F. Pixley.

Others who contributed to the book were Richard Kollodge, Marilyn L. Majeska, Michael Pleasants, and Catherine Schwartzstein, who edited chapters, and Shirley Kessel, who prepared the index.

Contents

Chapter 2. The Society and Its Environment 73
Robert K. Headley, Jr.

Chapter 3. The Economy 139
Tuyet L. Cosslett

Glossary 341

Index 343

List of Figures

Preface

The previous edition of *Cambodia: A Country Study* was compiled in 1972 when the ill-fated Khmer Republic (see Appendix B) was fighting for its life against the Khmer Rouge (see Appendix B). In the one and one-half decades since that time, profound upheavals have wrought substantial political changes in the country. These changes, and the regimes that sought to impose them, are only now beginning to be studied with objectivity. In addition, the quickening pace of negotiations concerning the future of the country suggests that a watershed period in its modern history may be approaching. It is, accordingly, time for a new country study, not only to catch up with the momentous developments of the past fifteen years, but also to establish some point of departure, some bench mark by which to interpret future events.

This is a completely new book, and, unlike the previous edition, it follows the standard, revised format of the entire country study series. It presents its narrative under five major concomitants of the Cambodian experience: historical setting, society and environment, economy, government and politics, and national security. Sources of information for this study included both monographs and serials, especially material published since 1975. Chapter bibliographies appear at the end of the book, and a brief, annotated bibliographic note on sources recommended for further reading is included at the end of each chapter. Measurements are given in the metric system; a conversion table is provided to assist readers who are unfamiliar with metric measurements (see table 1, Appendix A). A glossary is included.

It should be noted that, as a result of the Khmer Rouge policy of eradicating the traces of its predecessor and of establishing a ruthlessly self-sufficient, anti-modernistic regime, after mid-1975, statistical and quantitative data for Democratic Kampuchea are contradictory and virtually nonexistent. As for its successor, the People's Republic of Kampuchea, such data are only now becoming available, and they remain fragmentary and contradictory. Cambodia continues to be a desperately poor country, its infrastructure ravaged by war, and its thin stratum of educated citizens either in exile or nearly wiped out during the Khmer Rouge years; it is thus scarcely able to compile data that one has come to expect of other nations. Nevertheless, the country is making an effort to bind its wounds and to reestablish sovereignty over its territory, without enduring either a suffocating Vietnamese presence or a chilling reimposition of Khmer Rouge authority. More and better data should become available as Cambodia slowly rehabilitates itself and resumes its place in the Asian family of nations.

A word of explanation is needed concerning the use of "Cambodia" instead of "Kampuchea" to designate the country. According to historian David P. Chandler, both terms are derived from "Kambuja," a Sanskrit word thought to have been applied originally to a north Indian tribe. The selection of "Cambodia," therefore, was without ideological connotation. It is more recognizable to the English-speaking reader, and it adheres to the standard practice of the United States Board on Geographic Names (BGN), which also has been followed in the spelling of all place names. In April 1989, after the cut-off date of research for this book, Prime Minister Hun Sen of the People's Republic of Kampuchea announced that the name of the country had been changed to the State of Cambodia. In recent years some provinces have been combined, renamed, and then divided again several times. The most recent case is that of Bantay Meanchey, the formation of which—from parts of Batdambang, Siemreab-Otdar Meanchey, and Pouthisat—was announced in late 1987 to take effect in 1988. For the geographic terms occurring most frequently, such as names of provinces, the BGN designations together with the more common, journalistic equivalents are as follows:

BGN Name	Common Name
Batdambang	Battambang
Kampong Cham	Kompong Cham
Kampong Chhnang	Kompong Chnang
Kampong Saom	Kompong Som
Kampong Spoe	Kompong Speu
Kampong Thum	Kompong Thom
Kaoh Kong	Koh Kong
Kracheh	Kratie
Mondol Kiri	Mondolkiri
Otdar Meanchey	Oddar Meanchey
Pouthisat	Pursat
Rotanokiri	Ratanakiri
Stoeng Treng	Stung Treng
Takev	Takeo

Country Profile

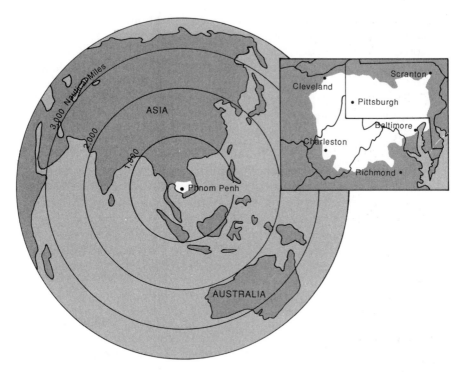

Country

Formal Name: Coalition Government of Democratic Kampuchea (CGDK) (insurgent coalition)
People's Republic of Kampuchea (PRK) (government in Phnom Penh)

Short Form: Cambodia

Term for Citizens: Cambodians

Capital: Phnom Penh

Date of Independence: November 9, 1953

Geography

Size: Total area 181,040 square kilometers, about size of Missouri; country shares 800-kilometer border with Thailand on north and west, 541-kilometer border with Laos on northeast, 1,228-kilometer border with Vietnam on east and southeast; coastline along Gulf of Thailand about 443 kilometers.

Topography: Most salient topographical feature lacustrine plain formed by inundations of Tonle Sap (Great Lake), measuring about 2,590 square kilometers during dry season to about 24,605 square kilometers during rainy season. This densely populated plain devoted to wet rice cultivation constitutes heartland of Cambodia. Most (about 75 percent) of country lies at elevations of less than 100 meters above sea level, except for Cardamom Mountains (highest elevation 1,771 meters), their north-south extension to the east, Elephant Range (elevation range 500–1,000 meters) and steep escarpment of Dangrek Mountains (average elevation 500 meters) along northern border with Thailand.

Climate: Temperatures range from 10°C to 38°C. Tropical monsoons: southwest monsoon blowing inland in northeasterly direction brings moisture-laden winds from Gulf of Thailand/Indian Ocean from May to October with period of heaviest precipitation September–October; northeast monsoon blowing in southwesterly direction toward coast ushers in dry season, November to March, with period of least rainfall January–February.

Society

Population: In 1987 estimates vary from 6.3 to 7.3 million with possibly more than 500,000 Cambodians scattered in Thailand and abroad as refugees; average annual growth targeted at 2.3 percent; estimated urban population of more than 10 percent; estimated population density averages about 36 per square kilometer.

Ethnic Groups: Ethnically homogeneous, more than 90 percent Khmer; national minorities comprise about 3 percent of total population; Cham (see Glossary), of Islamic faith, most significant minority group, other scattered tribal minorities in upland and forested areas. Reportedly some Vietnamese immigration since 1981–82. Some Chinese in urban areas, numbers unknown.

Languages: National language Khmer, a member of Mon-Khmer subfamily of Austroasiatic language group. Russian and Vietnamese taught in Phnom Penh and other urban areas.

Religion: Theravada Buddhism, suppressed by Khmer Rouge (see Appendix B), revived but controlled under successor regime; wats (temples) and monks privately supported; wats administered by lay committees; Buddhist clergy or *sangha* (see Glossary); chairman (*prathean*) heads ecclesiastical hierarchy.

Education: Rate of literacy about 48 percent. In late 1980s total estimated school enrollment 1.3 million (primary), 369,500 (secondary). Schooling follows Vietnamese model with three levels: primary grades 1-4; lower secondary education, grades 5-7; upper secondary education, grades 8-10; education at all levels hampered by lack of facilities, teachers, and instructional materials. Postsecondary education consists of twenty teacher-training schools, plus institutions offering professional or technical instruction. Soviet and Vietnamese instructors heavily represented in educational institutions. Admission to higher education based on political reliability.

Health: Average life expectancy 48.5 years (male 47 years, female 49.9 years) for the period 1985-90; some prevalent diseases are tuberculosis, malaria, infectious and parasitical illnesses; infant mortality 160 per thousand live births (1986); nonspecific gastro-enteritis accounts for disproportionate number of infant deaths; localized malnutrition and poor hygienic conditions exacerbate debility of population and susceptibility to illness. Total of 34 hospitals and 1,349 rural dispensaries nationwide; in countryside, network of primary care facilities being established with international help; hospitals planned or already established in provincial capitals, dispensaries at district (*srok*) level, first aid stations at village (*khum*) level; extension of health care greatly impeded by lack of trained personnel and inadequately developed infrastructure (especially clean water, and distribution or availability of medical supplies/equipment.)

Economy

General—Statistical economic data, including gross national product (GNP—see Glossary), gross domestic product (GDP—see Glossary) and balance of payments generally unavailable, lacking, or unreliable in late 1980s. Nation evolving toward socialistic central planning, but more than 50 percent of economy, especially retail trade and small scale manufacturing, remains in private sector. First Five-Year Program for Socioeconomic Restoration and Development (1986-90), hereafter called First Plan, inaugurated, with priority on increased cultivation of rice and rubber, increased exploitation of forest and aquatic resources; economically active population about 2.5 to 3 million. Collectivization of agriculture undertaken through organization of from seven to fifteen-families in solidarity groups (*krom samaki*) as basic production units.

Agriculture, Forestry, Fishing: About 80 percent of labor force engaged in agriculture, forestry, fishing. Main crop is paddy rice; output 2 million tons in 1986; area under cultivation 1.2 million hectares in 1987. Under First Plan, output expected to increase

7 percent annually to 350 kilograms per person by 1990. Production impeded by neglected irrigation systems during Pol Pot years, localized insecurity caused by forays of anti-Vietnamese Khmer insurgents, and lack of phosphate fertilizers. In 1986 principal food crops were maize, cassavas, sweet potatoes, groundnuts, beans, and sesame seeds. Principal commercial crop is rubber. Forests cover approximately 70 percent of land area; first reforestation project initiated in northeastern and southwestern regions of country. Fishing conducted in Tonle Sap, rivers, and offshore in Gulf of Thailand.

Industry: Industrial sector developing slowly because of lack of power and raw materials; accounts for less than 10 percent of labor force. In countryside, unknown number of rice-processing mills and sawmills reportedly back into operation by 1986; in urban areas about sixty state-owned factories produce light consumer goods such as plastic items, hand tools, soft drinks, cigarettes, textiles, nails, jute bags, soap, and basic pharmaceuticals; phosphate fertilizer plant, distillery, and brick tile plant reportedly operating; in 1987 small-scale artisans being collectivized in Phnom Penh, development plans call for opening of brewery, plywood, and cement factories.

Services: Total public sector employment (including state employees, industrial workers, artisans, party cadres, teachers, and armed forces personnel) amounts to about 8 percent of economically active population.

Resources: Limited: gemstones, gold, silver, phosphate, limestone, clay; possible deposits of salt and coal; unexploited deposits of iron and manganese ore, bauxite, and silicon reported; hydroelectric potential from Mekong and Basak rivers.

Exports: Approximately US$3 million in 1986; principal exports natural rubber (latex), timber, resin, maize, tobacco, and soybeans. Rubber and forest products offer best hope for expansion in near term; main export partners Vietnam, Soviet Union (purchases nearly entire Cambodian output of latex), and other countries belonging to the Council for Mutual Economic Assistance (CMEA, CEMA, or Comecon—Glossary).

Imports: Approximately US$17 million in 1986; principal imports foodstuffs, fuels, machinery, textiles, pharmaceuticals, and chemicals. Main import partners Vietnam, Soviet Union, and other Comecon countries, especially Poland and Czechoslovakia.

Balance of Payments: Negative trade balance from 1979 until 1987. In 1984 extended public debt US$503 million; debt service payments US$4 million.

Exchange Rate: Official rate 100 Cambodian riels per United States dollar; unofficial rate about 123 riels per dollar; Cambodian riel not negotiable in international money markets.

Transportation and Communications

Railroads: Two routes of one-meter-gauge-track: Phnom Penh-Kampong Saom route, 260 kilometers long; Phnom Penh-Batdambang-Sisophon route, 352 kilometers long; railroads disrupted during regime of Democratic Kampuchea but restored to service early 1980s. Both routes remain insecure and subject to sporadic guerrilla attacks.

Roads: Total 13,350 kilometers; about 2,600 kilometers paved (bituminous), 7,150 kilometers improved (crushed stone, gravel, earth), 3,600 kilometers unimproved; main roads paved but in varying states of disrepair.

Ports: Main seaport Kampong Saom, (Gulf of Thailand). Main riverine port Phnom Penh, at junction of Tonle Sab, Mekong, and Basak rivers; minor ports (Gulf of Thailand) Ream and Kampot. National merchant marine consists of three vessels with total displacement of 3,800 deadweight tons.

Inland Waterways: Total length about 3,982 kilometers; principal arteries are middle Mekong River (runs from Laos through Cambodia and Vietnam to South China Sea), and Tonle Sab and Basak rivers from Tonle Sap (Great Lake) to Cambodian-Vietnamese border; both wide (up to two kilometers) and navigable, with ferries at Kampong Cham, Tonle Bet, Sre Ambel, Stoeng Treng, and Phumi Prek Khsay (Neak Luong); precipitous falls and rapids occur near Laotian border and in vicinity of Kracheh city.

Civil Airports: Thirteen usable airfields, including 8 with permanent surface runways, 2 with runways 2,400 to 3,600 meters, 5 with runways 1,200 to 2,400 meters; main international airport Pochentong near Phnom Penh; secondary airports at Kang Keng at Ream, at Siemreab and Batdambang. National airline Air Kampuchea, inventory three Antonov-24s; scheduled air service to Batdambang and Ho Chi Minh City (Vietnam).

Telecommunications: In late 1980s, one earth satellite station, part of Intersputnik communications network; radio telephone link (via Intersputnik) between Phnom Penh and Ho Chi Minh City (Vietnam); about 7,300 telephones countrywide. One radio broadcasting station (''Voice of the Kampuchean People'') with medium and short wave capability; about 171,000 radio receivers countrywide, television service inaugurated with broadcasts twice a week in late 1980s.

Government and Politics

Two governments compete for internal legitimacy and for international recognition: Coalition Government of Democratic Kampuchea (CGDK—see Appendix B) and People's Republic of Kampuchea (PRK—see Appendix B).

CGDK: Tripartite coalition consisting of Party of Democratic Kampuchea (PDK—see Appendix B, or Khmer Rouge—see Appendix B), and two noncommunist movements, Khmer People's National Liberation Front (KPNLF—see Appendix B) and National United Front for an Independent, Neutral, Peaceful, and Cooperative Cambodia (Front Uni National pour un Cambodge Indépendant, Neutre, Pacifique, et Coopératif—FUNCINPEC—see Appendix B). CGDK recognized internationally by the United Nations and a few non-communist states; controls little territory except inaccessible guerrilla areas in northeastern and southwestern Cambodia; administers some camps along Thai border.

Government: A president and a prime minister; vice-president in charge of foreign affairs, and at next subordinate echelon, six coordinating committees established: culture and education, national defense, economy and finance, public health and social affairs, military affairs, and press and information affairs.

Politics: Coalition partners exist in uneasy alliance, united only by opposition to Vietnamese occupation forces and government in Phnom Penh; coordinating committees staffed by one member from each movement comprising CGDK.

Major International Memberships: United Nations and many of its specialized agencies; Asian Development Bank, Group of 77, General Agreement on Tariffs and Trade, World Bank (see Glossary), International Monetary Fund (see Glossary), Interpol, International Red Cross, International Telecommunications Union, and Nonaligned Movement.

PRK: Constitutes the government in Phnom Penh which exercises de facto control over most of Cambodian territory; recognized internationally by about three dozen Marxist and nonaligned states and revolutionary movements.

Government: Marxist government evolving toward socialism, sustained by large Vietnamese military presence. National Assembly,

117 members defined constitutionally as "supreme organ of state power," and body in which legislative authority vested; assembly selects members of Council of State that promulgates and interprets laws, the chairman of which serves as head of state; Council of State acts as secretariat for National Assembly and performs some assembly functions between parliamentary sessions. Council of Ministers, also responsible to National Assembly, exercises direct executive authority for administering government of the PRK down to local levels.

Politics: Kampuchean (or Khmer) People's Revolutionary Party (KPRP—see Appendix B) only political party permitted in late 1987 in areas under Phnomh Penh's control; functions at national level through Political Bureau (nine full and two candidate members) and Central Committee (thirty-one full and fourteen candidate members); mass auxiliary organizations foster patriotism and nurture party activism among population; most prominent of organization Kampuchean (or Khmer) United Front for National Construction and Defense (KUFNCD—see Appendix B); both KPRP and KUFNCD active down to local level and maintain nationwide network of committees at all provincial and district echelons. Other mass organizations include Kampuchean Federation of Trade Unions, Kampuchean People's Revolutionary Youth Union, Kampuchean Revolutionary Women's Association, and Kampuchean Revolutionary Youth Association.

Administrative Divisions: Two municipalities (Phnom Penh and Kampong Saom); eighteen provinces, subdivided into about 122 districts.

Legal System: Ministry of Justice, Office of Public Prosecutor, and People's Supreme Court exist at national level; at subordinate echelons, people's revolutionary courts established at provincial and municipal levels; court officials include president, vice-president and people's councillors. Separate system of military tribunals exist for armed forces, but in 1987 functions remained unknown.

Major International Memberships: None; nevertheless, government in Phnom Penh receives assistance from a number of communist and nonaligned states and from private international humanitarian organizations. Close bilateral relationship exists with Vietnam as result of Treaty of Peace, Friendship and Cooperation signed in February 1979.

National Security

Armed Forces of CGDK: In 1987 coalition forces remained unintegrated, with total numbers unknown. National Army of

Democratic Kampuchea (NADK—see Appendix B, also known as Khmer Rouge)—roughly 40,000 to 50,000 combatants in three to six divisions, distributed in four autonomous military regions. Khmer People's National Liberation Armed Forces (KPNLAF—see Appendix B)—strength waning; but conjecturally had 8,000 to 14,000 combatants organized into battalions and regiments, grouped administratively into 9 military regions. Sihanouk National Army (Armée Nationale Sihanoukiste—ANS—see Appendix B), strength increasing; has 7,000 to 11,000 combatants organized into a command structure and maneuver battalions grouped under 6 brigade headquarters.

Armed Forces of PRK: In 1987 military establishment comprised regular/main forces, provincial/regional forces, and village militia/local forces; embryonic coastal/riverine navy and air force existed; total military strength for all components unknown, but estimated to surpass 40,000 personnel; armed forces organized administratively into four military regions under Ministry of National Defense and General Staff in Phnom Penh.

Major Tactical Units of CGDK: Tactical units deployed usually comprise platoons or companies, occasionally single battalions. (People's Republic of Kampuchea): Seven understrength regular/main force divisions, with at least three deployed in border provinces of western Cambodia; several independent brigades and regiments; as many as four tank battalions, and combat support formations; naval forces one battalion; air force possibly two to four understrength squadrons; provincial/regional forces organized into battalions, generally deployed one per province, with greater number in border provinces; village militia/local forces organized into platoons and squads, generally deployed at subdistrict and village level; women heavily represented in militia/local forces.

Major Weapons/Equipment of CGDK: Small arms, light crew-served weapons, and equipment originating from China and possibly from Singapore.

Major Weapons/Equipment of PRK: Obsolescent tanks of Soviet or Chinese origin; armored personnel carriers of Soviet or United States origin; light to medium artillery pieces; small arms of Soviet origin; naval forces, small patrol and amphibious craft; air force, possibly MiG-21/FISHBED fighter aircraft, and Mi-8 (HIP) transport helicopters.

Security Expenditures of CGDK: Unknown; all military materiel assumed to be grant aid from China and from members of the Association of Southeast Asian Nations (ASEAN).

Security Expenditures of PRK: Unknown; all military materiel assumed to be grant aid from Soviet Union and Vietnam; estimated value of imported armaments US$150 million in 1986.

Foreign Troops and Advisers: (People's Republic of Kampuchea): Vietnamese expeditionary force numbering possibly 100,000 to 200,00 troops organized into 10 to 12 divisions under 4 Military Fronts; Vietnamese force to be withdrawn by 1990. Vietnamese military advisers with Cambodian units at least to battalion level; Warsaw Pact advisers at armed forces training institutions and possibly at upper defense echelons.

Internal Security: In 1987 insurgents of the Coalition Government of Democratic Kampuchea, backed by China and ASEAN nations, engaged in guerrilla warfare against People's Republic of Kampuchea government in Phnom Penh, and Vietnamese forces in Cambodia; some of country insecure because of sporadic guerrilla raids and ambushes, but guerrillas possessed insufficient strength or armaments to take and hold any urban area or to topple government.

Figure 1. Administrative Divisions of Cambodia, 1986

Introduction

ALTHOUGH THE LAND occupied by Cambodia has been populated for millennia, the area's history was unrecorded until the Chinese chronicles of the early Christian era. In the fewer than 2,000 years of its imperfectly documented existence, the Cambodian state has evolved along the lines of ascension, dominance, and retrogression inherent in all civilizations.

Historians surmise that by the first century A.D. a small number of Khmer (or Cambodian) states already existed on the fringes of the earliest recorded state in the region, the empire of Funan. Centered in the Mekong Delta of present-day Vietnam, Funan derived its power from commerce. With its port of Oc Eo on the Gulf of Thailand, Funan was well-placed to control maritime traffic between India and China. According to Chinese annals, Funan was a highly developed and prosperous state with an extensive canal system for transportation and irrigation, a fleet of naval vessels, a capital city with brick buildings, and a writing system based on Sanskrit. The inhabitants, whose adherence to Indian cultural institutions apparently coexisted with Mahayana Buddhism, were organized into a highly stratified society.

When the small Khmer states to the northwest of the Mekong Delta emerged into recorded history, it was to make war upon the declining empire of Funan. Between A.D. 550–650, these Khmer states overran their adversary, which fell apart, losing its tributary states on the Kra Isthmus and along the Gulf of Thailand.

Chaos and economic decline followed the fall of Funan, but the sequence of events over the next 500 years led to the ascension of the Cambodian state and its evolution into an increasingly powerful and dynamic entity. The first unified and distinctly Khmer polity to emerge after Funan was Chenla. It absorbed the Indianized cultural legacy of its predecessor and established its capital near the Tonle Sap (Great Lake), the heartland of Cambodia, then as now. Under expansionist rulers, its authority was pushed into the territories of present-day Thailand and Laos. The development of Chenla was not marked by an unrelieved accretion of power, however. Divisive forces quickly resulted in a split into Land (or Upper) Chenla and Water (or Lower) Chenla. Land Chenla demonstrated the greater vitality, controlled some thirty provincial cities, and sent emissaries to China under the Tang dynasty. Water Chenla slipped into vassalage to Java.

The historical ascension of the Khmer polity began during the early 800s. The initiator of the period was the first empire builder, Jayavarman II (A.D. 802–50), who carved out a feudal state generally encompassing modern Cambodia. Jayavarman revived the cult of Devaraja, an Indianized cultural institution that was intended to confer, through elaborate rituals and symbols, heavenly approbation or even divine status upon the ruler. Following the reign of Jayavarman II, the two Chenlas were reunited peacefully, and the Khmer polity continued to develop, establishing over time a priestly hierarchy, an armed force and police, a provincial administration of subordinate officials, a system of courts, corvée labor by the peasants, and a capital on the site of Angkor near the Tonle Sap.

The Khmer state reached its apogee in the Angkorian period—also called the empire of Angkor—during the period from the eleventh century to the thirteenth century, when it was ruled by a succession of able monarchs. The last great monarch of the Angkorian period was Jayavarman VII (1181–ca. 1218). He reversed the Cham encroachments that had taken place after the death of Suryavarman II (1113–50) and carried the war to the enemy, conquering Champa itself and briefly reducing it to a Khmer vassal state. At its greatest extent, the Angkorian empire of Jayavarman VII encompassed not only Champa on the coast of southern Vietnam but also extended north to the vicinity of Vientiane in present-day Laos and south to include the small trading city-states of the Malay Peninsula. Jayavarman continued the public works program of his predecessors, uniting his realm by elevated military causeways with resthouses at intervals. He also built hospitals for the aged and the infirm and sponsored the construction of Angkor Thom and the Bayon, the last major temples of Angkorian times and splendid edifices in their own right, but presaging the decadence that shortly set in (see The Angkorian Period, ch. 1).

Jayavarman VII's wars and public works exacted a heavy toll on the finances and the human labor force of the Angkorian empire. The drain of resources coincided with the gradual intrusion of Theravada Buddhism, with its egalitarian focus, at the expense of the Indianized cults that stressed a hierarchical, stratified society (see Buddhism, ch. 2). Whether it was this development or the inability of the Khmer monarchs to command the fealty of their subjects that led to a societal breakdown remains open to conjecture. Also coupled with these internal developments was the accelerated southward migration of the Thai, who, dislodged from their state in southwestern China by the Mongols in the mid-1200s, flooded into the Menam Chao Phraya Valley. Subject to internal and external pressures, the Khmer state became unable to defend itself at the very time its enemies were growing stronger. Thai attacks were stepped up around 1350, and they continued until Angkor itself was captured and sacked in 1430-31. The fall of Angkor ended the dominant period of the Khmer state. Thereafter, its borders shrank, and it controlled little more than the area around the Tonle Sap, the alluvial plain to the southeast, and some territory west of the Mekong River. To the east, the collapse of the kingdom of Champa in 1471 opened the Khmer lands of the Mekong Delta to the steady Vietnamese expansion southward.

The long waning of the Cambodian empire after the fall of Angkor is not well documented. The transfer of the capital from the Angkorian region around the Tonle Sap to the vicinity of Phnom Penh may have heralded the shift of emphasis from an agricultural to a trading society. Even with this change, the Khmer state retained some of its vitality into the seventeenth century, alternately trading and warring with its neighbors. By the eighteenth century, however, it had become a backwater buffer state, existing solely on the sufferance of its increasingly powerful neighbors, Thailand and Vietnam. The imposition of the French protectorate upon Cambodia prevented its neighbors from swallowing it completely.

Cambodia's status declined further under the French, however, when the last vestiges of its sovereignty were lost, especially after 1884, when Paris imposed another unequal treaty that went beyond the original protectorate of 1863. The newer pact limited the authority of the king, abolished slavery, stationed colonial officials in the countryside, and codified land ownership. Reaction to the 1884 treaty produced the only sustained rebellion during colonial times. Unrest persisted until 1886 and was put down with troops from Vietnam (see The French Protectorate, ch. 1). Thereafter, the French consolidated their grasp on the country, and Cambodia became merely a heavily taxed, efficient rice-producing colony, the inhabitants of which were known for their passivity.

As the Southeast Asian colonies of the European powers stood on the brink of World War II in 1940 and 1941, the utter powerlessness of Cambodia was illustrated by the fact that it was compelled to surrender its provinces of Siemreab and Batdambang (Battambang), which included some of the country's most fertile agricultural area, to Thailand, as a result of the brief Franco-Siamese War. In addition, some months later it was the French, not the Cambodians, who selected the candidate who would sit on the throne in Phnom Penh. Their choice was the young Prince Norodom Sihanouk, because French officials considered him more manipulable than the heir apparent. (Sihanouk was then a shy youth, well-disposed toward his role as figurehead monarch, and totally inexperienced in governing. His formidable international reputation lay far in the future.)

In March 1945, the Japanese swept aside the Vichy French administration in Cambodia (as elsewhere in Indochina), and they induced the young king to proclaim independence. The event offered little occasion for euphoria, however. The Japanese remained in control, and then, after the Japanese surrender, the French returned to reimpose their authority, granting the Cambodians, as consolation prizes in early 1946, the right to have a constitution and the right to form political parties.

In the late 1940s and the early 1950s, the struggle for independence in Cambodia took place on several levels. Two political parties were formed under princes of the royal house. The Liberal Party, the more conservative of the two, advocated an evolutionary approach to independence. The Democratic Party, the more radical one, favored the rapid attainment of independence and the formation of whatever political alliances might be necessary. Underground, Cambodian guerrillas took to the jungles to fight the returning French. The Khmer Issarak (see Appendix B), as these guerrillas were called, encompassed disaffected Cambodians from across the entire political spectrum. Meanwhile, the French managed to secure the return of Cambodia's two provinces lost to Thailand in 1941. In 1949, under increasing military pressure from the Viet Minh (see Appendix B) in neighboring Vietnam, the French granted Cambodia qualified self-government in certain areas and an autonomous zone in Batdambang and Siemreab.

Sihanouk continued the political struggle above ground, embarking upon a campaign for independence. Using a combination of private and public initiatives and grandiose gestures, he exacted grudging concessions from a French government increasingly hard-pressed in Indochina by its war against the Viet Minh. In November 1953, Sihanouk announced dramatically that independence had been gained, and he returned triumphantly from Paris to Phnom Penh.

Sihanouk quickly emerged as a leader of stature in his newly independent country. In an effort to gain a freer hand in the politics of his nation, a role he was not permitted to play as the ruler in a constitutional monarchy, he abdicated the throne in 1955 and formed a political movement, the Popular Socialist Community (Sangkum Riastre Niyum, or Sangkum). With control of the Sangkum, Sihanouk succeeded in having himself named both chief of state and head of government. For nearly sixteen years, from 1954 to 1970, he dominated Cambodian politics and ruled at the head of a highly authoritarian and centralized government.

In the countryside, Sihanouk kept the support of the people through his charismatic personality, his highly visible personal forays among the rural peasantry, and his adherence to the traditional symbols and institutions of the Khmer monarchy, such as public audiences and participation in time-honored ceremonies. Among the politicized urban elite, Sihanouk maintained power and kept his opponents off-balance through a range of manipulative stratagems, pitting them against one another when he could and co-opting them with government positions when he could not.

In spite of Sihanouk's efforts, the situation in Cambodia began to go awry in the mid- to late 1960s. Internally, the country had been savaged by economic reverses. The budget was chronically in deficit; United States aid had been terminated; and state socialism had stifled development (see Sihanouk's Peacetime Economy 1953–70, ch. 3). Prices for Cambodia's export commodities—rice and rubber—were declining. Numerous members of the youthful, educated elite were underemployed and dissatisfied. Among the politicized middle class, the military leadership, the intellectuals, and the students, opposition was developing to Sihanouk's authoritarianism. In the countryside, heavy taxation had ignited the shortlived Samlot Rebellion in Batdambang Province. Although suppressed ruthlessly, it refused to die out, and smoldered on in remote corners of Cambodia. Disaffected elements still were at large, and some of the country remained insecure. The radical wing of the Kampuchean (or Khmer) Communist Party, (KCP—see Appendix B), led by Saloth Sar (later to be known as Pol Pot), had gone underground and had taken up arms, unleashing its own insurgency against the Sihanouk regime. In the northeast, minority ethnic groups were alienated from the government in Phnom Penh because of its corvée labor, forced resettlement, and assimilationist policies (see Cambodia under Sihanouk, 1954–70, ch. 1).

Internationally, the picture was not much better. Sihanouk tried to maintain a nonaligned course in the country's foreign policy. During its first decade of independence, Cambodia had received aid from East and from West, and it was respected internationally. In the mid- to late 1960s, however, this neutrality was fast eroding, and Cambodia was about to be engulfed by the war in neighboring Vietnam. The country rapidly was becoming a logistical rear area and a safe haven for North Vietnamese and Viet Cong (see Appendix B) forces fighting the Saigon government. Cambodia was exposed to cross-border forays and airstrikes from South Vietnam to neutralize these enemy installations. The Cambodian port of Kampong Saom also was becoming the terminus for Chinese weapons and supplies that were then trucked, sometimes in

Cambodian army vehicles, overland to North Vietnamese and Viet Cong supply depots.

Sihanouk sought to adjust to the prevailing trends in Indochina. He sought to distance Cambodia from South Vietnam and accepted accommodation with North Vietnam and with the National Front for the Liberation of South Vietnam (NFLSVN—see Appendix B), the political arm of the Viet Cong. He broke relations with Washington, looked for support to Beijing—which was then distracted by its Cultural Revolution, and then resumed ties with Washington.

Events in Cambodia were moving out of control, however. When Sihanouk went abroad for a lengthy sojourn in January 1970 to solicit Soviet and Chinese assistance in curbing the presence of North Vietnamese sanctuaries on Cambodian territory, domestic opposition to his regime became more outspoken and soon acquired a momentum of its own. The entire Cambodian National Assembly, led by a rightist cabinet under Premier Lon Nol, voted on March 22 to bar the return of Sihanouk to the country. Cambodia's first post-independence era thus ended, and the country soon was plunged into a period of war, chaos, and human suffering perhaps unparalleled in its history.

The Lon Nol government that succeeded the fall of Sihanouk quickly abolished the monarchy and proclaimed itself the Khmer Republic (see Appendix B). It initially enjoyed wide support among the urban population, but it soon proved itself unequal to the tasks of governing and defending the country and capturing the allegiance of the Cambodian masses. The new government in Phnom Penh began by fanning anti-Vietnamese sentiment among the Khmer population, as a result of which countless numbers of civilian Vietnamese migrants in Cambodia were massacred. The government then turned against the North Vietnamese and the Viet Cong by calling publicly for their ouster from Cambodia and by initiating ineffectual military operations against them. Shortly thereafter, an offensive military thrust of the United States and South Vietnam into Cambodia dislodged North Vietnamese and Viet Cong units from their border sanctuaries; instead of driving them away from Cambodian territory, however, it pushed them deeper into the country, where they soon swept before them the ill-trained, ill-armed, and totally inexperienced Cambodian republican forces.

At the same time, two concurrent developments conspired to erode further the shaky position of the Khmer Republic. The first was that Sihanouk established a government-in-exile in Beijing, where he had fled following his ouster. There, he raised the standard of revolt against the republican regime in Phnom Penh, and he united in a common front with the armed Khmer communist rebels. Both sides saw the advantages to such an alliance of convenience. The Cambodian communists, dubbed the Khmer Rouge (see Appendix B) by Sihanouk, had ignited a small-scale insurgency in early 1968, but they had not been able to move beyond their redoubts in remote corners of Cambodia or to gain mass support in their first two years. Their alliance with Sihanouk, in a broad resistance front called the National United Front of Kampuchea (Front Uni National du Kampuchéa—FUNK—see Appendix B), transformed their forlorn rebellion, which was aided by Washington, into a war of national liberation against a puppet regime in Phnom Penh. At the same time, Sihanouk's name attracted to the FUNK cause Cambodians of every political persuasion, including many people without communist antecedents.

The second development, one with equally serious consequences for the Khmer Republic, was that the North Vietnamese quickly undertook the training of the Khmer Rouge guerrillas to transform them into a conventional fighting force. While this training program was underway, North Vietnamese units temporarily assumed the burden of keeping the Khmer republican forces at bay, an effort that did not tax them unduly. By 1973 the Khmer Rouge were conducting most combat operations against the Phnom Penh government by themselves.

The ill-fated Khmer Republic was unable to defend itself. By 1971 it was on the defensive, and it was losing ground steadily. Fleeing the fighting in the countryside, peasant refugees crowded into the government's shrinking strongholds around Phnom Penh and the provincial centers. Lon Nol's inept and corrupt regime went from one military defeat to another. By early 1975, the situation of the Khmer Republic was so precarious that Phnom Penh itself was invaded, and government control was limited to the provincial centers and to a patch of territory in western Cambodia around the Tonle Sap. In the following months, the Khmer Rouge steadily tightened the noose around the capital until all escape routes were cut off, and resistance collapsed. The fall of Phnom Penh in April 1975 marked the end of the Khmer Republic (see The Fall of Phnom Penh, ch. 1).

For the Cambodian people, the entry of the Khmer Rouge into the capital began the grimmest period in Cambodia's long history. The Khmer Rouge rulers of Democratic Kampuchea, as the regime that supplanted the Khmer Republic was called, envisioned a totally self-sufficient Cambodia. This self-sufficiency was to be achieved by accelerated agricultural production, which in turn would provide the wherewithal to develop the other sectors of the economy.

Self-sufficiency, however, was pursued with such single-minded ruthlessness that between 1 million and 3 million persons died because of purges, beatings, malnourishment, and overwork. To head off opposition to economic and social restructuring, the new regime hunted down and executed virtually anyone who had served the former government. The regime emptied the cities of inhabitants and forced the entire population into rudimentary, badly organized collectives in the countryside; untold numbers died, worked to death under slave labor conditions or executed for minor infractions of camp discipline. At the same time, the regime nurtured an acute paranoia that brooked no potential opposition but that prompted it to eradicate the educated middle class of Cambodia. When this eradication was accomplished, it turned on its own cadres at every echelon, torturing and executing thousands (see Revolutionary Terror, ch. 1). The regime's ruthless extermination of opponents, however, could not ensure its security; ultimately its own paranoia brought it down.

Regionally, the Khmer Rouge paranoia manifested itself in the exacerbation of tensions with Vietnam. During the war against the United States and its allies, commonalities of enemy and of ideology had enabled the Vietnamese and the Cambodians to bridge their mutual distrust. After April 1975, however, with the xenophobic Pol Pot factions of the KCP in control in Phnom Penh, the traditional Cambodian antipathy for the Vietnamese reemerged. The source of the friction was the recurrent cross-border forays by combatants from both sides into the Mekong Delta and the Parrot's Beak area. The Khmer Rouge regime viewed itself as threatened, its territory violated by Vietnam. Hanoi in turn felt compelled to deploy substantial military assets along the border, as fighting continued to erupt on both sides of the frontier. By mid-1978 Hanoi's patience was rapidly running out, as it became obliged to commit division-sized units to pacification missions along the Cambodian border.

Sometime in the fall of 1978, the leadership in Hanoi decided to mount a multi-division punitive expedition into Cambodia. To lend a veneer of political legitimacy to this military undertaking, Hanoi sponsored the establishment of an anti-Pol Pot movement called the Kampuchean (or Khmer) National United Front for National Salvation (KNUFNS—see Appendix B), made up of fugitive Cambodians who had fled the Khmer Rouge. Accompanied by token KNUFNS units, the Vietnamese launched their military campaign into Cambodia in late December 1978 (see Vietnamese Invasion of Cambodia, ch. 5). The Khmer Rouge proved surprisingly vulnerable to the onslaught, and Phnom Penh fell to Hanoi's forces in early January 1979. The Khmer Rouge, defeated militarily for the time being, but not destroyed, ignited a persistent insurgency in the remote regions of Cambodia. The country then embarked upon a decade-long period of fitful rehabilitation, made more precarious by the lack of resources, the enduring guerilla war, and the military occupation by Vietnam.

It was evident that the institutions of the new Cambodian regime, which called itself the People's Republic of Kampuchea (PRK—see Appendix B), were virtually identical to those of Vietnam. In the PRK, only a single, pro-Vietnamese political party was permitted. This party, the Kampuchean (or Khmer) People's Revolutionary Party (KPRP—see Appendix B), was headed by a political bureau with a secretariat and a general secretary in charge. It also had a central committee with a control commission to handle day-by-day affairs (see The Kampuchean, or Khmer, People's Revolutionary Party, ch. 4). The party was backed by a mass movement—the successor to KNUFNS, the Kampuchean (or Khmer) United Front for National Construction and Defense (KUFNCD—see Appendix B) and by a number of front organizations such as labor, women's, and youth groups. As in Vietnam, party and government were intertwined: the same individuals held concurrent leadership positions in both sectors. The Council of State was the highest government body; it reserved to itself the major decision-making authority. A Council of Ministers exercised cabinet functions and was responsible to a National Assembly elected from KPRP members. The National Assembly heard reports from ministers and from the rest of national leadership, but appeared to exercise little legislative authority (see Government Structure, ch. 4).

Cambodian rehabilitation and development were hampered by the civil war that plagued the country after the ouster of the Khmer Rouge. When the Vietnamese drove Pol Pot from power in their December 1978 invasion, they failed to administer the coup de grace to their adversaries, who regrouped their forces and initiated a guerrilla war against Hanoi's occupation forces. Despite their odious reputation and their abominable human rights record, the Khmer Rouge were able to attract guerrilla recruits to their ranks. The Khmer Rouge applied the same coercive measures in the remote areas of Cambodia under their control as those they had used when they ruled all of Cambodia, and they cast themselves as the sole nationalistic force opposing the Vietnamese occupation of Cambodia. In terms of the number of combatants they could muster, the Khmer Rouge, throughout the decade-long civil war, continued to be the largest single guerrilla force in the field.

For many Cambodians, however, the option of joining either the Khmer Rouge or the Vietnamese-installed regime was a Hobson's choice. Consequently, soon after Hanoi's invasion, two additional insurgent movements arose among the Khmer refugees who had fled both Hanoi's and Pol Pot's forces. One of these movements coalesced around the elderly nationalistic figure of Son Sann, a cabinet minister under Sihanouk. Son Sann's movement took the name Khmer People's National Liberation Front (KPNLF—see Appendix B), and its armed wing was called the Khmer People's National Liberation Armed Forces (KPNLAF—see Appendix B). In the meantime, a third insurgent force rallied under Sihanouk and his son Prince Norodom Ranariddh. Sihanouk's political movement was called for the National United Front for an Independent, Neutral, Peaceful, and Cooperative Cambodia (Front Uni National pour un Cambodge Indépendent, Neutre, Pacifique, et Coopératif—FUNCINPEC—see Appendix B), and his armed wing, the Sihanouk National Army (Armée Nationale Sihanoukiste—ANS—see Appendix B).

The three insurgent forces maintained their own separate structures; they initiated their own guerrilla campaigns against the PRK regime in Phnom Penh and its Vietnamese mentors. After several years of sustained pressure from the Association of Southeast Asian Nations (ASEAN) to form a unified front against the Vietnamese occupiers, the Khmer insurgent movements came together in an uneasy union, the Coalition Government of Democratic Kampuchea (CGDK—see Appendix B), in mid-1982. Sihanouk was chosen president of the CGDK; during the succeeding years, he launched an unending series of attempts to bring reconciliation to his divided country and to achieve some power-sharing arrangement agreeable to all four warring Khmer factions. Although the methods for achieving peace in Cambodia remained in dispute, there was agreement that the Vietnamese occupation forces must depart and that the Khmer Rouge must never again reimpose its brutal rule over Cambodia.

Cambodia's civil war had an international dimension as well. Arrayed on one side were the PRK, its Vietnamese allies who did much of the fighting and, by proxy, the Soviet Union. Arrayed on the other side were the CGDK, its ASEAN supporters, and China. Vietnam was involved because it had placed the PRK in power and because it feared being caught between a hostile China and a pro-Chinese Khmer Rouge regime. The Soviet Union was involved because of its treaty relationship with Hanoi and because it provided much of the military hardware used by the PRK and by the Vietnamese. ASEAN was involved because it feared a heavily armed, expansionist Vietnamese state, which might not stop at conquest of the Indochinese Peninsula. China was involved and became the chief supporter of the Khmer Rouge faction in the CGDK because it saw the PRK and Vietnam as two more links in the chain of Soviet client states being forged around it.

As the 1980s closed, there were hopeful signs that the situation in Cambodia might not be as intractable as it had seemed in previous years. For example, the international environment had changed considerably. Soviet withdrawals from Afghanistan and Mongolia, as well as the renewed dialogue between Moscow and Beijing, culminating in a Sino-Soviet summit in May 1989, allayed to some extent Beijing's fears of encirclement by client states of Moscow. China itself stepped back from its support of the Khmer Rouge regime of Democratic Kampuchea as the sole legitimate government of Cambodia, and seemingly accepted the Vietnamese-installed Phnom Penh regime as a partner in any postwar government. The United States continued to oppose the return of the Khmer Rouge to a position of dominance in a future government, but appeared to acquiesce in a power-sharing arrangement between the Phnom Penh regime and the non-communist resistance. Vietnam stepped up the pace of its troop withdrawal from Cambodia, ending its decade of occupation in September 1989—a year ahead of time.

Among the four competing Khmer factions who remained at an impasse over power-sharing in a post-occupation Cambodia, informal meetings in Jakarta in February and May 1989 produced a useful dialogue, but little agreement on matters of substance. The PRK, in an effort to attract the support of Prince Sihanouk and the non-communist resistance and to isolate the Khmer Rouge, amended the Constitution and changed the name of the country, the flag, and the national anthem in April 1989. The amended Constitution, however, upheld the dominant position of the incumbent Kampuchean, or Khmer, People's Revolutionary Party, and made no provision for the establishment of a multi-party system in the newly named State of Cambodia. As a result of these cosmetic gestures, plus a series of meetings between Prince Sihanouk and Prime Minister Hun Sen, as well as conciliatory utterances by Khmer Rouge leaders, the differences among all sides seem to have narrowed, and the hopes for a successful resolution of the Cambodian situation seemed to have progressed sufficiently for the French government to convene the Paris International Conference on Cambodia from July 30 to August 30, 1989.

The optimism on the eve of the conference—attended by nineteen countries including the United States, as well as the UN Secretary General and the four rival Cambodian factions, proved to be ill-founded. The forum expired amid the intransigence of the Khmer factions on five basic issues: verification of the Vietnamese troop withdrawal; establishment of provisions for a ceasefire in the fighting; determination of the status of Vietnamese residents in Cambodia; official characterization of the Khmer Rouge period as a genocide; and the establishment of a power-sharing arrangement among the four factions. The latter issue proved to be the major stumbling block. The non-communist resistance headed by Prince Sihanouk lobbied for the inclusion of the Khmer Rouge on the grounds that they already exercised a decisive presence in Cambodian affairs and that their exclusion from a future government would lead inevitably to a civil war between them and the coalition that opposed them. The Phnom Penh regime countered that to include the Khmer Rouge in a postwar government would lead to a repetition of the cruelty and repression they wrought during the Democratic Kampuchea period. Thus, the impasse continued, and the failure of the Paris conference brought negotiations to an end for the time being. The State of Cambodia, in a preliminary fashion, however, cast about for a renewal of the dialogue by reconvening informal talks in Jakarta.

In the meantime, pessimistic forecasts of a civil war in Cambodia following the Paris conference, the Vietnamese troop withdrawal, and the end of the dry season, seemed to be borne out. On the western frontier with Thailand, Khmer resistance forces took to the field with renewed aggressiveness, capturing in succession a number of border towns. The single-minded purposefulness of the Khmer Rouge in the rebel offensive came as no surprise. What astonished foreign observers, however, was the unexpected combativeness of the Khmer People's National Liberation Armed Forces, which in previous years had been reduced to ineffectuality by the bickering of its leaders. As this book goes to press, the Thai-Cambodian border remains in turmoil, with the Phnom Penh regime in a defensive posture—increasingly hard-pressed to contain rebel actions and confronting increased speculation from foreign observers as to whether it can hold its own or indeed survive without outside help.

December 28, 1989   Russell R. Ross
                                           Andrea Matles Savada

Chapter 1. Historical Setting

A gate of the Angkor Thom temple complex, circa A.D. 1200

THE KHMER PEOPLE were among the first in Southeast Asia to adopt religious ideas and political institutions from India and to establish centralized kingdoms encompassing large territories. The earliest known kingdom in the area, Funan, flourished from around the first century to the sixth century A.D. It was succeeded by Chenla, which controlled large areas of modern Cambodia, Vietnam, Laos, and Thailand (known as Siam until 1939). The golden age of Khmer civilization, however, was the period from the ninth to the thirteenth century, when the kingdom of Kambuja, which gave Kampuchea, or Cambodia, its name, ruled large territories from its capital in the region of Angkor in western Cambodia.

Under Jayavarman VII (1181–ca. 1218), Kambuja reached its zenith of political power and cultural creativity. Following Jayavarman VII's death, Kambuja experienced gradual decline. Important factors were the aggressiveness of neighboring peoples (especially the Thai, or Siamese), chronic interdynastic strife, and the gradual deterioration of the complex irrigation system that had ensured rice surpluses. The Angkorian monarchy survived until 1431, when the Thai captured Angkor Thom and the Cambodian king fled to the southern part of his country.

The fifteenth century to the nineteenth century was a period of continued decline and territorial loss. Cambodia enjoyed a brief period of prosperity during the sixteenth century because its kings, who built their capitals in the region southeast of the Tonle Sap (Great Lake) along the Mekong River, promoted trade with other parts of Asia. This was the period when Spanish and Portuguese adventurers and missionaries first visited the country. But the Thai conquest of the new capital at Lovek in 1594 marked a downturn in the country's fortunes, and Cambodia became a pawn in power struggles between its two increasingly powerful neighbors, Siam and Vietnam. Vietnam's settlement of the Mekong Delta led to its annexation of that area at the end of the seventeenth century. Cambodia thereby lost some of its richest territory and was cut off from the sea. Such foreign encroachments continued through the first half of the nineteenth century because Vietnam was determined to absorb Khmer land and to force the inhabitants to accept Vietnamese culture. Such imperialistic policies created in the Khmer an abiding suspicion of their eastern neighbors that flared into violent confrontation after the Khmer Rouge (see Appendix B) established its regime in 1975.

3

In 1863 King Norodom signed an agreement with the French to establish a protectorate over his kingdom. The country gradually came under French colonial domination. During World War II, the Japanese allowed the French government (based at Vichy) that collaborated with the Nazis to continue administering Cambodia and the other Indochinese territories, but they also fostered Khmer nationalism. Cambodia enjoyed a brief period of independence in 1945 before Allied troops restored French control. King Norodom Sihanouk, who had been chosen by France to succeed King Monivong in 1941, rapidly assumed a central political role as he sought to neutralize leftist and republican opponents and attempted to negotiate acceptable terms for independence from the French. Sihanouk's ''royal crusade for independence'' resulted in grudging French acquiescence to his demands for a transfer of sovereignty. A partial agreement was struck in October 1953. Sihanouk then declared that independence had been achieved and returned in triumph to Phnom Penh. The following year, as a result of the Geneva Conference on Indochina, Cambodia was able to bring about the withdrawal of the Viet Minh (see Appendix B) troops from its territory and to withstand any residual impingement upon its sovereignty by external powers.

In order to play a more active role in national politics, Sihanouk abdicated in 1955 and placed his father, Norodom Suramarit, on the throne. Now only a prince, Sihanouk organized his own political movement, the Popular Socialist Community, (Sangkum Reastr Niyum, or Sangkum), which won all the seats in the National Assembly in the 1955 election. The Sangkum dominated the political scene until the late 1960s. Sihanouk's highly personal ruling style made him immensely popular with the people, especially in rural villages. Although the Sangkum was backed by conservative interests, Sihanouk included leftists in his government, three of whom—Khieu Samphan, Hou Yuon, and Hu Nim—later became leaders of the Khmer Rouge. In 1963 he announced the nationalization of banking, foreign trade, and insurance in a socialist experiment that dried up foreign investment and alienated the right wing. In foreign relations, Sihanouk pursued a policy of neutrality and nonalignment. He accepted United States economic and military aid, but he also promoted close relations with China and attempted to keep on good terms with the Democratic Republic of Vietnam (North Vietnam). The principal objectives of his foreign policy were to preserve Cambodia's independence and to keep the country out of the widening conflict in neighboring Vietnam. Relations with Washington grew stormy in the early 1960s. In 1963 the prince rejected further United States aid, and, two years later, he severed diplomatic relations.

Both the domestic and the international situations had deteriorated by the late 1960s. The increasingly powerful right wing challenged Sihanouk's control of the political system. Peasant resentment over harsh tax collection measures and the expropriation of land to build a sugar refinery led to a violent revolt in 1967 in the northwestern province of Batdambang (Battambang). The armed forces, commanded by General Lon Nol (who was also prime minister), quelled the revolt, but a communist-led insurgency spread throughout the country. The spillover of the Second Indochina War (or Vietnam War) into the Cambodian border areas also was becoming a serious problem. Apparently one factor in Sihanouk's decision to reestablish relations with Washington in 1969 was his fear of further incursions by the North Vietnamese and the Viet Cong (see Appendix B). In March 1970, however, he was overthrown by General Lon Nol and other right-wing leaders, who seven months later abolished the monarchy and established the Khmer Republic (see Appendix B).

The Khmer Republic faced not only North Vietnamese and Viet Cong combat units but also an effective, homegrown communist movement that grew more lethal as time went on. The Cambodian communists, whom Sihanouk had labeled Khmer Rouge, traced their movement back to the struggle for independence and the creation in 1951, under Vietnamese auspices, of the Kampuchean (or Khmer) People's Revolutionary Party (KPRP—see Appendix B). During the early 1960s, however, a group of Paris-trained communist intellectuals, of whom the most important were Saloth Sar (known as Pol Pot after 1976), Khieu Samphan, and Ieng Sary, seized control of the party. They gradually purged or neutralized rivals whom they considered too subservient to Vietnam. After the March 1970 coup d'état that toppled Sihanouk, the Khmer Rouge formed a united front with the ousted leader, a move that won them the goodwill of peasants who were still loyal to the prince.

Despite massive United States aid to the newly proclaimed Khmer Republic and the bombing of North Vietnamese and Khmer Rouge installations and troop concentrations in the countryside, the Phnom Penh regime rapidly lost most of the country's territory to the communists. In January 1975 communist forces laid siege to Phnom Penh, and in succeeding months they tightened the noose around the capital. On April 1, 1975, President Lon Nol left the country. Sixteen days later Khmer Rouge troops entered the city.

The forty-four months the Khmer Rouge were in power was a period of unmitigated suffering for the Khmer people. Although the severity of revolutionary policies varied from region to region because of ideological differences and the personal inclinations of local leaders, hundreds of thousands of people starved, died from disease, or were executed. "New people" (the intelligentsia and those from the cities—those new to the rural areas), being considered politically unreliable, were special targets of terror and of a harsh, unremitting regime of forced labor. In 1977 Pol Pot launched a bloody purge within the communist ranks that accounted for many deaths. The slaughter of the Vietnamese minority living in Cambodia and the Khmer Rouge's aggressive incursions into Vietnam led to fighting with Vietnam in 1977 and 1978. In December 1978, Vietnamese forces invaded the country. On January 7, 1979, they captured Phnom Penh and began to establish the People's Republic of Kampuchea (PRK—see Appendix B; fig. 1). The Khmer Rouge fled to isolated corners of the country and resumed their guerrilla struggle, which continued in the late 1980s.

Prehistory and Early Kingdoms

Archaeological evidence indicates that parts of the region now called Cambodia were inhabited during the first and second millennia B.C. by peoples having a Neolithic culture. By the first century A.D., the inhabitants had developed relatively stable, organized societies, which had far surpassed the primitive stage in culture and technical skills. The most advanced groups lived along the coast and in the lower Mekong River valley and delta regions, where they cultivated irrigated rice and kept domesticated animals.

Scholars believe that these people may have been Austroasiatic in origin and related to the ancestors of the groups who now inhabit insular Southeast Asia and many of the islands of the Pacific Ocean. They worked metals, including both iron and bronze, and possessed navigational skills. Mon-Khmer people, who arrived at a later date, probably intermarried with them. The Khmer who now populate Cambodia may have migrated from southeastern China to the Indochinese Peninsula before the first century A.D. They are believed to have arrived before their present Vietnamese, Thai, and Lao neighbors (see fig. 2).

Early Indianized Kingdom of Funan

At about the time that the ancient peoples of Western Europe were absorbing the classical culture and institutions of the Mediterranean, the peoples of mainland and insular Southeast Asia were responding to the stimulus of a civilization that had arisen in northern India during the previous millennium. The Britons, Gauls, and Iberians experienced Mediterranean influences directly, through conquest by and incorporation into the Roman Empire. In contrast, the Indianization of Southeast Asia was a slower process than the Romanization of Europe because there was no period of direct Indian rule and because land and sea barriers that separated the region from the Indian subcontinent are considerable. Nevertheless, Indian religion, political thought, literature, mythology, and artistic motifs gradually became integral elements in local Southeast Asian cultures. The caste system never was adopted, but Indianization stimulated the rise of highly-organized, centralized states.

Funan, the earliest of the Indianized states, generally is considered by Cambodians to have been the first Khmer kingdom in the area. Founded in the first century A.D., Funan was located on the lower reaches of the Mekong River in the delta area. Its capital, Vyadhapura, probably was located near the present-day town of Phumi Banam in Prey Veng Province. The earliest historical reference to Funan is a Chinese description of a mission that visited the country in the third century A.D. The name Funan derives from the Chinese rendition of the old Khmer word *bnam* (mountain). What the Funanese called themselves, however, is not known.

During this early period in Funan's history, the population was probably concentrated in villages along the Mekong River and along the Tonle Sab River below the Tonle Sap. Traffic and communications were mostly waterborne on the rivers and their delta tributaries. The area was a natural region for the development of an economy based on fishing and rice cultivation. There is considerable evidence that the Funanese economy depended on rice surpluses produced by an extensive inland irrigation system. Maritime trade also played an extremely important role in the development of Funan. The remains of what is believed to have been the kingdom's main port, Oc Eo (now part of Vietnam), contain Roman as well as Persian, Indian, and Greek artifacts.

By the fifth century A.D., the state exercised control over the lower Mekong River area and the lands around the Tonle Sap. It also commanded tribute from smaller states in the area now comprising northern Cambodia, southern Laos, southern Thailand, and the northern portion of the Malay Peninsula.

Indianization was fostered by increasing contact with the subcontinent through the travels of merchants, diplomats, and learned Brahmans (Hindus of the highest caste traditionally assigned to the priesthood). Indian immigrants, believed to have arrived in the fourth and the fifth centuries, accelerated the process. By the

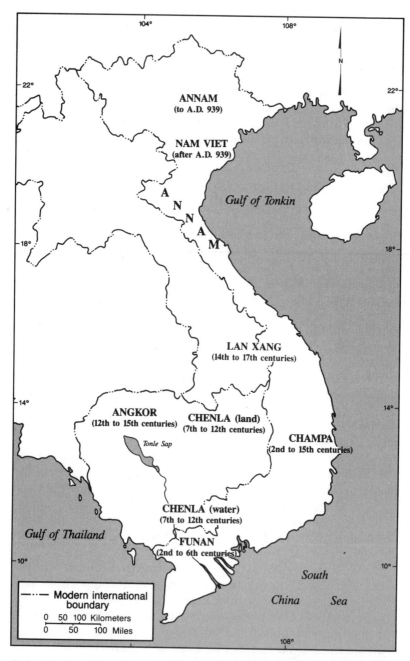

Source: Based on information from John F. Cady, *Southeast Asia: Its Historical Development*, New York, 1964.

Figure 2. Early States of Indochina

fifth century, the elite culture was thoroughly Indianized. Court ceremony and the structure of political institutions were based on Indian models. The Sanskrit language was widely used; the laws of Manu, the Indian legal code, were adopted; and an alphabet based on Indian writing systems was introduced.

Funan reached its zenith in the fifth century A.D. Beginning in the early sixth century, civil wars and dynastic strife undermined Funan's stability, making it relatively easy prey to incursions by hostile neighbors. By the end of the seventh century, a northern neighbor, the kingdom of Chenla, had reduced Funan to a vassal state.

The Successor State of Chenla

The people of Chenla also were Khmer. Once they established control over Funan, they embarked on a course of conquest that continued for three centuries. They subjugated central and upper Laos, annexed portions of the Mekong Delta, and brought what are now western Cambodia and southern Thailand under their direct control.

The royal families of Chenla intermarried with their Funanese counterparts and generally preserved the earlier political, social, and religious institutions of Funan. In the eighth century A.D., however, factional disputes at the Chenla court resulted in the splitting of the kingdom into rival northern and southern halves. According to Chinese chronicles, the two parts were known as Land (or Upper) Chenla and Water (or Lower) Chenla. Land Chenla maintained a relatively stable existence, but Water Chenla underwent a period of constant turbulence.

Late in the eighth century A.D., Water Chenla was subjected to attacks by pirates from Java, Sumatra, and the Malay Peninsula. By the beginning of the ninth century, it had apparently become a vassal of the Sailendra dynasty of Java. The last of the Water Chenla kings allegedly was killed around A.D. 790 by a Javanese monarch whom he had offended. The ultimate victor in the strife that followed was the ruler of a small Khmer state located north of the Mekong Delta. His assumption of the throne as Jayavarman II (ca. A.D. 802–50) marked the liberation of the Khmer people from Javanese suzerainty and the beginning of a unified Khmer nation.

The Angkorian Period

The Angkorian period lasted from the early ninth century to the early fifteenth century A.D. In terms of cultural accomplishments and political power, this was the golden age of Khmer civilization.

The great temple cities of the Angkorian region, located near the modern town of Siemreab, are a lasting monument to the greatness of Jayavarman II's successors. (Even the Khmer Rouge, who looked on most of their country's past history and traditions with hostility, adopted a stylized Angkorian temple for the flag of Democratic Kampuchea. A similar motif is found in the flag of the PRK). The kingdom founded by Jayavarman II also gave modern-day Cambodia, or Kampuchea, its name. During the early ninth to the mid-fifteenth centuries, it was known as Kambuja, originally the name of an early north Indian state, from which the current forms of the name have been derived.

Possibly to put distance between himself and the seaborne Javanese, Jayavarman II settled north of the Tonle Sap. He built several capitals before establishing one, Hariharalaya, near the site where the Angkorian complexes were built. Indravarman I (A.D. 877–89) extended Khmer control as far west as the Korat Plateau in Thailand, and he ordered the construction of a huge reservoir north of the capital to provide irrigation for wet rice cultivation. His son, Yasovarman I (A.D. 889–900), built the Eastern Baray (reservoir or tank), evidence of which remains to the present time. Its dikes, which may be seen today, are more than 6 kilometers long and 1.6 kilometers wide. The elaborate system of canals and reservoirs built under Indravarman I and his successors were the key to Kambuja's prosperity for half a millennium. By freeing cultivators from dependence on unreliable seasonal monsoons, they made possible an early "green revolution" that provided the country with large surpluses of rice. Kambuja's decline during the thirteenth and fourteenth centuries probably was hastened by the deterioration of the irrigation system. Attacks by Thai and other foreign peoples and the internal discord caused by dynastic rivalries diverted human resources from the system's upkeep, and it gradually fell into disrepair.

Suryavarman II (1113–50), one of the greatest Angkorian monarchs, expanded his kingdom's territory in a series of successful wars against the kingdom of Champa in central Vietnam, the kingdom of Nam Viet in northern Vietnam, and the small Mon polities as far west as the Irrawaddy River of Burma. He reduced to vassalage the Thai peoples who had migrated into Southeast Asia from the Yunnan region of southern China and established his suzerainty over the northern part of the Malay Peninsula. His greatest achievement was the construction of the temple city complex of Angkor Wat. The largest religious edifice in the world, Angkor Wat is considered the greatest single architectural work in Southeast Asia. Suryavarman II's reign was followed, however,

by thirty years of dynastic upheaval and an invasion by the neighboring Cham (see Glossary), who destroyed the city of Angkor in
1177.

The Cham ultimately were driven out and conquered by Jayavarman VII, whose reign (1181-ca. 1218) marked the apogee of Kambuja's power. Unlike his predecessors, who had adopted the cult
of the Hindu god-king, Jayavarman VII was a fervent patron of
Mahayana Buddhism. Casting himself as a bodhisattva (see Glossary), he embarked on a frenzy of building activity that included
the Angkor Thom complex and the Bayon, a remarkable temple
whose stone towers depict 216 faces of buddhas, gods, and kings.
He also built over 200 rest houses and hospitals throughout his kingdom. Like the Roman emperors, he maintained a system of roads
between his capital and provincial towns. According to historian
George Coedès, "No other Cambodian king can claim to have
moved so much stone." Often, quality suffered for the sake of size
and rapid construction, as is revealed in the intriguing but poorly
constructed Bayon.

Carvings show that everyday Angkorian buildings were wooden
structures not much different from those found in Cambodia today.
The impressive stone buildings were not used as residences by members of the royal family. Rather, they were the focus of Hindu or
Buddhist cults that celebrated the divinity, or buddhahood, of the
monarch and his family. Coedès suggests that they had the dual
function of both temple and tomb. Typically, their dimensions
reflected the structure of the Hindu mythological universe. For
example, five towers at the center of the Angkor Wat complex
represent the peaks of Mount Meru, the center of the universe;
an outer wall represents the mountains that ring the world's edge;
and a moat depicts the cosmic ocean. Like many other ancient
edifices, the monuments of the Angkorian region absorbed vast
reserves of resources and human labor and their purpose remains
shrouded in mystery.

Angkorian society was strictly hierarchical. The king, regarded
as divine, owned both the land and his subjects. Immediately below
the monarch and the royal family were the Brahman priesthood
and a small class of officials, who numbered about 4,000 in the
tenth century. Next were the commoners, who were burdened with
heavy corvée (forced labor) duties. There was also a large slave
class that, like the nameless multitudes of ancient Egypt, built the
enduring monuments.

After Jayavarman VII's death, Kambuja entered a long period
of decline that led to its eventual disintegration. The Thai were
a growing menace on the empire's western borders. The spread

of Theravada Buddhism, which came to Kambuja from Sri Lanka by way of the Mon kingdoms, challenged the royal Hindu and Mahayana Buddhist cults. Preaching austerity and the salvation of the individual through his or her own efforts, Theravada Buddhism did not lend doctrinal support to a society ruled by an opulent royal establishment maintained through the virtual slavery of the masses.

In 1353 a Thai army captured Angkor. It was recaptured by the Khmer, but wars continued and the capital was looted several times. During the same period, Khmer territory north of the present Laotian border was lost to the Lao kingdom of Lan Xang. In 1431 the Thai captured Angkor Thom. Thereafter, the Angkorian region did not again encompass a royal capital, except for a brief period in the third quarter of the sixteenth century.

Cambodia's Struggle for Survival, 1432–1887

The more than four centuries that passed from the abandonment of Angkor around the mid-fifteenth century to the establishment of a protectorate under the French in 1863 are considered by historians to be Cambodia's "dark ages," a period of economic, social, and cultural stagnation when the kingdom's internal affairs came increasingly under the control of its aggressive neighbors, the Thai and the Vietnamese. By the mid-nineteenth century, Cambodia had become an almost helpless pawn in the power struggles between Thailand and Vietnam and probably would have been completely absorbed by one or the other if France had not intervened, giving Cambodia a colonially dominated "lease on life." Fear of racial and cultural extinction has persisted as a major theme in modern Cambodian thought and helps to explain the intense nationalism and xenophobia of the Khmer Rouge during the 1970s. Establishment in 1979 of the People's Republic of Kampuchea, a Vietnamese-dominated satellite state, can be seen as the culmination of a process of Vietnamese encroachment that was already well under way by the seventeenth century.

The process of internal decay and foreign encroachment was gradual rather than precipitous and was hardly evident in the fifteenth century when the Khmer were still powerful. Following the fall of Angkor Thom, the Cambodian court abandoned the region north of the Tonle Sap, never to return except for a brief interlude in the late sixteenth century. By this time however, the Khmer penchant for monument building had ceased. Older faiths such as Mahayana Buddhism and the Hindu cult of the god-king had been supplanted by Theravada Buddhism, and the Cambodians had become part of the same religious and cultural cosmos as the Thai. This similarity did not prevent intermittent warfare between the two kingdoms, however. During the sixteenth century Cambodian armies, taking advantage of Thai troubles with the Burmese, invaded the Thai kingdom several times.

In the meantime, following the abandonment of the Angkorian sites, the Khmer established a new capital several hundred kilometers to the southeast on the site of what is now Phnom Penh. This new center of power was located at the confluence of the Mekong and the Tonle Sab rivers. Thus, it controlled the river commerce of the Khmer heartland and the Laotian kingdoms and had access, by way of the Mekong Delta, to the international trade routes that linked the China coast, the South China Sea, and the Indian Ocean. A new kind of state and society emerged, more open to the outside world and more dependent on commerce as a source of wealth than its inland predecessor. The growth of maritime trade with China during the Ming dynasty (1368–1644) provided lucrative opportunities for members of the Cambodian elite who controlled royal trading monopolies. The appearance of Europeans in the region in the sixteenth century also stimulated commerce.

King Ang Chan (1516–66), one of the few great Khmer monarchs of the post-Angkorian period, moved the capital from Phnom Penh to Lovek. Portuguese and Spanish travelers who visited the city, located on the banks of the Tonle Sab, a river north of Phnom Penh, described it as a place of fabulous wealth. The products traded there included precious stones, metals, silk and cotton, incense, ivory, lacquer, livestock (including elephants), and rhinoceros horn (prized by the Chinese as a rare and potent medicine). By the late sixteenth and early seventeenth centuries, Lovek contained flourishing foreign trading communities of Chinese, Indonesians, Malays, Japanese, Arabs, Spanish, and Portuguese. They were joined later in the century by the English and the Dutch.

Because the representatives of practically all these nationalities were pirates, adventurers, or traders, this was an era of stormy cosmopolitanism. Hard-pressed by the Thai, King Sattha (1576–94) surrounded himself with a personal guard of Spanish and Portuguese mercenaries, and in 1593 asked the Spanish governor of the Philippines for aid. Attracted by the prospects of establishing a Spanish protectorate in Cambodia and of converting the monarch to Christianity, the governor sent a force of 120 men, but Lovek had already fallen to the Thai when they arrived the following year. The Spanish took advantage of the extremely confused situation to place one of Sattha's sons on the throne in 1597. Hopes of making the country a Spanish dependency were dashed, however, when the Spaniards were massacred two years later by an equally belligerent contingent of Malay mercenaries.

The Thai, however, had dealt a fatal blow to Cambodian independence by capturing Lovek in 1594. With the posting of a Thai military governor in the city, a degree of foreign political control was established over the kingdom for the first time. Cambodian chronicles describe the fall of Lovek as a catastrophe from which the nation never fully recovered.

Domination by Thailand and by Vietnam

More than their conquest of Angkor a century and a half earlier, the Thai capture of Lovek marked the beginning of a decline in Cambodia's fortunes. One possible reason for the decline was the labor drain imposed by the Thai conquerors as they marched thousands of Khmer peasants, skilled artisans, scholars, and members of the Buddhist clergy back to their capital of Ayutthaya. This practice, common in the history of Southeast Asia, crippled Cambodia's ability to recover a semblance of its former greatness. A new Khmer capital was established at Odongk (Udong), south of Lovek, but its monarchs could survive only by entering into what amounted to vassal relationships with the Thai and with the Vietnamese. In common parlance, Thailand became Cambodia's ''father'' and Vietnam its ''mother.''

By the late fifteenth century, the Vietnamese—who, unlike other Southeast Asian peoples, had patterned their culture and their civilization on those of China—had defeated the once-powerful kingdom of Champa in central Vietnam. Thousands of Chams fled into Khmer territory. By the early seventeenth century, the Vietnamese had reached the Mekong Delta, which was inhabited by Khmer people. In 1620 the Khmer king Chey Chettha II (1618–28) married a daughter of Sai Vuong, one of the Nguyen lords (1558–1778), who ruled southern Vietnam for most of the period of the restored Le dynasty (1428–1788). Three years later, Chey Chettha allowed the Vietnamese to establish a custom-house at Prey Nokor, near what is now Ho Chi Minh City (until 1975, Saigon). By the end of the seventeenth century, the region was under Vietnamese administrative control, and Cambodia was cut off from access to the sea. Trade with the outside world was possible only with Vietnamese permission.

There were periods in the seventeenth and the eighteenth centuries, when Cambodia's neighbors were preoccupied with internal or external strife, that afforded the beleaguered country a breathing spell. The Vietnamese were involved in a lengthy civil war until 1674, but upon its conclusion they promptly annexed sizable areas of contiguous Cambodian territory in the region of the Mekong Delta. For the next one hundred years they used the alleged mistreatment of Vietnamese colonists in the delta as a pretext for their continued expansion. By the end of the eighteenth century, they had extended their control to include the area encompassed in the late 1980s by the Socialist Republic of Vietnam (Vietnam).

Thailand, which might otherwise have been courted as an ally against Vietnamese incursions in the eighteenth century, was itself involved in a new conflict with Burma. In 1767 the Thai capital of Ayutthaya was besieged and destroyed. The Thai quickly recovered, however, and soon reasserted their dominion over Cambodia. The youthful Khmer king, Ang Eng (1779–96), a refugee at the Thai court, was installed as monarch at Odongk by Thai troops. At the same time, Thailand quietly annexed Cambodia's three northernmost provinces. In addition, the local rulers of the northwestern provinces of Batdambang and Siemreab (Siemreap) became vassals of the Thai king, and these areas came under the Thai sphere of influence.

A renewed struggle between Thailand and Vietnam for control of Cambodia in the nineteenth century resulted in a period when Vietnamese officials, working through a puppet Cambodian king, ruled the central part of the country and attempted to force Cambodians to adopt Vietnamese customs. Several rebellions against Vietnamese rule ensued. The most important of these occurred in 1840 to 1841 and spread through much of the country. After two years of fighting, Cambodia and its two neighbors reached an accord that placed the country under the joint suzerainty of Thailand and Vietnam. At the behest of both countries, a new monarch, Ang Duong (1848–59), ascended the throne and brought a decade of peace and relative independence to Cambodia.

In their arbitrary treatment of the Khmer population, the Thai and the Vietnamese were virtually indistinguishable. The suffering and the dislocation caused by war were comparable in many ways to similar Cambodian experiences in the 1970s. But the Thai and the Vietnamese had fundamentally different attitudes concerning their relationships with Cambodia. The Thai shared with the Khmer a common religion, mythology, literature, and culture. The Chakri kings at Bangkok wanted Cambodia's loyalty and tribute, but they had no intention of challenging or changing its people's values or way of life. The Vietnamese viewed the Khmer people as barbarians to be civilized through exposure to Vietnamese culture, and they regarded the fertile Khmer lands as legitimate sites for colonization by settlers from Vietnam.

The French Protectorate

France's interest in Indochina in the nineteenth century grew out of its rivalry with Britain, which had excluded it from India and had effectively shut it out of other parts of mainland Southeast Asia. The French also desired to establish commerce in a region that promised so much untapped wealth and to redress the Vietnamese state's persecution of Catholic converts, whose welfare was a stated aim of French overseas policy. The Nguyen dynasty's repeated refusal to establish diplomatic relations and the violently anti-Christian policies of the emperors Minh Mang (1820-41), Thieu Tri (1841-47), and Tu Duc (1848-83) impelled the French to engage in gunboat diplomacy that resulted, in 1862, in the establishment of French dominion over Saigon and over the three eastern provinces of the Cochinchina (Mekong Delta) region.

In the view of the government in Paris, Cambodia was a promising backwater. Persuaded by a missionary envoy to seek French protection against both the Thai and the Vietnamese, King Ang Duong invited a French diplomatic mission to visit his court. The Thai, however, pressured him to refuse to meet with the French when they finally arrived at Odongk in 1856. The much-publicized travels of the naturalist Henri Mouhot, who visited the Cambodian court, rediscovered the ruins at Angkor, and journeyed up the Mekong River to the Laotian kingdom of Luang Prabang from 1859 to 1861, piqued French interest in the kingdom's alleged vast riches and in the value of the Mekong as a gateway to China's southwestern provinces. In August 1863, the French concluded a treaty with Ang Duong's successor, Norodom (1859-1904). This agreement afforded the Cambodian monarch French protection (in the form of a French official called a resident—in French résident) in exchange for giving the French rights to explore and to exploit the kingdom's mineral and forest resources. Norodom's coronation, in 1864, was an awkward affair at which both French and Thai representatives officiated. Although the Thai attempted to thwart the expansion of French influence, their own influence over the monarch steadily dwindled. In 1867 the French concluded a treaty with the Thai that gave the latter control of Batdambang Province and of Siemreab Province in exchange for their renunciation of all claims of suzerainty over other parts of Cambodia. Loss of the northwestern provinces deeply upset Norodom, but he was beholden to the French for sending military aid to suppress a rebellion by a royal pretender.

In June 1884, the French governor of Cochinchina went to Phnom Penh, Norodom's capital, and demanded approval of a

Gate of the Dead,
Angkor Thom, twelfth century
Courtesy Mr. and Mrs.
Robert E. Hammerquist

Villager resting near
pre-Angkorian ruins
Courtesy Bill Herod

treaty with Paris that promised far-reaching changes such as the abolition of slavery, the institution of private land ownership, and the establishment of French *résidents* in provincial cities. Mindful of a French gunboat anchored in the river, the king reluctantly signed the agreement. Local elites opposed its provisions, however, especially the one dealing with slavery, and they fomented rebellions throughout the country during the following year. Though the rebellions were suppressed, and the treaty was ratified, passive resistance on the part of the Cambodians postponed implementation of the reforms it embodied until after Norodom's death.

The French Colonial Period, 1887–1953

In October 1887, the French proclaimed the Union Indochinoise, or Indochina Union, comprising Cambodia and the three constituent regions of Vietnam: Tonkin, Annam, and Cochinchina. (Laos was added to the Indochina Union after being separated from Thai suzerainty in 1893.) Cambodia's chief colonial official, responsible to the Union's governor general and appointed by the Ministry of Marine and Colonies in Paris, was a resident general (*résident supérieur*). Residents, or local governors, were posted in all the principal provincial centers. In 1897 the incumbent resident general complained to Paris that Norodom was no longer capable of ruling and received permission to assume the king's authority to issue decrees, collect taxes, and appoint royal officials. Norodom and his successors were left with hollow, figurehead roles as head of state and as patron of the Buddhist religion. The colonial bureaucracy expanded rapidly. French nationals naturally held the highest positions, but even on the lower rungs of the bureaucracy Cambodians found few opportunities because the colonial government preferred to hire Vietnamese.

When Norodom died in 1904, the French passed over his sons and set his brother Sisowath (1904–27) on the throne. Sisowath's branch of the royal family was considered more cooperative than that of Norodom because the latter was viewed as partly responsible for the revolts of the 1880s and because Norodom's favorite son, Prince Yukanthor, had stirred up publicity abroad about French colonial injustices. During their generally peaceful reigns, Sisowath and his son Monivong (1927–41) were pliant instruments of French rule. A measure of the monarchs' status was the willingness of the French to provide them annually with complimentary rations of opium. One of the few highlights of Sisowath's reign was French success in getting Thailand's King Chulalongkorn to sign a new treaty in 1907 returning the northwestern provinces of Batdambang and Siemreab to Cambodia.

The Colonial Economy

Soon after establishing their protectorate in 1863, the French realized that Cambodia's hidden wealth was an illusion and that Phnom Penh would never become the Singapore of Indochina. Aside from collecting taxes more efficiently, the French did little to transform Cambodia's village-based economy. Cambodians paid the highest taxes per capita in Indochina, and in 1916 a nonviolent tax revolt brought tens of thousands of peasants into Phnom Penh to petition the king for a reduction. The incident shocked the French, who had lulled themselves into believing that the Cambodians were too indolent and individualistic to organize a mass protest. Taxes continued to be sorely resented by the Cambodians. In 1925 villagers killed a French resident after he threatened to arrest tax delinquents (see The French Protectorate, 1863–1954, ch. 5). For poor peasants, the corvée service—a tax substitute—of as many as ninety days a year on public works projects, was an onerous duty.

According to Hou Yuon (a veteran of the communist movement who was murdered by the Khmer Rouge after they seized power in 1975), usury vied with taxes as the chief burden upon the peasantry. Hou's 1955 doctoral thesis at the University of Paris was one of the earliest and most thorough studies of conditions in the rural areas during the French colonial era. He argued that although most landholdings were small (one to five hectares), poor and middle-class peasants were victims of flagrantly usurious practices that included effective interest rates of 100 to 200 percent. Foreclosure reduced them to the status of sharecroppers or landless laborers. Although debt slavery and feudal landholding patterns had been abolished by the French, the old elites still controlled the countryside. According to Hou, "the great feudal farms, because of their precapitalist character, are disguised as small and medium-sized farms, in the form of tenancies and share-farms, and materially are indistinguishable from other small and medium-seized farms." Whether or not the countryside was as polarized in terms of class (or property) as Hou argues is open to debate, but it is clear that great tension and conflict existed despite the smiles and the easygoing manner of Khmer villagers.

To develop the economic infrastructure, the French built a limited number of roads and a railroad that extended from Phnom Penh through Batdambang to the Thai border. The cultivation of rubber and of corn were economically important, and the fertile provinces of Batdambang and Siemreab became the rice baskets of Indochina. The prosperous 1920s, when rubber, rice, and corn were in demand overseas, were years of considerable economic growth, but the world depression after 1929 caused great suffering, especially among rice cultivators whose falling incomes made them more than ever the victims of moneylenders.

Industry was rudimentary and was designed primarily to process raw materials such as rubber for local use or export. There was considerable immigration, which created a plural society similar to those of other Southeast Asian countries. As in British Burma and Malaya, foreigners dominated the developed sectors of the economy. Vietnamese came to serve as laborers on rubber plantations and as clerical workers in the government. As their numbers increased, Vietnamese immigrants also began to play important roles in the economy as fishermen and as operators of small businesses. The Chinese had been in Cambodia for several centuries before the imposition of French rule, and they had dominated precolonial commerce. This arrangement continued under the French, because the colonial government placed no restrictions on the occupations in which they could engage. Chinese merchants and bankers in Cambodia developed commercial networks that extended throughout Indochina as well as overseas to other parts of Southeast Asia and to mainland China.

The Emergence of Nationalism

In stark contrast to neighboring Cochinchina and to the other Vietnamese-populated territories of Indochina, Cambodia was relatively quiescent politically during the first four decades of the twentieth century. The carefully maintained fiction of royal rule was probably the major factor. Khmer villagers, long inured to abuses of power, believed that as long as a monarch occupied the throne ''all was right with the world.'' Low literacy rates, which the French were extremely reluctant to improve, also insulated the great majority of the population from the nationalist currents that were sweeping other parts of Southeast Asia.

Nevertheless, national consciousness was emerging among the handful of educated Khmer who composed the urban-based elite. Restoration of the monuments at Angkor, which the historian David P. Chandler suggests was France's most valuable legacy to the colony, awakened Cambodians' pride in their culture and in their past achievements. Many of the new elite were graduates of the Lycée Sisowath in Phnom Penh, where resentment of the favored treatment given Vietnamese students resulted in a petition to King Monivong during the 1930s. Significantly, the most articulate of the early nationalists, were Khmer Krom (see Appendix B)—members of the Cambodian minority who lived in Cochinchina. In 1936 Son Ngoc Thanh and another Khmer Krom named Pach Chhoeun, began publishing *Nagaravatta* (Angkor Wat), the first Khmer-language newspaper. In its editorials, *Nagaravatta* mildly condemned French colonial policies, the prevalence of usury in the rural areas, foreign domination of the economy, and the lack of opportunities for educated Khmer. Much of the paper's journalistic wrath was directed toward the Vietnamese for their past exploitation of Cambodia and for their contemporary monopolization of civil service and of professional positions.

The Khmer were fortunate in escaping the suffering endured by most other Southeast Asian peoples during World War II. After the establishment of the Vichy regime in France in 1940, Japanese forces moved into Vietnam and displaced French authority. In mid-1941, they entered Cambodia but allowed Vichy French colonial officials to remain at their administrative posts. The pro-Japanese regime in Thailand, headed by Prime Minister Field Marshal Luang Plaek Phibunsonggram, requested assurances from the Vichy regime that, in the event of an interruption of French sovereignty, Cambodian and Laotian territories formerly belonging to Thailand would be returned to Bangkok's authority. The request was rejected. In January 1941, a Thai force invaded Cambodia. The land fighting was indecisive, but the Vichy French defeated the Thai navy in an engagement in the Gulf of Thailand (see The Japanese Occupation, 1941–45, ch. 5). At this point, Tokyo intervened and compelled the French authorities to agree to a treaty ceding the province of Batdambang and part of the province of Siemreab to Thailand in exchange for a small compensation. The Cambodians were allowed to retain Angkor. Thai aggression, however, had minimal impact on the lives of most Cambodians outside the northwestern region.

King Monivong died in April 1941. Although his son, Prince Monireth, had been considered the heir apparent, the French chose instead Norodom Sihanouk, the great grandson of King Norodom. Sihanouk was an ideal candidate from their point of view because of his youth (he was nineteen years old), his lack of experience, and his pliability.

Japanese calls of "Asia for the Asiatics" found a receptive audience among Cambodian nationalists, although Tokyo's policy in Indochina was to leave the colonial government nominally in charge. When a prominent, politically active Buddhist monk, Hem Chieu, was arrested and unceremoniously defrocked by the French authorities in July 1942, the editors of *Nagaravatta* led a demonstration demanding his release. They as well as other nationalists apparently overestimated the Japanese willingness to back them, for the Vichy authorities quickly arrested the demonstrators and gave Pach Chhoeun, one of the *Nagaravatta* editors, a life sentence (see The Japanese Occupation, 1941–45, ch. 5). The other editor, Son Ngoc Thanh, escaped from Phnom Penh and turned up the following year in Tokyo.

In a desperate effort to enlist local support in the final months of the war, the Japanese dissolved the French colonial administration on March 9, 1945, and urged Cambodia to declare its independence within the Greater East Asia Co-Prosperity Sphere. Four days later, King Sihanouk decreed an independent Kampuchea (the original Khmer pronunciation of Cambodia). Son Ngoc Thanh returned from Tokyo in May, and he was appointed foreign minister. On August 15, 1945, the day Japan surrendered, a new government was established with Son Ngoc Thanh acting as prime minister. When an Allied force occupied Phnom Penh in October, Thanh was arrested for collaboration with the Japanese and was sent into exile in France to remain under house arrest. Some of his supporters went to northwestern Cambodia, then still under Thai control, where they banded together as one faction in the Khmer Issarak (see Appendix B) movement, originally formed with Thai encouragement in the 1940s.

The Struggle for Independence

Cambodia's situation at the end of the war was chaotic. The Free French, under General Charles de Gaulle, were determined to recover Indochina, though they offered Cambodia and the other Indochinese protectorates a carefully circumscribed measure of self-government. Convinced that they had a "civilizing mission," they envisioned Indochina's participation in a French Union of former colonies that shared the common experience of French culture. Neither the urban professional elites nor the common people, however, were attracted by this arrangement. For Cambodians of practically all walks of life, the brief period of independence, from March to October of 1945, was an invigorating breath of fresh air. The lassitude of the Khmer was a thing of the past.

In Phnom Penh, Sihanouk, acting as head of state, was placed in the extremely delicate position of negotiating with the French for full independence while trying to neutralize party politicians and supporters of the Khmer Issarak and Viet Minh who considered him a French collaborator. During the tumultuous period between 1946 and 1953, Sihanouk displayed the remarkable aptitude for political survival that sustained him before and after his fall

Angkor Wat from the causeway
Courtesy Mr. and Mrs. Robert E. Hammerquist

from power in March 1970. The Khmer Issarak was an extremely heterogeneous guerrilla movement, operating in the border areas. The group included indigenous leftists, Vietnamese leftists, anti-monarchical nationalists (Khmer Serei—see Appendix B) loyal to Son Ngoc Thanh, and plain bandits taking advantage of the chaos to terrorize villagers. Though their fortunes rose and fell during the immediate postwar period (a major blow was the overthrow of a friendly leftist government in Bangkok in 1947), by 1954 the Khmer Issarak operating with the Viet Minh by some estimates controlled as much as 50 percent of Cambodia's territory.

In 1946 the French allowed the Cambodians to form political parties and to hold elections for a Consultative Assembly that would advise the monarch on drafting the country's constitution. The two major parties were both headed by royal princes. The Democratic Party, led by Prince Sisowath Yuthevong, espoused immediate independence, democratic reforms, and parliamentary government. Its supporters were teachers, civil servants, politically active members of the Buddhist priesthood, and others whose opinions had been greatly influenced by the nationalistic appeals of *Nagaravatta* before it was closed down by the French in 1942. Many Democrats sympathized with the violent methods of the Khmer Issarak. The Liberal Party, led by Prince Norodom Norindeth, represented the interests of the old rural elites, including large landowners. They preferred continuing some form of the colonial relationship with France, and advocated gradual democratic reform. In the Consultative Assembly election held in September 1946, the Democrats won fifty out of sixty-seven seats.

With a solid majority in the assembly, the Democrats drafted a constitution modeled on that of the French Fourth Republic. Power was concentrated in the hands of a popularly elected National Assembly. The king reluctantly proclaimed the new constitution on May 6, 1947. While it recognized him as the ''spiritual head of the state,'' it reduced him to the status of a constitutional monarch, and it left unclear the extent to which he could play an active role in the politics of the nation. Sihanouk would turn this ambiguity to his advantage in later years, however.

In the December 1947 elections for the National Assembly, the Democrats again won a large majority. Despite this, dissension within the party was rampant. Its founder, Prince Yuthevong, had died and no clear leader had emerged to succeed him. During the period 1948 to 1949, the Democrats appeared united only in their opposition to legislation sponsored by the king or his appointees. A major issue was the king's receptivity to independence within the French Union, proposed in a draft treaty offered by the French in late 1948. Following dissolution of the National Assembly in September 1949, agreement on the pact was reached through an exchange of letters between King Sihanouk and the French government. It went into effect two months later, though National Assembly ratification of the treaty was never secured.

The treaty granted Cambodia what Sihanouk called ''fifty percent independence'': by it, the colonial relationship was formally ended, and the Cambodians were given control of most administrative functions. Cambodian armed forces were granted freedom of action within a self-governing autonomous zone comprising Batdambang and Siemreab provinces, which had been recovered from Thailand after World War II, but which the French, hard-pressed elsewhere, did not have the resources to control. Cambodia was still required to coordinate foreign policy matters with the High Council of the French Union, however, and France retained a significant measure of control over the judicial system, finances, and customs. Control of wartime military operations outside the autonomous zone remained in French hands. France was also permitted to maintain military bases on Cambodian territory. In 1950 Cambodia was accorded diplomatic recognition by the United States and by most noncommunist powers, but in Asia only Thailand and the Republic of Korea (South Korea) extended recognition.

The Democrats won a majority in the second National Assembly election in September 1951, and they continued their policy of opposing the king on practically all fronts. In an effort to win greater popular approval, Sihanouk asked the French to release nationalist Son Ngoc Thanh from exile and to allow him to return to his country. He made a triumphant entry into Phnom Penh on October 29, 1951. It was not long, however, before he began demanding withdrawal of French troops from Cambodia. He reiterated this demand in early 1952 in *Khmer Krok* (Khmer Awake) a weekly newspaper that he had founded. The newspaper was forced to cease publication in March, and Son Ngoc Thanh fled the capital with a few armed followers to join the Khmer Issarak. Branded alternately a communist and an agent of the United States Central Intelligence Agency (CIA) by Sihanouk, he remained in exile until Lon Nol established the Khmer Republic in 1970.

In June 1952, Sihanouk announced the dismissal of his cabinet, suspended the constitution, and assumed control of the government as prime minister. Then, without clear constitutional sanction, he dissolved the National Assembly and proclaimed martial law in January 1953. Sihanouk exercised direct rule for almost three years, from June 1952 until February 1955. After dissolution of the assembly, he created an Advisory Council to supplant the legislature and appointed his father, Norodom Suramarit, as regent.

In March 1953, Sihanouk went to France. Ostensibly, he was traveling for his health; actually, he was mounting an intensive campaign to persuade the French to grant complete independence. The climate of opinion in Cambodia at the time was such that if he did not achieve full independence quickly, the people were likely to turn to Son Ngoc Thanh and the Khmer Issarak, who were fully committed to attaining that goal. At meetings with the French president and with other high officials, the French suggested that Sihanouk was unduly "alarmist" about internal political conditions. The French also made the thinly veiled threat that, if he continued to be uncooperative, they might replace him. The trip appeared to be a failure, but on his way home by way of the United States, Canada, and Japan, Sihanouk publicized Cambodia's plight in the media.

To further dramatize his "royal crusade for independence," Sihanouk, declaring that he would not return until the French gave assurances that full independence would be granted, left Phnom Penh in June to go into self-imposed exile in Thailand. Unwelcome in Bangkok, he moved to his royal villa near the ruins of Angkor in Siemreab Province. Siemreab, part of the autonomous military zone established in 1949, was commanded by Lieutenant

Colonel Lon Nol, formerly a right-wing politician who was becoming a prominent, and in time would be an indispensable, Sihanouk ally within the military. From his Siemreab base, the king and Lon Nol contemplated plans for resistance if the French did not meet their terms.

Sihanouk was making a high-stakes gamble, for the French could easily have replaced him with a more pliable monarch; however, the military situation was deteriorating throughout Indochina, and the French government, on July 3, 1953, declared itself ready to grant full independence to the three states of Cambodia, Vietnam, and Laos. Sihanouk insisted on his own terms, which included full control of national defense, the police, the courts, and financial matters. The French yielded: the police and the judiciary were transferred to Cambodian control at the end of August, and in October the country assumed full command of its military forces. King Sihanouk, now a hero in the eyes of his people, returned to Phnom Penh in triumph, and independence day was celebrated on November 9, 1953. Control of residual matters affecting sovereignty, such as financial and budgetary affairs, passed to the new Cambodian state in 1954.

Cambodia under Sihanouk, 1954–70

Sihanouk continues to be one of the most controversial figures in Southeast Asia's turbulent, and often tragic, postwar history. Admirers view him as one of the country's great patriots, whose insistence on strict neutrality kept Cambodia out of the maelstrom of war and out of the revolution in neighboring Vietnam for more than fifteen years before he was betrayed by his close associate, Lon Nol. Critics attack him for his vanity, eccentricities, and intolerance of any political views different from his own. One such critic, Michael Vickery, asserts that beneath the neutralist rhetoric Sihanouk presided over a regime that was oppressively reactionary and, in some instances, as violent in its suppression of political opposition as the Khmer Rouge. According to Vickery, the royal armed forces under Lon Nol slaughtered women and children in pro-Khmer Issarak regions of Batdambang in 1954 using methods that were later to become routine under Pol Pot. Another critical observer, Milton E. Osborne, writing as an Australian expatriate in Phnom Penh during the late 1960s, describes the Sihanouk years in terms of unbridled greed and corruption, of a foreign policy inspired more by opportunism than by the desire to preserve national independence, of an economy and a political system that were rapidly coming apart, and of the prince's obsession with making outrageously mediocre films—one of which starred himself and his wife, Princess Monique.

Sihanouk was all of these things—patriot, neutralist, embodiment of the nation's destiny, eccentric, rigid defender of the status quo, and promoter of the worst sort of patron-client politics. He believed that he single-handedly had won Cambodia's independence from the French. The contributions of other nationalists, such as Son Ngoc Thanh and the Viet Minh, were conveniently forgotten. Sihanouk also believed he had the right to run the state in a manner not very different from that of the ancient Khmer kings— that is, as an extension of his household. Unlike the ancient "god-kings," however, he established genuine rapport with ordinary Cambodians. He made frequent, often impromptu, trips throughout the country, visiting isolated villages, chatting with peasants, receiving petitions, passing out gifts, and scolding officials for mismanagement. According to British author and journalist William Shawcross, Sihanouk was able to create a "unique brand of personal populism." To ordinary Cambodians, his eccentricities, volatility, short temper, sexual escapades, and artistic flights of fancy were an expression of royal charisma rather than an occasion for scandal. Sihanouk's delight in making life difficult for foreign diplomats and journalists, moreover, amused his subjects. Ultimately, the eccentric humanity of Sihanouk was to contrast poignantly with the random brutality of his Khmer Rouge successors.

The Geneva Conference

Although Cambodia had achieved independence by late 1953, its military situation remained unsettled. Noncommunist factions of the Khmer Issarak had joined the government, but communist Viet Minh activities increased at the very time French Union forces were stretched thin elsewhere. In April 1954, several Viet Minh battalions crossed the border into Cambodia. Royalist forces engaged them but could not force their complete withdrawal. In part, the communists were attempting to strengthen their bargaining position at the Geneva Conference that had been scheduled to begin in late April.

The Geneva Conference was attended by representatives of Cambodia, North Vietnam, the Associated State of Vietnam (the predecessor of the Republic of Vietnam, or South Vietnam), Laos, the People's Republic of China, the Soviet Union, France, Britain, and the United States. One goal of the conference was to restore a lasting peace in Indochina. The discussions on Indochina began on May 8, 1954. The North Vietnamese attempted to get representation for the resistance government that had been established in the south, but failed. On July 21, 1954, the conference reached an agreement calling for a cessation of hostilities in Indochina. With respect to Cambodia, the agreement stipulated that all Viet Minh military forces be withdrawn within ninety days and that Cambodian resistance forces be demobilized within thirty days. In a separate agreement signed by the Cambodian representative, the French and the Viet Minh agreed to withdraw all forces from Cambodian soil by October 1954.

In exchange for the withdrawal of Viet Minh forces, the communist representatives in Geneva wanted full neutrality for Cambodia and for Laos that would prevent the basing of United States military forces in these countries. On the eve of the conference's conclusion, however, the Cambodian representative, Sam Sary, insisted that, if Cambodia were to be genuinely independent, it must not be prohibited from seeking whatever military assistance it desired (Cambodia had earlier appealed to Washington for military aid). The conference accepted this point over North Vietnam's strenuous objections. In the final agreement, Cambodia accepted a watered-down neutrality, vowing not to join any military alliance "not in conformity with the principles of the Charter of the United Nations" or to allow the basing of foreign military forces on its territory "as long as its security is not threatened."

The conference agreement established the International Control Commission (officially called the International Commission for Supervision and Control) in all the Indochinese countries. Made up of representatives from Canada, Poland, and India, it supervised the cease-fire, the withdrawal of foreign troops, the release of prisoners of war, and overall compliance with the terms of the agreement. The French and most of the Viet Minh forces were withdrawn on schedule in October 1954.

Domestic Developments

The Geneva agreement also stipulated that general elections should be held in Cambodia during 1955 and that the International Control Commission should monitor them to ensure fairness. Sihanouk was more determined than ever to defeat the Democrats (who, on the basis of their past record, were expected to win the election). The king attempted unsuccessfully to have the constitution amended. On March 2, 1955, he announced his abdication in favor of his father, Norodom Suramarit. Assuming the title of *samdech* (prince), Sihanouk explained that this action was necessary in order to give him a free hand to engage in politics.

To challenge the Democrats, Prince Sihanouk established his own political machine, the oddly named Sangkum Reastr Niyum (Popular Socialist Community), commonly referred to as the Sangkum. The name is odd because its most important components were right-wing parties that were virulently anticommunist. The Sang-kum's emergence in early 1955 unified most right-wing groups under the prince's auspices. In the September election, Sihanouk's new party decisively defeated the Democrats, the Khmer Indepen-dence Party of Son Ngoc Thanh, and the leftist Pracheachon (Citizens') Party, winning 83 percent of the vote and all of the seats in the National Assembly.

Khmer nationalism, loyalty to the monarch, struggle against in-justice and corruption, and protection of the Buddhist religion were major themes in Sangkum ideology. The party adopted a particu-larly conservative interpretation of Buddhism, common in the Ther-avada countries of Southeast Asia, that the social and economic inequalities among people were legitimate because of the workings of karma (see Buddhism, ch. 2). For the poorer classes, virtuous and obedient conduct opened up the possibility of being born into a higher station in a future life. The appeal to religion won the allegiance of the country's many Buddhist priests, who were a par-ticularly influential group in rural villages.

As the 1960s began, organized political opposition to Sihanouk and the Sangkum virtually had disappeared. According to Vick-ery, the Democratic Party disbanded in 1957 after its leaders— who had been beaten by soldiers—requested the privilege of join-ing the Sangkum.

Despite its defense of the status quo, especially the interests of rural elites, the Sangkum was not an exclusively right-wing organi-zation. Sihanouk included a number of leftists in his party and government. Among these were future leaders of the Khmer Rouge. Hu Nim and Hou Yuon served in several ministries between 1958 and 1963, and Khieu Samphan served briefly as secretary of state for commerce in 1963.

Sihanouk's attitude toward the left was paradoxical. He often declared that if he had not been a prince, he would have become a revolutionary. Sihanouk's chronic suspicion of United States in-tentions in the region, his perception of revolutionary China as Cambodia's most valuable ally, his respect for such prominent and capable leftists as Hou, Hu, and Khieu, and his vague notions of "royal socialism" all impelled him to experiment with socialist poli-cies. In 1963 the prince announced the nationalization of bank-ing, foreign trade, and insurance as a means of reducing foreign control of the economy. In 1964 a state trading company, the Na-tional Export-Import Corporation, was established to handle for-eign commerce. The declared purposes of nationalization were to give Khmer nationals, rather than Chinese or Vietnamese, a greater role in the nation's trade, to eliminate middlemen and to conserve foreign exchange through the limiting of unnecessary luxury imports. As a result of this policy, foreign investment quickly disappeared, and a kind of "crony socialism" emerged somewhat similar to the "crony capitalism" that evolved in the Philippines under President Ferdinand Marcos. Lucrative state monopolies were parceled out to Sihanouk's most loyal retainers, who "milked" them for cash.

Sihanouk was headed steadily for a collision with the right. To counter charges of one-man rule, the prince declared that he would relinquish control of candidate selection and would permit more than one Sangkum candidate to run for each seat in the September 1966 National Assembly election. The returns showed a surprising upsurge in the conservative vote at the expense of more moderate and left-wing elements, although Hou, Hu, and Khieu were reelected by their constituencies. General Lon Nol became prime minister.

Out of concern that the right wing might cause an irreparable split within the Sangkum and might challenge his domination of the political system, Sihanouk set up a "counter government" (like the British "shadow cabinet") packed with his most loyal personal followers and with leading leftists, hoping that it would exert a restraining influence on Lon Nol. Leftists accused the general of being groomed by Western intelligence agencies to lead a bloody anticommunist coup d'état similar to that of General Soeharto in Indonesia. Injured in an automobile accident, Lon Nol resigned in April 1967. Sihanouk replaced him with a trusted centrist, Son Sann. This was the twenty-third successive Sangkum cabinet and government to have been appointed by Sihanouk since the party was formed in 1955.

Nonaligned Foreign Policy

Sihanouk's nonaligned foreign policy, which emerged in the months following the Geneva Conference, cannot be understood without reference to Cambodia's past history of foreign subjugation and its very uncertain prospects for survival as the war between North Vietnam and South Vietnam intensified. Soon after the 1954 Geneva Conference, Sihanouk expressed some interest in integrating Cambodia into the framework of the Southeast Asia Treaty Organization (SEATO), which included Cambodia, Laos, and South Vietnam within the "treaty area," although none of these states was a signatory. But meetings in late 1954 with India's Prime Minister Jawaharlal Nehru and Burma's Premier U Nu made him receptive to the appeal of nonalignment. Moreover, the prince was somewhat uneasy about a United States-dominated

alliance that included one old enemy, Thailand, and encompassed another, South Vietnam, each of which offered sanctuary to anti-Sihanouk dissidents.

At the Bandung Conference in April 1955, Sihanouk held private meetings with Premier Zhou Enlai of China and Foreign Minister Pham Van Dong of North Vietnam. Both assured him that their countries would respect Cambodia's independence and territorial integrity. His experience with the French, first as a client, then as the self-proclaimed leader of the "royal crusade for independence," apparently led him to conclude that the United States, like France, would eventually be forced to leave Southeast Asia. From this perspective, the Western presence in Indochina was only a temporary interruption of the dynamics of the region—continued Vietnamese (and perhaps even Thai) expansion at Cambodia's expense. Accommodation with North Vietnam and friendly ties with China during the late 1950s and the 1960s were tactics designed to counteract these dynamics. China accepted Sihanouk's overtures and became a valuable counterweight to growing Vietnamese and Thai pressure on Cambodia.

Cambodia's relations with China were based on mutual interests. Sihanouk hoped that China would restrain the Vietnamese and the Thai from acting to Cambodia's detriment. The Chinese, in turn, viewed Cambodia's nonalignment as vital in order to prevent the

31

encirclement of their country by the United States and its allies. When Premier Zhou Enlai visited Phnom Penh in 1956, he asked the country's Chinese minority, numbering about 300,000, to cooperate in Cambodia's development, to stay out of politics, and to consider adopting Cambodian citizenship. This gesture helped to resolve a sensitive issue—the loyalty of Cambodian Chinese— that had troubled the relationship between Phnom Penh and Beijing. In 1960 the two countries signed a Treaty of Friendship and Nonaggression. After the Sino-Soviet rift Sihanouk's ardent friendship with China contributed to generally cooler ties with Moscow.

China was not the only large power to which Sihanouk looked for patronage, however. Cambodia's quest for security and nation-building assistance impelled the prince to search beyond Asia and to accept help from all donors as long as there was no impingement upon his country's sovereignty. With this end in mind, Sihanouk turned to the United States in 1955 and negotiated a military aid agreement that secured funds and equipment for the Royal Khmer Armed Forces (Forces Armées Royales Khmères— FARK—see Appendix B). A United States Military Assistance Advisory Group (MAAG) was established in Phnom Penh to supervise the delivery and the use of equipment that began to arrive from the United States. By the early 1960s, aid from Washington constituted 30 percent of Cambodia's defense budget and 14 percent of total budget inflows (see The First Indochina War, 1945–54, ch. 5).

Relations with the United States, however, proved to be stormy. United States officials both in Washington and in Phnom Penh frequently underestimated the prince and considered him to be an erratic figure with minimal understanding of the threat posed by Asian communism. Sihanouk easily reciprocated this mistrust because several developments aroused his suspicion of United States intentions toward his country.

One of these developments was the growing United States influence within the Cambodian armed forces. The processing of equipment deliveries and the training of Cambodian personnel had forged close ties between United States military advisers and their Cambodian counterparts. Military officers of both nations also shared apprehensions about the spread of communism in Southeast Asia. Sihanouk considered FARK to be Washington's most powerful constituency in his country. The prince also feared that a number of high-ranking, rightist FARK officers led by Lon Nol were becoming too powerful and that, by association with these officers, United States influence in Cambodia was becoming too deeply rooted.

A second development included the repetition of overflights by United States and South Vietnamese military aircraft within Cambodian airspace and border incursions by South Vietnamese troops in hot pursuit of Viet Cong insurgents who crossed into Cambodian territory when military pressure upon them became too sustained. As the early 1960s wore on, this increasingly sensitive issue contributed to the deterioration of relations between Phnom Penh and Washington.

A third development was Sihanouk's own belief that he had been targeted by United States intelligence agencies for replacement by a more pro-Western leader. Evidence to support this suspicion came to light in 1959 when the government discovered a plot to overthrow Sihanouk. The conspiracy involved several Khmer leaders suspected of American connections. Among them were Sam Sary, a leader of right-wing Khmer Serei troops in South Vietnam; Son Ngoc Thanh, the early nationalist leader once exiled into Thailand; and Dap Chhuon, the military governor of Siemreab Province. Another alleged plot involved Dap Chhuon's establishment of a "free" state that would have included Siemreab Province and Kampong Thum (Kampong Thom) Province and the southern areas of Laos that were controlled by the rightist Laotian prince, Boun Oum.

These developments, magnified by Sihanouk's abiding suspicions, eventually undermined Phnom Penh's relations with Washington. In November 1963, the prince charged that the United States was continuing to support the subversive activities of the Khmer Serei in Thailand and in South Vietnam, and he announced the immediate termination of Washington's aid program to Cambodia. Relations continued to deteriorate, and the final break came in May 1965 amid increasing indications of airspace violations by South Vietnamese and by United States aircraft and of ground fighting between Army of the Republic of Vietnam (ARVN) troops and Viet Cong insurgents in the Cambodian border areas.

In the meantime, Cambodia's relations with North Vietnam and with South Vietnam, as well as the rupture with Washington, reflected Sihanouk's efforts to adjust to geopolitical realities in Southeast Asia and to keep his country out of the escalating conflict in neighboring South Vietnam. In the early to mid-1960s, this effort required a tilt toward Hanoi because the government in Saigon tottered on the brink of anarchy. In the cities, the administration of Ngo Dinh Diem and the military regimes that succeeded it had become increasingly ineffectual and unstable, while in the countryside the government forces were steadily losing ground to the Hanoi-backed insurgents. To observers in Phnom Penh, South

Vietnam's short-term viability was seriously in doubt, and this compelled a new tack in Cambodian foreign policy. First, Cambodia severed diplomatic ties with Saigon in August 1963. The following March, Sihanouk announced plans to establish diplomatic relations with North Vietnam and to negotiate a border settlement directly with Hanoi. These plans were not implemented quickly, however, because the North Vietnamese told the prince that any problem concerning Cambodia's border with South Vietnam would have to be negotiated directly with the National Front for the Liberation of South Vietnam (NFLSVN—see Appendix B). Cambodia opened border talks with the front in mid-1966, and the latter recognized the inviolability of Cambodia's borders a year later. North Vietnam quickly followed suit. Cambodia was the first foreign government to recognize the NFLSVN's Provisional Revolutionary Government after it was established in June 1969. Sihanouk was the only foreign head of state to attend the funeral of Ho Chi Minh, North Vietnam's deceased leader, in Hanoi three months later.

In the late 1960s, while preserving relations with China and with North Vietnam, Sihanouk sought to restore a measure of equilibrium by improving Cambodia's ties with the West. This shift in course by the prince represented another adjustment to prevailing conditions in Southeast Asia. North Vietnamese and Viet Cong forces were increasing their use of sanctuaries in Cambodia, which also served as the southern terminus of the Ho Chi Minh Trail, their logistical resupply route originating in North Vietnam. Cambodian neutrality in the conflict thus was eroding, and China, preoccupied with its Cultural Revolution, did not intercede with Hanoi. On Cambodia's eastern border, South Vietnam, surprisingly, had not collapsed, even in the face of the communist Tet Offensive in 1968, and President Nguyen Van Thieu's government was bringing a measure of stability to the war-ravaged country. As the government in Phnom Penh began to feel keenly the loss of economic and military aid from the United States, which had totaled about US$400 million between 1955 and 1963, it began to have second thoughts about the rupture with Washington. The unavailability of American equipment and spare parts was exacerbated by the poor quality and the small numbers of Soviet, Chinese, and French substitutes.

In late 1967 and in early 1968, Sihanouk signaled that he would raise no objection to hot pursuit of communist forces by South Vietnamese or by United States troops into Cambodian territory. Washington, in the meantime, accepted the recommendation of the United States Military Assistance Command—Vietnam

(MACV) and, beginning in March 1969, ordered a series of air-strikes (dubbed the Menu series) against Cambodian sanctuaries used by the North Vietnamese and the Viet Cong. Whether or not these bombing missions were authorized aroused considerable controversy, and assertions by the Nixon administration that Sihanouk had "allowed" or even "encouraged" them were disputed by critics such as British journalist William Shawcross. On a diplomatic level, however, the Menu airstrikes did not impede bilateral relations from moving forward. In April 1969, Nixon sent a note to the prince affirming that the United States recognized and respected "the sovereignty, neutrality and territorial integrity of the Kingdom of Cambodia with its present frontiers." Shortly thereafter, in June 1969, full diplomatic relations were restored between Phnom Penh and Washington.

The Cambodian Left: The Early Phases

The history of the communist movement in Cambodia can be divided into six phases: the emergence of the Indochinese Communist Party (ICP —see Appendix B), whose members were almost exclusively Vietnamese, before World War II; the ten-year struggle for independence from the French, when a separate Cambodian communist party, the Kampuchean (or Khmer) People's Revolutionary Party (KPRP—see Appendix B), was established under Vietnamese auspices; the period following the Second Party Congress of the KPRP in 1960, when Saloth Sar (Pol Pot after 1976) and other future Khmer Rouge leaders gained control of its apparatus; the revolutionary struggle from the initiation of the Khmer Rouge insurgency in 1967–68 to the fall of the Lon Nol government in April 1975; the Democratic Kampuchea regime, from April 1975 to January 1979; and the period following the Third Party Congress of the KPRP in January 1979, when Hanoi effectively assumed control over Cambodia's government and communist party.

Much of the movement's history has been shrouded in mystery, largely because successive purges, especially during the Democratic Kampuchea period, have left so few survivors to recount their experiences. One thing is evident, however; the tension between Khmer and Vietnamese was a major theme in the movement's development. In the three decades between the end of World War II and the Khmer Rouge victory, the appeal of communism to Western-educated intellectuals (and to a lesser extent its more inchoate attraction for poor peasants) was tempered by the apprehension that the much stronger Vietnamese movement was using communism as an ideological rationale for dominating the Khmer.

35

The analogy between the Vietnamese communists and the Nguyen dynasty, which had legitimized its encroachments in the nineteenth century in terms of the "civilizing mission" of Confucianism, was persuasive. Thus, the new brand of indigenous communism that emerged after 1960 combined nationalist and revolutionary appeals and, when it could afford to, exploited the virulent anti-Vietnamese sentiments of the Khmers. Khmer Rouge literature in the 1970s frequently referred to the Vietnamese as *yuon* (barbarian), a term dating from the Angkorian period.

In 1930 Ho Chi Minh founded the Vietnamese Communist Party by unifying three smaller communist movements that had emerged in Tonkin, in Annam, and in Cochinchina during the late 1920s. The name was changed almost immediately to the ICP, ostensibly to include revolutionaries from Cambodia and Laos. Almost without exception, however, all the earliest party members were Vietnamese. By the end of World War II, a handful of Cambodians had joined its ranks, but their influence on the Indochinese communist movement and on developments within Cambodia was negligible.

Viet Minh units occasionally made forays into Cambodia bases during their war against the French, and, in conjunction with the leftist government that ruled Thailand until 1947, the Viet Minh encouraged the formation of armed, left-wing Khmer Issarak bands. On April 17, 1950 (twenty-five years to the day before the Khmer Rouge captured Phnom Penh), the first nationwide congress of the Khmer Issarak groups convened, and the United Issarak Front was established. Its leader was Son Ngoc Minh (possibly a brother of the nationalist Son Ngoc Thanh), and a third of its leadership consisted of members of the ICP. According to the historian David P. Chandler, the leftist Issarak groups, aided by the Viet Minh, occupied a sixth of Cambodia's territory by 1952; and, on the eve of the Geneva Conference, they controlled as much as one half of the country.

In 1951 the ICP was reorganized into three national units—the Vietnam Workers' Party, the Lao Itsala, and the KPRP. According to a document issued after the reorganization, the Vietnam Workers' Party would continue to "supervise" the smaller Laotian and Cambodian movements. Most KPRP leaders and rank-and-file seem to have been either Khmer Krom, or ethnic Vietnamese living in Cambodia. The party's appeal to indigenous Khmers appears to have been minimal.

According to Democratic Kampuchea's version of party history, the Viet Minh's failure to negotiate a political role for the KPRP at the 1954 Geneva Conference represented a betrayal of the

Ruins of the Bayon Temple, thirteenth century
Courtesy Mr. and Mrs. Robert E. Hammerquist

Cambodian movement, which still controlled large areas of the countryside and which commanded at least 5,000 armed men. Following the conference, about 1,000 members of the KPRP, including Son Ngoc Minh, made a "Long March" into North Vietnam, where they remained in exile. In late 1954, those who stayed in Cambodia founded a legal political party, the Pracheachon Party, which participated in the 1955 and the 1958 National Assembly elections. In the September 1955 election, it won about 4 percent of the vote but did not secure a seat in the legislature. Members of the Pracheachon were subject to constant harassment and to arrests because the party remained outside Sihanouk's Sangkum. Government attacks prevented it from participating in the 1962 election and drove it underground. Sihanouk habitually labeled local leftists the Khmer Rouge (see Appendix B), a term that later came to signify the party and the state headed by Pol Pot, Ieng Sary, Khieu Samphan, and their associates.

During the mid-1950s, KPRP factions, the "urban committee" (headed by Tou Samouth), and the "rural committee" (headed by Sieu Heng), emerged. In very general terms, these groups espoused divergent revolutionary lines. The prevalent "urban" line, endorsed by North Vietnam, recognized that Sihanouk, by virtue of his success in winning independence from the French, was a genuine national leader whose neutralism and deep distrust of the

United States made him a valuable asset in Hanoi's struggle to "liberate" South Vietnam. Champions of this line hoped that the prince could be persuaded to distance himself from the right wing and to adopt leftist policies. The other line, supported for the most part by rural cadres who were familiar with the harsh realities of the countryside, advocated an immediate struggle to overthrow the "feudalist" Sihanouk. In 1959 Sieu Heng defected to the government and provided the security forces with information that enabled them to destroy as much as 90 percent of the party's rural apparatus. Although communist networks in Phnom Penh and in other towns under Tou Samouth's jurisdiction fared better, only a few hundred communists remained active in the country by 1960.

The Paris Student Group

During the 1950s, Khmer students in Paris organized their own communist movement, which had little, if any, connection to the hard-pressed party in their homeland. From their ranks came the men and women who returned home and took command of the party apparatus during the 1960s, led an effective insurgency against Sihanouk and Lon Nol from 1968 until 1975, and established the regime of Democratic Kampuchea.

Pol Pot, who rose to the leadership of the communist movement in the 1960s, was born in 1928 (some sources say in 1925) in Kampong Thum Province, north of Phnom Penh. He attended a technical high school in the capital and then went to Paris in 1949 to study radio electronics (other sources say he attended a school for printers and typesetters and also studied civil engineering). Described by one source as a "determined, rather plodding organizer," he failed to obtain a degree, but, according to the Jesuit priest, Father François Ponchaud, he acquired a taste for the classics of French literature as well as for the writings of Marx.

Another member of the Paris student group was Ieng Sary. He was a Chinese-Khmer born in 1930 in South Vietnam. He attended the elite Lycée Sisowath in Phnom Penh before beginning courses in commerce and politics at the Institut d'Etudes Politiques in France. Khieu Samphan, considered "one of the most brilliant intellects of his generation," was born in 1931 and specialized in economics and politics during his time in Paris. In talent he was rivaled by Hou Yuon, born in 1930, who was described as being "of truly astounding physical and intellectual strength," and who studied economics and law. Son Sen, born in 1930, studied education and literature; Hu Nim, born in 1932, studied law.

These men were perhaps the most educated leaders in the history of Asian communism. Two of them, Khieu Samphan and Hou

Yuon, earned doctorates from the University of Paris; Hu Nim obtained his degree from the University of Phnom Penh in 1965. In retrospect, it seems enigmatic that these talented members of the elite, sent to France on government scholarships, could launch the bloodiest and most radical revolution in modern Asian history. Most came from landowner or civil servant families. Pol Pot and Hou Yuon may have been related to the royal family. An older sister of Pol Pot had been a concubine at the court of King Monivong. Three of the Paris group forged a bond that survived years of revolutionary struggle and intraparty strife, Pol Pot and Ieng Sary married Khieu Ponnary and Khieu Thirith (also known as Ieng Thirith), purportedly relatives of Khieu Samphan. These two well-educated women also played a central role in the regime of Democratic Kampuchea.

The intellectual ferment of Paris must have been a dizzying experience for young Khmers fresh from Phnom Penh or the provinces. A number sought refuge in the dogma of orthodox Marxism-Leninism. At some time between 1949 and 1951, Pol Pot and Ieng Sary joined the French Communist Party, the most tightly disciplined and Stalinist of Western Europe's communist movements. In 1951 the two men went to East Berlin to participate in a youth festival. This experience is considered to have been a turning point in their ideological development. Meeting with Khmers who were fighting with the Viet Minh (and whom they subsequently judged to be too subservient to the Vietnamese), they became convinced that only a tightly disciplined party organization and a readiness for armed struggle could achieve revolution. They transformed the Khmer Students' Association (KSA), to which most of the 200 or so Khmer students in Paris belonged, into a platform for nationalist and leftist ideas. In 1952 Pol Pot, Hou Yuon, Ieng Sary, and other leftists gained notoriety by sending an open letter to Sihanouk calling him the "strangler of infant democracy." A year later, the French authorities closed down the KSA. In 1956, however, Hou Yuon and Khieu Samphan helped to establish a new Marxist-oriented group, the Khmer Students' Union.

The doctoral dissertations written by Hou Yuon and Khieu Samphan express basic themes that were later to become the cornerstones of the policy adopted by Democratic Kampuchea. The central role of the peasants in national development was espoused by Hou Yuon in his 1955 thesis, "The Cambodian Peasants and Their Prospects for Modernization," which challenged the conventional view that urbanization and industrialization are necessary precursors of development. The major argument in Khieu Samphan's 1959 thesis, "Cambodia's Economy and Industrial Development," was that the country had to become self-reliant and had to end its economic dependency on the developed world. In its general contours, Khieu's work reflected the influence of a branch of the "dependency theory" school, which blamed lack of development in the Third World on the economic domination of the industrialized nations.

The KPRP Second Congress

After returning to Cambodia in 1953, Pol Pot threw himself into party work first in Kampong Cham Province (Kompong Cham) and then in Phnom Penh under Tou Samouth's "urban committee." His comrades, Ieng Sary and Hou Yuon, became teachers at a new private high school, the Lycée Kambuboth, which Hou Yuon helped to establish. Khieu Samphan returned from Paris in 1959, taught as a member of the law faculty of the University of Phnom Penh, and started a left-wing, French-language publication, *L'Observateur*. The paper soon acquired a reputation in Phnom Penh's small academic circle. The following year, the government closed the paper, and Sihanouk's police publicly humiliated Khieu by undressing and photographing him in public—as Shawcross notes, "not the sort of humiliation that men forgive or forget." Yet the experience did not prevent Khieu from advocating cooperation with Sihanouk in order to promote a united front against United States activities in South Vietnam. As mentioned, Khieu Samphan, Hou Yuon, and Hu Nim tried to "work through the system" by joining the Sangkum and by accepting posts in the prince's government. Hardliners like Pol Pot, Ieng Sary, and Son Sen advocated resistance.

In late September 1960, twenty-one leaders of the KPRP held a secret congress in a vacant room of the Phnom Penh railroad station. This pivotal event remains shrouded in mystery because its outcome has become an object of contention (and considerable historical rewriting) between pro-Vietnamese and anti-Vietnamese Khmer communist factions. The question of cooperation with, or resistance to, Sihanouk was thoroughly discussed. Tou Samouth, who advocated a policy of cooperation, was elected general secretary of the KPRP that was renamed the Workers' Party of Kampuchea (WPK—see Appendix B). His ally, Nuon Chea (also known as Long Reth), became deputy general secretary; however, Pol Pot and Ieng Sary were named to the Political Bureau to occupy the third and the fifth highest positions in the renamed party's hierarchy. The name change is significant. By calling itself a workers' party, the Cambodian movement claimed equal status with the Vietnam Workers' Party. The pro-Vietnamese regime of the

People's Republic of Kampuchea (PRK—see Appendix B) implied in the 1980s that the September 1960 meeting was nothing more than the second congress of the KPRP.

On July 20, 1962, Tou Samouth disappeared. He may have been the victim of Sihanouk's police, but some observers suggest that Pol Pot, who had built up a strong faction within the party, had him eliminated. In February 1963, at the WPK's second congress, Pol Pot was chosen to succeed Tou Samouth as the party's general secretary. Tou's allies, Nuon Chea and Keo Meas, were removed from the Central Committee and replaced by Son Sen and Vorn Vet. From then on, Pol Pot and loyal comrades from his Paris student days controlled the party center, edging out older veterans whom they considered excessively pro-Vietnamese.

In July 1963, Pol Pot and most of the central committee left Phnom Penh to establish an insurgent base in Rotanokiri (Ratanakiri) Province in the northeast. This is a region inhabited by tribal minorities, the Khmer Loeu (see Appendix B), whose rough treatment (including resettlement and forced assimilation) at the hands of the central government made them willing recruits for a guerrilla struggle. In 1965 Pol Pot made a visit of several months duration to North Vietnam and China. He probably received some training in China, which must have enhanced his prestige when he returned to the WPK's liberated areas. Despite friendly relations between Sihanouk and the Chinese, the latter kept Pol Pot's visit a secret from Sihanouk. In September 1966, the party changed its name a second time, to the Kampuchean (or Khmer) Communist Party (KCP—see Appendix B). Adopting the label "communist" suggested that the Cambodian movement was more advanced than Vietnam's (which was merely a "workers' party"), and was on the same level as China's.

Into the Maelstrom: Insurrection and War, 1967-75

By the mid-1960s, Sihanouk's delicate balancing act was beginning to go awry. Regionally, the presence of large-scale North Vietnamese and Viet Cong logistical bases on Cambodian territory and the use of Kampong Saom (then Sihanoukville) as a port of disembarkation for supplies being sent to communist troops, as well as the covert intelligence-gathering, sabotage missions, and overflights by South Vietnamese and United States teams had made a sham of Cambodian neutrality. Domestically, Sihanouk's sporadic harassment of the leftists and the withdrawal of his endorsement from all candidates in the 1966 elections cost the radicals their chance for victory and alienated them from the prince as well. Sihanouk also lost the support of the rightists by his failure to come to grips with the deteriorating economic situation in the country and with the growing North Vietnamese and Viet Cong military presence in Cambodia. In addition to these regional developments and the clash of interests among Phnom Penh's politicized elite, social tensions also were creating a favorable environment for the growth of a domestic communist insurgency in the rural areas.

In early 1967, an insurrection broke out in the area around Samlot in Batdambang, a province long noted for the presence of large landowners and great disparities of wealth. Local resentment focused on tax collections and on the decision of the revenue-starved government to expropriate land to build a sugar refinery near Samlot. In January 1967, irate villagers attacked a tax collection brigade—an incident that recalled the 1925 murder of the French resident in the area. With the probable encouragement of local communist cadres, the insurrection quickly spread through the whole region. Sihanouk was on one of his frequent sojourns in France, and Lon Nol, the prime minister, responded harshly. After returning home in March 1967, Sihanouk personally supervised counterinsurgency measures. He later mentioned, in an offhand way, that the effectiveness of the royal armed forces had restored the peace but that approximately 10,000 people had died.

The insurgency was not suppressed completely. It spread rapidly from Batdambang to the southern and to the southwestern provinces of Pouthisat (Pursat), Kampong Chhnang (Kompong Chang), Kampong Cham, Kampong Spoe (Kompong Speu), Kampot, and the central province of Kampong Thum. By the end of 1968, unrest was reported in eleven of the country's eighteen provinces. The Khmer Loeu regions of Mondol Kiri (Mondolkiri) Province and Rotanokiri Province fell almost entirely under KCP control by the end of the decade.

In January 1968, the communists established the Revolutionary Army of Kampuchea (RAK—see Appendix B; The Second Indochina War, 1954–75, ch. 5). During Sihanouk's last two years in power, the RAK obtained minimal assistance from the North Vietnamese, the Viet Cong, and the Chinese. Although North Vietnam had established a special unit in 1966 to train the Cambodian communists, it was extremely reluctant to alienate Sihanouk at a time when vital supplies were passing through the port of Kampong Saom and along the Ho Chi Minh Trail to the Viet Cong bases along the Cambodia-Vietnam border. Beijing and Moscow also were providing Sihanouk with arms, many of which were being used against the insurgents. The indifference of the world communist movement to the Cambodian struggle from 1967 to 1969

made a permanent impression on Pol Pot and other Khmer Rouge
leaders.

The March 1970 Coup d'Etat

Sihanouk was away on a trip to Moscow and Beijing when General Lon Nol launched a successful coup d'état. On the morning
of March 18, 1970, the National Assembly was hastily convened,
and voted unanimously to depose Sihanouk as head of state. Lon
Nol, who had been serving as prime minister, was granted emergency powers. Sirik Matak, an ultraconservative royal prince who
in 1941 had been passed over by the French in favor of his cousin
Norodom Sihanouk as king, retained his post as deputy prime
minister. The new government emphasized that the transfer of
power had been totally legal and constitutional, and it received the
recognition of most foreign governments.

Most middle-class and educated Khmers in Phnom Penh had
grown weary of Sihanouk and apparently welcomed the change
of government. But he was still popular in the villages. Days after
the coup, the prince, now in Beijing, broadcast an appeal to the
people to resist the usurpers. Demonstrations and riots occurred
throughout the country. In one incident on March 29, an estimated
40,000 peasants began a march on the capital to demand Sihanouk's
reinstatement. They were dispersed, with many casualties, by contingents of the armed forces and the Khmer Serei.

From Beijing, Sihanouk proclaimed his intention to create a
National United Front of Kampuchea (Front Uni National du
Kampuchéa—FUNK—see Appendix B). In the prince's words,
this front would embrace "all Khmer both inside and outside the
country—including the faithful, religious people, military men,
civilians, and men and women who cherish the ideals of independence, democracy, neutrality, progressivism, socialism, Buddhism,
nationalism, territorial integrity, and anti-imperialism." A coalition, brokered by the Chinese, was hastily formed between the
prince and the KCP. On May 5, 1970, the actual establishment
of FUNK and of the Royal Government of National Union of Kampuchea (Gouvernement Royal d'Union Nationale du Kampuchéa—
GRUNK—see Appendix B), were announced. Sihanouk assumed
the post of GRUNK head of state, appointing Penn Nouth, one
of his most loyal supporters, as prime minister. Khieu Samphan
was designated deputy prime minister, minister of defense, and
commander in chief of the GRUNK armed forces (though actual military operations were directed by Pol Pot). Hu Nim became minister of information, and Hou Yuon assumed multiple
responsibilities as minister of interior, communal reforms, and

cooperatives. GRUNK claimed that it was not a government-in-exile because Khieu Samphan and the insurgents remained inside Cambodia.

For Sihanouk and the KCP, this was an extremely useful marriage of convenience. Peasants, motivated by loyalty to the monarchy, rallied to the FUNK cause. The appeal of the Sihanouk-KCP coalition grew immensely after October 9, 1970, when Lon Nol abolished the monarchy and redesignated Cambodia as the Khmer Republic. The concept of a republic was not popular with most villagers, who had grown up with the idea that something was seriously awry in a Cambodia without a monarch.

GRUNK operated on two tiers. Sihanouk and his loyalists remained in Beijing, although the prince did make a visit to the "liberated areas" of Cambodia, including Angkor Wat, in March 1973. The KCP commanded the insurgency within the country. Gradually, the prince was deprived of everything but a passive, figurehead role in the coalition. The KCP told people inside Cambodia that expressions of support for Sihanouk would result in their liquidation, and when the prince appeared in public overseas to publicize the GRUNK cause, he was treated with almost open contempt by Ieng Sary and Khieu Samphan. In June 1973, the prince told the Italian journalist Oriana Fallaci that when "they [the Khmer Rouge] no longer need me, they will spit me out like a cherry pit!" By the end of that year, Sihanouk loyalists had been purged from all of GRUNK's ministries.

The Widening War

The 1970 coup d'état that toppled Sihanouk dragged Cambodia into the vortex of a wider war. The escalating conflict pitted government troops, now renamed the Khmer National Armed Forces (Forces Armées Nationales Khmères—FANK—see Appendix B), initially against the North Vietnamese and the Viet Cong, and subsequently against the old RAK, now revitalized and renamed the Cambodian People's National Liberation Armed Forces (CPNLAF—see Appendix B).

As combat operations quickly disclosed, the two sides were mismatched. The inequality lay not so much in sheer numbers. Thousands of young urban Cambodians flocked to join FANK in the months following the coup and, throughout its five-year life, the republican government forces held a numerical edge over their opponents, the padded payrolls and the phantom units reported in the press notwithstanding. Instead, FANK was outclassed in training and leadership. With the surge of recruits, the government forces expanded beyond their capacity to absorb the new inductees. Later, given the press of tactical operations and the need to replace combat casualties, there was insufficient time to impart needed skills to individuals or to units, and lack of training remained the bane of FANK's existence until its collapse. While individual soldiers and some government units fought bravely, their leaders—with notable exceptions—were both corrupt and incompetent. Arrayed against an armed force of such limited capability was arguably the best light infantry in the world at the time—the North Vietnamese and the Viet Cong. And when these forces were supplanted, it was by the tough, rigidly indoctrinated peasant army of the CPNLAF with its core of Khmer Rouge leaders.

With the fall of Sihanouk, the North Vietnamese and the Viet Cong became alarmed at the prospect of a pro-Western regime that might allow the United States to establish a military presence on their western flank. To prevent this from happening, they began transferring their military installations away from the border area to locations deeper within Cambodian territory. A new command center was established at the city of Kracheh (Kratié). On April 29, 1970, South Vietnamese and United States units unleashed a multi-pronged offensive into Cambodia to destroy the Central Office for South Vietnam (COSVN), the headquarters for North Vietnamese and Viet Cong combat operations in South Vietnam. Extensive logistical installations and large amounts of supplies were found and destroyed, but as reporting from the United States MACV subsequently disclosed, still larger amounts of material already had been moved deeper into Cambodia.

The North Vietnamese army turned on the republican government forces, and by June 1970, three months after the coup, they and the CPNLAF had swept FANK from the entire northeastern third of the country. After defeating the government forces, they turned newly won territories over to the local insurgents. The Khmer Rouge also established "liberated areas" in the south and the southwestern parts of the country, where they operated independently of the Vietnamese. The KCP's debt to the North Vietnamese after March 1970 was one that Pol Pot was loath to acknowledge; however, it is clear that without North Vietnamese and Viet Cong assistance, the revolutionary struggle would have dragged on much longer than it did.

United States bombing of enemy troop dispositions in Cambodia—particularly in the summer of 1973, when intense aerial bombardment (known as Arclight) was used to halt a Khmer Rouge assault on Phnom Penh—bought time for the Lon Nol government, but did not stem the momentum of the communist forces. United States official documents give a figure of 79,959 sorties by B-52 and F–111 aircraft over the country, during which a total of 539,129 tons of ordnance were dropped, about 350 percent of the tonnage (153,000 tons) dropped on Japan during World War II. Many of the bombs that fell in Cambodia struck relatively uninhabited mountain or forest regions; however, as declassified United States Air Force maps show, others fell over some of the most densely inhabited areas of the country, such as Siemreab Province, Kampong Chhnang Province, and the countryside around Phnom Penh. Deaths from the bombing are extremely difficult to estimate, and figures range from a low of 30,000 to a high of 500,000. Whatever the real extent of the casualties, the Arclight missions over Cambodia, which were halted in August 15, 1973, by the United States Congress, delivered shattering blows to the structure of life in many of the country's villages, and, according to some critics, drove the Cambodian people into the arms of the Khmer Rouge.

The bombing was by far the most controversial aspect of the United States presence in Cambodia. In his book *Sideshow*, William Shawcross provides a vivid image of the hellish conditions, especially in the months of January to August 1973, when the Arclight sorties were most intense. He claims that the bombing contributed to the forging of a brutal and singlemindedly fanatical Khmer Rouge movement. However, his arguments have been disputed by several United States officials—including the former ambassador to Cambodia, Emory C. Swank, and the former Air Force commander in Thailand, General John W. Vogt—in an appendix to the second volume of the memoirs of then Secretary of State, Henry Kissinger.

From the Khmer Rouge perspective, however, the severity of the bombings was matched by the treachery of the North Vietnamese. The Cambodian communists had refused to take part in the Paris peace talks. When North Vietnam and the United States signed the Paris Peace Accords on January 27, 1973, bombing missions over Vietnam and Laos were terminated. The fighter bombers and other aircraft thus released were diverted to strike Khmer Rouge positions in Cambodia.

Early Khmer Rouge Atrocities

One of the earliest accounts of life under the Khmer Rouge was written in 1973 by a school administrator, Ith Sarin, who had joined the movement after becoming disillusioned with Lon Nol and the Khmer Republic, then rose to the status of candidate member of the KCP, but left the party and returned to Phnom Penh after nine months in the underground. His work, *Regrets for the Khmer Soul* (in Khmer, *Sranaoh Pralung Khmer*), revealed the secrecy with which the Khmer Rouge concealed the existence of the communist party, which they referred to by the sinister term Angkar Loeu (High Organization), or simply, Angkar. The KCP Central Committee was referred to as the Kena Mocchhim (or Committee Machine, *mocchhim* being derived from the Western term, "machine").

Territories under Angkar control were well organized. Ith Sarin described a five-level hierarchy of Angkar-controlled bodies reaching from the six areas, or *phumphaek* (see Glossary) into which the country was divided down to the hamlet, or *phum* level. The Angkar imposed a grim regime in which hatred for Lon Nol, the Americans, and, at times, the North Vietnamese "allies" was assiduously cultivated. Expressions of support for Sihanouk were firmly discouraged and people were encouraged to spy on each other. Discipline was unremittingly harsh. Ith Sarin concluded from his experience that the great majority of the people did not like the Angkar and the collective way of life it imposed, that they despaired that Sihanouk would ever return to power, and that they would support the Khmer Republic if it carried out genuine reforms. Oddly, Lon Nol's security forces banned the book for a time on the grounds that it was "pro-communist." Although this was not true, it did provide a foretaste of what the entire Cambodian population would endure after April 1975.

Disturbing stories of Khmer Rouge atrocities began to surface as the communists prepared to deal the coup de grace to the Khmer Republic. In March 1974, they captured the old capital city of Odongk north of Phnom Penh, destroyed it, dispersed its 20,000 inhabitants into the countryside, and executed the teachers and civil servants. The same year, they brutally murdered sixty people, including women and children, in a small village called Sar Sarsdam in Siemreab Province. A similar incident was reported at Ang Snuol, a town west of the capital. Other instances of what one observer, Donald Kirk, described as a "sweeping, almost cosmic policy" of indiscriminate terror, were recounted by refugees who fled to Phnom Penh or across the Thai border. Kirk contrasted this behavior with the Viet Cong's use of "a modicum of care and precision" in applying terror in South Vietnam (for instance, assassination of landlords or of South Vietnamese officials). Atrocity stories, however, were considered to be anticommunist propaganda by many, if not most, Western journalists and other observers; nevertheless, Phnom Penh's population swelled to as many as 2.5 million people as terrified refugees sought to escape not only the United States bombing and the ground fighting, but the harshness of life under the Angkar.

The Fall of Phnom Penh

The Khmer Rouge initiated their dry-season offensive to capture the beleaguered Cambodian capital on January 1, 1975. Their troops controlled the banks of the Mekong River, and they were able to rig ingenious mines to sink convoys bringing relief supplies of food, fuel, and ammunition to the slowly starving city. After the river was effectively blocked in early February, the United States began airlifts of supplies. This was extremely risky because of Khmer Rouge rockets. The communists also fired rockets and shells into the city, causing many civilian deaths. Doomed units of republican soldiers dug in around the capital; many of them had run out of ammunition, and they were overrun as the Khmer Rouge advanced. American observers, who generally had little esteem for FANK officer corps, were impressed by the determination of the Khmer enlisted men to fight to the end.

On April 1, 1975, President Lon Nol resigned and left the country. His exit was prompted by fear of certain death if he fell into Khmer Rouge hands. The communists had included him among "seven traitors" who were marked for execution. (The others were non-communist, nationalist leaders Sirik Matak, Son Ngoc Thanh, In Tam, Prime Minister Long Boret, Cheng Heng, who became head of state after Sihanouk's ouster, and Sosthene Fernandez, the FANK commander in chief). Saukham Khoy became acting president of a government that had less than three weeks to live. Last-minute efforts on the part of the United States to arrange a peace agreement involving Sihanouk ended in failure. On April 12, United States embassy personnel were evacuated by helicopter. The ambassador, John Gunther Dean, invited high officials of the Khmer Republic to join them. But Sirik Matak, Long Boret, Lon Non (Lon Nol's brother), and most members of Lon Nol's cabinet declined. They chose to share the fate of their people. All were executed soon after Khmer Rouge units entered Phnom Penh on April 17, 1975.

Democratic Kampuchea, 1975-78

Mid-April is the beginning of the Cambodian new year, the year's most festive celebration. For many Cambodians, the fall of Phnom Penh promised both a new year and a new era of peace. The people of Phnom Penh and of other cities waited in anticipation for the appearance of their new rulers. The troops who entered the capital on April 17 were mostly grim-faced youths clad in black with the checkered scarves that had become the uniform of the movement. Their unsmiling demeanor quickly dispelled popular enthusiasm. People began to realize that, in the eyes of the victors, the war was not over; it was just beginning, and the people were the new enemy. According to Father Ponchaud, as the sense of consternation and dread grew, it seemed that "a slab of lead had fallen on the city."

Evacuation of Phnom Penh began immediately. The black-clad troops told the residents that they would move only about "two or three kilometers" outside the city and would return in "two or three days." Other witnesses report being told that the evacuation was because of the threat of an American bombing and that they did not have to lock their houses since the Khmer Rouge would "take care of everything" until they returned. The roads out of the city were clogged with evacuees. Phnom Penh—the population of which, numbering 2.5 million people, included as many as 1.5 million wartime refugees living with relatives or in shanty-towns around the urban center—was soon emptied. Similar evacuations occurred at Batdambang, Kampong Cham, Siemreab, Kampong Thum, and the country's other towns and cities.

There were no exceptions to the evacuation. Even Phnom Penh's hospitals were emptied of their patients. The Khmer Rouge provided transportation for some of the aged and the disabled, and they set up stockpiles of food outside the city for the refugees; however, the supplies were inadequate to sustain the hundreds of thousands of people on the road. Even seriously injured hospital patients, many without any means of conveyance, were summarily forced to leave regardless of their condition. According to Khieu Samphan, the evacuation of Phnom Penh's famished and disease-racked population resulted in 2,000 to 3,000 deaths, which is probably an understatement. The foreign community, about 800 persons, was quarantined in the French embassy compound, and by the end of the month the foreigners were taken by truck to the Thai border. Khmer women who were married to foreigners were allowed to accompany their husbands, but Khmer men were not permitted to leave with their foreign wives.

Promises that urban residents forced into the countryside would be allowed to return home were never kept. Instead, the town dwellers, regarded as politically unreliable "new people," were put to work in forced labor battalions throughout the country. One refugee, for example, recalled that her family was sent to the region around Moung Roessei in Batdambang Province to clear land and grow rice.

Aside from the alleged threat of United States air strikes, the Khmer Rouge justified the evacuations in terms of the impossibility of transporting sufficient food to feed an urban population of between 2 and 3 million people. Lack of adequate transportation meant that, instead of bringing food to the people (tons of it lay in storehouses in the port city of Kampong Saom, according to

Father Ponchaud), the people had to be brought to (and had to grow) the food. But there were other, more basic motivations. The Khmer Rouge was determined to turn the country into a nation of peasants in which the corruption and parasitism of city life would be completely uprooted. In addition, Pol Pot wanted to break up the "enemy spy organizations" that allegedly were based in the urban areas. Finally, it seems that Pol Pot and his hard-line associates on the KCP Political Bureau used the forced evacuations to gain control of the city's population and to weaken the position of their factional rivals within the communist party. Had Phnom Penh been controlled by one of the more moderate communist leaders, the exodus might not have taken place when it did.

The regime immediately seized and executed as many Khmer Republic civil servants, police, and military officers as it could find. Evacuees who had been associated with the Lon Nol government had to feign peasant or working-class backgrounds to avoid certain death. One refugee wrote that she and her family, who came from the middle or upper middle class, dyed their city clothes black (like those of peasants) to help them escape detection. In one incident, soon after the fall of Phnom Penh, more than 300 former military officers were told to put on their dress uniforms in order to "meet Sihanouk." Instead, they were taken to a jungle clearing in Batdambang Province and were machine-gunned or clubbed to death. The wives and the children of people with government backgrounds were also killed, apparently to eliminate people who might harbor feelings of revenge toward the regime.

According to refugee accounts, the rate of killing had decreased by the summer of 1975. Some civil servants and educated people were sent to "reeducation centers" and, if they showed "genuine" contrition, were put in forced labor battalions. There were new killings, however, in late 1975 and in early 1976. Many of the victims were educated people, such as schoolteachers. During the entire Democratic Kampuchea period from 1975 to 1978, cadres exercised the power of life and death, especially over "new people," for whom threats of being struck with a pickax or an ax handle and of being "put in a plastic bag" were a part of everyday life. In order to save ammunition, firearms were rarely used. People were murdered for not working hard, for complaining about living conditions, for collecting or stealing food for their own use, for wearing jewelry, for having sexual relations, for grieving over the loss of relatives or friends, or for expressing religious sentiments. Sick people were often eliminated. The killings often, if not usually, occurred without any kind of trial, and they continued, uninterrupted, until the 1979 Vietnamese invasion. People who displeased the Angkar, or its local representatives, customarily received a formal warning (*kosang*) to mend their ways. More than two warnings resulted in being given an "invitation," which meant certain death. In 1977 and 1978 the violence reached a climax as the revolutionaries turned against each other in bloody purges.

Revolutionary Terror

Estimates of the number of people who perished under the Khmer Rouge vary tremendously. A figure of three million deaths between 1975 and 1979 was given by the Vietnamese-sponsored Phnom Penh regime, the PRK. Father Ponchaud suggested 2.3 million. Amnesty International estimated 1.4 million dead; the United States Department of State, 1.2 million. Khieu Samphan and Pol Pot, who could be expected to give underestimations, cited figures of 1 million and 800,000, respectively. In 1962 the year of the last census taken before Cambodia was engulfed by war, the population of the country was cited at 5.7 million. Ten years later, in 1972, the population was estimated to have reached 7.1 million. Using Pol Pot's rather modest figure of 800,000 deaths, about 11 percent of the population would have died from unnatural causes between 1975 and 1978. By contrast, Amnesty International's figure would yield a death rate of almost 20 percent of the population; Father Ponchaud's, of approximately 32 percent. The revolution was easily, in proportion to the size of the country's population, the bloodiest in modern Asian history.

As is evident from the accounts of refugees, the greatest causes of death were hunger, disease, and exposure. Many city people could not survive the rigors of life in the countryside, the forced marches, and the hard physical labor. People died from the bites of venomous snakes, drowned in flooded areas during the rainy season, and were killed by wild beasts in jungle areas. Many fell victim to malaria. Others died in the fighting between Vietnam and Cambodia in 1978 and in 1979. Nonetheless, executions accounted for hundreds of thousands of victims and perhaps for as many as 1 million. Western journalists have been shown "killing fields" containing as many as 16,000 bodies.

Society under the Angkar

The social transformation wrought by the Khmer Rouge, first, in the areas that they occupied during the war with Lon Nol and, then, in varying degrees, throughout the country, was far more radical than anything attempted by the Russian, Chinese, or Vietnamese revolutions. According to Pol Pot, five classes existed in prerevolutionary Cambodia—peasants, workers, bourgeoisie,

51

capitalists, and feudalists. Postrevolutionary society, as defined by the 1976 Constitution of Democratic Kampuchea, consisted of workers, peasants, and "all other Kampuchean working people." No allowance was made for a transitional stage such as China's "New Democracy" in which "patriotic" landlord or bourgeois elements were permitted to play a role in socialist construction. Sihanouk writes that in 1975 he, Khieu Samphan, and Khieu Thirith went to visit Zhou Enlai, who was gravely ill. Zhou warned them not to attempt to achieve communism suddenly by one "great leap forward" without intermediate steps, as China had done with disastrous results in the late 1950s. Khieu Samphan and Khieu Thirith "just smiled an incredulous and superior smile." Khieu Samphan and Son Sen later boasted to Sihanouk that "we will be the first nation to create a completely communist society without wasting time on intermediate steps."

Although conditions varied from region to region, a situation that was, in part, a reflection of factional divisions that still existed within the KCP during the 1970s, the testimony of refugees reveals that the most salient social division was between the politically suspect "new people," those driven out of the towns after the communist victory, and the more reliable "old people," the poor and lower middle-class peasants who had remained in the countryside. Despite the ideological commitment to radical equality, KCP members and the armed forces constituted a clearly recognizable elite. The working class was a negligible factor because of the evacuation of the urban areas and the idling of most of the country's few factories. The one important working class group in prerevolutionary Cambodia—laborers on large rubber plantations—traditionally had consisted mostly of Vietnamese emigrants and thus was politically suspect.

The number of people, including refugees, living in the urban areas, on the eve of the communist victory probably was somewhat more than 3 million, in a wartime population that has been estimated at between 5.7 and 7.3 million. As mentioned, despite their rural origins, the refugees were considered "new people"— that is, people unsympathetic to Democratic Kampuchea. Some doubtless passed as "old people" after returning to their native villages, but the Khmer Rouge seem to have been extremely vigilant in recording and keeping track of the movements of families and of individuals. The lowest unit of social control, the *krom* (group), consisted of ten to fifteen nuclear families whose activities were closely supervised by a three-person committee. The committee chairman was selected by the KCP. This grass roots leadership was required to note the social origin of each family under its jurisdiction and to report it to persons higher up in the Angkar hierarchy. The number of "new people" may initially have been as high as 2.5 million.

The "new people" were treated as slave laborers. They were constantly moved, were forced to do the hardest physical labor, and worked in the most inhospitable, fever-ridden parts of the country, such as forests, upland areas, and swamps. "New people" were segregated from "old people," enjoyed little or no privacy, and received the smallest rice rations. When the country experienced food shortages in 1977, the "new people" suffered the most. The medical care available to them was primitive or nonexistent. Families often were separated because people were divided into work brigades according to age and sex and sent to different parts of the country. "New people" were subjected to unending political indoctrination and could be executed without trial. The creation of what amounted to a slave class suggests continuity between the Cambodian revolution and the country's ancient history. Like the Khmer Rouge leadership, the god-kings of Angkor had commanded armies of slaves. Pol Pot boasted in 1977 that "if our people can make Angkor, they can make anything."

The situation of the "old people" under Khmer Rouge rule was more ambiguous. Refugee interviews reveal cases in which villagers were treated as harshly as the "new people," enduring forced labor, indoctrination, the separation of children from parents, and executions; however, they were generally allowed to remain in their native villages. Because of their age-old resentment of the urban and rural elites, many of the poorest peasants probably were sympathetic to Khmer Rouge goals. In the early 1980s, visiting Western journalists found that the issue of peasant support for the Khmer Rouge was an extremely sensitive subject that officials of the People's Republic of Kampuchea had little inclination to discuss.

On the basis of interviews with refugees from different parts of the country as well as other sources, Vickery has argued that there was a wide regional variation in the severity of policies adopted by local Khmer Rouge authorities. Ideology had something to do with the differences, but the availability of food, the level of local development, and the personal qualities of cadres also were important factors. The greatest number of deaths occurred in undeveloped districts, where "new people" were sent to clear land. While conditions were hellish in some localities, they apparently were tolerable in others. Vickery describes the Eastern Zone, which was dominated by pro-Vietnamese cadres, as one in which the extreme policies of the Pol Pot leadership were not adopted (at least until 1978, when the Eastern leadership was liquidated in a bloody purge). Executions were few, "old people" and "new people" were treated largely the same, and food was made available to the entire population. Although the Southwestern Zone was an original center of power of the Khmer Rouge, and cadres administered it with strict discipline, random executions were relatively rare, and "new people" were not persecuted if they had a cooperative attitude. In the Western Zone and in the Northwestern Zone, conditions were harsh. Starvation was widespread in the latter zone because cadres sent rice to Phnom Penh rather than distributed it to the local population. In the Northern Zone and in the Central Zone, there seem to have been more executions than there were victims of starvation. Little reliable information emerged on conditions in the Northeastern Zone, one of the most isolated parts of Cambodia (see fig. 3).

On the surface, society in Democratic Kampuchea was strictly egalitarian. The Khmer language, like many in Southeast Asia, has a complex system of usages to define speakers' rank and social status. These usages were abandoned. People were encouraged to call each other "friend," or "comrade" (in Khmer, *mit* or *met*), and to avoid traditional signs of deference such as bowing or folding the hands in salutation. Language was transformed in other ways. The Khmer Rouge invented new terms. People were told they must "forge" (*lot dam*) a new revolutionary character, that they were the "instruments" (*opokar*) of the Angkar, and that nostalgia for prerevolutionary times (*cchoeu sttak aram,* or "memory sickness") could result in their receiving Angkar's "invitation."

As in other revolutionary states, however, some people were "more equal" than others. Members and candidate members of the KCP, local-level leaders of poor peasant background who collaborated with the Angkar, and members of the armed forces had a higher standard of living than the rest of the population. Refugees agree that, even during times of severe food shortage, members of the grass-roots elite had adequate, if not luxurious, supplies of food. One refugee wrote that "pretty new bamboo houses" were built for Khmer Rouge cadres along the river in Phnom Penh. According to Craig Etcheson, an authority on Democratic Kampuchea, members of the revolutionary army lived in self-contained colonies, and they had a "distinctive warrior-caste ethos." Armed forces units personally loyal to Pol Pot, known as the "Unconditional Divisions," were a privileged group within the military.

Given the severity of their revolutionary ideology, it is surprising that the highest ranks of the Khmer Rouge leadership exhibited a talent for cronyism that matched that of the Sihanouk-era elite. Pol Pot's wife, Khieu Ponnary, was head of the Association of Democratic Khmer Women and her younger sister, Khieu Thirith, served as minister of social action. These two women are considered among the half-dozen most powerful personalities in Democratic Kampuchea. Son Sen's wife, Yun Yat, served as minister for culture, education and learning. Several of Pol Pot's nephews and nieces were given jobs in the Ministry of Foreign Affairs. One of Ieng Sary's daughters was appointed head of the Calmette Hospital although she had not graduated from secondary school. A niece of Ieng Sary was given a job as English translator for Radio Phnom Penh although her fluency in the language was extremely limited. Family ties were important, both because of the culture and because of the leadership's intense secretiveness and distrust of outsiders, especially of pro-Vietnamese communists. Greed was also a motive. Different ministries, such as the Ministry of Foreign Affairs and the Ministry of Industry, were controlled and exploited by powerful Khmer Rouge families. Administering the diplomatic corps was regarded as an especially profitable fiefdom.

Religious and Minority Communities

Article 20 of the 1976 Constitution of Democratic Kampuchea guaranteed religious freedom, but it also declared that "all reactionary religions that are detrimental to Democratic Kampuchea and the Kampuchean People are strictly forbidden." About 85 percent of the population follows the Theravada school of Buddhism (see Buddhism, ch. 2). Before 1975 the Khmer Rouge tolerated the activities of the community of Buddhist monks, or *sangha* (see Glossary), in the liberated areas in order to win popular support. This changed abruptly after the fall of Phnom Penh. The country's 40,000 to 60,000 Buddhist monks, regarded by the regime as social parasites, were defrocked and forced into labor brigades. Many monks were executed; temples and pagodas were destroyed or turned into storehouses or jails. Images of the Buddha were defaced and dumped into rivers and lakes. People who were discovered praying or expressing religious sentiments in other ways were often killed. The Christian and Muslim communities also were persecuted. The Roman Catholic cathedral of Phnom Penh was completely razed. The Khmer Rouge forced Muslims to eat pork, which they regard as an abomination. Many of those who refused were killed. Christian clergy and Muslim leaders were executed.

The Khmer Rouge's treatment of minorities seems to have varied from group to group. The Vietnamese endured the greatest suffering. Tens of thousands were murdered in regime-organized massacres. Most of the survivors fled to Vietnam. The Cham, a Muslim

Source: Based on information from Michael Vickery, *Cambodia: 1975–82,* Boston, 1984, and Elizabeth Becker, *When the War Was Over,* New York, 1986.

Figure 3. Khmer Rouge Administrative Zones for Democratic Kampuchea, 1975–78

minority who are the descendants of migrants from the old state of Champa, were forced to adopt the Khmer language and customs. Their communities, which traditionally had existed apart from Khmer villages, were broken up. Forty thousand Cham were killed in two districts of Kampong Cham Province alone. Thai minorities living near the Thai border also were persecuted.

Despite the fact that Chinese and Sino-Khmers had dominated the Cambodian economy for centuries and could be considered exploiters of the peasantry, the Khmer Rouge apparently did not single them out for harsh treatment. The war drove most rural Chinese into the cities, and after the forced evacuations they and their urban compatriots were regarded as "new people." They shared the same hardships as Khmers, however. Phnom Penh's close relationship with China was probably a factor in the regime's reluctance to persecute them openly.

In the late 1980s, little was known of Khmer Rouge policies toward the tribal peoples of the northeast, the Khmer Loeu. Pol Pot established an insurgent base in the tribal areas of Rotanokiri Province in the early 1960s, and he may have had a substantial Khmer Loeu following (see The Cambodian Left: The Early Phases, this ch.). Predominately animist peoples with few ties to the Buddhist culture of the lowland Khmers, the Khmer Loeu had resented Sihanouk's attempts to "civilize" them. Cambodia expert Serge Thion notes that marriage to a tribal person was considered "final proof of unconditional loyalty to the party." Khieu Samphan may have been married to a tribal woman.

Education and Health

Like the radical exponents of the Cultural Revolution in China during the 1960s, the Khmer Rouge regarded traditional education with unalloyed hostility. After the fall of Phnom Penh, they executed thousands of teachers. Those who had been educators prior to 1975 survived by hiding their identities. Aside from teaching basic mathematical skills and literacy, the major goal of the new educational system was to instill revolutionary values in the young. For a regime at war with most of Cambodia's traditional values, this meant that it was necessary to create a gap between the values of the young and the values of the nonrevolutionary old.

In a manner reminiscent of George Orwell's *1984,* the regime recruited children to spy on adults. The pliancy of the younger generation made them, in the Angkar's words, the "dictatorial instrument of the party." In 1962 the communists had created a special secret organization, the Alliance of Democratic Khmer Youth, that, in the early 1970s, changed its name to the Alliance of Communist Youth of Kampuchea. Pol Pot considered Alliance alumni as his most loyal and reliable supporters, and used them to gain control of the central and of the regional KCP apparatus. The powerful Khieu Thirith, minister of social action, was responsible for directing the youth movement.

Hardened young cadres, many little more than twelve years of age, were enthusiastic accomplices in some of the regime's worst atrocities. Sihanouk, who was kept under virtual house arrest in Phnom Penh between 1976 and 1978, wrote in *War and Hope* that his youthful guards, having been separated from their families and given a thorough indoctrination, were encouraged to play cruel games involving the torture of animals. Having lost parents, siblings, and friends in the war and lacking the Buddhist values of their elders, the Khmer Rouge youth also lacked the inhibitions that would have dampened their zeal for revolutionary terror.

Health facilities in the years 1975 to 1978 were abysmally poor. Many physicians either were executed or were prohibited from practicing. It appears that the party and the armed forces elite had access to Western medicine and to a system of hospitals that offered reasonable treatment but ordinary people, especially "new people," were expected to use traditional plant and herbal remedies that usually were ineffective. Some bartered their rice rations and personal possessions to obtain aspirin and other simple drugs.

The Economy

In its general contours, Democratic Kampuchea's economic policy was similar to, and possibly inspired by, China's radical Great Leap Forward that carried out immediate collectivization of the Chinese countryside in 1958. During the early 1970s, the Khmer Rouge established "mutual assistance groups" in the areas they occupied. After 1973 these were organized into "low-level cooperatives" in which land and agricultural implements were lent by peasants to the community but remained their private property. "High-level cooperatives," in which private property was abolished and the harvest became the collective property of the peasants, appeared in 1974. "Communities," introduced in early 1976, were a more advanced form of high-level cooperative in which communal dining was instituted. State-owned farms also were established.

Far more than had the Chinese communists, the Khmer Rouge relentlessly pursued the ideal of economic self-sufficiency, in their case the version that Khieu Samphan had outlined in his 1959 doctoral dissertation. Extreme measures were taken. Currency was abolished, and domestic trade or commerce could be conducted only through barter. Rice, measured in tins, became the most important medium of exchange, although people also bartered gold, jewelry, and other personal possessions. Foreign trade was almost completely halted, though there was a limited revival in late 1976 and early 1977. China was the most important trading partner, but commerce amounting to a few million dollars was also conducted with France, with Britain, and with the United States through a Hong Kong intermediary.

From the Khmer Rouge perspective, the country was free of foreign economic domination for the first time in its 2,000-year history. By mobilizing the people into work brigades organized in a military fashion, the Khmer Rouge hoped to unleash the masses' productive forces. There was an "Angkorian" component to economic policy. That ancient kingdom had grown rich and powerful because it controlled extensive irrigation systems that produced surpluses of rice. Agriculture in modern Cambodia depended, for the most part, on seasonal rains. By building a nationwide system of irrigation canals, dams, and reservoirs, the leadership believed it would be possible to produce rice on a year-round basis. It was the "new people" who suffered and sacrificed the most to complete these ambitious projects.

Although the Khmer Rouge implemented an "agriculture first" policy in order to achieve self-sufficiency, they were not, as some observers have argued, "back-to-nature" primitivists. Although the 1970–75 war and the evacuation of the cities had destroyed or idled most industry, small contingents of workers were allowed to return to the urban areas to reopen some plants. Like their Chinese counterparts, the Cambodian communists had great faith in the inventive power and the technical aptitude of the masses, and they constantly published reports of peasants' adapting old mechanical parts to new uses. Much as the Chinese had attempted unsuccessfully to build a new steel industry based on backyard furnaces during the Great Leap Forward, the Khmer Rouge sought to move industry to the countryside. Significantly, the seal of Democratic Kampuchea displayed not only sheaves of rice and irrigation sluices, but also a factory with smokestacks.

Politics under the Khmer Rouge

By the April 1975 communist victory, Pol Pot and his close associates occupied the most important positions in the KCP and in the state hierarchies. He had been KCP general secretary since February 1963. His associates functioned as the party's Political Bureau, and they controlled a majority of the seats on the Central Committee. Khieu Thirith's management of youth groups meant that Pol Pot had ample reserves of zealous young cadres, "the nucleus and wick of the struggle," committed to imposing the party center's will throughout the country. But his domination of the revolutionary movement was not complete. In different areas of the country, especially in the Eastern Zone, pro-Vietnamese and veteran Khmer Issarak commanders were jealous of their independence. They questioned, and at times openly defied, his policies of revolutionary terror and hostility toward Vietnam. The highest ranks of the party were not free of dissension.

Like Joseph Stalin in the late 1920s and in the 1930s, Pol Pot initiated a purge of his opponents, both imagined and real. In terms of the number of people liquidated in relation to the total population, the Khmer Rouge terror was far bloodier than Stalin's. Through the 1970s, and especially after mid-1975, the party was shaken by factional struggles. There were even armed attempts to topple Pol Pot. The resultant purges reached a crest in 1977 and 1978 when hundreds of thousands of people, including some of the most important KCP leaders, were executed.

Establishing Democratic Kampuchea

The communists had exercised real power behind the facade, since its establishment in 1970, of the Royal Government of National Union of Kampuchea, (Governement Royal d'Union Nationale du Kampuchéa—GRUNK—see Appendix B). It remained formally in control of the country until the proclamation of the Constitution of Democratic Kampuchea on January 5, 1976. Three months later, on April 2, Sihanouk resigned as head of state. Sihanouk remained under comfortable, but insecure, house arrest in Phnom Penh, until he departed for China on the last flight before Vietnamese forces captured the city on January 7, 1979.

Khieu Samphan described the 1976 Constitution as "not the result of any research on foreign documents, nor . . . the fruit of any research by scholars. In fact the people—workers, peasants, and Revolutionary Army—wrote the Constitution with their own hands." It was a brief document of sixteen chapters and twenty-one articles that defined the character of the state; the goals of economic, social and cultural policies; and the basic tenets of foreign policy. The "rights and duties of the individual" were briefly defined in Article 12. They included none of what are commonly regarded as guarantees of political human rights except the statement that "men and women are equal in every respect." The document declared, however, that "all workers" and "all peasants" were "masters" of their factories and fields. An assertion that "there is absolutely no unemployment in Democratic Kampuchea" rings true in light of the regime's massive use of forced labor.

The Constitution defined Democratic Kampuchea's foreign policy principles in Article 21, the document's longest, in terms of "independence, peace, neutrality, and nonalignment." It pledged the country's support to anti-imperialist struggles in the Third World. In light of the regime's aggressive attacks against Vietnamese, Thai, and Lao territory during 1977 and 1978, the promise to "maintain close and friendly relations with all countries sharing a common border" bore little resemblance to reality.

Governmental institutions were outlined very briefly in the Constitution. The legislature, the Kampuchean People's Representative Assembly (KPRA), contained 250 members "representing workers, peasants, and other working people and the Kampuchean Revolutionary army." One hundred and fifty KPRA seats were allocated for peasant representatives; fifty, for the armed forces; and fifty, for worker and other representatives. The legislature was to be popularly elected for a five-year term. Its first and only election was held on March 20, 1976. "New people" apparently were not allowed to participate.

The executive branch of government also was chosen by the KPRA. It consisted of a state presidium "responsible for representing the state of Democratic Kampuchea inside and outside the country." It served for a five-year term, and its president was head of state. Khieu Samphan was the first and only person to serve in this office, which he assumed after Sihanouk's resignation. The judicial system was composed of "people's courts," the judges for which were appointed by the KPRA, as was the executive branch.

The Constitution did not mention regional or local government institutions. After assuming power, the Khmer Rouge abolished the old provinces (*khet*) and replaced them with seven zones; the Northern Zone, Northeastern Zone, Northwestern Zone, Central Zone, Eastern Zone, Western Zone, and Southwestern Zone. There were also two other regional-level units: the Kracheh Special Region Number 505 and, until 1977, the Siemreab Special Region Number 106. The zones were divided into *damban* (regions) that were given numbers. Number One, appropriately, encompassed the Samlot region of the Northwestern Zone (including Batdambang Province), where the insurrection against Sihanouk had erupted in early 1967. With this exception, the *damban* appear to have been numbered arbitrarily.

The *damban* were divided into *srok* (districts), *khum* (subdistricts), and *phum* (villages), the latter usually containing several hundred people. This pattern was roughly similar to that which existed under Sihanouk and the Khmer Republic, but inhabitants of the villages were organized into *krom* (groups) composed of ten to fifteen families. On each level, administration was directed by a three-person committee (*kanak,* or *kena*). KCP members occupied committee posts at the higher levels. Subdistrict and village committees were often staffed by local poor peasants, and, very rarely, by "new people." Cooperatives (*sahakor*), similar in jurisdictional area to the *khum,* assumed local government responsibilities in some areas.

An Elusive Party

To most people inside and outside Democratic Kampuchea, the communist party was known simply as the Angkar Loeu. The party's commitment to revolution was expressed in the terminology of the 1976 Constitution, but no mention was made of a specifically Marxist-Leninist ideology. The KCP's real leaders and identity were kept closely guarded secrets from non-members until 1977. Head of state Khieu Samphan was a front—Sihanouk describes him as a "bit player"—for the most important leader, Saloth Sar, whose appearances and speeches were not publicized in the official media. Under the name Pol Pot, Saloth Sar was elected to a seat in the KPRA in March 1976 as a representative of rubber plantation workers, and he became Democratic Kampuchea's prime minister the following month.

The histories of most revolutionary movements contain a clandestine theme, but rarely have any approached the near-paranoia of the Cambodian communists. In part, this reflected the profound distrust with which Pol Pot and his associates regarded people outside their small, closed circle that had begun its association in Paris in the 1950s. Also, there may have been an unwillingness to risk the support of a still-conservative peasantry by publicly embracing Marxism-Leninism. The most important reason for the obsession with secrecy, however, was intraparty strife—the KCP's continuing failure to resolve factional differences and to achieve consensus on its mission and policies. Even more than the future, however, the past was a focus of bitter controversy: how much should the KCP acknowledge its debt to the Vietnamese communists?

On September 18, in a speech mourning the death of Mao Zedong, Pol Pot announced that the Angkar was "Marxist-Leninist" and that it enjoyed "fraternal relations" with the Chinese Communist Party. But it was not until a year later, in September 1977, that Pol Pot revealed the existence of the KCP and its history in a five-hour recorded radio speech. He stated that the KCP was seventeen years old and that its founding date had been September 30, 1960. He noted that the KCP's decision to disclose its real identity had been encouraged by "foreign friends" (the Chinese) who wanted the KCP to take credit for the revolutionary victory.

Pol Pot's mention of the September 1960 founding date was extremely significant. Within the party ranks, September 30, 1951, traditionally had been recognized as its founding date. This was the day when the Kampuchean (or Khmer) People's Revolutionary Party (KPRP—see Appendix B) was established following the reorganization of the Indochinese Communist Party (ICP—see Appendix B). The September 1960 meeting had been considered the KPRP's second congress, but in the September–October 1976 edition of the party's official journal, *Tung Padevat* (Revolutionary

Flag), the date of birth of the KPRP was given as September 30, 1960. *Tung Padevat* declared that the new founding date was adopted because "we must arrange the history of the party into something clean and perfect, in line with our policies of independence and self-mastery." Pol Pot's speech a year later gave official sanction to this view.

Another party journal, *Tung Kraham* (Red Flag), mentioned the traditional founding date, September 30, 1951, in its September 1976 issue. The argument over the birth date reflected deep factional divisions within the KCP. Backers of the 1951 birth date, if not pro-Vietnamese, were at least willing to recognize their movement's past dependence on Vietnamese support. Pol Pot and his associates adopted the 1960 birthday to emphasize the party's Cambodian identity and to distance it from any association with the Vietnamese communists. The party's official history, or *"Black Book,"* published in 1978 after pro-Vietnamese elements had been liquidated, stated that the KCP had severed fraternal party relations with the Vietnam Workers' Party as early as 1973.

Intraparty Conflict

On the eve of its 1975 victory against the Lon Nol forces, the KCP was, in terms of personnel, ideological viewpoints, and factional loyalties, quite heterogeneous. Etcheson, in *The Rise and Demise of Democratic Kampuchea*, identifies six factions: the Pol Pot group (members of which he labels "Stalinists"); internationalists (pro-Vietnamese elements who were based in Hanoi after 1954, and who returned to the country when the FUNK united front was declared in 1970); veterans of the leftist Khmer Issarak (who remained in the country after 1954, mostly in the southern and in western parts of the country); veterans of the Pracheachon Party founded in 1954 (which had contested Sihanouk's Sangkum openly until being driven underground in the 1960s); pro-Chinese or Maoist elements (including Paris-group intellectuals Hou Yuon and Hu Nim); and the pro-Sihanouk Khmer Rumdo (see Appendix B). Ben Kiernan, another analyst of Cambodia, identifies three factions: the Pol Pot faction, the pro-Vietnamese communists, and the adherents of the Chinese Cultural Revolution model. The roles of ideology and of conflicting party lines in factional struggles, however, should not be overemphasized. Behind doctrinal differences lay the dynamics of personal rivalry and the strong sense of patron-client loyalty that has always characterized Cambodian politics.

Although the Revolutionary Army of Kampuchea (RAK) was "reestablished" in July 1975 to bring all Khmer Rouge units formally under central authority, real control of regional armed forces remained in the hands of the zone party committee heads. The most important center of regional resistance to the Pol Pot-dominated party center was the Eastern Zone, comprising part or all of the old provinces of Prey Veng, Svay Rieng, Kandal, and Kampong Cham that adjoined Vietnam. Its leader was So Phim, a pro-Vietnamese internationalist.

Differences between the Eastern Zone revolutionaries and the other Khmer Rouge were readily apparent by 1975. While the uniforms of Pol Pot loyalists and their allies were black, the uniforms of the Eastern Zone were a distinctive green. In addition, cadre behavior toward the civilian population in the Eastern Zone was generally exemplary. It seems that some of the Eastern cadres were sympathetic to Sihanouk; refugee Molyda Szymusiak wrote that during the evacuation of Phnom Penh, a "Sihanouk Khmer" soldier advised her relatives (who were distantly related to the royal family) to accompany him to Prey Veng Province on Cambodia's southern border.

At least two coups d'état against the center were attempted—in July and in September, 1975. The latter incident involved Eastern Zone troops. After April 1975, Hou Yuon, one of the original Paris group, disappeared. His colleague, Hu Nim, who was tortured and killed in the Tuol Sleng detention center in 1977, indicated in his confession that Hou Yuon had been liquidated for opposing the extremism of the center's policies.

Pol Pot loyalists occupied most of the important positions in the new government that was formed after the March 20, 1976, elections; however, Vorn Vet, a pro-Vietnamese leader, was appointed second vice premier with responsibility over six ministry-level economic committees, and he also headed the special Phnom Penh capital zone. So Phim, a longtime rival of Pol Pot within the communist movement, was first vice president of the presidium and a member of the KCP Political Bureau. (The second vice president, Nhim Ros, was a Pol Pot loyalist who commanded the Northwestern Zone.) The year 1976 appears to have been a time initially of retreat for the faction led by Pol Pot. Many communists were alienated by his authoritarian behavior. Article 4 of the Constitution, "Democratic Kampuchea applies the collective principle in leadership and in work," apparently reflects this opinion. In relation to what had gone before and what was to come, policies during 1976 were moderate. The terror eased. Relations with Hanoi were placed on a friendlier footing. Trade and diplomatic relations were expanded.

On September 27, 1976, Pol Pot resigned as premier "for reasons of health." Nuon Chea, the pro-Vietnamese deputy premier, became acting premier. Little is known of the intense factional maneuvering that was occurring at this time, but by late October 1976, Pol Pot had regained his post. On October 22, his comeback was confirmed with his issuance of a statement in his capacity as prime minister condemning China's "counterrevolutionary Gang of Four," who had been arrested in Beijing on October 6.

The influence of China on Democratic Kampuchea's internal politics apparently was a crucial, though little understood, factor in Pol Pot's defeat of his pro-Vietnamese rivals. Etcheson and Kiernan have suggested, in separate articles, that radicals in the Chinese Communist Party may have backed pro-Vietnamese Internationalist elements in the KCP in 1976 because they were interested in preserving good relations with Hanoi. The fall of the radicals in October 1976, a month after Mao Zedong's death, brought in the moderates, led by Deng Xiaoping. As the subsequent break between Beijing and Hanoi shows, Deng was inclined to regard Vietnam as an agent of Soviet "hegemonism." Chinese support of the Pol Pot faction may have been a crucial element in its ability to triumph over the pro-Vietnamese communists in the fall of 1976. From an ideological standpoint, the pragmatic Deng Xiaoping and the ultra-radical Pol Pot were polar opposites, but from the geopolitical perspective, the post-Mao Zedong leadership recognized the value of having a well-armed Cambodian thorn in the side of Vietnam. Immediately after making his September 27, 1977, speech revealing the KCP's existence, Pol Pot, accompanied by Ieng Sary and Vorn Vet, visited Beijing, where he acknowledged the importance of Maoist thought to the Cambodian revolution. In early 1978, the Chinese sent substantial military aid, which included armor, artillery, and antitank guns.

The Purge

In 1975 Pol Pot concluded an alliance with the party head of the Southwestern Zone, Ta Mok, who was a Khmer Issarak veteran and, like Pol Pot, was strongly anti-Vietnamese. During 1977 and 1978, Ta Mok provided the backing that enabled Pol Pot to liquidate the opposition within the KCP and to initiate new terrorism against the local population. In February 1977, Southwestern cadres went into the Eastern, Northern, and Western zones to purge local Khmer Rouge. Four months later, the same process was begun in the Northwestern Zone. The purges intensified following an abortive coup d'état in August.

After the fall of the capital, Ta Mok's lieutenant, a former high school teacher who assumed the name Mit (Comrade) Deuch, became head of the secret police, and established the Tuol Sleng interrogation and detention center on the site of a former Phnom Penh high school. In the 1975 to 1976 period, Tuol Sleng's meticulous records show that 2,404 "antiparty elements" were tortured and executed. The terror escalated in 1977, when the number of victims rose to 6,330. In the first six months of 1978, records show that 5,765 people were killed; records for the latter half of that year have not been discovered. The victims who passed through Tuol Sleng from mid-1975 to January 1979 numbered about 20,000. Among those who met death in the infamous prison were Paris alumni Hu Nim and (presumably) Hou Yuon. Similar centers were set up throughout the country (Tuol Sleng's code designation, S-21, suggests that at least twenty other similar sites had been established). Molyda Szymusiak writes that a new wave of terror began in the Batdambang region after cadres arrived from the south. The Sala Som Niat, a school for political education was converted into an extermination center where local communists were tortured and executed. The pattern in these centers was much the same: victims were tortured, forced to write often absurd confessions, and then killed. A young British teacher, captured in a yacht off the Cambodian coast, confessed at Tuol Sleng that he had been recruited by the Central Intelligence Agency (CIA) of the United States when he was twelve years old; he was subsequently murdered. Hu Nim was forced to confess that he had become a CIA agent in 1957.

The Eastern Zone apparently remained largely unaffected by the purge until May 1978, when So Phim led a revolt that provoked massive retaliation by Pol Pot and his Southwestern henchmen. In the bloodiest purge of the entire 1975 to 1978 period, as many as 100,000 people in the Eastern Zone—labeled people with "Khmer bodies but Vietnamese minds"—were liquidated or were deported to face certain death in other parts of the country. Most of the victims were political cadres, "new people," and Vietnamese or part-Vietnamese residents. So Phim reportedly committed suicide as he faced capture. Some of his subordinates, including Heng Samrin, the leader of the PRK after 1979, fled to Vietnam.

The Fall of Democratic Kampuchea

Immediately following the Khmer Rouge victory in 1975, there were skirmishes between their troops and Vietnamese forces. A number of incidents occurred in May 1975. The Cambodians launched attacks on the Vietnamese islands of Phu Quoc and Tho

The Tuol Sleng detention center, a grim reminder of Democratic Kampuchea Courtesy Bill Herod

Brick detention cubicles in the Tuol Sleng detention center (Note leg iron in the middle cubicle.) Courtesy Bill Herod

Chu and intruded into Vietnamese border provinces. In late May, at about the same time that the United States launched an air strike against the oil refinery at Kampong Saom, following the *Mayaguez* incident, Vietnamese forces seized the Cambodian island of Poulo Wai. The following month, Pol Pot and Ieng Sary visited Hanoi. They proposed a friendship treaty between the two countries, an idea that met with a cool reception from Vietnam's leaders. Although the Vietnamese evacuated Poulo Wai in August, incidents continued along Cambodian's northeastern border. At the instigation of the Phnom Penh regime, thousands of Vietnamese also were driven out of Cambodia.

Relations between Cambodia and Vietnam improved in 1976, in part because of Pol Pot's preoccupation with intraparty challenges. In May Cambodian and Vietnamese representatives met in Phnom Penh in order to establish a commission to resolve border disagreements. The Vietnamese, however, refused to recognize the Brévié Line—the colonial-era demarcation of maritime borders between the two countries—and the negotiations broke down. In late September, however, a few days before Pol Pot was forced to resign as prime minister, air links were established between Phnom Penh and Hanoi.

With Pol Pot back in the forefront of the regime in 1977, the situation rapidly deteriorated. Incidents escalated along all of Cambodia's borders. Khmer Rouge forces attacked villages in the border areas of Thailand near Aranyaprathet. Brutal murders of Thai villagers, including women and children, were the first widely reported concrete evidence of Khmer Rouge atrocities. There were also incidents along the Laotian border. At approximately the same time, villages in Vietnam's border areas underwent renewed attacks. In turn, Vietnam launched air strikes against Cambodia. In September, border fighting resulted in as many as 1,000 Vietnamese civilian casualties. The following month, the Vietnamese counterattacked in a campaign involving a force of 20,000 personnel. Vietnamese defense minister General Vo Nguyen Giap underestimated the tenacity of the Khmer Rouge, however, and was obliged to commit an additional 58,000 reinforcements in December. On January 6, 1978, Giap's forces began an orderly withdrawal from Cambodian territory. The Vietnamese apparently believed they had "taught a lesson" to the Cambodians, but Pol Pot proclaimed this a "victory" even greater than that of April 17, 1975.

Faced with growing Khmer Rouge belligerence, the Vietnamese leadership decided in early 1978 to support internal resistance to the Pol Pot regime, with the result that the Eastern Zone became a focus of insurrection. War hysteria reached bizarre levels within

Democratic Kampuchea. In May 1978, on the eve of So Phim's Eastern Zone uprising, Radio Phnom Penh declared that if each Cambodian soldier killed thirty Vietnamese, only 2 million troops would be needed to eliminate the entire Vietnamese population of 50 million. It appears that the leadership in Phnom Penh was seized with immense territorial ambitions, i.e., to recover the Mekong Delta region, which they regarded as Khmer territory.

Massacres of ethnic Vietnamese and of their sympathizers by the Khmer Rouge intensified in the Eastern Zone after the May revolt. In November, Vorn Vet led an unsuccessful coup d'état. There were now tens of thousands of Cambodian and Vietnamese exiles on Vietnamese territory. On December 3, 1978, Radio Hanoi announced the formation of the Kampuchean (or Khmer) National United Front for National Salvation (KNUFNS—see Appendix B). This was a heterogeneous group of communist and noncommunist exiles who shared an antipathy to the Pol Pot regime and a virtually total dependence on Vietnamese backing and protection. The KNUFNS provided the semblance, if not the reality, of legitimacy for Vietnam's invasion of Democratic Kampuchea and for its subsequent establishment of a satellite regime in Phnom Penh (see The Vietnamese Invasion of Cambodia, ch. 5).

In the meantime, as 1978 wore on, Cambodian bellicosity in the border areas surpassed Hanoi's threshold of tolerance. Vietnamese policy makers opted for a military solution and, on December 22, Vietnam launched its offensive with the intent of overthrowing Democratic Kampuchea. An invasion force of 120,000, consisting of combined armor and infantry units with strong artillery support, drove west into the level countryside of Cambodia's southeastern provinces. After a seventeen-day blitzkrieg, Phnom Penh fell to the advancing Vietnamese on January 7, 1979. From new redoubts in the mountain and jungle fastness of Cambodia's periphery, Pol Pot and other Khmer Rouge leaders regrouped their units, issued a new call to arms, and reignited a stubborn insurgency against the regime in power as they had done in the late 1960s. For the moment, however, the Vietnamese invasion had accomplished its purpose of deposing an unlamented and particularly loathsome dictatorship. A new administration under the mentorship of Hanoi was quickly established, and it set about competing, both domestically and internationally, with the Khmer Rouge as the legitimate government of Cambodia. Peace still eluded the war-ravaged nation, however, and although the insurgency set in motion by the Khmer Rouge proved unable to topple the new Vietnamese-backed regime in Phnom Penh, it did nonetheless keep the country in a permanent state of insecurity. The fledgling Khmer administration, weak and lacking in manpower and in resources, was propped up by a substantial Vietnamese military force and civilian advisory effort. As events in the 1980s progressed, the main preoccupations of the new regime were survival, restoring the economy, and combating the Khmer Rouge insurgency by military and by political means. The fostering of activity to meet these imperatives and the building of institutions are described in subsequent chapters (see The People's Republic of Kampuchea, ch. 4; The Vietnamese Invasion of Cambodia, ch. 5).

* * *

Probably the most definitive account of Cambodian history in English is David P. Chandler's *A History of Cambodia,* which covers this subject from the earliest centuries to the attainment of independence. An earlier work, Martin Herz's *A Short History of Cambodia from the Days of Angkor to the Present,* is somewhat dated but contains highly specific material on the early Sihanouk years. The sections on Cambodia in D.G.E. Hall's classic, *A History of South-East Asia,* are also useful. Hall's parallel treatments of Vietnamese and Thai history provide interesting perspective. George Coedès' *Angkor: An Introduction* and *The Making of South East Asia* are informative on the ancient kingdoms. The former provides good descriptions of the monuments of Angkor, their architectural motifs, and their religious significance. For an understanding of the rise of communism in Cambodia an essential source is Ben Kiernan's *How Pol Pot Came to Power.*

William Shawcross's *Sideshow: Kissinger, Nixon, and the Destruction of Cambodia* is a critical account of United States involvement in the country before and during the years, 1970 to 1975, when Lon Nol was in power. Another perspective is provided by Henry Kissinger in *White House Years* and in *Years of Upheaval.*

A large number of books have been written on the horrors of the Democratic Kampuchea period. Molyda Szymusiak's *The Stones Cry Out* is one of the most gripping. Others include François Ponchaud's *Cambodia: Year Zero* and Sydney Schanberg's *The Death and Life of Dith Pran.* The film ''The Killing Fields'' is also based on the experiences in Cambodia during and after the war of Dith Pran—journalist Schanberg's cameraman in wartime Phnom Penh. Norodom Sihanouk's *War and Hope* provides another close-up. Useful scholarly treatments of the period include Craig Etcheson's perspective on the Khmer Rouge, *The Rise and Demise of Democratic Kampuchea;* two collections of essays, *Peasants and Politics in*

Kampuchea, 1942–81, edited by Ben Kiernan and Chanthou Boua; and *Revolution and Its Aftermath in Kampuchea,* edited by David P. Chandler and Ben Kiernan. One well-reviewed account of life in Democratic Kampuchea and the transition to its successor regime is Elizabeth Becker's *When the War Was Over;* another account, equally well-regarded by critics, addressing the abiding enmity between Cambodia and Vietnam is Nayan Chanda's *Brother Enemy.* Familiarity with both sources is essential for an understanding of what occurred in Cambodia after 1975. (For further information and complete citations, see Bibliography.)

Chapter 2. The Society and Its Environment

Members of the ethnic Cham minority near Kampong Cham

SINCE 1975 CAMBODIA has suffered through one of the most catastrophic periods in its long history. The takeover of the country by the communist Khmer Rouge (see Appendix B) in 1975, its violent aftermath, and the constant warfare between communist and noncommunist factions has resulted in widespread and major changes in the Cambodian social fabric. The country was plunged into a dark age from which it was slowly emerging in the late 1980s.

Under the Khmer Rouge, the entire social structure of the country suffered radical and massive changes. An estimated 1 million to 2 million Cambodians died during the first three-and-one-half years of communist rule. Traditional family life was violently disrupted and virtually abolished between 1975 and 1979. Nuclear families—the most important units of Cambodian society—were broken up and were replaced with communal groupings. About 97 percent of the population was forced into communal economic programs. Urban dwellers were driven into the countryside in mass marches that caused great suffering and many deaths. Rural society was reorganized into interfamilial units known as *krom* (groups). Urban Cambodians, ethnic minorities, and educated people suffered especially harsh treatment. The ethnic Chinese, because they were engaged extensively in small businesses and were mainly urban dwellers, were targets for communist persecution, as were the Cham (see Glossary), a prominent ethnic minority group. Educated people were special targets for extermination, and most of the teachers and physicians fled the country or were massacred. Those who showed evidence of Western influence, such as using the English language, were suspect. Although freedom of religion was guaranteed in theory under the Khmer Rouge, in fact Buddhism and other religions were repressed ruthlessly. Temples were destroyed or put to secular uses, and monks were defrocked and forced do manual labor.

The Vietnamese invasion in December 1978 ameliorated the situation somewhat. As a result of the invasion, the Khmer Rouge government of Democratic Kampuchea was overthrown, and the People's Republic of Kampuchea (PRK—see Appendix B) under Heng Samrin was installed in 1979. The PRK allowed considerably more freedom than had its predecessor. In the late 1980s, Marxist-Leninist socialism as it existed in Vietnam was the goal of the PRK government in Phnom Penh. The regime was not pushing hard to convert the country, but was planning a gradual conversion instead. Religions were allowed to function. The government allowed Buddhist monks to return to their temples, although narrow limits were placed on those who could become monks and on aspects of ritual. The education system, which had suffered almost total destruction under the Khmer Rouge, was reconstituted, and the number of students attending formal classes rose dramatically in the early 1980s. The public health service was functioning again in the mid-1980s, and modern medical services were available although trained medical personnel and some medicines continued to be in short supply. The shortage of medical personnel was partially filled by foreign doctors and technicians. The PRK did not neglect to court ethnic minorities. Members of one of the Khmer Loeu (or highland Khmer) tribal minorities were made leaders in several northeastern provinces, and members of the Cham minority served in the central government.

Environment

Cambodia covers 181,040 square kilometers in the southwestern part of the Indochina peninsula. It lies completely within the tropics; its southernmost points are only slightly more than 10° above the equator. Roughly square in shape, the country is bounded on the north by Thailand and by Laos, on the east and southeast by Vietnam, and on the west by the Gulf of Thailand and by Thailand. Much of the country's area consists of rolling plains. Dominant features are the large, almost centrally located, Tonle Sap (Great Lake) and the Mekong River, which traverses the country from north to south.

The climate is monsoonal and has marked wet and dry seasons of relatively equal length. Both temperature and humidity generally are high throughout the year. Forest covers about two-thirds of the country, but it has been somewhat degraded in the more readily accessible areas by a method called slash-and-burn agriculture.

Topography

Cambodia falls within several well-defined geographic regions. The largest part of the country—about 75 percent of the total—consists of the Tonle Sap Basin and the Mekong Lowlands. To the southeast of this great basin is the Mekong Delta, which extends through Vietnam to the South China Sea. The basin and delta regions are rimmed with mountain ranges to the southwest (the Cardamom Mountains, the Elephant Range) and to the north (Dangrek Mountains). Higher land to the northeast and to the east merges into the Central Highlands of southern Vietnam (see fig. 4).

The Tonle Sap Basin-Mekong Lowlands region consists chiefly of plains with elevations generally of less than 100 meters. As the elevation increases, the terrain becomes more rolling and dissected.

The Cardamom Mountains in the southwest, oriented generally in a northwest-southeast direction, rise to more than 1,500 meters. The highest mountain in Cambodia—Phnom Aural, at 1,771 meters—is in the eastern part of this range. The Elephant Range, an extension running toward the south and the southeast from the Cardamom Mountains, rises to elevations of between 500 and 1,000 meters. These two ranges are bordered on the west by a narrow coastal plain that contains Kampong Saom Bay, which faces the Gulf of Thailand. This area was largely isolated until the opening of the port of Kampong Saom (formerly called Sihanoukville) and the construction of a road and railroad connecting Kampong Saom, Kampot, Takev, and Phnom Penh in the 1960s.

The Dangrek Mountains at the northern rim of the Tonle Sap Basin consist of a steep escarpment with an average elevation of about 500 meters, the highest points of which reach more than 700 meters. The escarpment faces southward and is the southern edge of the Korat Plateau in Thailand. The watershed along the escarpment marks the boundary between Thailand and Cambodia. The main road through a pass in the Dangrek Mountains at O Smach connects northwestern Cambodia with Thailand. Despite this road and those running through a few other passes, in general the escarpment impedes easy communication between the two countries. Between the western part of the Dangrek and the northern part of the Cardamom ranges, however, lies an extension of the Tonle Sap Basin that merges into lowlands in Thailand, which allows easy access from the border to Bangkok.

The Mekong Valley, which offers a communication route between Cambodia and Laos, separates the eastern end of the Dangrek Mountains and the northeastern highlands. To the southeast, the basin joins the Mekong Delta, which, extending into Vietnam, provides both water and land communications between the two countries.

Climate

Cambodia's climate—like that of the rest of Southeast Asia—is dominated by the monsoons, which are known as tropical wet and dry because of the distinctly marked seasonal differences. The monsoonal airflows are caused by annual alternating high pressure and low pressure over the Central Asian landmass. In summer, moisture-laden air—the southwest monsoon—is drawn landward from the Indian Ocean. The flow is reversed during the winter, and the northeast monsoon sends back dry air. The southwest monsoon brings the rainy season from mid-May to mid-September or to early October, and the northeast monsoon flow of drier and cooler air lasts from early November to March. The southern third of the country has a two-month dry season; the northern two-thirds, a four-month one. Short transitional periods, which are marked by some difference in humidity but by little change in temperature, intervene between the alternating seasons. Temperatures are fairly uniform throughout the Tonle Sap Basin area, with only small variations from the average annual mean of around 25°C. The maximum mean is about 28°C; the minimum mean, about 22°C. Maximum temperatures of higher than 32°C, however, are common and, just before the start of the rainy season, they may rise to more than 38°C. Minimum temperatures rarely fall below 10°C. January is the coldest month, and April is the warmest. Typhoons—tropical cyclones—that often devastate coastal Vietnam rarely cause damage in Cambodia (see fig. 5).

The total annual rainfall average is between 100 and 150 centimeters, and the heaviest amounts fall in the southeast. Rainfall from April to September in the Tonle Sap Basin-Mekong Lowlands area averages 130 to 190 centimeters annually, but the amount varies considerably from year to year. Rainfall around the basin increases with elevation. It is heaviest in the mountains along the coast in the southwest, which receive from 250 to more than 500 centimeters of precipitation annually as the southwest monsoon reaches the coast. This area of greatest rainfall, however, drains mostly to the sea; only a small quantity goes into the rivers flowing into the basin. The relative humidity is high at night throughout the year; usually it exceeds 90 percent. During the daytime in the dry season, humidity averages about 50 percent or slightly lower, but it may remain about 60 percent in the rainy period.

Drainage

Except for the smaller rivers in the southeast, most of the major rivers and river systems in Cambodia drain into the Tonle Sap or into the Mekong River. The Cardamom Mountains and Elephant Range form a separate drainage divide. To the east the rivers flow into the Tonle Sap, while on the west they flow into the Gulf of Thailand. Toward the southern end of the Elephant Mountains, however, because of the topography, some small rivers flow southward on the eastern side of the divide.

The Mekong River in Cambodia flows southward from the Cambodia-Laos border to a point below Kracheh city, where it turns west for about 50 kilometers and then turns southwest to

Phnom Penh. Extensive rapids run above Kracheh city. From Kampong Cham the gradient slopes very gently, and inundation of areas along the river occurs at flood stage—June through November—through breaks in the natural levees that have built up along its course. At Phnom Penh four major water courses meet at a point called the Chattomukh (Four Faces). The Mekong River flows in from the northeast and the Tonle Sab—a river emanating from the Tonle Sap—flows in from the northwest. They divide into two parallel channels, the Mekong River proper and the Basak River, and flow independently through the delta areas of Cambodia and Vietnam to the South China Sea.

The flow of water into the Tonle Sab is seasonal. In September or in October, the flow of the Mekong River, fed by monsoon rains, increases to a point where its outlets through the delta cannot handle the enormous volume of water. At this point, the water pushes northward up the Tonle Sab and empties into the Tonle Sap, thereby increasing the size of the lake from about 2,590 square kilometers to about 24,605 square kilometers at the height of the flooding (see fig. 6). After the Mekong's waters crest—when its downstream channels can handle the volume of water—the flow reverses, and water flows out of the engorged lake.

As the level of the Tonle Sap retreats, it deposits a new layer of sediment. The annual flooding, combined with poor drainage immediately around the lake, transforms the surrounding area into marshlands unusable for agricultural purposes during the dry season. The sediment deposited into the lake during the Mekong's flood stage appears to be greater than the quantity carried away later by the Tonle Sab River. Gradual silting of the lake would seem to be occurring; during low-water level, it is only about 1.5 meters deep, while at flood stage it is between 10 and 15 meters deep.

Regional Divisions

Cambodia's boundaries in 1987 were for the most part based upon those recognized by France and by neighboring countries during the colonial period. The 800-kilometer boundary with Thailand, coincides with a natural feature, the watershed of the Dangrek Mountains, only in its northern sector. The 541-kilometer border with Laos and the 1,228-kilometer border with Vietnam result largely from French administrative decisions and do not follow major natural features. Border disputes have broken out in the past between Cambodia and Thailand as well as between, Cambodia and Vietnam.

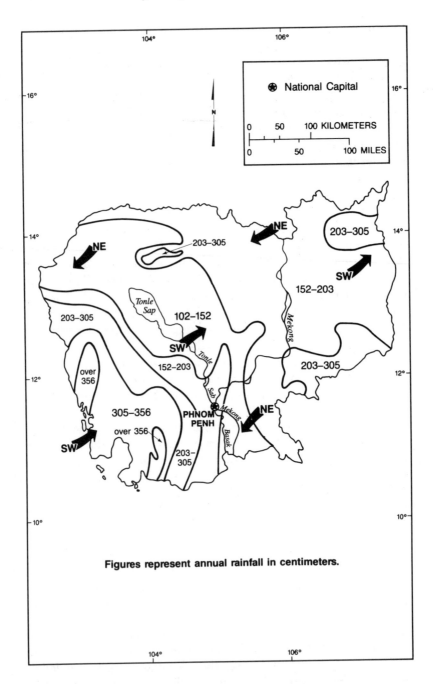

Figure 5. Annual Rainfall and Monsoon Airflow

Population

Between 1874 and 1921, the total population increased from about 946,000 to 2.4 million. By 1950 it had increased to between 3,710,107 and 4,073,967, and in 1962 it had reached 5.7 million. From the 1960s until 1975, the population of Cambodia increased by about 2.2 percent yearly, the lowest increase in Southeast Asia. By 1975 when the Khmer Rouge took power, it was estimated at 7.3 million. Of this total an estimated one million to two million reportedly died between 1975 and 1978. In 1981 the PRK gave the official population figure as nearly 6.7 million, although approximately 6.3 million to 6.4 million is probably a more accurate one. The average annual rate of population growth from 1978 to 1985 was 2.3 percent (see table 2, Appendix A). Life expectancy at birth was 44.2 years for males and 43.3 years for females in 1959. By 1970 life expectancy had increased by about 2.5 years since 1945. The greater longevity for females apparently reflected improved health practices during maternity and childbirth.

In 1959 about 45 percent of the population was under 15 years of age; by 1962 this figure had increased slightly to 46 percent. In 1962 an estimated 52 percent of the population was between 15 and 64 years of age, while 2 percent was older than 65. The percentage of males and females in the three groups was almost the same.

The population of Cambodia has been fairly homogeneous. In 1962 about 80 percent of the population was ethnic Khmer. The remaining 20 percent included Chinese, Vietnamese, Cham, Khmer Loeu (see Appendix B), Europeans. By 1981 as a result of the Vietnamese repatriation in 1970 to 1971 and the deaths and emigration of large numbers of Cham and Chinese, ethnic Khmer accounted for about 90 percent or more of the population.

Dynamics

Rapid and drastic population movements occurred in the early 1970s, when large numbers of rural Cambodians fled to the cities to escape the fighting in the countryside, and between 1975 and 1979, when the government forcibly relocated urban dwellers to rural sites throughout the country. Large scale emigration also occurred between 1975 and 1979.

Distribution

Population density varies throughout Cambodia. The national average in 1972 was about 22 persons per square kilometer. At one end of the density scale were the provinces around Phnom Penh,

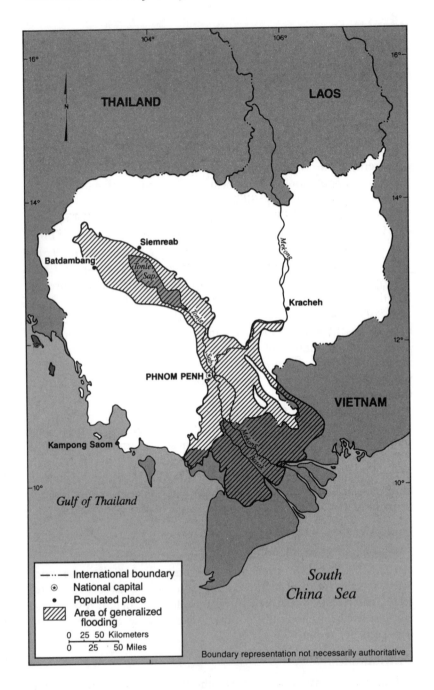

Figure 6. Annual Flooding Around Tonle Sap, 1985

where the number of inhabitants per square kilometer could reach as many as 500, but more generally varied between 200 and 500. At the lower end of the scale were outlying provinces, like Rotanokiri (Ratanakiri) and Mondol Kiri (Mondolkiri) in the northeast and Kaoh Kong in the southwest, where the density was as low as zero to five persons per square kilometer. For almost two-thirds of the country, the density was approximately five persons per square kilometer (see table 3, Appendix A).

Ethnic Khmer were concentrated in central and in southeastern Cambodia. The Cham lived in their own towns and sections in larger cities. The Chinese lived mainly in urban centers; in Phnom Penh they were concentrated around the markets. The Vietnamese tended to live in their own villages and in certain sections of Phnom Penh. The Khmer Loeu were concentrated in the northeastern and southwestern areas of Cambodia.

Migration and Refugees

Over the decades, some movement of the rural population in Cambodia—either to urban areas in quest of employment or to other villages in search of more favorable agricultural sites—has been customary. Many highland tribal groups practice slash-and-burn agriculture that requires movement to a new area once the soil is exhausted in a given location. Warfare in the early 1970s drove large numbers of rural people to the cities in search of safety. The population of Phnom Penh, for example, increased from 393,995 in 1962 to about 1.2 million in 1971, but had decreased to about 500,000 by 1985. With their takeover in April 1975, the Khmer Rouge forced most of the population out of Phnom Penh into the countryside, where large numbers either died because of hardship or were executed. Many such population movements were forced upon the populace under the Khmer Rouge regime. Many Cambodians who had left the country to study abroad became de facto emigrants when the communists took over. Thousands more fled into neighboring Thailand and Vietnam in 1975 and at the time of the Vietnamese invasion in late 1978. Cham, Vietnamese, and Chinese communities alike were persecuted, and their members were killed, under the Khmer Rouge. Forced repatriation in 1970 and deaths during the Khmer Rouge era reduced the Vietnamese population in Cambodia from between 250,000 and 300,000 in 1969 to a reported 56,000 in 1984. Postwar emigration of Vietnamese civilians to Cambodia remained a subject of controversy. Some social scientists believed that the number of Vietnamese in Cambodia in 1988 had reached at least the prewar level, and, indeed, many Khmer feared that even more Vietnamese immigrants would inundate their population.

During the Khmer Rouge era, about 50,000 Cambodians fled to Thailand, and an estimated 150,000 fled to Vietnam. As soon as the Khmer Rouge regime began to crumble under the onslaught of the Vietnamese in late 1978, a massive exodus of Cambodians began. About 630,000—braving hostile fire, minefields, bandits, and border guards—left the country between 1979 and 1981. In subsequent years, about 208,000 resettled in other countries; these included 136,000 in the United States, 32,000 in France, and 13,000 each in Australia and in Canada.

In late 1987, about 265,000 Cambodians—about 150,000 of them below the age of 15—remained in Thailand. The Khmer refugees were supported by the United Nations Border Relief Operation (which assumed the task from the United Nations High Commissioner for Refugees in the early 1980s) and private agencies at an annual cost of US$36 million in 1986. The refugees were grouped in nine camps on the Thailand side of that country's common border with Cambodia. Of the nine installations, the most prominent was Khao-I-Dang, located near Aranyaprathet, Prachin Buri Province, Thailand. It was controlled by the Thai military, and its inhabitants were the only ones to be regarded legally as refugees by the Thai government. In 1987 Khao-I-Dang had a population of about 21,000 to 25,000 (down from a peak of 130,000 at its founding in 1979), of whom about 12,000 to 15,000 were eligible for resettlement.

The other eight camps were under the control of the three Khmer resistance factions (see Coalition Government of Democratic Kampuchea, ch. 4; Coalition Government Resistance Forces, ch. 5). These camps were considered reception centers rather than bona fide refugee facilities by the Thai government, and their inmates, unlike the residents of Khao-I-Dang, were considered displaced persons rather than refugees. Of these eight installations, five were controlled by the Khmer Rouge; two, by the Khmer People's National Liberation Front (KPNLF—see Appendix B); and one, by the Sihanouk National Army (Armée Nationale Sihanoukiste— ANS—see Appendix B). Khmer insurgents freely visited the camps controlled by their own resistance factions and used them as rest and recuperation centers.

The Khmer Rouge camps sheltered between 50,000 and 60,000 inhabitants. Access to them was granted grudgingly, if at all, even to United Nations officials. Occasional visiting journalists reported in the 1980s that an atmosphere of repression and fear prevailed at these facilities. The largest Khmer Rouge installation, located on the southwestern part of the border between Cambodia and Thailand, was known as Site 8 and held about 30,000 persons. Smaller installations, inhabited by 20,000 or more people altogether, were reported at Na Trao and Huay Chan, in Sisaket Province, Thailand, and at the seldom-visited encampments of Borai and in Ta Luen, Trat Province, Thailand.

The KPNLF controlled two camps containing a total of about 160,000 persons. The principal installation was Site 2, with a population of between 145,000 and 150,000 and an environment noted for its rampant lawlessness. Site 2 was located in the vicinity of Ta Phraya, Prachin Buri Province, Thailand, and, at one time in the early 1980s, held the largest concentration Cambodians outside of Phnom Penh.

The lone camp controlled by the ANS was Site B, also known as "Green Hill," which was located about 50 kilometers north of Ta Phraya and had a population of between 40,000 and 50,000. Site B was considered by observers to be the most orderly and well-managed of the refugee camps; it offered more living space, including room for personal gardens, than did the others.

Social Structure and Organization

The ethnic groups that constitute Cambodian society possess a number of economic and demographic commonalities—for example, Chinese merchants play middlemen in many economic cycles, but they also preserve differences in their social and cultural institutions. The major differences among these groups lie in social organization, language, and religion. The majority of the inhabitants of Cambodia are settled in fairly permanent villages near the major bodies of water in the Tonle Sap Basin-Mekong Lowlands region. The contemporary locations of major Khmer population centers date back to antiquity according to geographer Jacques Nepote. He points out that contemporary Khmer Krom (see Appendix B) settlements are located in the same areas as the ancient site of Funan, and that the Khmer settlements extending from Phnom Penh in a southeastern direction are located where pre-Angkorian archaeological sites are clustered (see Prehistory and Early Kingdoms, ch. 1). The Khmer Loeu live in widely scattered villages that are abandoned when the cultivated land in the vicinity is exhausted.

The permanently settled Khmer and Cham villages usually are located on or near the banks of a river or other bodies of water. Cham villages usually are made up almost entirely of Cham, but Khmer villages, especially in central and in southeastern Cambodia, typically include sizable Chinese communities. In his study of the coastal Chinese in Kampot Province and in Kaoh Kong Province, French geographer Roland Pourtier points out that the Chinese dwellings and shops—usually in the same structures—are located at the center of the town or village, while the Khmer houses are scattered at some distance from the center. He also finds that there are some villages made up almost entirely of Chinese.

The Khmer

Household and Family Structure

In the late 1980s, the nuclear family, consisting of a husband and a wife and their unmarried children, probably continued to be the most important kin group within Khmer society. The family is the major unit of both production and consumption. Within this unit are the strongest emotional ties, the assurance of aid in the event of trouble, economic cooperation in labor, sharing of produce and income, and contribution as a unit to ceremonial obligations. A larger grouping, the personal kindred that includes a nuclear family with the children, grandchildren, grandparents, uncles, aunts, first cousins, nephews, and nieces, may be included in the household. Family organization is weak, and ties between related families beyond the kindred are loosely defined at best. There is no tradition of family names, although the French tried to legislate their use in the early twentieth century. Most Khmer genealogies extend back only two or three generations, which contrasts with the veneration of ancestors by the Vietnamese and by the Chinese. Noble families and royal families, some of which can trace their descent for several generations, are exceptions.

The individual Khmer is surrounded by a small inner circle of family and friends who constitute his or her closest associates, those he would approach first for help. In rural communities, neighbors—who are often also kin—may be important, too, and much of housebuilding and other heavy labor intensive tasks are performed by groups of neighbors. Beyond this close circle are more distant relatives and casual friends. In rural Cambodia, the strongest ties a Khmer may develop—besides those to the nuclear family and to close friends—are those to other members of the local community. A strong feeling of pride—for the village, for the district, and province—usually characterizes Cambodian community life. There is much sharing of religious life through the local Buddhist temple, and there are many cross-cutting kin relations within the community. Formerly, the Buddhist priesthood, the national armed forces, and, to a lesser extent, the civil service all served to connect the Khmer to the wider national community. The priesthood

88

served only males, however, while membership in some components of the armed forces and in the civil service was open to women as well.

Two fictive relationships in Cambodia transcend kinship boundaries and serve to strengthen interpersonal and interfamily ties. A Khmer may establish a fictive child-parent or sibling relationship called *thoa* (roughly translating as adoptive parent or sibling). The person desiring to establish the *thoa* relationship will ask the other person for permission to enter into the relationship. The *thoa* relationship may become as close as the participants desire. The second fictive relationship is that of *kloeu* (close male friend). This is similar, in many ways, to becoming a blood brother. A person from one place may ask a go-between in another place to help him establish a *kloeu* relationship with someone in that place. Once the participants agree, a ceremony is held that includes ritual drinking of water into which small amounts of the participants' blood have been mixed and bullets and knives have been dipped; prayers are also recited by an *achar* (or ceremonial leader) before witnesses. The *kloeu* relationship is much stronger than the *thoa*. One *kloeu* will use the same kinship terms when addressing his *kloeu's* parents and siblings as he would when addressing his own. The two friends can call upon each other for any kind of help at any time. The *kloeu* relationship apparently is limited to some rural parts of Cambodia and to Khmer-speaking areas in Thailand. As of the late 1980s, it may have become obsolete. The female equivalent of *kloeu* is *mreak*.

Legally, the husband is the head of the Khmer family, but the wife has considerable authority, especially in family economics. The husband is responsible for providing shelter and food for his family; the wife is generally in charge of the family budget, and she serves as the major ethical and religious model for the children, especially the daughters. In rural areas, the male is mainly responsible for such activities as plowing and harrowing the rice paddies, threshing rice, collecting sugar palm juice, caring for cattle, carpentry, and buying and selling cows and chickens. Women are mainly responsible for pulling and transplanting rice seedlings, harvesting and winnowing rice, tending gardens, making sugar, weaving, and caring for the household money. Both males and females may work at preparing the rice paddies for planting, tending the paddies, and buying and selling land.

Ownership of property among the rural Khmer was vested in the nuclear family. Descent and inheritance is bilateral. Legal children might inherit equally from their parents. The division of property was theoretically equal among siblings, but in practice the oldest child might inherit more. Each of the spouses might bring inherited land into the family, and the family might acquire joint land during the married life of the couple. Each spouse was free to dispose of his or her land as he or she chose. A will was usually oral, although a written one was preferred.

Private ownership of land was abolished by the Khmer Rouge in the 1970s. Such ownership is also not recognized by the PRK government, which for example, refused to support former owners when they returned and found others living on and working their land. Some peasants were able to remain on their own land during the Khmer Rouge era, however, and generally they were allowed to continue to work the land as if it were their own property. In 1987 the future of private ownership of land remained in doubt. According to Cambodia scholar Michael Vickery, the PRK government planned to collectivize in three stages. The first stage involved allotting land to families at the beginning of the season and allowing the cultivators to keep the harvest. The second stage involved allotting land to each family according to the number of members. The families in the interfamily units known as solidarity groups (*krom samaki*) were to work to prepare the fields, but subsequently each family was responsible for the upkeep of its own parcel of land. At this stage, each family could dispose of its own produce. In the final stage, all labor was to be performed in common, and at the end of the season any remuneration was distributed according to a work point system. Livestock at this stage would still belong to the family. By 1984 the first stage groups accounted for 35 percent of the rural population, but the third level accounted for only 10 percent of the farms (see Agriculture, ch. 3).

Housing

The nuclear family, in rural Cambodia, typically lives in a rectangular house that may vary in size from four by six meters to six by ten meters. It is constructed of a wooden frame with gabled thatch roof and walls of woven bamboo. Khmer houses typically are raised on stilts as much as three meters for protection from annual floods. Two ladders or wooden staircases provide access to the house. The steep thatch roof overhanging the house walls protects the interior from rain. Typically a house contains three rooms separated by partitions of woven bamboo. The front room serves as a living room used to receive visitors, the next room is the parents' bedroom, and the third is for unmarried daughters. Sons sleep anywhere they can find space. Family members and neighbors work together to build the house, and a house-raising ceremony is held upon its completion. The houses of poorer persons may contain only a single large room. Food is prepared in a separate kitchen located near the house but usually behind it. Toilet facilities consist of simple pits in the ground, located away from the house, that are covered up when filled. Any livestock is kept below the house.

Chinese and Vietnamese houses in Cambodian town and villages typically are built directly on the ground and have earthen, cement, or tile floors, depending upon the economic status of the owner. Urban housing and commercial buildings may be of brick, masonry, or wood.

Diet

Dietary habits appear to be basically the same among the Khmer and other ethnic groups, although the Muslim Cham do not eat pork. The basic foods are rice—in several varieties fish, and vegetables, especially trakuon (water convolvulus). Rice may be less thoroughly milled than it is in many other rice-eating countries, and consequently it contains more vitamins and roughage. The average rice consumption per person per day before 1970 was almost one-half kilogram. Fermented fish in the form of sauce or of paste are important protein supplements to the diet. Hot peppers, lemon grass, mint, and ginger add flavor to many Khmer dishes; sugar is added to many foods. Several kinds of noodles are eaten. The basic diet is supplemented by vegetables and by fruits—bananas, mangoes, papayas, rambutan, and palm fruit—both wild and cultivated, which grow abundantly throughout the country. Beef, pork, poultry, and eggs are added to meals on special occasions, or, if the family can afford it, daily. In the cities, the diet has been affected by many Western items of food. French, Chinese, Vietnamese, and Indian cuisine were available in Phnom Penh in pre-Khmer Rouge days.

Rural Khmer typically eat several times a day; the first meal consists of a piece of fruit or cake, which workers eat after arriving at the fields. The first full meal is at about 9:00 or 10:00 in the morning; it is prepared by the wife or daughter and brought to the man in the field. Workers eat a large meal at about noon in the field and then have supper with their families after returning home around 5:00 P.M.

Before the early 1970s, the Cambodian people produced a food supply that provided an adequate diet, although children gave evidence of caloric underconsumption and of a deficiency in B vitamins. During the Khmer Rouge era, malnutrition increased, especially among the people who were identified as "new people" by the authorities (see Society under the Angkar, ch. 1). Collective meals were introduced by 1977. Food rations for the new people were meager. Refugees' statements contain the following descriptions: "[daily rations of] a tin of boiled rice a day mixed with . . . sauce"; "we ate twice a day, boiled soup and rice only"; "one tin of rice a day shared between three people. Never any meat or fruit"; "Ration was two tins of rice between four persons per day with fish sauce." People were reduced to eating anything they could find—insects, small mammals, arachnids, crabs, and plants.

The food situation improved under the PRK, although in the regime's early years there were still serious food shortages. International food donations improved the situation somewhat. In 1980 monthly rice rations distributed by the government averaged only one to two kilograms per person. People supplemented the ration by growing secondary crops such as corn and potatoes, by fishing, by gathering fruit and vegetables, and by collecting crabs and other edible animals. A 1984 estimate reported that as many as 50 percent of all young people in Cambodia were undernourished.

Dress

The traditional Khmer costume consisted of a shirt or blouse and a skirt-like lower garment—*sampot* for women and sarong for men, a tube-shaped garment about a meter wide and as much as three meters in circumference. Made of cotton or of silk in many different styles and patterns, it is pulled on over the legs and fastened around the waist. On ceremonial occasions, elegant *sampot* and sarong, embroidered with gold or silver threads, may be worn with a long piece of material gathered at the waist, passed between the legs, and tucked into the waistband in back. Members of the urban middle and upper classes may wear Western-style clothing at work and more traditional clothing at home.

At home both sexes wear the *sampot* and the sarong. In rural areas, working men and women may wear loose-fitting pants and shirts or blouses. Many men wear Western-style pants or shorts. A third essential part of Khmer dress is the *krama*, or long scarf, that is worn around the neck, over the shoulders, or wrapped turban-style around the head. School children wear Western-style clothing to school. The boys wear shirts and shorts; the girls wear skirts and blouses.

The Khmer Rouge were noted for their unisex black "pajamas." Their typical garb was the peasant outfit of collarless black shirt— baggy trousers and checkered *krama* (a scarf knotted loosely about the neck). French anthropologist Marie Alexandrine Martin reported that the wearing of brightly colored clothing was prohibited under the Khmer Rouge and that women, young and old, wore black, dark blue, or maroon *sampot* with short-sleeved plain blouses.

*Riverine village
and fishermen
Courtesy Bill Herod*

*Rural women and children,
ca. 1958
Courtesy National Archives*

Women were forbidden to wear Western-style pants at any time. The conical hat characteristic of the Vietnamese has been adopted to a certain extent by Khmer in the provinces adjacent to Vietnam.

Families

The birth of a child is a happy event for the family. According to traditional beliefs, however, confinement and childbirth expose the family, and especially the mother and the child to harm from the spirit world. A woman who dies in childbirth—crosses the river (*chhlong tonle*) in Khmer—is believed to become an evil spirit. In traditional Khmer society, a pregnant woman respects a number of food taboos and avoids certain situations. These traditions remain in practice in rural Cambodia, but they have become weakened in urban areas.

No extensive information exists on birth control or on the use of contraceptives in Cambodia. Before the Khmer Rouge takeover, no organizations in Cambodia were known to be concerned with family planning. Traditional Khmer families were normally smaller than Chinese or Vietnamese families; the desired number of children was five. Reports suggest that several methods of contraception are currently available in Cambodia and that these are practiced in the PRK (see Public Health, this ch.). A recent study of Cambodian women in France reported that 91 percent of the sample wished to use some method of birth control and that 74 percent knew of at least one method. The most common methods used in that group were the oral contraceptive pill and some form of sterilization. It is not known to what extent the attitudes of this group reflect those of Cambodian women in general.

A Cambodian child may be nursed until he or she is between two and four years of age. Up to the age of three or four, the child is given considerable physical affection and freedom. There is little corporal punishment. After reaching the age of about four, children are expected to feed and bathe themselves and to control their bowel functions. Children around five years of age also may be expected to help look after younger siblings. Children's games emphasize socialization or skill rather than winning and losing.

Most children begin school when they are seven or eight. By the time they reach this age, they are familiar with the society's norms of politeness, obedience, and respect toward their elders and toward Buddhist monks. The father at this time begins his permanent retreat into a relatively remote, authoritarian role. By age ten, a girl is expected to help her mother in basic household tasks; a boy knows how to care for the family's livestock and can do farm work under the supervision of older males.

In precommunist days, parents exerted complete authority over their children until the children were married, and the parents continued to maintain some control well into the marriage. Punishment was meted out sparingly, but it might have involved physical contact. Age difference was strictly recognized. The proper polite vocabulary was used in the precommunist period, and special generational terms for "you" continued to be used in the late 1980s. Younger speakers had to show respect to older people, including siblings, even if their ages differed by only a few minutes.

Between the ages of seven and nineteen, but most commonly between the ages of eleven and nineteen, a boy may become a temple servant and go on to serve a time as a novice monk. Having a son chosen for such a position is a great honor for the parents, and earns the individual son much merit (see Religion, this ch.).

Formerly, and perhaps still in some rural areas, a ceremony marked the entrance of a girl into puberty. Upon the onset of menstruation, a girl would participate in a ritual called *chol mlup* (entering the shadow). Certain foods were taboo at this time, and she would be isolated from her family for a period of a few days to six months. After the period of seclusion, she was considered marriageable.

Adolescent children usually play with members of the same sex. The main exception to this occurs during festivals, especially happy ones such as the New Year Festival, when boys and girls take part in group games. Young people then have the opportunity to begin looking for future mates. Virginity is highly valued in brides, and premarital sex is deplored. The girl who becomes pregnant out of wedlock brings shame to her family.

The choice of a spouse is a complex one for the young male, and it may involve not only his parents and his friends, as well as those of the young woman, but also a matchmaker. A young man can decide on a likely spouse on his own and then ask his parents to arrange the marriage negotiations, or the young person's parents may make the choice of spouse, giving the child little to say in the selection. In theory, a girl may veto the spouse her parents have chosen.

Courtship patterns differ between rural and urban Khmer. Attitudes in the larger cities have been influenced by Western ideas of romantic love that do not apply in the countryside. A man usually marries between the ages of nineteen and twenty-five, a girl between the ages of sixteen and twenty-two. Marriage between close blood relatives is forbidden. After a spouse has been selected, a go-between meets with the parents and broaches the subject of marriage. Then each family investigates the other to make sure its child is marrying into a good family. When both sides agree to the marriage and presents have been exchanged and accepted, the families consult an *achar* to set the wedding date. In rural areas, there is a form of bride-service; that is, the young man may take a vow to serve his prospective father-in-law for a period of time.

The traditional wedding is a long and colorful affair. Formerly it lasted three days, but in the 1980s it more commonly lasted a day and a half. The ceremony begins in the morning at the home of the bride and is directed by the *achar*. Buddhist priests offer a short sermon and recite prayers of blessing. Parts of the ceremony involve ritual hair cutting, tying cotton threads soaked in holy water around the bride's and groom's wrists, and passing a candle around a circle of happily married and respected couples to bless the union. After the wedding, a banquet is held. In the city, the banquet is held at a restaurant; in the country, it is held in a temporary shelter and is prepared by the two families. Newlyweds traditionally move in with the wife's parents and may live with them up to a year, until they can build a new house nearby. These patterns changed drastically under the communists. The Khmer Rouge divided families and separated the men from the women. The father, mother, and children frequently were separated for many months. A man and woman often did not have time to consummate a marriage, and sexual relations were limited by long separations. Extramarital relations and even flirtations between young people were heavily punished.

Divorce is legal, relatively easy to obtain, but not common. Divorced persons are viewed with some disapproval, and they are not invited to take part in the blessing of a newlywed couple. Some of the grounds for divorce are incompatibility, prolonged absence without good reason, abandonment by either partner, refusal of the husband to provide for the family, adultery, immoral conduct, and refusal, for more than a year, to permit sexual intercourse. A magistrate may legalize the divorce. Each spouse retains whatever property he or she brought into the marriage. Property acquired jointly is divided equally. Divorced persons may remarry, but the woman must wait ten months. Custody of minor children is usually given to the mother. Both parents continue to have an obligation to contribute financially toward the rearing and education of the child.

In theory a man may have multiple wives if he can afford them, but this is rare in practice; the first wife may veto the taking of a second wife. Concubinage also exists, although it is more frequent in the cities. While second wives have certain legal rights, concubines have none.

As the married couple moves through life they have children, nurture and train them, educate them, and marry them off. When they become too old to support themselves, they may invite the youngest child's family to move in and to take over running the household. At this stage in their lives, they enjoy a position of high status, they help care for grandchildren, and they devote more time in service to the wat (temple).

Death is not viewed with the great outpouring of grief common to Western society; it is viewed as the end of one life and as the beginning of another life that one hopes will be better. Buddhist Khmer usually are cremated, and their ashes are deposited in a stupa in the temple compound. A corpse is washed, dressed, and placed in a coffin, which may be decorated with flowers and with a photograph of the deceased. White pennant-shaped flags, called "white crocodile flags," outside a house indicate that someone in that household has died. A funeral procession consisting of an *achar,* Buddhist monks, members of the family, and other mourners accompanies the coffin to the crematorium. The spouse and the children show mourning by shaving their heads and by wearing white clothing. Relics such as teeth or pieces of bone are prized by the survivors, and they are often worn on gold chains as amulets.

Social Stratification and Social Mobility

Social strata in precommunist Cambodia may be viewed as constituting a spectrum, with an elite group or upper class at one end and a lower class consisting of rural peasants and unskilled urban workers at the other end. The elite group was composed of high-ranking government, military, and religious leaders, characterized by high prestige, wealth, and education or by members one of the royal or noble families. Each one of the subgroups had its own internal ranking system. Before the ouster of Sihanouk in 1970, the highest ranks of the elite group were filled largely by those born into them. The republican regime in the early 1970s invalidated all royal and noble titles, and the only titles of social significance legally in use in connection with the elite group were those gained through achievement. Military and government titles tended to replace royal and noble titles. In spite of the legislated loss of titles, however, wide public recognition of the royalty and the nobility continued. The deferential linguistic usages and the behavior styles directed toward members of these groups persisted through the 1970s and, to a limited extent, were still present in the late 1980s.

In the early 1970s, the senior military officers, some of whom were also members of the aristocracy, replaced the hereditary aristocracy as the most influential group in the country. To some extent, this upper stratum of the upper class was closed, and it was extremely difficult to move into it and to attain positions of high power. The closed nature of the group frustrated many members of the small intellectual elite. This group, positioned at the lower end of the elite group, consisted of civil servants, professional people, university students, and some members of the Buddhist hierarchy. It had become large enough to be politically influential by the 1970s, for example, student strikes were serious enough in 1972 to force the government to close some schools.

Somewhere in the middle of this social spectrum was a small middle class, which included both Khmer and non-Khmer of medium prestige. Members of this class included businessmen, white-collar workers, teachers, physicians, most of the Buddhist clergy, shopkeepers, clerks, and military officers of lower and middle rank. Many Chinese, Vietnamese, and members of other ethnic minorities belonged to the middle class. The Khmer were a majority only among the military and among the civil servants.

The lower class consisted of rural small farmers, fishermen, craftsmen, and blue-collar urban workers. The majority of Cambodians belonged to this group. Most of the members of the lower class were Khmer, but other ethnic groups, including most of the Cham, Khmer Loeu, some Vietnamese, and a few Chinese, were included. This class was virtually isolated from, and was uninterested in, the activities of the much smaller urban middle and upper classes.

Within the lower class, fewer status distinctions existed; those that did depended upon attributes such as age, sex, moral behavior, and religious piety. Traditional Buddhist values were important on the village level. Old age was respected, and older men and women received deferential treatment in terms of language and behavior. All else being equal, males generally were accorded a higher social status than females. Good character—honesty, generosity, compassion, avoidance of quarrels, chastity, warmth— and personal religious piety also increased status. Generosity toward others and to the wat was important. Villagers accorded respect and honor to those whom they perceived as having authority or prestige. Buddhist monks and nuns, teachers, high-ranking government officials, and members of the hereditary aristocracy made up this category. Persons associated with those who possessed prestige tended to derive prestige and to be accorded respect therefrom.

The Khmer language reflects a somewhat different classification of Khmer society based on a more traditional model and characterized by differing linguistic usages (see Languages, this ch.). This classification divided Cambodian society into three broad categories: royalty and nobility, clergy, and laity. The Khmer language had—and to a lesser extent still has—partially different lexicons for each of these groups. For example, *nham* (to eat) was used when speaking of oneself or to those on a lower social level; *pisa* (to eat) was used when speaking politely of someone else; *chhan* (to eat) was used of Buddhist clergy, and *saoy* (to eat) was used of royalty. The Khmer Rouge attempted to do away with the different lexicons and to establish a single one for all; for example, they tried to substitute a single, rural word, *hop* (to eat), for all of the above words.

Social mobility was played out on an urban stage. There was little opportunity among the majority of the rural Cambodians to change social status; this absence of opportunity was a reflection of traditional Buddhist fatalism. A man could achieve higher status by entering the monkhood or by acquiring an education and then entering the military or the civil service. Opportunities in government service, especially for white-collar positions, were highly prized by Cambodian youths. The availability of such positions did not keep pace with the number of educated youths, however, and in the late 1960s and the early 1970s this lag began to cause widespread dissatisfaction.

The Khmer Rouge characterized Cambodians as being in one of several classes: the feudal class (members of the royal family and high government or military officials); the capitalist class (business people); the petite bourgeoisie (civil servants, professionals, small business people, teachers, servants, and clerics); peasant class (the rich, the mid-level, and the poor, based on whether or not they could hire people to work their land and on whether or not they had enough food); the worker class (the independent worker, the industrial worker, and the party members); and the "special" classes (revolutionary intellectuals, military and police officials, and Buddhist monks).

Other Ethnic Groups

The Cham

The Cham people in Cambodia descend from refugees of the kingdom of Champa, which once ruled much of Vietnam between Cao Ha in the north and Bien Hoa in the south. In 1471 Champa was conquered by the Vietnamese, and many Cham fled to Cambodia. Cham scholar Po Dharma points out that the Cham have lived in Cambodia since at least 1456. They settled along the Tonle Sap and Mekong rivers and in Batdambang, Pouthisat, Takev, Kampot, Kampong Cham, Kampong Thum, and Kampong Chhnang provinces. At some time before the seventeenth century, the Cambodian Cham and some of those in adjacent Vietnam converted to Islam, probably as a result of contacts with their Malay kin who had embraced that religion centuries earlier (see Religion, this ch.).

Friendly relations prevailed between the Cham and the Khmer for centuries even though, because of the Cham religion, little intermarriage occurred. Under the Khmer Republic (see Appendix B) of 1970 to 1975, one of the elite military units was made up of members of the Cham and other ethnic minorities. The Khmer Rouge tried, without much success, to recruit the Cham during the struggle with the Khmer Republic. The Cham were singled out for particularly brutal repression under the Khmer Rouge regime, and large numbers were killed. The PRK actively courted the Cham, and in 1987 a Cham was a member of the party Central Committee and minister of agriculture. Cham sources estimate that in the 1980, in addition to the Cham in Cambodia and in Vietnam, there were 3,000 Cham in Malaysia, 2,000 in the United States, 1,000 in Western Europe, 500 in Canada, and several hundred in Indonesia.

Po Dharma divides the Cambodian Cham into two groups— the orthodox and the traditional—based on their religious practices. The orthodox group, which makes up about one-third of the total number of Cham in the country, were located mainly in the Phnom Penh-Odongk area and in the provinces of Takev and Kampot. The traditional Cham were scattered throughout the midsection of the country in the provinces of Batdambang, Kampong Thum, Kampong Cham, and Pouthisat.

The Cham of both groups typically live in villages inhabited only by other Cham; the villages may be along the shores of water courses, or they may be inland. The Cham refer to the former as *play krong* (river villages) and to the latter as *play ngok* (upper villages). The inhabitants of the river villages engage in fishing, in raising rice, and in growing vegetables, especially onions. They trade fish to local Khmer for rice. The women in these villages earn money by weaving. The Cham who live inland support themselves by various means, depending on the village. Some villages specialize in metal working; others raise fruit trees or vegetables. The Cham also often serve as butchers of cattle for their Khmer Buddhist neighbors and are, in some areas, regarded as skillful water buffalo breeders.

Cham dress is distinctive. The main item of clothing for both sexes is a sarong-like garment called a batik, which is worn knotted at the waist. Men wear shirts over the batik, and women wear close-fitting blouses that are open at the throat and have tight sleeves. The characteristic headdress is a turban or scarf.

Cham society is matriarchal with matrilineal descent. There is some trace of an earlier clan system. Parents permit their daughters a considerable amount of freedom of choice in marriage. The parents of the girl usually make the marriage overtures to the boy. A Cham marriage involves little ceremony. Among the Muslim Cham, the girl's parents ask the groom if he accepts their daughter in marriage, and he is expected to answer yes. The imam acts as a witness. This simple ceremony is followed by a feast. Residence is matrilocal; the young man goes to live with his wife's family. Females inherit the family property.

The Khmer Loeu

The Khmer Loeu are the non-Khmer highland tribes in Cambodia. Although the origins of this group are not clear, some believe that the Mon-Khmer-speaking tribes were part of the long migration of these people from the northwest. The Austronesian-speaking groups, Rade and Jarai, apparently came to coastal Vietnam and then moved west, forming wedges among some of the Mon-Khmer groups. The Khmer Loeu are found mainly in the northeastern provinces of Rotanokiri, Stoeng Treng, and Mondol Kiri. The Cambodian government coined the word Khmer Loeu—literally "Highland Khmer"—in the 1960s in order to create a feeling of unity between the highland tribal groups and the ruling lowland ethnic Khmer. Traditionally the Khmer have referred to these groups as *phnong* and *samre,* both of which have pejorative meanings. Some of the highland groups, in fact, are related in language to the Khmer, but others are from a very different linguistic and cultural background (see Languages, this ch.).

Khmer Loeu form the majority population in Rotanokiri and Mondol Kiri provinces, and they also are present in substantial numbers in Kracheh and Stoeng Treng provinces (see fig. 7). Their total population in 1969 was estimated at 90,000 persons. In 1971 the number of Khmer Loeu was estimated variously between 40,000 and 100,000 persons. Population figures were unavailable in 1987, but the total probably was nearly 100,000 persons.

Most Khmer Loeu live in scattered temporary villages that have only a few hundred inhabitants. These villages usually are governed by a council of local elders or by a village headman.

The Khmer Loeu cultivate a wide variety of plants, but the main crop is dry or upland rice grown by the slash-and-burn method. Hunting, fishing, and gathering supplement the cultivated vegetable foods in the Khmer Loeu diet. Houses vary from huge multifamily longhouses to small single-family structures. They may be built close to the ground or on stilts.

101

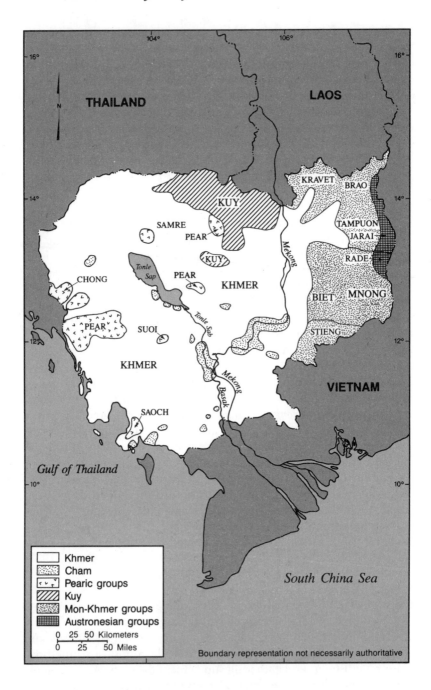

Figure 7. Ethno-Linquistic Groups of Cambodia, 1983

During the period of the French Protectorate, the French did not interfere in the affairs of the Khmer Loeu (see The French Protectorate, ch. 1). Reportedly, French army commanders considered the Khmer Loeu as an excellent source of personnel for army outposts, and they recruited large numbers to serve with the French forces. Many Khmer Loeu continued this tradition by enlisting in the Cambodian army.

In the 1960s, the Cambodian government carried out a broad civic action program—for which the army had responsibility—among the Khmer Loeu in Mondol Kiri, Rotanokiri, Stoeng Treng, and Kaoh Kong provinces. The goals of this program were to educate the Khmer Loeu, to teach them Khmer, and eventually to assimilate them into the mainstream of Cambodian society. There was some effort at resettlement; in other cases, civil servants went out to live with individual Khmer Loeu groups to teach their members Khmer ways. Schools were provided for some Khmer Loeu communities, and in each large village a resident government representative disseminated information and encouraged the Khmer Loeu to learn the lowland Khmer way of life. Civil servants sent to work among the Khmer Loeu often viewed the assignment as a kind of punishment.

In the late 1960s, an estimated 5,000 Khmer Loeu in eastern Cambodia rose in rebellion against the government and demanded self-determination and independence. The government press reported that local leaders loyal to the government had been assassinated. Following the rebellion, the hill people's widespread resentment of ethnic Khmer settlers caused them to refuse to cooperate with the Cambodian army in its suppression of rural unrest. Both the Khmer and the Vietnamese communists took advantage of this disaffection, and they actively recruited Khmer Loeu into their ranks. In late 1970, the government forces withdrew from Rotanokiri and Mondol Kiri provinces and abandoned the area to the rapidly growing Khmer communist insurgent force, the Revolutionary Army of Kampuchea (RAK—see Appendix B), and to its Vietnamese mentors (see Into the Maelstrom: ch. 1; Insurrection and War, 1967–75, ch. 1; National Army of Democratic Kampuchea, ch. 5). There is some evidence that in the 1960s and in the 1970s the Front Uni pour la Libération des Races Opprimés (FULRO—United Front for the Liberation of Oppressed Races) united tribes in the mountainous areas of southern Vietnam and had members from Khmer Loeu groups as well as from the Cham in Cambodia.

In the early 1980s, Khmer Rouge propaganda teams infiltrated the northeastern provinces and encouraged rebellion against the central government. In 1981 the government structure included four Khmer Loeu province chiefs, all reportedly from the Brao group, in the northeastern provinces of Mondol Kiri, Rotanokiri, Stoeng Treng, and Preah Vihear. According to a 1984 resolution of the PRK National Cadres Conference entitled "Policy Toward Ethnic Minorities," the minorities were considered an integral part of the Cambodian nation, and they were to be encouraged to participate in collectivization. Government policy aimed to transform minority groups into modern Cambodians. The same resolution called for the elimination of illiteracy, with the stipulations that minority languages be respected and that each tribe be allowed to write, speak, and teach in its own language.

The major Khmer Loeu groups in Cambodia are the Kuy, Mnong, Stieng, Brao, Pear, Jarai, and Rade. All but the last two speak Mon-Khmer languages (see Language, this ch.).

In the late 1980s, about 160,000 Kuy lived in the northern Cambodian provinces of Kampong Thum, Preah Vihear, and Stoeng Treng as well as in adjacent Thailand. (Approximately 70,000 Kuy had been reported in Cambodia itself in 1978.) Most of the Kuy have been assimilated into the predominant culture of the country in which they live. Many are Buddhists, and the majority practice wet-rice cultivation. They have the reputation of being skilled blacksmiths.

The Brao, including the Tampuon subgroup, inhabit northeastern Cambodia and adjacent Laos. In 1962 the Brao population in Laos was estimated at about 9,000 persons. In 1984 it was reported that the total Brao population was between 10,000 and 15,000 persons. About 3,000 Brao reportedly moved into Cambodia from Laos in the 1920s. The Brao live in large villages centered on a communal house. They cultivate dry-rice and produce some pottery. They appear to have a bilateral kinship system.

A total of 23,000 Mnong were thought to be living in Cambodia and in Vietnam in the early 1980s. In Cambodia the Mnong are found in Mondol Kiri, Kracheh, and Kampong Cham provinces in villages consisting of several longhouses each of which is divided into compartments that house nuclear families. The Mnong practice dry-rice farming, and some also cultivate a wide variety of vegetables, fruits, and other useful plants as secondary crops. Some subgroups weave cloth. At least two of the Mnong subgroups have matrilineal descent. Monogamy is the predominant form of marriage, and residence is usually matrilocal. Wealth distinctions are measured by the number of buffalo that a notable person sacrifices on a funereal or ceremonial occasion as a mark of status and as a means of eliciting social approval. Slavery is known to have existed in the past, but the system allowed a slave to gain freedom. The Stieng are closely related to the Mnong. Both groups straddle the Cambodian-Vietnamese border, and their languages belong to the same subfamily of Mon-Khmer. In 1978 the Cambodian Stieng numbered about 20,000 persons in all. The Stieng cultivate dry-field rice. Their society is apparently patriarchal; residence after marriage is patrilocal if a bride-price was paid. The groups have a very loose political organization; each village has its own leaders and tribunals.

Several small groups, perhaps totalling no more than 10,000 people in Cambodia and southeastern Thailand, make up the Pearic group. The main members are the Pear in Batdambang, Pouthisat, and Kampong Thum provinces; the Chong in Thailand and Batdambang Province; the Saoch in Kampot Province; the Samre in what was formerly Siemreab Province (now part of Siemreab-Otdar Meanchey Province); and the Suoi in Kampong Chhnang Province. Some believe that this group constitutes the remnant of the pre-Khmer population of Cambodia. Many members of the Pearic group grow dry-field rice, which they supplement by hunting and by gathering. They have totemic clans, each headed by a chief who inherited his office patrilineally. Marriage occurs at an early age; there is a small bride-price. Residence may be matrilocal until the birth of the first child, or it may be patrilocal as it is among the Saoch. The village headman is the highest political leader. The Saoch have a council of elders who judge infractions of traditional law. Two chief sorcerers, whose main function is to control the weather, play a major role in Pearic religion. Among the Saoch, a corpse is buried instead of being burned as among the Khmer.

The Austronesian groups of Jarai and Rade form two of the largest ethnic minorities in Vietnam. Both groups spill over into northeastern Cambodia, and they share many cultural similarities. The total Jarai population stands at about 200,000; the Rade number about 120,000. According to 1978 population figures, there were 10,000 Jarai and 15,000 Rade in Cambodia in the late 1970s. They live in longhouses containing several compartments occupied by matrilineally linked nuclear families. There may be twenty to sixty longhouses in one village. The Rade and Jarai cultivate dry-field rice and secondary crops such as maize. Both groups have exogamous matrilineal descent groups (consanguineous kin groups that acknowledge a traditional bond of common descent in the maternal line and within which they do not marry). Women initiate marriage negotiations, and residence is matrilocal. Each village has its own political hierarchy and is governed by an oligarchy of the leading families. In the past, sorcerers known as the ''kings of fire and water'' exerted political power that extended beyond an individual village. The Rade and the Jarai have been involved intimately in the FULRO movement, and many of the leaders in the movement are from these two groups.

The Chinese

The Chinese in Cambodia formed the country's largest ethnic minority in the late 1960s and in the early 1970s. In the late 1960s, an estimated 425,000 ethnic Chinese lived in Cambodia, but by 1984, as a result of warfare, Khmer Rouge and Vietnamese persecution, and emigration, only about 61,400 Chinese remained in the country. Sixty percent of the Chinese were urban dwellers engaged mainly in commerce; the other 40 percent were rural residents working as shopkeepers, as buyers and processors of rice, palm sugar, fruit, and fish, and as moneylenders. In 1963 William Willmott, an expert on overseas Chinese communities, estimated that 90 percent of the Chinese in Cambodia were involved in commerce and that 92 percent of those involved in commerce in Cambodia were Chinese. The Chinese in Kampot Province and in parts of Kaoh Kong Province also cultivated black pepper and fruit (especially rambutans, durians, and coconuts), and they engaged in salt-water fishing. In rural Cambodia, the Chinese were moneylenders, and they wielded considerable economic power over the ethnic Khmer peasants through usury. Studies in the 1950s disclosed that Chinese shopkeepers would sell to peasants on credit at interest rates of from 10 to 20 percent a month. In 1952 according to Australian political analyst Ben Kiernan, the Colonial Credit Office found in a survey that 75 percent of the peasants in Cambodia were in debt. There seemed to be little distinction between Chinese and Sino-Khmer (offspring of mixed Chinese and Khmer marriages) in the moneylending and shopkeeping enterprises.

The Chinese in Cambodia represented five major linguistic groups, the largest of which was the Teochiu (accounting for about 60 percent), followed by the Cantonese (accounting for about 20 percent), the Hokkien (accounting for about 7 percent), and the Hakka and the Hainanese (each accounting for about 4 percent). Those belonging to certain Chinese linguistic groups in Cambodia tended to gravitate to certain occupations. The Teochiu, who made up about 90 percent of the rural Chinese population, ran village stores, controlled rural credit and rice-marketing facilities, and grew vegetables. In urban areas they were often engaged in such enterprises as the import-export business, the sale of pharmaceuticals, and street peddling. The Cantonese, who were the majority Chinese group before the Teochiu migrations began in the late 1930s, lived mainly in the city. Typically, the Cantonese engaged in transportation and in construction, for the most part as mechanics or carpenters. The Hokkien community was involved in import-export and in banking, and it included some of the country's richest Chinese. The Hainanese started out as pepper growers in Kampot Province, where they continued to dominate that business. Many moved to Phnom Penh, where, in the late 1960s, they reportedly had a virtual monopoly on the hotel and restaurant business. They also often operated tailor shops and haberdasheries. In Phnom Penh, the newly-arrived Hakka were typically folk dentists, sellers of traditional Chinese medicines, and shoemakers.

Distinction by dialect group also has been important historically in the administrative treatment of the Chinese in Cambodia. The French brought with them a system devised by the Vietnamese Emperor Gia Long (1802–20) to classify the local Chinese according to areas of origin and dialect. These groups were called *bang* (or congregations by the French) and had their own leaders for law, order, and tax-collecting. In Cambodia every Chinese was required to belong to a *bang*. The head of a *bang*, known as the *ong bang*, was elected by popular vote; he functioned as an intermediary between the members of his *bang* and the government. Individual Chinese who were not accepted for membership in a *bang* were deported by the French authorities.

The French system of administering the Chinese community was terminated in 1958. During the 1960s, Chinese community affairs tended to be handled, at least in Phnom Penh, by the Chinese Hospital Committee, an organization set up to fund and to administer a hospital established earlier for the Chinese community. This committee was the largest association of Chinese merchants in the country, and it was required by the organization's constitution to include on its fifteen-member board six from the Teochiu dialect group, three from the Cantonese, two from the Hokkien, two from the Hakka, and two from the Hainanese. The hospital board constituted the recognized leadership of Phnom Penh's Chinese community. Local Chinese school boards in the smaller cities and towns often served a similar function.

In 1971 the government authorized the formation of a new body, the Federated Association of Chinese of Cambodia, which was the first organization to embrace all of Cambodia's resident Chinese. According to its statutes, the federation was designed to "aid Chinese nationals in the social, cultural, public health, and medical fields," to administer the property owned jointly by the Chinese community in Phnom Penh and elsewhere, and to promote friendly relations between Cambodians and Chinese. With leadership that could be expected to include the recognized leaders of the national Chinese community, the federation was believed likely to continue the trend, evident since the early 1960s, to transcend dialect group allegiance in many aspects of its social, political, and economic programs.

Generally, relations between the Chinese and the ethnic Khmer were good. There was some intermarriage, and a sizable proportion of the population in Cambodia was part Sino-Khmer, who were assimilated easily into either the Chinese or the Khmer community. Willmott assumes that a Sino-Khmer elite dominated commerce in Cambodia from the time of independence well into the era of the Khmer Republic.

The Khmer Rouge takeover was catastrophic for the Chinese community for several reasons. When the Khmer Rouge took over a town, they immediately disrupted the local market. According to Willmott, this disruption virtually eliminated retail trade ''and the traders (almost all Chinese) became indistinguishable from the unpropertied urban classes.'' The Chinese, in addition to having their major livelihood eradicated, also suffered because of their class membership. They were mainly well-educated urban merchants, thus possessing three characteristics that were anathema to the Khmer Rouge. Chinese refugees have reported that they shared the same brutal treatment as other urban Cambodians under the Khmer Rouge regime and that they were not especially singled out as an ethnic group until after the Vietnamese invasion. Observers believe that the anti-Chinese stance, of the Vietnamese government and of its officials in Phnom Penh, makes it unlikely that a Chinese community on the earlier scale will reappear in Cambodia in the near future.

The Vietnamese

Enmity has existed between the Khmer and the Vietnamese for centuries, but this antagonism did not hinder the growth of a sizable Vietnamese community scattered throughout southeastern and central Cambodia. According to an American scholar on Southeast Asia, Donald J. Steinberg, an estimated 291,596 Vietnamese, constituting more than 7 percent at the total population, resided in Cambodia in 1950. They were concentrated in Phnom Penh, and in Kandal, Prey Veng, and Kampong Cham provinces.

The Khmer have shown more antipathy toward the Vietnamese than toward the Chinese or toward their other neighbors, the Thai. Several factors explain this attitude. The expansion of Vietnamese power has resulted historically in the loss of Khmer territory. The Khmer, in contrast, have lost no territory to the Chinese and little

An oxcart driver wears the checkered scarf that distinguishes Cambodians from their Thai or Vietnamese neighbors. Courtesy Bill Herod

Mother and child symbolize a renascent nation. Courtesy Bill Herod

to the Thai. No close cultural or religious ties exist between Cambodia and Vietnam. The Vietnamese fall within the Chinese culture sphere, rather than within the Indian, where the Thai and the Khmer belong. The Vietnamese differ from the Khmer in mode of dress, in kinship organization, and in many other ways—for example the Vietnamese are Mahayana Buddhists. Although Vietnamese lived in urban centers such as Phnom Penh, a substantial number lived along the lower Mekong and Basak rivers as well as on the shores of the Tonle Sap, where they engaged in fishing. Much of the manpower on French-owned rubber plantations was provided by the Vietnamese, who also were employed by the French as lower level civil servants and as white collar workers in private businesses.

Other Groups

The Europeans and the Indians constituted the smallest ethnic minorities in Cambodia prior to 1975. In 1950 there were about 4,500 Europeans and about 2,500 Indians in addition to small numbers of other Asians in that country. More than 90 percent of the Europeans lived in Phnom Penh, and the next largest number lived in Kampong Cham. A small Burmese minority, the Kola, was found in unspecified numbers in the gem-mining areas of Batdambang and Rotanokiri provinces in prewar days. Many of the Europeans served as technical advisers to the Cambodian government, or they worked for Western businesses. The Indians often were involved in moneylending and in small businesses, such as those that sold books and cloth. In the 1980s, Soviet and East European advisers supported the PRK government, but no accurate estimate of their numbers was available.

Languages

The majority of Cambodians, even those who are not ethnic Khmer, speak Khmer, the official language of the country. Ethnic Khmer living in Thailand, in Vietnam, and in Laos speak dialects of Khmer that are more or less intelligible to Khmer speakers from Cambodia. Minority languages include Vietnamese, Cham, several dialects of Chinese, and the languages of the various hill tribes (see Other Ethnic Groups, this ch.).

Austroasiatic-Mon-Khmer

Khmer belongs to the Mon-Khmer family of the Austroasiatic phylum of languages. American linguists David Thomas and Robert Headley have divided the Mon-Khmer family into nine branches: Pearic in western Cambodia and eastern Thailand;

Khmer in Cambodia, Thailand, Vietnam, and Laos; Bahnaric in Vietnam, Laos, and Cambodia; Katuic in Vietnam, Laos, and Cambodia; Khmuic in Laos, Thailand, and China; Monic in Burma and Thailand; Palaungic in Burma, China, and Thailand; Khasi in Assam (India); and Viet-Muong in Vietnam. Of the languages in the Mon-Khmer family, Vietnamese has the largest number of speakers (about 47 million); Khmer, has the next largest (about 8 million).

Khmer, in contrast to Vietnamese, Thai, Lao, and Chinese, is nontonal. Native Khmer words may be composed of one or two syllables. Khmer is uninflected, but it has a rich system of affixes, including infixes, for derivation. Generally speaking, Khmer has nouns (including pronouns as a special subcategory), verbs (including stative verbs or adjectives), adverbs, and various kinds of words called particles (including verbal auxiliaries, prepositions, conjunctions, final particles, and interjections). Many Khmer words change, chameleon-like, from one part of speech to another, depending on the context. The normal word order is subject-verb-object. Adjectival modifiers follow the nouns they modify.

Khmer, like its neighbors, Thai, Lao, and Burmese, has borrowed extensively from other languages, especially the Indic languages of Sanskrit and Pali. Khmer uses Sanskrit and Pali roots much as English and other West European languages use Latin and Greek roots to derive new, especially scientific, words. Khmer has also borrowed terms—especially financial, commercial, and cooking terms—from Chinese. In the nineteenth and twentieth centuries, Khmer borrowed from French as well. These latter borrowings have been in the realm of material culture, especially the names for items of modern Western technology, such as *buuzii* (spark plug) from the French *bougie.*

Khmer is written in a script derived from a south Indian alphabet. The language has symbols for thirty-three consonants, twenty-four dependent vowels, twelve independent vowels, and several diacritics. Most consonants have reduced or modified forms, called subscripts, when they occur as the second member of a consonant cluster. Vowels may be written before, after, over, or under a consonant symbol.

Some efforts to standardize Khmer spelling have been attempted, but inconsistencies persist, and many words have more than one accepted spelling. A two-volume dictionary prepared under the direction of the Venerable Chuon Nath of the Buddhist Institute in Phnom Penh is the standard work on Khmer lexicography.

Khmer is divided into three stages—Old Khmer (seventh to twelfth century A.D.), Middle Khmer (twelfth to seventeenth century A.D.), and Modern Khmer (seventeenth century to the present). It is likely that Old Khmer was the language of Chenla. What the language of Funan was is not at all certain, but it was probably a Mon-Khmer language. The earliest inscription in Khmer, found at Angkor Borei in Takev Province south of Phnom Penh, dates from A.D. 611 (see Prehistory and Early Kingdoms, ch. 1).

Austronesian

The Austronesian languages are spread over vast areas of Asia and the Pacific, from Madagascar to Easter Island and from Taiwan to Malaysia. Four Austronesian languages—Cham, Jarai, Rade, and Malay—are spoken in Cambodia. Cham is spoken by the largest number of people. Before 1975, there were about 100,000 speakers of Western Cham. Western Cham is the term used to distinguish (at least two mutually related dialects of) the Cham spoken in Cambodia and that used in adjacent inland Vietnam from Eastern Cham spoken in the coastal areas of central Vietnam. Western Cham is written in Arabic script, or, since the late 1960s and the early 1970s, in a romanized script devised by Protestant missionaries. The traditional Cham script, based on an Indian script, is still known and used by the Eastern Cham in Vietnam, but it has been lost by the Western Cham.

The Cham language is also nontonal. Words may contain one, two, or three syllables. Cham contains much linguistic borrowing from Arabic, Malay, and Khmer. The normal word order is subject-verb-object, and, as in Khmer, modifying adjectives follow the nouns that they modify. Most Cham in Cambodia are bilingual in Cham and in Khmer and many also know Arabic and Malay. Rade and Jarai, close relatives of Cham, are spoken by several thousand members of both ethnic groups in northeastern Cambodia. Both languages are written in romanized scripts based on the Vietnamese alphabet. Rade and Jarai have rich oral literatures, and the former has two epic tales that have been transcribed and published.

Religion

Buddhism

Origins of Buddhism on the Indian Subcontinent

Theravada Buddhism is the religion of virtually all of the ethnic Khmer, who constitute about 90 percent or more of the Cambodian population. Buddhism originated in what are now north India and

Nepal during the sixth century B.C. It was founded by a Sakya prince, Siddhartha Gautama (563–483 B.C.; his traditional dates are 623–543 B.C., also called the Gautama Buddha), who, at the age of twenty-nine, after witnessing old age, sickness, death, and meditation, renounced his high status and left his wife and infant son for a life of asceticism. After years of seeking truth, he is said to have attained enlightenment while sitting alone under a *bo* tree. He became the Buddha—"the enlightened"—and formed an order of monks, the *sangha* (see Glossary), and later an order of nuns. He spent the remainder of his life as a wandering preacher, dying at the age of eighty.

Buddhism began as a reaction to Hindu doctrines and as an effort to reform them. Nevertheless, the two faiths share many basic assumptions. Both view the universe and all life therein as parts of a cycle of eternal flux. In each religion, the present life of an individual is a phase in an endless chain of events. Life and death are merely alternate aspects of individual existence marked by the transition points of birth and death. An individual is thus continually reborn, perhaps in human form, perhaps in some non-human form, depending upon his or her actions in the previous life. The endless cycle of rebirth is known as *samsara* (wheel of life). Theravada Buddhism is a tolerant, non prescriptive religion that does not require belief in a supreme being. Its precepts require that each individual take full responsibility for his own actions and omissions. Buddhism is based on three concepts: dharma (the doctrine of the Buddha, his guide to right actions and belief); karma (the belief that one's life now and in future lives depends upon one's own deeds and misdeeds and that as an individual one is responsible for, and rewarded on the basis of, the sum total of one's acts and omissions in all one's incarnations past and present); and *sangha,* the ascetic community within which man can improve his karma.

The Buddha added the hope of escape—a way to get out of the endless cycle of pain and sorrow—to the Brahmanic idea of *samsara.* The Buddhist salvation is nirvana, a final extinction of one's self. Nirvana may be attained by achieving good karma through earning much merit and avoiding misdeeds. A Buddhist's pilgrimage through existence is a constant attempt to distance himself or herself from the world and finally to achieve complete detachment, or nirvana.

The fundamentals of Buddhist doctrine are the Four Noble Truths: suffering exists; craving (or desire) is the cause of suffering; release from suffering can be achieved by stopping all desire; and enlightenment—buddhahood—can be attained by following the Noble Eightfold Path (right views, right intention, right speech, right action, right livelihood, right effort, right mindfulness, and right concentration), which constitutes a middle way between sensuality and asceticism. Enlightenment consists of knowing these truths. The average layperson cannot hope for nirvana after the end of this life, but can—by complying, as best he or she is able to, with the doctrine's rules of moral conduct—hope to improve his or her karma and thereby better his condition in the next incarnation.

The doctrine of karma holds that, through the working of a just, automatic, and impersonal cosmic law, one's actions in this incarnation and in all previous ones will determine which position in the hierarchy of living things one will occupy in the next incarnation. An individual's karma can be improved through certain acts and omissions. By following the five precepts or commandments, a Buddhist can better his or her karma. These commandments are: do not kill, do not steal, do not indulge in forbidden sexual pleasures, do not tell lies, and do not take intoxicants or stupefying drugs or liquors.

The most effective way to work actively to improve one's karma is to earn merit. Any act of benevolence or generosity can gain merit for the doer. Cambodian Buddhists tend to regard opportunities for earning merit as primarily connected with interaction with the *sangha,* contributing to its support through money, goods, and labor, and participating in its activities. Some of the favorite ways for a male to earn merit are to enter the *sangha* as a monk (after the age of twenty) or as a novice, or to live in the wat as a temple servant; in the case of a female (usually the elderly), the favorite way is to become a nun. Other activities that gain merit include sponsoring a monk or novice, contributing to a wat, feeding members of the *sangha* at a public meal, and providing food for either of the two daily meals of the *sangha.*

In his first sermon to his followers, the Buddha described a moral code, the dharma, which the *sangha* was to teach after him. He left no designated successor. Indian emperor Asoka (273–232 B.C.) patronized the *sangha* and encouraged the teaching of the Buddha's philosophy throughout his vast empire; by 246 B.C., the new religion had reached Sri Lanka. The Tripitaka, the collection of basic Buddhist texts, was written down for the first time in Sri Lanka during a major Buddhist conference in the second or first century B.C. By the time of the conference, a schism had developed separating Mahayana (Greater Path) Buddhism from more conservative Theravada (Way of the Elders, or Hinayana—Lesser Path) faction or Buddhism. The Mahayana faction reinterpreted the original

Young Buddhist monks pause at a temple entrance.
Courtesy Bill Herod

Khmer - are the predominant ethnic group in
Cambodia, accounting for approximately 90% of the 14.2 million.
A language -

teachings of the Buddha and added a type of deity called a bodhisattva (see Glossary) to large numbers of other buddhas. The Mahayana adherents believe that nirvana is available to everyone, not just to select holy men. Mahayana Buddhism quickly spread throughout India, China, Korea, Japan, Central Asia, and to some parts of Southeast Asia. According to the Venerable Pang Khat, Theravada Buddhism reached Southeast Asia as early as the second or third century A.D., while Mahayana Buddhism did not arrive in Cambodia until about A.D. 791. In Southeast Asia, Mahayana Buddhism carried many Brahman beliefs with it to the royal courts of Funan, of Champa, and of other states. At this time, Sanskrit words were added to the Khmer and to the Cham languages. Theravada Buddhism (with its scriptures in the Pali language), remained influential in Sri Lanka, and by the thirteenth century it had spread into Burma, Thailand, Laos, and Cambodia, where it supplanted Mahayana Buddhism.

Cambodian Adaptations

Cambodian Buddhism has no formal administrative ties with other Buddhist bodies, although Theravada monks from other countries, especially Thailand, Laos, Burma, and Sri Lanka, may participate in religious ceremonies in order to make up the requisite number of clergy. Cambodian Buddhism is organized nationally

115

in accordance with regulations formulated in 1943 and modified in 1948. During the monarchical period, the king led the Buddhist clergy. Prince Sihanouk continued in this role even after he had abdicated and was governing as head of state. He appointed both the heads of the monastic orders and other high-ranking clergy. After the overthrow of Sihanouk in 1970, the new head of state, Lon Nol, appointed these leaders.

Two monastic orders constituted the clergy in Cambodia. The larger group, to which more than 90 percent of the clergy belonged, was the Mohanikay. The Thommayut order was far smaller. The Thommayut was introduced into the ruling circles of Cambodia from Thailand in 1864; it gained prestige because of its adoption by royalty and by the aristocracy, but its adherents were confined geographically to the Phnom Penh area. Among the few differences between the two orders is stricter observance by the Thommayut bonzes (monks) of the rules governing the clergy. In 1961 the Mohanikay had more than 52,000 ordained monks in some 2,700 wat, whereas the Thommayut order had 1,460 monks in just over 100 wat. In 1967 more than 2,800 Mohanikay wat and 320 Thommayut wat were in existence in Cambodia. After Phnom Penh, the largest number of Thommayut wat were found in Batdambang, Stoeng Treng, Prey Veng, Kampot, and Kampong Thum provinces.

Each order has its own superior and is organized into a hierarchy of eleven levels. The seven lower levels are known collectively as the *thananukram;* the four higher levels together are called the *rajagana.* The Mohanikay order has thirty-five monks in the *rajagana;* the Thommayut has twenty-one. Each monk must serve for at least twenty years to be named to these highest levels.

The cornerstones of Cambodian Buddhism are the Buddhist bonze and the wat. Traditionally, each village has a spiritual center—a wat—where from five to more than seventy bonzes reside. A typical wat in rural Cambodia consists of a walled enclosure containing a sanctuary, several residences for bonzes, a hall, a kitchen, quarters for nuns, and a pond. The number of monks varies according to the size of the local population. The sanctuary, which contains an altar with statues of the Buddha and, in rare cases, a religious relic, is reserved for major ceremonies and usually only for the use of bonzes. Other ceremonies, classes for monks and for laity, and meals take place in the hall. Stupas containing the ashes of extended family members are constructed near the sanctuary. Fruit trees and vegetable gardens tended by local children are also part of the local wat. The main entrance, usually only for ceremonial use, faces east; other entrances are located at other points around the wall. There are no gates.

Steinberg notes the striking ratio of bonzes to the total population of Cambodia. In the late 1950s, an estimated 100,000 bonzes (including about 40,000 novices) served a population of about 5 million. This high proportion undoubtedly was caused in large part by the ease with which one could enter and leave the *sangha*. Becoming a bonze and leaving the *sangha* are matters of individual choice although, in theory, nearly all Cambodian males over sixteen serve terms as bonzes. Most young men do not intend to become fully ordained bonzes (*bhikkhu*), and they remain as monks for less than a year. Even a son's temporary ordination as a bonze brings great merit to his parents, however, and is considered so important that arrangements are made at a parent's funeral if the son has not undergone the process while the parent was living. There are two classes of bonzes at a wat—the novices (*samani* or *nen*) and the *bhikkhu*. Ordination is held from mid-April to mid-July, during the rainy season.

Buddhist monks do not take perpetual vows to remain monks, although, in fact, some become monks permanently. Traditionally, they became monks early in life. It is possible to become a novice at as young an age as seven, but in practice thirteen is the earliest age for novices. A *bhikkhu* must be at least twenty. The monk's life is regulated by Buddhist law, and life in the wat adheres to a rigid routine. A *bhikkhu* follows 227 rules of monastic discipline as well as the 10 basic precepts. These include the five precepts that all Buddhists should follow. The five precepts for monastic asceticism prohibit eating after noon, participating in any entertainment (singing, dancing, and watching movies or television), using any personal adornments, sleeping on a luxurious bed, and handling money. In addition, a monk also is expected to be celibate. Furthermore, monks supposedly avoid all involvement in political affairs. They are not eligible to vote or to hold any political office, and they may not witness a legal document or give testimony in court. Since the person of a monk is considered sacred, he is considered to be outside the normal civil laws and public duties that affect lay people. Some of these practices have changed in the modern period, however, and in the 1980s Buddhist monks have been active even in the PRK government.

Women are not ordained, but older women, especially widows, can become nuns. They live in wat and play an important role in the everyday life of the temple. Nuns shave their heads and eyebrows and generally follow the same precepts as monks. They may prepare the altars and do some of the housekeeping chores.

Role of Buddhism in Cambodian Life

Buddhist monks traditionally were called upon to perform a number of functions in Cambodian life. They participated in all formal village festivals, ceremonies, marriages, and funerals. They also might have participated in ceremonies to name infants and in other minor ceremonies or rites of passage. Monks did not lead the ceremonies, however, because that role was given to the *achar,* or master of ceremonies; the monk's major function was to say prayers of blessing. They were often healers and, in traditional Khmer culture, they were the practitioners whose role was closest to that of modern psychiatrists. They might also have been skilled in astrology. The monk traditionally occupied a unique position in the transmission of Khmer culture and values. By his way of life, he provided a living model of the most meritorious behavior a Buddhist could follow. He also provided the laity with many opportunities for gaining merit. For centuries monks were the only literate people residing in rural communities; they acted as teachers to temple servants, to novices, and to newly ordained monks. Until the 1970s, most literate Cambodian males gained literacy solely through the instruction of the *sangha.*

After independence from France, young Cambodian intellectuals changed their attitude toward the clergy. In describing a general shift away from Buddhism in the late 1950s and the early 1960s, Vickery cites the early work of anthropologist May Mayko Ebihara and his own observations. He suggests that the Khmer Rouge was able to instill antireligious feelings in younger males because the latter were losing interest in becoming monks even during their teenage years, the traditional temporary period of service. The monks themselves had abandoned some of their traditional restrictions and had become involved in politics. At intervals during the colonial period, some monks had demonstrated or had rebelled against French rule, and in the 1970s monks joined pro-government demonstrations against the communists. Anticlerical feelings reached their highest point among the Khmer Rouge, who at first attempted to indoctrinate monks and to force them to pass anticlerical ideas on to the laity. Under the Khmer Rouge regime, monks were expelled forcibly from the wat and were compelled to do manual labor. Article 20 of the 1976 Constitution of Democratic Kampuchea permitted freedom of religion but banned all reactionary religions, that were "detrimental to the country." The minister of culture stated that Buddhism was incompatible with the revolution and was an instrument of exploitation. Under this regime, to quote the Finnish Inquiry Commission, "The practice of religion was forbidden and the pagodas were systematically destroyed.'' Observers estimated that 50,000 monks died during the Khmer Rouge regime. The status of Buddhism and of religion in general after the Vietnamese invasion was at least partially similar to its status in pre-Khmer Rouge times.

According to Michael Vickery, who has written positively about the PRK, public observance of Buddhism and of Islam has been reestablished, and government policies allow Cambodians freedom to believe or not to believe in Buddhism. Vickery cites some differences in this reestablished Buddhism. Religious affairs are overseen by the PRK's Kampuchean (or Khmer) United Front for National Construction and Defense (KUFNCD—see Appendix B), the mass organization that supports the state by organizing women, youths, workers, and religious groups (see The Kampuchean, or Khmer, United Front for National Construction and Defense, ch. 4). In 1987 there was only a single Buddhist order because the Thommayut order had not been revived. The organization of the clergy also had been simplified. The *sangharaja* (primate of the Buddhist clergy) had been replaced by a *prathean* (chairman). Communities that wanted a wat had to apply to a local front committee for permission. The wat were administered by a committee of the local laity. Private funds paid for the restoration of the wat damaged during the war and the Khmer Rouge era, and they supported the restored wat. Monks were ordained by a hierarchy that has been reconstituted since an initial ordination in September 1979 by a delegation from the Buddhist community in Vietnam. The validity of this ordination continues to be questioned. In general, there are only two to four monks per wat, which is fewer than before 1975. In 1981 about 4,930 monks served in 740 wat in Cambodia. The Buddhist General Assembly reported 7,000 monks in 1,821 active wat a year later. In 1969 by contrast, observers estimated that 53,400 monks and 40,000 novice monks served in more than 3,000 wat. Vickery sums up his observations on the subject by noting that, ''The government has kept its promise to allow freedom for traditional Buddhism, but does not actively encourage it.''

Martin offers another, more pessimistic, view of the religious situation in the late 1980s. In a 1986 study, she asserts that the PRK showed outsiders only certain aspects of religious freedom; she also states that the few wat that were restored had only two or three old monks in residence and that public attendance was low. The monks were allowed to leave the wat only for an hour in the mornings, to collect their food, or during holy days. Lay people who practiced their faith were about the same ages as the monks, and they were allowed to visit the wat only in the evenings.

A government circular had also instructed civil servants to stop celebrating the traditional New Year Festival. Some traditional Buddhist festivals still were tolerated, but the state collected a 50 percent tithe on donations. Martin believes that Buddhism was threatened externally by state repression and by nonsupport and internally by invalid clergy. She noted that the two Buddhist superiors, Venerable Long Chhim and Venerable Tep Vong, were both believed to be from Vietnam. Venerable Tep Vong was concurrently the superior of the Buddhist clergy, vice president of the PRK's Khmer National Assembly, and vice president of the KUFNCD National Council. She quoted a refugee from Batdambang as having said, ''During the meetings, the Khmer administrative authorities, accompanied by the Vietnamese experts, tell you, 'Religion is like poison, it's like opium; it's better to give the money to the military, so they can fight'.''

Buddhism is still strong among the various Cambodian refugee groups throughout the world, although some younger monks, faced with the distractions of a foreign culture, have chosen to leave the clergy and have become laicized. In the United States in 1984, there were twelve Cambodian wat with about twenty-one monks. In the 1980s, a Cambodian Buddhist wat was constructed near Washington, D.C., financed by a massive outpouring of donations from Cambodian Buddhists throughout North America. This wat is one of the few outside Southeast Asia that has the consecrated boundary within which ordinations may be performed.

Most of the major Cambodian annual festivals are connected with Buddhist observances. The *chol chnam* (New Year Festival) takes place in mid-April; it was one of the few festivals allowed under the Khmer Rouge regime. The *phchun ben,* celebrated in September or in October, is a memorial day for deceased ancestors and for close friends. *Meak bochea,* in January or February, commemorates the last sermon of the Buddha. *Vissakh bochea,* in April or in May, is the triple anniversary of the birth, death, and enlightenment of the Buddha. The *chol vossa* takes place in June or in July; it marks the beginning of a penitential season during which the monks must remain within the temple compounds. The *kathen* marks the end of this season; celebrated in September, it features offerings, especially of robes, to the monks. The *kathen* was still celebrated in the PRK in the late 1980s.

Cambodian Buddhism exists side-by-side with, and to some extent intermingles with, pre-Buddhist animism and Brahman practices. Most Cambodians, whether or not they profess to be Buddhists (or Muslims), believe in a rich supernatural world. When ill, or at other times of crisis, or to seek supernatural help, Cambodians may enlist the aid of a practitioner who is believed to be able to propitiate or obtain help from various spirits. Local spirits are believed to inhabit a variety of objects, and shrines to them may be found in houses, in Buddhist temples, along roads, and in forests.

Several types of supernatural entities are believed to exist; they make themselves known by means of inexplicable sounds or happenings. Among these phenomena are *khmoc* (ghosts), *pret* and *besach* (particularly nasty demons, the spirits of people who have died violent, untimely, or unnatural deaths), *arak* (evil spirits, usually female), *neak ta* (tutelary spirits residing in inanimate objects), *mneang phteah* (guardians of the house), *meba* (ancestral spirits), and *mrenh kongveal* (elf-like guardians of animals). All spirits must be shown proper respect, and, with the exception of the *mneang phteah* and *mrenh kongveal,* they can cause trouble ranging from mischief to serious life-threatening illnesses. An important way for living people to show respect for the spirits of the dead is to provide food for the spirits. If this food is not provided, the spirit can cause trouble for the offending person. For example, if a child does not provide food for the spirit of its dead mother, that spirit can cause misfortunes to happen to the child.

Aid in dealing with the spirit world may be obtained from a *kru* (shaman or spirit practitioner), an *achar* (ritualist), *thmup* (witch, sorcerer or sorceress), or a *rup arak* (medium, usually male). The *kru* is a kind of sorcerer who prepares charms and amulets to protect the wearer from harm. He can cure illnesses, find lost objects, and prepare magic potions. Traditionally, Cambodians have held strong beliefs about protective charms. Amulets are worn routinely by soldiers to ward off bullets, for example. The *kru* are believed to have the power to prepare an amulet and to establish a supernatural link between it and the owner. A *kru* may acquire considerable local prestige and power. Many *kru* are former Buddhist monks.

Another kind of magical practitioner is the *achar,* a specialist in ritual. He may function as a kind of master of ceremonies at a wat and as a specialist in conducting spirit worship rituals connected with life-cycle ceremonies. *Rup arak* are mediums who can be possessed by supernatural beings and communicate with the spirit world. The *thmup* are sorcerers who cause illnesses.

Fortunetellers and astrologers—*haor teay*—are important in Cambodian life. They are consulted about important decisions such as marriages, building a new house, or going on a long journey. They are believed to be able to foretell future events and to determine lucky or unlucky days for various activities.

Villagers are sensitive to the power and to the needs of the spirit world. According to observations by an American missionary in the early 1970s, villagers consulted the local guardian spirit to find out what the coming year would bring, a new province chief held a ceremony to ask the protection of the spirits over the province, and soldiers obtained magic cloths and amulets from mediums and shamans to protect them from the bullets of the enemy. Before embarking on a mission against enemy forces, a province chief might burn incense and call on a spirit for aid in defeating the enemy. Examples of Brahman influences were various rituals concerned with the well-being of the nation carried out by the ruler and the *baku* (a Brahman priestly group attached to the royal court). These rituals were reportedly stopped after Sihanouk's ouster in 1970 (see The March 1970 Coup d'Etat, ch. 1).

Chinese Religion

Mahayana Buddhism is the religion of the majority of Chinese and Vietnamese in Cambodia. Elements of other religious practices, such as veneration of folk heros and ancestors, Confucianism, and Taoism mix with Chinese and Vietnamese Buddhism.

In the Chinese home, ancestors and household gods are honored during prescribed times to help unite the extended family and to gain help from the dead, who can intercede for the living. Taoism teaches meditation and the use of magic to gain happiness, wealth, health, and immortality. Confucianism, part social philosophy and part religion, stresses religious ritual and pays great attention to the veneration of ancestors and of great figures of the past.

Chinese Mahayana Buddhism has become intertwined with Taoist and with Confucian beliefs. Adherents honor many buddhas, including the Gautama Buddha, and they believe in a paradise after death. They also believe in bodhisattvas—people who have nearly attained nirvana, but who stay back to help save others.

Islam

Islam is the religion of the Cham (also called Khmer Islam) and Malay minorities. According to Po Dharma, there were 150,000 to 200,000 Muslims in Cambodia as late as 1975. Persecution under the Khmer Rouge eroded their numbers, however, and by the late 1980s they probably had not regained their former strength. All of the Cham Muslims are Sunnis of the Shafii school. Po Dharma divides the Muslim Cham in Cambodia into a traditionalist branch and an orthodox branch.

The Cham have their own mosques. In 1962 there were about 100 mosques in the country. At the end of the nineteenth century, the Muslims in Cambodia formed a unified community under the authority of four religious dignitaries—*mupti, tuk kalih, raja kalik,* and *tvan pake.* A council of notables in Cham villages consisted of one *hakem* and several *katip, bilal,* and *labi.* The four high dignitaries and the *hakem* were exempt from personal taxes, and they were invited to take part in major national ceremonies at the royal court. When Cambodia became independent, the Islamic community was placed under the control of a five-member council that represented the community in official functions and in contacts with other Islamic communities. Each Muslim community has a *hakem* who leads the community and the mosque, an imam who leads the prayers, and a *bilal* who calls the faithful to the daily prayers. The peninsula of Chrouy Changvar near Phnom Penh is considered the spiritual center of the Cham, and several high Muslim officials reside there. Each year some of the Cham go to study the Quran at Kelantan in Malaysia, and some go on to study in, or make a pilgrimage to, Mecca. According to figures from the late 1950s, about 7 percent of the Cham had completed the pilgrimage and could wear the fez or turban as a sign of their accomplishment.

The traditional Cham retain many ancient Muslim or pre-Muslim traditions and rites. They consider Allah as the all-powerful God, but they also recognize other non-Islamic deities. They are closer, in many respects, to the Cham of coastal Vietnam than they are to other Muslims. The religious dignitaries of the traditional Cham (and of the Cham in Vietnam) dress completely in white, and they shave their heads and faces. These Cham believe in the power of magic and sorcery, and they attach great importance to magical practices in order to avoid sickness or slow or violent death. They believe in many supernatural powers. Although they show little interest in the pilgrimage to Mecca and in the five daily prayers, the traditional Cham do celebrate many Muslim festivals and rituals.

The orthodox Cham have adopted a more orthodox religion largely because of their close contacts with, and intermarriages with, the Malay community. In fact, the orthodox Cham have adopted Malay customs and family organization, and many speak the Malay language. They send pilgrims to Mecca, and they attend international Islamic conferences. Conflicts between the traditional and the orthodox Cham increased between 1954 and 1975. For example, the two groups polarized the population of one village, and each group eventually had its own mosque and separate religious organization.

According to Cham sources, 132 mosques were destroyed during the Khmer Rouge era, many others were desecrated, and Muslims were not allowed to worship. In the PRK, Islam has been given the same freedom as Buddhism. Vickery believes that about 185,000

Cham lived in Cambodia in the mid-1980s and that the number of mosques was about the same then as it was before 1975. In late 1987, there were six mosques in the Phnom Penh area and a "good number" in the provinces, but Muslim dignitaries were thinly stretched; only 20 of the previous 113 most prominent Cham clergy in Cambodia survived the Khmer Rouge period.

Other Religions

Christianity, introduced into Cambodia by Roman Catholic missionaries in 1660, made little headway, at least among the Buddhists. In 1972 there were probably about 20,000 Christians in Cambodia, most of whom were Roman Catholics. Before the repatriation of the Vietnamese in 1970 and 1971, possibly as many as 62,000 Christians lived in Cambodia. According to Vatican statistics, in 1953, members of the Roman Catholic Church in Cambodia numbered 120,000, making it, at the time, the second largest religion in the country. In April 1970, just before repatriation, estimates indicate that about 50,000 Catholics were Vietnamese. Many of the Catholics remaining in Cambodia in 1972 were Europeans—chiefly French. Steinberg reported, also in 1953, that an American Unitarian mission maintained a teacher-training school in Phnom Penh, and Baptist missions functioned in Batdambang and Siemreab provinces. A Christian and Missionary Alliance mission was founded in Cambodia in 1923; by 1962 the mission had converted about 2,000 people.

American Protestant missionary activity increased in Cambodia, especially among some of the hill tribes and among the Cham, after the establishment of the Khmer Republic. The 1962 census, which reported 2,000 Protestants in Cambodia, remains the most recent statistic for the group. In 1982 French geographer Jean Delvert reported that three Christian villages existed in Cambodia, but he gave no indication of the size, location, or type of any of them. Observers reported that in 1980 there were more registered Khmer Christians among the refugees in camps in Thailand than in all of Cambodia before 1970. Kiernan notes that, until June 1980, five weekly Protestant services were held in Phnom Penh by a Khmer pastor, but that they had been reduced to a single weekly service after police harassment. His estimates suggest that in 1987 the Christian community in Cambodia had shrunk to only a few thousand members.

Highland tribal groups, most with their own local religious systems, probably number fewer than 100,000 persons. The Khmer Loeu have been loosely described as animists, but most tribal groups have their own pantheon of local spirits. In general they see their world filled with various invisible spirits (often called *yang*), some benevolent, others malevolent. They associate spirits with rice, soil, water, fire, stones, paths, and so forth. Sorcerers or specialists in each village contact these spirits and prescribe ways to appease them. In times of crisis or change, animal sacrifices may be made to placate the anger of the spirits. Illness is often believed to be caused by evil spirits or sorcerers. Some tribes have special medicine men or shamans who treat the sick. In addition to belief in spirits, villagers believe in taboos on many objects or practices. Among the Khmer Loeu, the Rade and Jarai groups have a well developed hierarchy of spirits with a supreme ruler at its head.

Education

Public School System

Traditional education in Cambodia was handled by the local wat, and the bonzes were the teachers. The students were almost entirely young boys, and the education was limited to memorizing Buddhist chants in Pali. During the period of the French protectorate, an educational system based on the French model was inaugurated alongside the traditional system. Initially, the French neglected education in Cambodia. Only seven high school students graduated in 1931, and only 50,000 to 60,000 children were enrolled in primary school in 1936. In the years immediately following independence, the number of students rapidly increased. Vickery suggests that education of any kind was considered an "absolute good" by all Cambodians and that this attitude eventually created a large group of unemployed or underemployed graduates by the late 1960s.

From the early twentieth century until 1975, the system of mass education operated on the French model. The educational system was divided into primary, secondary, higher, and specialized levels. Public education was under the jurisdiction of the Ministry of Education, which exercised full control over the entire system; it established syllabi, hired and paid teachers, provided supplies, and inspected schools. An inspector of primary education, who had considerable authority, was assigned to each province. Cultural committees under the Ministry of Education were responsible for "enriching the Cambodian language."

Primary education, divided into two cycles of three years each, was carried out in state-run and temple-run schools. Successful completion of a final state examination led to the award of a certificate after each cycle. The primary education curriculum consisted of arithmetic, history, ethics, civics, drafting, geography, hygiene,

Vong Dantrey percussion ensemble accompanies classical ballet rehearsal.
Courtesy Bill Herod

language, and science. In addition, the curriculum included physical education and manual work. French language instruction began in the second year. Khmer was the language of instruction in the first cycle, but French was used in the second cycle and thereafter. By the early 1970s, Khmer was used more widely in primary education. In the 1980s, primary school ran from the first to the fourth grade. Theoretically one primary school served each village. Secondary education also was divided into two cycles, one of four years taught at a college, followed by one of three years taught at a lycée. Upon completion of the first cycle, students could take a state examination. Successful candidates received a secondary diploma. Upon completion of the first two years of the second cycle, students could take a state examination for the first baccalaureate, and, following their final year, they could take a similar examination for the second baccalaureate. The Cambodian secondary curriculum was similar to that found in France. Beginning in 1967, the last three years of secondary school were split up into three sections according to major subjects—letters, mathematics and technology; agriculture; and biology. In the late 1960s and the early 1970s, the country emphasized a technical education. In the PRK, secondary education was reduced to six years (see table 4, Appendix A).

Students at rehearsal during a revival of classical ballet
Courtesy Bill Herod

Higher education lagged well behind primary and secondary education, until the late 1950s. The only facility in the country for higher education before the 1960s was the National Institute of Legal, Political, and Economic Studies, which trained civil servants. In the late 1950s, it had about 250 students. Wealthy Cambodians and those who had government scholarships sought university-level education abroad. Students attended schools in France, but after independence increasing numbers enrolled at universities in the United States, Canada, China, the Soviet Union, and the German Democratic Republic (East Germany). By 1970 six universities with a total enrollment of nearly 9,000 students served Cambodia. The largest, the University of Phnom Penh, had nearly 4,570 male students and more than 730 female students in eight departments—letters and humanities, science and technology, law and economics, medicine, pharmacy, commercial science, teacher training, and higher teacher training. Universities operated in the provinces of Kampong Cham, Takev, Batdambang; and in Phnom Penh, the University of Agricultural Sciences and the University of Fine Arts offered training. The increased fighting following the 1970 coup closed the three provincial universities.

During the Khmer Rouge regime, education was dealt a severe setback, and the great strides made in literacy and in education during the two decades following independence were obliterated systematically. Schools were closed, and educated people and teachers were subjected to, at the least, suspicion and harsh treatment and, at the worst, execution. At the beginning of the 1970s, more than 20,000 teachers lived in Cambodia; only about 5,000 of the teachers remained 10 years later. Soviet sources report that 90 percent of all teachers were killed under the Khmer Rouge regime. Only 50 of the 725 university instructors, 207 of the 2,300 secondary school teachers, and 2,717 of the 21,311 primary school teachers survived. The meager educational fare was centered on precepts of the Khmer revolution; young people were rigidly indoctrinated, but literacy was neglected, and an entire generation of Cambodian children grew up illiterate. After the Khmer Rouge were driven from power, the educational system had to be re-created from almost nothing. Illiteracy had climbed to more than 40 percent, and most young people under the age of 14 lacked any basic education.

Education began making a slow comeback, following the establishment of the PRK. In 1986 the following main institutions of higher education were reported in the PRK: the Faculty of Medicine and Pharmacy (reopened in 1980 with a six-year course of study); the Chamcar Daung Faculty of Agriculture (opened in 1985); the Kampuchea-USSR Friendship Technical Institute (which includes technical and engineering curricula), the Institute of Languages (Vietnamese, German, Russian, and Spanish are taught); the Institute of Commerce, the Center for Pedagogical Education (formed in 1979); the Normal Advanced School; and the School of Fine Arts. Writing about the educational system under the PRK, Vickery states, ''Both the government and the people have demonstrated enthusiasm for education . . . . The list of subjects covered is little different from that of prewar years. There is perhaps more time devoted to Khmer language and literature than before the war and, until the 1984–85 school year, at least, no foreign language instruction.'' He notes that the secondary school syllabus calls for four hours of foreign language instruction per week in either Russian, German, or Vietnamese but that there were no teachers available.

Martin describes the educational system in the PRK as based very closely on the Vietnamese model, pointing out that even the terms for primary and secondary education have been changed into direct translations of the Vietnamese terms. Under the PRK regime, according to Martin, the primary cycle had four instead of six classes, the first level of secondary education had three instead of four classes, and the second level of secondary education had

(Top) Survivor of the Khmer Rouge upheaval (Bottom left) Ballet student rehearses hand movements (Bottom right) Youthful monk near roadside shrine All photos, courtesy Bill Herod

three classes. Martin writes that not every young person could go to school because schooling both in towns and in the countryside required enrollment fees. Civil servants pay 25 riels (for value of the riel—see Glossary) per month to send a child to school, and others pay up to 150 riels per month. Once again, according to Martin, "Access to tertiary studies is reserved for children whose parents work for the regime and have demonstrated proof of their loyalty to the regime." She writes that, from the primary level on, the contents of all textbooks except for alphabet books was politically oriented and dealt "more specifically with Vietnam." From the beginning of the secondary cycle, Vietnamese language study was compulsory.

Buddhist Education

Before the French organized a Western-style educational system, the Buddhist wat, with monks as teachers, provided the only formal education in Cambodia. The monks traditionally regarded their main educational function as the teaching of Buddhist doctrine and history and the importance of gaining merit. Other subjects were regarded as secondary. At the wat schools, young boys—girls were not allowed to study in these institutions—were taught to read and to write Khmer, and they were instructed in the rudiments of Buddhism.

In 1933 a secondary school system for novice monks was created within the Buddhist religious system. Many wat schools had so-called Pali schools that provided three years of elementary education from which the student could compete for entrance into the Buddhist lycées. Graduates of these lycées could sit for the entrance examination to the Buddhist University in Phnom Penh. The curriculum of the Buddhist schools consisted of the study of Pali, of Buddhist doctrine, and of Khmer, along with mathematics, Cambodian history and geography, science, hygiene, civics, and agriculture. Buddhist instruction was under the authority of the Ministry of Religion.

Nearly 600 Buddhist primary schools, with an enrollment of more than 10,000 novices and with 800 monks as instructors, existed in 1962. The Preah Suramarit Buddhist Lycée—a four-year institution in Phnom Penh founded in 1955—included courses in Pali, in Sanskrit, and in Khmer, as well as in many modern disciplines. In 1962 the student body numbered 680. The school's graduates could continue their studies in the Preah Sihanouk Raj Buddhist University created in 1959. The university offered three cycles of instruction; the doctoral degree was awarded after successful completion of the third cycle. In 1962 there were 107 students enrolled in the Buddhist University. By the 1969–70 academic year, more than 27,000 students were attending Buddhist religious elementary schools, 1,328 students were at Buddhist lycées, and 176 students were enrolled at the Buddhist University.

The Buddhist Institute was a research institution formed in 1930 from the Royal Library. The institute contained a library, record and photograph collections, and a museum. Several commissions were part of the institute. A folklore commission published collections of Cambodian folktales, a Tripitaka Commission completed a translation of the Buddhist canon into Khmer, and a dictionary commission produced a definitive two-volume dictionary of Khmer. No information was available in 1987 regarding the fate of the temple schools, but it is doubtful that they were revived after the fall of the Khmer Rouge regime.

Private Education

For a portion of the urban population in Cambodia, private education was important in the years before the communist takeover. Some private schools were operated by ethnic or religious minorities—Chinese, Vietnamese, European, Roman Catholic, and Muslim—so that children could study their own language, culture, or religion. Other schools provided education to indigenous children who could not gain admission to a public school. Attendance at some of the private schools, especially those in Phnom Penh, conferred a certain amount of prestige on the student and on the student's family.

The private educational system included Chinese-language schools, Vietnamese-language (often Roman Catholic) schools, French-language schools, English-language schools, and Khmer-language schools. Enrollment in private primary schools rose from 32,000 in the early 1960s to about 53,500 in 1970, although enrollment in private secondary schools dropped from about 19,000 to fewer than 8,700 for the same period. In 1962 there were 195 Chinese schools, 40 Khmer schools, 15 Vietnamese schools, and 14 French schools operating in Cambodia. Private secondary education was represented by several high schools, notably the Lycée Descartes in Phnom Penh.

All of the Vietnamese schools in Phnom Penh and some of the Chinese schools there were closed by government decree in 1970. There was no information available in 1987 that would have indicated the presence of any private schools in the PRK, although there was some private instruction, especially in foreign languages.

Health and Welfare

The government made a great effort to train new medical personnel, especially nurses and midwives, following independence in 1953. By the late 1950s, however, infant mortality reportedly was as high as 50 percent. Dysentery, malaria, yaws, tuberculosis, trachoma, various skin diseases, and parasitic diseases were common. Inadequate nutrition, poor sanitary conditions, poor hygiene practices, and a general lack of adequate medical treatment combined to give the average Cambodian a life expectancy of about forty-six years by the late 1960s. This figure represented a significant increase from the thirty-year life expectancy reported a decade earlier. The catastrophic effects of the war and Khmer Rouge rule reversed this positive trend. During the unrest, many Western-trained physicians were killed or fled the country. Modern medicines were in short supply, and traditional herbal remedies were used.

Public Health

According to traditional Cambodian beliefs, disease may be caused by some underlying spiritual cause. Evil spirits or "bad air" are believed to cause many diseases and can be expelled from the body of a sick person by trained practitioners, who may be traditional healers—bonzes, former bonzes, herbalists, folk healers—or Western-trained doctors and nurses. Aside from a wide variety of herbal remedies, traditional healing practices include scraping the skin with a coin, ring, or other small object; sprinkling or spraying water on the sick person; and prayer. The use of cupping glasses (in French, *ventouse*) continued in widespread use in the late 1980s.

Sanitation practices in rural Cambodia are often primitive. The water supply is the main problem; rivers and streams are common sources of drinking water and of water for cooking. These water sources are often the same ones used for bathing, washing clothes, and disposing of waste products. Adequate sewage disposal is nonexistent in most rural and suburban areas. Sanitary conditions in the largest urban areas—Phnom Penh, Batdambang city, and Kampong Cham city—were much improved over the conditions in the rural areas, however. By the early 1970s, Phnom Penh had three water purification plants, which were adequate for the peacetime population but could not provide safe water when the city's population increased significantly in the mid-1970s. The city had regular garbage collection, and sewage was usually disposed of in septic tanks.

132

The medical situation in Cambodia faced its first crisis at the time of independence in 1953. Many French medical personnel departed, and few trained Cambodians were left to replace them. In addition to a lack of personnel, a shortage of medical supplies and facilities threatened health care. To correct the first problem, in 1953 the government established a school of medicine and a school of nursing, the Royal Faculty of Medicine of Cambodia (which became the Faculty of Medicine, Pharmacy, and Paramedical Science in 1972, and probably the Faculty of Medicine and Pharmacy which reopened in 1980). The first class of candidates for the degree of doctor of medicine was enrolled in 1958. In 1962 this school became part of the University of Phnom Penh, and in 1967 it expanded its teaching program to include training for dentists and for medical specialists (see Public School System, this ch.). By the late 1960s, trained Cambodian instructors began replacing foreign personnel at the Faculty of Medicine, and by 1971 thirty-three Cambodian medical instructors represented sixteen specialized branches of medical study.

A school for training nurses and midwives was operating before 1970. This institution also trained sanitation agents, who received four years of medical training with emphasis on sanitation and on preventive medicine. These agents provided medical services for areas where there were no doctors or clinics. The number of nurses trained almost quintupled between 1955 and 1970. In Cambodia, nursing careers had been primarily reserved for men, but the number of women entering the field greatly increased after 1955. Midwives delivered almost half of the babies in the early 1970s. In March 1970, eighty-one pharmacists practiced in government-controlled areas. By 1971 the number had dropped to sixty three.

Cambodia never has had an adequate number of hospitals or clinics. In 1930 there was only a single 450-bed hospital serving Phnom Penh. By 1953 however, 122 public medical establishments operated in Cambodia, and, between 1955 and 1970, many improvements were made by the royal government. Old hospital buildings were replaced or repaired, and new ones were constructed. In 1962 provincial hospitals, along with many infirmaries, operated in all but three provincial capitals. By March 1970, 29 hospitals, with a total of 6,186 beds, were in operation; by September 1971, however, only 13 still functioned.

Phnom Penh had greater hospital resources than other parts of the country. In the late 1960s, hospitals served inhabitants in the surrounding area as well as residents of the city. At that time, seven hospitals (including five teaching institutions), several private clinics, twenty-two public dispensaries or infirmaries, and six military infirmaries operated as well. The major hospitals in Phnom Penh were the Preah Ket Mealea Hospital, the largest in the country with 1,000 beds, which was built in 1893; the 500-bed Soviet-Khmer Friendship Hospital, built in 1960; the Preah Monivong military hospital complexes; the French-operated Calmette Hospital; a Buddhist monks' hospital; and a Chinese hospital. Eight of the eighteen operating theaters in Cambodia in the late 1960s were in Phnom Penh.

A leprosarium in Kampong Cham Province provided care for about 2,000 patients, and the Sonn Mann Mental Hospital at Ta Khmau provided care for 300 patients. In 1971 Sonn Mann had about 1,100 patients and a staff of six doctors, twenty-two nurses, one midwife, fifty-four administrative employees, and eighty-nine guards.

Modern medical practices and pharmaceuticals have been scarce in Cambodia since the early 1970s. The situation deteriorated so badly between 1975 and 1979 that the population had to resort to traditional remedies. A Cambodian refugee described a hospital in Batdambang Province in the early days of the Khmer Rouge regime: ". . . the sick were thrown into a big room baptized 'Angkar Hospital,' where conditions were miserable. Phnom Srok had one, where there were 300 to 600 sick people 'nursed' by Red Khmer, who used traditional medicines produced from all sorts of tree rooths [sic]. Only few stayed alive. The Red Khmer explained to us that the healing methods of our ancestors must be used and that nothing should be taken from the Western medicine." International aid produced more medicine after 1979, and there was a flourishing black market in medicines, especially antibiotics, at exorbitant prices. Three small pharmaceutical factories in Phnom Penh in 1983 produced about ten tons of pharmaceuticals. Tetracycline and ampicillin were being produced in limited amounts in Phnom Penh, according to 1985 reports. The PRK government emphasized traditional medicine to cover the gap in its knowledge of modern medical technologies. Each health center on the province, district, and subdistrict level had a *kru* (teacher), specializing in traditional herbal remedies, attached to it. An inventory of medicinal plants was being conducted in each province in the late 1980s.

In 1979 according to observer Andrea Panaritis, of the more than 500 physicians practicing in Cambodia before 1975, only 45 remained. In the same year, 728 students returned to the Faculty of Medicine. The faculty, with practically no trained Cambodian instructors available, relied heavily on teachers, advisers, and material aid from Vietnam. Classes were being conducted in both

Khmer and French; sophisticated Western techniques and surgical methods were taught alongside traditional Khmer healing methods. After some early resistance, the medical faculty and students seemed to have accepted the importance of preventive medicine and public health. The improvement in health care under the PRK was illustrated by a Soviet report about the hospital in Kampong Spoe. In 1979 it had a staff of three nurses and no doctor. By 1985 the hospital had a thirty-three-member professional staff that included a physician from Vietnam and two doctors and three nurses from Hungary. The Soviet-Khmer Friendship Hospital reopened with sixty beds in mid-1982. By 1983 six adequate civilian hospitals in Phnom Penh and nineteen dispensaries scattered around the capital provided increasing numbers of medical services. Well-organized provincial hospitals also were reported in Batdambang, Takev, Kampong Thum, and Kandal provinces. Panaritis reports that rudimentary family planning existed in the PRK in the mid-1980s, and that obstetrics stressed prenatal and nutritional care. The government did not actively promote birth control, but requests for abortions and tubal ligations have been noted in some reports. Condoms and birth control pills were available, although the pills had to be brought in from Bangkok or Singapore.

As of late 1987, the government in Phnom Penh had disseminated no information on the spread of the Acquired Immuno-Deficiency Syndrome (AIDS or HIV virus) in Cambodia. In addition, the list of common illnesses in Cambodia, as reported by international organizations, does not mention Karposi's sarcoma and pneumo-cystic pneumonia (PCP), the most common complications resulting from infection by the HIV virus. The risk to the Cambodian population of contamination by carriers of the HIV virus carriers comes from two sources. The more likely of the two consists of infected, illegal border-crossers, including insurgents, from Thailand, where authorities identified a hundred cases of AIDS in 1987 (triple the number in 1986). Less likely is the risk of infection from legal travelers. Cambodia remains a closed country, and access by foreigners (except for Vietnamese, Soviet, and East European visitors) is limited to a few scholars and to members of international and private aid organizations.

Welfare Programs

Steinberg cites twelfth-century King Jayavarman VII as having begun a public welfare system in Cambodia. Jayavarman built public rest houses along the roads, distributed rice to the needy, and banned tax collectors from places where the sick were cared for.

Beginning in 1936, the French colonial authorities passed legislation affecting the hours of work, the wages, and the worker's compensation for foreign employees. Later, Cambodians were covered. A system of family allotments was instituted in 1955. Under this system, employers were required to contribute a monthly sum for the welfare of the worker's family.

A few welfare organizations were established in Cambodia under the Sihanouk regime. In 1949 the National Mutual Help Association was founded to provide money, food, and clothing to the needy. In 1951 the Cambodian Red Cross was organized to provide aid to disaster victims, especially those suffering from floods. The Women's Mutual Health Association was formed in 1953. It was associated with the Preah Ket Mealea Hospital in Phnom Penh, where it provided prenatal and child care. During the 1950s, the Association of Vietnamese in Cambodia opened a dispensary in Phnom Penh. The most ubiquitous source of assistance for the average Cambodian, however, was the network of Buddhist wats that extended down to the grass roots level. Also, relatives and, in the case of the Chinese, extended families and business associations provided assistance to needy members.

In the PRK under the government's gradual evolution toward Marxist-Leninist socialism, the ability of the wat to extend charitable aid was seriously impaired because these institutions existed in conditions of near penury, following their active suppression under the Khmer Rouge, and they were barely tolerated by the PRK regime. Instead, fragmentary evidence suggests that public welfare was decentralized and, because of the paucity of resources, received only small amounts in funds from the central government. According to available literature, the care of needy persons was entrusted to local party and government committees and, at the lowest echelon, to *krom samaki* (solidarity groups). Leaders at these grass-roots levels thus were able to evaluate true need and to extend aid varying from in-kind assistance to informal job placement. Such decentralization avoided the bureaucratization of welfare but, at the same time, it carried its own potential for abuse because aid could be apportioned on the basis of fidelity to regime and to party, or even to enforce loyalty to local leaders. The extension to the local level of such social services, however, indicated that the PRK was slowly extending its presence in the countryside, thus reinforcing its claim of nationhood, and its control over its territory and over Cambodian society at large.

* * *

The most important published sources on the geography of Cambodia are Ashok K. Dutt's collection of articles in *Southeast Asia: Realm of Contrasts* and David J. Steinberg's chapters in *Cambodia, Its People, Its Society, Its Culture.* Among the major resources on Cambodian society are Jean Delvert's *Le Cambodge,* a major study of Cambodian peasants; May Mayko Ebihara's dissertation, "Svay: A Khmer Village in Cambodia"; and Gabrielle Martel's *Lovea, village des environs d'Angkor.* Frank M. Le Bar, Gerald C. Hickey, and John K. Musgrave's *Ethnic Groups of Mainland Southeast Asia* provides useful but somewhat dated sketches of the Khmer and several of the ethnic minorities in Cambodia. *Cambodge: Faits et Problèmes de Population* by Jacques Migozzi and "Kampuchea: A Country Adrift" by Ea Meng Try are useful studies of the population of Cambodia before and after the Khmer Rouge takeover. The various works of Michael Vickery, Ben Kiernan, and Marie Martin provide data on Cambodia under the Khmer Rouge and PRK regimes. (For further information and complete citations, see Bibliography.)

Chapter 3. The Economy

Economic activity in Cambodia: Collecting palm sugar in a bamboo ampong, net fishing on the Mekong River, selling in a village market.

THE ECONOMY OF CAMBODIA in the late 1980s was dominated by subsistence agriculture; the industrial sector was still in its infancy. After it came to power in 1979, the new, Vietnamese-installed government in Phnom Penh set restoration of the nation's self-sufficiency in food, a situation that the country had enjoyed throughout prewar times, as a major goal. A persistent guerrilla war and a ravaged infrastructure impeded the achievement of this goal and of economic recovery in general, however. At the Fifth Party Congress of the Kampuchean (or Khmer) People's Revolutionary Party (KPRP—see Appendix B), held in Phnom Penh from October 13 to October 16, 1985, General Secretary Heng Samrin laid claim to some "important successes in agricultural production" in his political report. At the same time, he acknowledged that the country's "backward and unbalanced" economy still faced tremendous difficulties, including shortages of fuel, spare parts, raw materials, skilled labor, and a cadre of professionals possessing technical expertise and economic management skills. In short, the country's material and technical bases had not been restored to prewar levels. Prior to its adjournment, the KPRP Congress adopted the First Five-Year Program of Socioeconomic Restoration and Development (1986–90), hereafter referred to as the First Plan.

In 1987 there were signs that reforms legalizing private enterprise were revitalizing the country's economy. Small industrial enterprises reopened, and transportation and telecommunication systems were partially restored. As private market activities resumed, the population of Phnom Penh grew from 50,000 in 1978—the last year of the Pol Pot regime—to 700,000. Economic revitalization also occurred at Kampong Saom (formerly known as Sihanoukville), Cambodia's only seaport and its second largest city, which resumed its pre-1975 industrial and shipping activities.

Economic rehabilitation has been precarious and has been plagued by uncontrollable factors, such as adverse weather and serious security problems. In 1987 a severe drought in Southeast Asia reduced Cambodia's rice production. According to a senior official of the Ministry of Agriculture, estimated production of milled rice fell that year to approximately 1 million tons, about 300,000 tons below the level of fiscal year (FY—see Glossary) 1986. (Cambodia needs at least 1.9 million tons of rice annually for a population of 6.5 million).

The prospects for Cambodia's economic revitalization were poor in the late 1980s. The country's infrastructure was both weak and unstable. Factories and workshops, lacking electricity and supplies, operated only intermittently and at low capacity. The economy relied heavily—and almost completely after 1980—on foreign aid from communist countries, particularly the Soviet Union and the Socialist Republic of Vietnam (Vietnam); Western nations, Japan, and China had terminated economic assistance to Cambodia in 1980 to protest the presence of Vietnamese troops in that country. According to General Secretary Samrin, Cambodia would require "dozens of years" to restore its economy and to accomplish "a gradual passage toward socialism." Internationally, Cambodia in the future may have the option of joining the Council for Mutual Economic Assistance (CMEA, CEMA, or Comecon—see Glossary). If the Vietnamese troops leave, the country also may be offered some form of economic cooperation by other Asian and Western nations. In either case, however, Cambodia is very poor, produces little, and is not likely to prove an enticing economic partner. For this reason, in the forging of new economic links with the East and with the West, the country is likely to be relegated to a passive role, and the initiative will probably belong to the larger states, who will decide on what terms to share their largesse with Cambodia.

Because of insufficient and inconsistent—and therefore unreliable—data, analysis of Cambodia's war-torn economy can only be tentative. In the late 1980s, key economic indicators were missing or were difficult to reconcile, particularly for the Pol Pot period (1975–78). Since 1979 government economic publications have been scarce, and official statistics represent targets and estimates spelled out in the country's economic development plans rather than actual figures.

Economic Setting

Seasonal monsoons and diverse topography significantly influence Cambodia's economy (see Environment, ch. 2). The southwest monsoon brings the rainy season (May to October), which is suitable for planting and growing the rice seedlings, and the northeast monsoon sends back dry air (November to March), which makes possible the paddy harvest.

The country's lakes and rivers also affect the economy. They are an abundant source of fish, a mainstay of the Cambodian diet, and they make possible irrigated agriculture, on which the country depends for its livelihood (see Climate, ch. 2). The principal waterway, the Mekong River, is an important trade route and avenue of communication. Since ancient times, the Tonle Sap (Great Lake), the Tonle Sab and the Mekong rivers, and their tributaries have been centers of economic and political power. Phnom Penh—the site of the royal residence, the administrative capital, and, in general, the locus of power, of culture, and of business—is situated at the junction of the Tonle Sab and the Mekong.

Natural Resources

Metals and Minerals

In general, Cambodia's mineral resources appear to be limited. In the late 1950s and throughout the 1960s, however, exploration by Chinese experts in Kampong Thum Province disclosed commercially exploitable deposits of iron ore amounting to about 5.2 million tons. Western sources indicated possible reserves of high-grade iron ore, ranging from 2.5 million to 4.8 million tons, in the northern part of the country. Chinese explorations also revealed manganese ore reserves, estimated at about 120,000 tons, in Kampong Thum Province.

Deposits of phosphate, limestone, and clay of exploitable quality and quantity have also been reported. A few thousand tons of phosphate are extracted annually in Kampot Province and are processed locally or at a small plant in Batdambang Province. In addition, salt and coal also may be present in Cambodia's geological strata. Rubies, sapphires, and zircons have been mined since at least the late 1800s, mostly at Ba Kev, Stoeng Treng Province, and at Pailin, Batdambang Province. Limited gold and silver deposits have been reported in several parts of the country.

Hydroelectric Power

The country's hydroelectric generating potential is considerable, especially from the swift current of the middle Mekong River where it flows through Stoeng Treng and Kracheh provinces. Other sites of minor importance are on rivers in the highlands of the northeastern and north-central parts of the country. Although the Tonle Sap is Cambodia's dominant hydraulic feature, the rivers flowing into this great lake have little or no exploitable potential. In general, development of the country's water potential appears to be more important for the expansion of irrigation than for the production of electricity.

Petroleum

In late 1969, the Cambodian government granted a permit to a French company to explore for petroleum in the Gulf of Thailand.

By 1972 none had been located, and exploration ceased when the Khmer Republic (see Appendix B) fell in 1975. Subsequent oil and gas discoveries in the Gulf of Thailand and in the South China Sea, however, could spark renewed interest in Cambodia's offshore area, especially because the country is on the same continental shelf as its Southeast Asian oil-producing neighbors.

Forestry

Another natural resource is the forests, which cover approximately 70 percent of the country and which potentially constitute a second pillar of the economy in addition to the primary one, agriculture (see table 5). A survey in the 1960s disclosed that Cambodia had more than 13 million hectares of forests that contained many species of tropical growth and trees but not teak or other valuable sources of hardwood. Some destruction of the forest environment undoubtedly occurred in the war that followed in the 1970s, but its extent has not been determined. Most of the heavy fighting took place in areas uncovered by dense tropical jungle. As of late 1987, forest resources had not yet been fully exploited because of poor security in the countryside and a lack of electrical and mechanical equipment, such as power tools and lumber trucks. Nevertheless, the Cambodian government reportedly has discussed with Vietnam the possibility of coordinated reforestation programs.

Timber and firewood are the main forest products. Timber is considered one of the four economic initiatives of the government's First Plan. Timber production was projected to reach a peak of 200,000 cubic meters in 1990.

Labor Force

Cambodia ranks among the least populated Asian nations with an estimated 1987 population of only about 6.3 million to 6.4 million. Its density of approximately 36 persons per square kilometer is about one-fifth of Vietnam's population density of 187 persons per square kilometer. The First Plan set the population growth rate at 2.8 percent per year, up from the average annual growth rate of 2.3 percent for the 1978 to 1985 period (see Population, ch. 2).

In 1987 observers estimated that about 34.5 percent of the population was under 15 years of age and that 3 percent was 62.5 or older. An estimated 63 percent of the population (or about 4 million people) were between the ages of 15 and 64. The economically active segment of the population, the work force, was probably around 3 million people, or 46 percent of the total population. This estimated percentage of the labor force remained relatively constant from 1962—when the census showed a work force of 2.5

million people out of a total population of 5.73 million—until the 1980s.

In 1983 all public-sector employees, including state employees, armed forces personnel, industrial workers, artisans, teachers, and party cadres, accounted for approximately 8 percent of an economically active population of between 2.5 million and 3 million. Approximately 80 percent of the work force was engaged in agriculture, in forestry, and in fishing.

A critical shortage of qualified and professional personnel emerged as technicians, engineers, skilled workers, and trained managers either fled the country or fell victim to executions under the Pol Pot regime. In 1980 the Ministry of Agriculture had only 200 technicians, down from a total of 1,600 in 1975.

Moreover, the continuing conflict diverted part of the work force to combat zones or to security-related projects (see Military Developments in Postwar Cambodia, ch. 5). In March 1984, the government initiated a forced-labor program, employing civilians in "national defense work" to seal the 830 kilometers of frontier with Thailand. This project, code-named K–5, diverted from the labor force a number of conscripts (aged 18 to 45) ranging from 25,000 to 30,000 for each province, or as high as 3,000 for each district of Cambodia. The labor shortage constituted a major impediment to economic progress, a point stressed by Heng Samrin at the Fifth Party Congress when he said that "Labor . . . is scattered at present in order to face the needs of the struggle," adding that the "lack of qualified labor and specialized cadres . . . has prevented us from ensuring that current works satisfy the requirements for development."

Economic Developments after Independence

The predominance of agriculture and the lack—or neglect—of real industrial development have characterized Cambodia's modern economy since independence in 1953. Wet rice cultivation traditionally has played a key role in peasant subsistence, in national self-sufficiency in food production, in trade relations with other states, and in governmental revenues for national development. Conversely, the government has made few attempts to industrialize the nation.

After Cambodia became independent in 1953, the country's economic policies were shaped by the succession of governments that followed. Prince Sihanouk opted for unconditional aid from the East and from the West, and the nation made modest strides. The Lon Nol government would have adhered to a laissez-faire doctrine, but it was overwhelmed by the war around it. The Khmer

Rouge (see Appendix B) adopted a fanatical and doctrinaire self-reliance, and the Cambodian people and nation were ravaged by it. The post-1979 government of the People's Republic of Kampuchea (PRK—see Appendix B), with its Vietnamese mentors, acquiesced to a pragmatic combination of socialism and small-scale capitalism, and the country achieved some limited rehabilitative goals. In the late 1980s, government policies fundamentally relied upon the nation's own sparse resources—chiefly agriculture, a nascent industrial base, and modest foreign aid from Comecon countries and non-governmental international organizations.

Sihanouk's Peacetime Economy, 1953-70

Sihanouk's political neutrality, which formed the cornerstone of his foreign policy, had a significant effect on Cambodia's economic development. Sihanouk insisted that the economic dimension of neutrality meant either total rejection of international aid (as practiced by Burma under Ne Win) or acceptance of foreign economic assistance from all countries without strings attached. Indeed, during the first decade that he was in power in newly independent Cambodia (1953-63), the prince carefully practiced his "purer form of neutrality between East and West" in seeking foreign economic assistance for development (see Cambodia under Sihanouk, 1954-70, ch. 1).

→ In 1963 however, Cambodia's economy started to stagnate when Sihanouk decided to link his economic neutrality policy to the country's territorial integrity and border security. He rejected further assistance from the United States, because Washington supported the Republic of Vietnam (South Vietnam), and from Thailand, with which Cambodia had continuous frontier disputes. In a related move, Sihanouk nationalized trading companies, banks, insurance, and major industries, thereby causing economic deterioration between 1963 and 1969. The 1967 Samlot (Batdambang) revolt and the February 1970 government decision to demonetize (or exchange) the old 500 riel (for value of the riel—see Glossary) banknotes were crucial events contributing to the end of the Sihanouk era (see Into the Maelstrom: Insurrection and War, 1967-75, ch. 1; The Second Indochina War, 1954-75, ch. 5).

During his tenure after independence, Sihanouk used the country's ill-defined constitution to monitor all government activities of any consequence and to bend the government's decision-making process to his advantage. During the course of nation building, political aims often prevailed over strictly economic objectives. For example, prior to 1967, the government assigned higher priority to social improvements, such as health and education, than it did

*Young peasant woman
pauses during the rice harvest
Courtesy Bill Herod*

*A fruit vendor
awaits customers in a
Phnom Penh marketplace
Courtesy Bill Herod*

to national economic growth. The government later gave higher priority to the productive sectors of agriculture and industry in economic plans for the 1968–72 periods; however, because of war, the government did not implement these plans.

Nonetheless, between 1952 and 1969, Cambodia's gross national product (GNP—see Glossary) grew an average of 5 percent a year in real terms, with growth higher during the 1950s than during the 1960s. In addition, the service sector played an important role in Sihanouk's mixed economic system in contrast to its position under the regimes of Pol Pot and of Heng Samrin, who considered the service sector insignificant and "unproductive." In 1968 the service sector accounted for more than 15 percent of gross domestic product (GDP—see Glossary), agriculture accounted for 36 percent, and manufacturing for 12 percent.

Agriculture developed under a degree of paternalism from Sihanouk, who donated farm equipment to various villages and, in return, received respect and affection from the peasants. In general, however, Cambodian agriculture subsisted without much help from the government. In 1969 approximately 80 percent of rice farmers owned the land they cultivated, and the landholding for each family averaged slightly more than two hectares. The farmers used simple and rudimentary implements that were well suited to their needs and to the light weight of their draft animals. Overall, the peasants were remarkably self-sufficient.

Farmers began to cultivate more land, causing rice production to increase from an average of 1.4 million tons in 1955 to 2.4 million tons in 1960. Production remained at that level throughout the 1960s. Rice yield per hectare, however, remained low—less than 1.2 tons per hectare—during the 1952–69 period. Little was done to increase yield through the use of irrigation, chemical fertilizers, or improved seeds and implements. Average yields in Batdambang and Kampong Cham provinces, however, were 50 percent higher than the national average because of better soil fertility and, in the case of Batdambang, larger average landholdings and greater use of machines in cultivation.

Industrial and infrastructural development benefited from foreign economic assistance. In general, the government avoided ambitious plans and focused on small enterprises to meet local needs and to reduce foreign imports. In June 1956, the Chinese provided Phnom Penh with US$22.4 million in equipment as part of an ongoing program of industrial economic assistance. In addition, they helped build a textile mill and a glass plant in the 1960s. During this period, other nations contributed through aid programs of their own. Czechoslovakia granted loans for the construction of tractor assembly plants, tire-production facilities, and a sugar refinery. Other aid donors were the Soviet Union, Yugoslavia, France, the Federal Republic of Germany (West Germany), Japan, and Australia. United States economic assistance to Cambodia amounted to more than US$350 million for the 1955 to 1962 period, and it was invested mostly in the areas of public health, education, and agricultural development. To avoid the appearance of undue dependence upon foreign aid, Cambodia insisted upon "project sharing," that is, participation of its own in specific enterprises, such as the French-sponsored oil refinery and truck assembly plant at Sihanoukville. This stipulation imposed by Phnom Penh also had the effect of holding down the scale of many aid projects and the amounts of loans extended to the Cambodian government.

The government also used foreign assistance to expand the country's transportation and communication networks. France helped to develop Sihanoukville, Cambodia's second largest port, which opened in 1960, and the United States constructed a highway linking the port to Phnom Penh. In addition, the Cambodians, with French and West German assistance, built a railway from Sihanoukville to the capital.

Despite Sihanouk's claims of economic progress, Cambodia's industrial output in 1968 amounted to only 12 percent of GNP, or only one-third of agricultural production. Rice and rubber were the country's two principal commodity exports and foreign-exchange earners during the Sihanouk era.

The Wartime Economy, 1970–75

The war that engulfed the rest of Indochina spread to Cambodia in April 1970, shortly after the coup that deposed Prince Sihanouk. Wartime conditions had a major impact on the country's economy, especially on the export sector. Production and export of virtually all commodities dropped sharply, as insecurity spread throughout the countryside. Intense combat in the nation's most densely populated farming areas caused a large segment of the peasant population to flee to cities and to towns. By 1975 the population of Phnom Penh had swollen to 2 million, from just 50,000 in 1955. Moreover, the war seriously dislocated the economic system. Food shortages arose as insurgents interrupted the transportation of crops from the countryside to the main marketing centers. Increasing budgetary expenditures, skyrocketing inflation, shrinking export earnings, and a rising balance-of-payments deficit plagued the war-torn economy.

The war's most damaging effect was on rice production. In 1972 Cambodia needed to import rice (from Japan and from Thailand) for the first time since independence. Fighting reduced the amount of land under rice cultivation to fewer than 800,000 hectares in 1972, far less than the approximately 3 million hectares that had been under cultivation in 1969. The 1972 rice harvest amounted to only 26.8 percent of the 1969 harvest. Exports of natural rubber, the country's second leading foreign-exchange earner, ceased shortly after hostilities began in 1970. The war destroyed extensive rubber plantations and damaged rubber-processing facilities.

In late 1970, Lon Nol, who succeeded Sihanouk, continued to liberalize the economy in an effort to save the country from economic disaster. This endeavor was a continuation of the policies he had enacted as head of the government of "national salvation" in August 1969. Under Lon Nol's direction, Phnom Penh limited the control and the authority of the state export-import agency (Société nationale d'exportation et d'importation—SONEXIM), which had been established in 1964 to administer foreign trade, to denationalize banks and industries, to encourage private foreign investments, and to allow greater private participation in the economy. The new economic policies of the Khmer Republic gradually reversed the pattern of state socialism that had formed the keystone of Sihanouk's domestic policies.

On October 29, 1971, the government implemented a comprehensive program of reforms to stabilize the economy. These reforms included increased import taxes on all nonessential commodities; increased interest rates on bank deposits and on commercial loans; elimination of credit to state enterprises and to public utilities; introduction of a flexible currency exchange system; and simplification of the import system to facilitate the movement of goods. The emphasis of the program was to restore monetary stability in the face of rising inflation, financial speculation, black markets, and other economic problems caused by the war. In a change of policy, the government also moved toward greater involvement with international and with regional organizations and sought support from the World Bank (see Glossary), the International Monetary Fund (see Glossary), and the Asian Development Bank.

As the war progressed, Lon Nol's government aimed major economic measures mainly at improving the overall food supply situation and at maintaining public confidence in the continued availability of essential consumer items. To ensure adequate domestic supplies, in November 1971 Phnom Penh suspended grants of export licenses for major export commodities, such as rice, corn, and cattle. Although the move helped maintain stocks of essential commodities in the capital and in provincial centers, supplies were small relative to demand.

The Lon Nol government had earlier declared in principle that it maintained a policy of "strict neutrality" and would accept foreign assistance from "all countries which love peace and justice." As early as April 20, 1970, Cambodia formally requested military and economic aid from Washington to help cope with growing war expenditures and with an increasing budgetary deficit. As military activity in the country intensified, the United States became Cambodia's largest donor and supplier. Moscow, however, sent medical equipment and, in October 1971, the Soviets renewed a financial agreement with the republican regime. The Economic Support Fund, to which the United Nations (UN), the United States, Britain, Japan, New Zealand, Thailand, and Malaysia pledged their contributions, provided US$21 million in auxiliary relief. Other nations, including Italy, Israel, West Germany, and Switzerland, provided funds mostly to assist war victims. France earmarked its aid for the maintenance of French educational programs and cultural institutions. Nevertheless, these palliative measures fell far short of what was needed. By 1975 the economy had collapsed, and the country was surviving mainly on imported food financed by the United States government.

The Economy under the Khmer Rouge, 1975-79

Under the leadership of the Khmer Rouge, Cambodia underwent a brutal and radical revolution. When the communist forces took power in Phnom Penh in April 1975, their immediate goals were to overhaul the social system and to revitalize the national economy. The economic development strategy of the Khmer Rouge was to build a strong agricultural base supported by local small industries and handicrafts. As explained by Deputy Premier Ieng Sary, the regime was "pursuing radical transformation of the country, with agriculture as the base. With revenues from agriculture we are building industry which is to serve the development of agriculture." This strategy was also the focus of a doctoral thesis written by future Khmer Rouge leader Khieu Samphan at the University of Paris in 1959. Samphan argued that Cambodia could only achieve economic and industrial development by increasing and expanding agricultural production. The new communist government implemented the tenets of this thesis; it called for a total collectivization of agriculture and for a complete nationalization of all sectors of the economy.

Strict adherence to the principle of self-reliance constituted the central goal of the Khmer Rouge regime. A Phnom Penh radio broadcast in early May (about a month after the Khmer Rouge arrived in the capital) underscored the importance of Cambodian self-reliance and boasted that during the war the Khmer Rouge had used scrap iron and wrecked military vehicles to manufacture their own bullets and mines. The statement made it clear that the policy of self-reliance would continue in peacetime. In another move aimed at reducing foreign influence on the country, the regime announced on May 10 that it would not allow foreigners to remain in Cambodia but that the measure was only temporary; and it added, "We shall reconsider the question [of allowing foreigners to enter the country] after the re-establishment of diplomatic, economic and commercial relations with other countries." Although Cambodia resumed diplomatic relations with a number of nations, the new government informed the UN General Assembly on October 6, 1975, that it was neutral and economically self-sufficient and would not ask for aid from any country. On September 9, however, the Chinese ambassador arrived in Cambodia, and there were soon reports that China was providing aid to the Khmer Rouge. Estimates of the number of Chinese experts in Cambodia after that time ranged from 500 to 2,000. The policy of self-reliance also meant that the government organized the entire population into forced-labor groups to work in paddies and on other land to help the country reach its goal of food self-sufficiency.

The Khmer Rouge, as soon as it took power on April 17, 1975, emptied Phnom Penh (of its approximately 2 million residents) as well as other cities and towns, and forced the people into the countryside. This overnight evacuation was motivated by the urgent need to rebuild the country's war-torn economy and by the Khmer Rouge peasantry's hostility toward the cities. According to a Khmer Rouge spokesman at the French embassy on May 10, the evacuation was necessary to "revolutionize" and to "purify" the urban residents and to annihilate Phnom Penh, which "Cambodian peasants regarded as a satellite of foreigners, first French, and then American, and which has been built with their sweat without bringing them anything in exchange." The only people who were not ordered to leave the city were those who operated essential public services, such as water and electricity.

Other Khmer Rouge leaders rationalized the evacuation as a matter of self-reliance. They told the Swedish ambassador in early 1976 that "they didn't have any transportation facilities to bring food to the people, and so the logical thing was to bring the people to the food, i.e., to evacuate them all and make them get out into the ricefields." Indeed, when the evacuees reached their destinations, they were immediately mobilized to clear land, to harvest rice crops, to dig and restore irrigation canals, and to build and repair dikes in preparation for the further expansion of agriculture.

Oxcarts remain a primary conveyance in rural Cambodia.
(Upturned wagon tongue characterizes Cambodian oxcarts.)
Courtesy Bill Herod

The rice crop in November 1976 was reported to be good in relation to earlier years. At the same time, plantations producing cotton, rubber, and bananas were established or rehabilitated.

While the Khmer Rouge gave high priority to agriculture, it neglected industry. Pol Pot sought "to consolidate and perfect [existing] factories," rather than to build new ones. About 100 factories and workshops were put back into production; most of them (except a Chinese-built cement plant, a gunnysack factory, and textile mills in Phnom Penh and in Batdambang) were repair and handicraft shops revived to facilitate agricultural development.

Cambodia's economic revolution was much more radical and ambitious than that in any other communist country. In fact, Khmer Rouge leader Premier Ieng Sary explained that Cambodia wanted "to create something that never was before in history. No model exists for what we are building. We are not imitating either the Chinese or the Vietnamese model." The state or cooperatives owned all land; there were no private plots as in China or in the Soviet Union. The constitution, adopted in December 1975 and proclaimed in January 1976, specifically stated that the means of production were the collective property of the state (see Democratic Kampuchea, 1975–78, ch. 1).

The Cambodian economic system was unique in at least two respects. First, the government abolished private ownership of land. The Khmer Rouge believed that, under the new government, Cambodia should be a classless society of "perfect harmony" and that private ownership was "the source of egoist feelings and consequently social injustices." Second, Cambodia was a cashless nation; the government confiscated all republican era currency. Shops closed, and workers received their pay in the form of food rations, because there was no money in circulation.

On August 12, 1975, fewer than four months after the Khmer Rouge had taken power, Khieu Samphan claimed that, within a year or two, Cambodia would have sufficient food supplies and would be able to export some of its products. To achieve this goal in record time, large communes comprising several villages replaced village cooperatives, which had formed in the areas controlled by the Khmer Rouge in 1973 and which had spread throughout the country by 1975. Unlike China and Vietnam, which had introduced collectivization gradually over several years, Cambodia imposed the system hastily and without preparation.

The Khmer Rouge, in line with the slogan, "If we have dikes, we will have water; if we have water, we will have rice; if we have rice, we can have absolutely everything," organized the workers into three "forces." The first force comprised unmarried men (ages fifteen to forty) who were assigned to construct canals, dikes, and dams. The second force consisted of married men and women who were responsible for growing rice near villages. The third force was made up of people forty years of age and older who were assigned to less arduous tasks, such as weaving, basket-making, or watching over the children. Children under the age of fifteen grew vegetables or raised poultry. Everyone had to work between ten and twelve hours a day, and some worked even more, often under adverse, unhealthy conditions.

On September 27, 1977, in a major speech celebrating the anniversary of the Kampuchean (or Khmer) Communist Party (KCP—see Appendix B), Khmer Rouge leader Pol Pot asserted that, "Our entire people, our entire revolutionary army and all our cadres live under a collective regime through a communal support system." He then listed the government's achievements in rebuilding the economy and concluded that, "Though not yet to the point of affluence, our people's standard of living has reached a level at which people are basically assured of all needs in all fields."

Measuring the economic performance of the Khmer Rouge regime was impossible because statistics were not available, and no monetary transactions or bookkeeping were carried out. The economic life described by foreign diplomats, by Western visitors, and by Cambodian refugees in Thai camps ranged from spartan to dismal. Phnom Penh became a ghost town of only about 10,000 people. There were no shops, post offices, telephones, or telegraph services. Frequent shortages of water and of electricity occurred in all urban areas, and the government prohibited movement across provincial borders, except for that of trucks distributing rice and fuel.

Conditions in the cooperatives varied considerably from place to place. In some areas, cooperative members had permission to cultivate private plots of land and to keep livestock. In others, all property was held communally. Conditions were most primitive in the new economic zones, where city dwellers had been sent to farm virgin soil and where thousands of families lived in improvised barracks (see Democratic Kampuchea, 1975–78, ch. 1).

Cambodia made progress in improving the country's irrigation network and in expanding its rice cultivation area. Phnom Penh radio claimed that a network of ditches, canals, and reservoirs had been constructed throughout the country "like giant checkerboards, a phenomenon unprecedented in the history of our Cambodia." Still, rice production and distribution were reported to be unsatisfactory. Rice harvests were poor in 1975 and 1978, when the worst floods in seventy years struck the Mekong Valley. Even after the better harvests of 1976 and 1977, however, rice distribution was unequal, and the government failed to reach the daily ration of 570 grams per person. (The daily ration of rice per person actually varied by region from 250 to 500 grams.) Party leaders, cadres, soldiers, and factory workers ate well, but children, the sick, and the elderly suffered from malnutrition and starvation. There also were reports that the government was stockpiling rice in preparation for war with Vietnam and exporting it to China in exchange for military supplies. This diverted rice could have been one explanation for the people's meager rice ration.

At the end of 1978, when Vietnamese troops invaded Cambodia, the ensuing turbulence completely disrupted the nation's economic activity, particularly in the countryside, which once again became a war theater traversed by a massive population movement. Agricultural production was again a major casualty, with the result that there was a severe food crisis in 1979.

Economic Role of the Kampuchean People's Revolutionary Party

After the fall of Pol Pot and the establishment of the People's Republic of Kampuchea in January 1979, the Kampuchean (or

Khmer) People's Revolutionary Party (KPRP—see Appendix B), led by General Secretary Heng Samrin, set Cambodia's economic development policies. Party congresses adopted these policies at meetings in January 1979, May 1981, and October 1985. A new Constitution, which the National Assembly approved in June 1981, defined Cambodia's new socialist direction and the role of the state in economic affairs. Then, after six more years of struggling with an economy of survival and subsistence, KPRP leaders presented their First Plan, which represented a systematic and rational party effort at centrally planning and improving the economy.

New Economic Policy and System

In contrast to Pol Pot's radical, doctrinaire approach to economic development, Heng Samrin and the leaders of the Kampuchean (or Khmer) National United Front for National Salvation (KNUFNS—see Appendix B), the umbrella group of anti-Pol Pot forces sponsored by Hanoi, sought to rally public support by formulating a policy that would be pragmatic, realistic, and flexible. In an eleven-point program promulgated shortly before the Vietnamese invasion of Cambodia, the front articulated the economic guidelines that would mark its tenure in power. These guidelines advocated a gradual transformation to socialism; a "planned economy with markets"; the restoration of banks, of currency, and of trade; the abolition of forced labor; the introduction of an eight-hour workday; and pay based on work performed.

The KPRP socialist economy accepted the private sector. At a May 1980 agriculture conference, Samrin reviewed the effectiveness of the solidarity groups (*krom samaki*), production units of seven to fifteen families, united in a common endeavor to raise food or to produce goods. These production units had been organized in line with the policy of moving toward socialism. He affirmed that each member of these groups would receive at least one hectare of land to cultivate for communal purposes, plus a private plot not exceeding a quarter of a hectare on which to grow vegetables or to graze livestock. Also, a July 1980 planning conference called for a policy of "simultaneous development of family (private) economy and national (socialized) economy." The conference also decided that the state should buy agricultural products from the peasants and should sell them manufactured goods at free-market prices.

The KPRP further clarified its economic policy at its Fourth Party Congress (its first since taking power in Phnom Penh) from May 26 to May 29, 1981. It declared that the nation's economic system had three main parts—the state economy, the collective economy,

Lunchtime in Phnom Penh
Courtesy Bill Herod

and the family economy, and that each of these parts "had its own significant role."

The state economy covered large-scale agricultural production, all industrial production, the communications and transportation networks, finance, and domestic and foreign trade. To facilitate economic transactions nationwide, the state restored the banking system in November 1979, and it reintroduced currency in March 1980. The KPRP acknowledged that the state economy was small and said that it should be expanded. The party leaders, however, aware of the pitfalls of central planning, warned against "over-expansion and disregard for real needs, production conditions, management ability, and economic capability."

The collective economy—the largest of the three elements—was assigned an important role in agricultural rehabilitation and development. It consisted of solidarity groups in agriculture, fishing, forestry, and handicrafts. These groups also assumed the task of collective purchase and sale.

The family-run economy included the home economies of the peasants, most retail businesses, individual artisans, handicrafts, repair shops, and small trade. Although the 1981 Constitution stated that the land and other natural resources were state property, it gave the citizens usufruct rights to land allotted for a house and garden by the state. In some cases, agricultural workers were also allowed to borrow an extra plot of land from the state, to produce food on it, and to keep the harvest for their own consumption.

Private enterprise also made a modest beginning under Cambodia's hybrid economic system. Citizens were allowed to buy and to sell agricultural produce and handicrafts. The law guaranteed workers the right to keep their wages, their other income and their property. Encouraged and protected by the state, hundreds of small shops and factories, each employing a few workers, opened for business in Phnom Penh and in other urban areas.

This inchoate private sector played such an important role in the national economic recovery that party leaders urged its official recognition, at the Fifth Congress in October 1985, as a means of mitigating the weaknesses of the state-run economy. Thus, the government added a fourth component—private economy—to the economic system and legitimized it with a constitutional amendment in February 1986.

First Plan, 1986–90

The First Five-Year Program of Socioeconomic Restoration and Development (1986–90), or First Plan, originated in February 1984, when the heads of the state planning commissions of Vietnam, Laos, and Cambodia met in Ho Chi Minh City (formerly Saigon) and agreed to coordinate their 1986 to 1990 economic plans. Heng Samrin formally announced Cambodia's plan in his political report to the congress.

The plan was intended to open a new phase of the Cambodian revolution; it gave highest priority to agricultural production, calling it "the first front line," and focused on the four sectors of food, rubber, fishing, and timber (see table 6). It set production targets for each sector. During the plan period, food production was to increase 7 percent a year to keep up with a targeted 2.8 percent annual population growth rate, which did not seem to have been reached by 1987. The plan projected that by 1990, rubber farming would expand to 50,000 hectares in order to produce 50,000 tons of latex; timber production would reach 200,000 cubic meters; jute production would increase to 15,000 tons; and fish production would amount to 130,000 tons. As in the past, the plan labeled agriculture and forestry as the real force of the national economy.

The plan was less specific for the industrial sector. It did not set industrial production targets, except that for electrical output, which was projected to reach 300 million kilowatt hours per year in 1990. The plan called attention to the need for selective restoration of existing industrial production capabilities and for proposed progressive construction of a small to medium industrial base, which would be more appropriate to the country's situation.

The plan placed increased emphasis on the distribution of goods. Trade organizations were to be perfected at all levels, and socialist trading networks were to be expanded in all localities. In particular, the trade relationship between the state and the peasantry was to be improved and consolidated in accordance with the motto, "For the peasantry, selling rice and agricultural products to the state is patriotism; for the state, selling goods and delivering them directly to the people is being responsible to the people."

The plan also required that investment be directed toward the improvement of the infrastructure, particularly toward the reconstruction of communication lines and waterworks. Road, inland waterways, and railroad networks had to be restored to serve the national economy and defense.

Last, but not least, the plan cited "export and thrift" (without elaboration), as the two primary policies to be followed in order to solve the national budget deficit. The plan implied that, into the 1990s, exports would have to consist principally of agricultural and forestry products, to which some value might be added by low-technology processing. "Thrift," although undefined, could, in the future, include some kind of government savings plan, with incentives for small depositors, to absorb surplus riels generated by Cambodia's considerable free-market and black-market sectors.

Heng Samrin, like his predecessors, Sihanouk and Pol Pot, urged Cambodians to undertake the task of economic restoration "in the spirit of mainly relying on one's own forces." Unlike Sihanouk and Pol Pot, however, the KPRP leader stressed economic and technical cooperation with Vietnam. He believed such cooperation would be "an indispensable factor" in the development of agriculture and of forestry in Cambodia. Heng Samrin also advocated better economic cooperation with the Soviet Union and with other socialist countries.

Agriculture

Agriculture, accounting for 90 percent of GDP in 1985 and employing approximately 80 percent of the work force, is the traditional mainstay of the economy. Rice, the staple food, continued to be the principal commodity in this sector. Rice production, a vital economic indicator in Cambodia's agrarian society, frequently fell far short of targets, causing severe food shortages in 1979, 1981, 1984, and 1987. The plan's 1987 target for the total area to be devoted to rice cultivation was 1.77 million hectares, but the actual area under cultivation in 1987 amounted to only 1.15 million hectares (see table 7, Appendix A). After 1979 and through the late 1980s, the agricultural sector performed poorly. Adverse weather conditions, insufficient numbers of farm implements and of draft animals, inexperienced and incompetent personnel, security problems, and government collectivization policies all contributed to low productivity.

Collectivization and Solidarity Groups

Collectivization of the agricultural sector under the Heng Samrin regime included the formation of solidarity groups. As small aggregates of people living in the same locality, known to one another, and able to a certain extent to profit collectively from their work, they were an improvement over the dehumanized, forced-labor camps and communal life of the Pol Pot era. The organization of individuals and families into solidarity groups also made sense in the environment of resources-poor, postwar Cambodia. People working together in this way were able to offset somewhat the shortages of manpower, draft animals, and farm implements (see New Economic and Policy System, this ch.).

In 1986 more than 97 percent of the rural population belonged to the country's more than 100,000 solidarity groups. Unlike the large communes of the Khmer Rouge, the solidarity groups were relatively small. They consisted initially of between twenty and fifty families and were later reduced to between seven and fifteen families. The groups were a form of ''peasants' labor association,'' the members of which continued to be owners of the land and of the fruits of their labor. According to a Soviet analyst, the solidarity groups ''organically united'' three forms of property—the land, which remained state property; the collectively owned farm implements and the harvest; and the individual peasant's holding, each the private property of a peasant family.

In theory, each solidarity group received between ten and fifteen hectares of common land, depending upon the region and land availability. This land had to be cultivated collectively, and the harvest had to be divided among member families according to the amount of work each family had contributed as determined by a work point system. In dividing the harvest, allowance was made first for those who were unable to contribute their labor, such as the elderly and the sick, as well as nurses, teachers, and administrators. Some of the harvest was set aside as seed for the following season, and the rest was distributed to the workers. Those who performed heavy tasks and who consequently earned more work points received a greater share of the harvest than those who worked on light tasks. Women without husbands, however, received enough to live on even if they did little work and earned few work points. Work points also were awarded, beyond personal labor, to individuals or to families who tended group-owned livestock or who lent their own animals or tools for solidarity group use.

Each member family of a solidarity group was entitled to a private plot of between 1,500 and 2,000 square meters (depending upon the availability of land) in addition to land it held in common with other members. Individual shares of the group harvest and of the produce from private plots were the exclusive property of the producers, who were free to consume, store, barter, or sell them.

The solidarity groups evolved into three categories, each distinct in its level of collectivization and in its provisions for land tenure. The first category represented the highest level of collective labor. Member families of each solidarity group in this category undertook all tasks from plowing to harvesting. Privately owned farm implements and draft animals continued to be individual personal property, and the owners received remuneration for making them available to the solidarity group during the planting and the harvesting seasons. Each group also had collectively owned farm implements, acquired through state subsidy.

The second category was described as "a transitional form from individual to collective form" at the KPRP National Conference in November 1984. This category of group was different from the first because it distributed land to member families at the beginning of the season according to family size. In this second category, group members worked collectively only on heavy tasks, such as plowing paddy fields and transplanting rice seedlings. Otherwise, each family was responsible for the cultivation of its own land allotment and continued to be owner of its farm implements and animals, which could be traded by private agreement among members. Some groups owned a common pool of rice seeds, contributed by member families, and of farm implements, contributed by the state. The size of the pool indicated the level of the group's collectivization. The larger the pool, the greater the collective work. In groups that did not have a common pool of rice and tools, productive labor was directed primarily to meeting the family's needs, and the relationship between the agricultural producers and the market or state organizations was very weak.

The third category was classified as the family economy. As in the second category, the group allocated land to families at the beginning of the season, and farm implements continued to be their private property. In this third category, however, the family cultivated its own assigned lot, owned the entire harvest, and sold its surplus directly to state purchasing organizations. In the solidarity groups of this category, there was no collective effort, except in administrative and sociocultural matters.

The government credited the solidarity group system with rehabilitating the agricultural sector and increasing food production. The system's contribution to socialism, however, was less visible and significant. According to Chhea Song, deputy minister of agriculture, a mere 10 percent of the solidarity groups really worked collectively in the mid-1980s (seven years after solidarity groups had come into operation). Seventy percent of the solidarity groups performed only some tasks in common, such as preparing the fields and planting seeds. Finally, 20 percent of the agricultural workers farmed their land as individuals and participated in the category of the family economy.

Rice Production and Cultivation

In 1987 statistics on rice production were sparse, and they varied depending upon sources. Cambodian government figures were generally lower than those provided by the UN Food and Agriculture Organization (FAO) for the period from 1979 to 1985 (see table 8, Appendix A).

Political and technical factors account for the discrepancies. Data collection in the war-torn nation is difficult because of the lack of trained personnel. Moreover, representatives of international and of foreign relief organizations are not permitted to travel beyond Phnom Penh, except with special permission, because of security and logistics problems. In addition, international and Cambodian sources use different benchmarks in calculating rice production. FAO computes the harvest by calendar year; Cambodian officials and private observers base their calculations on the harvest season, which runs from November to February and thus extends over two calendar years. Last of all, a substantial statistical difference exists between milled rice and paddy (unmilled rice) production, compounding problems in compiling accurate estimates. In terms of weight, milled rice averages only 62 percent of the original unmilled paddy. Estimates sometimes refer to these two kinds of rice interchangeably.

Despite statistical discrepancies, there is consensus that annual unmilled rice production during the 1979 to 1987 period did not reach the 1966 level of 2.5 million tons. Nevertheless, since 1979, Cambodian rice production has increased gradually (except during the disastrous 1984 to 1985 season), and the nation in the late 1980s had just begun to achieve a precarious self-sufficiency, if estimates were borne out (see table 9, Appendix A).

A woman cuts and
wraps cakes of soap
Courtesy Bill Herod

A machinist plies her trade
Courtesy Bill Herod

Cambodia's cultivated rice land can be divided into three areas. The first and richest (producing more than one ton of rice per hectare) covers the area of the Tonle Sap Basin and the provinces of Batdambang, Kampong Thum, Kampong Cham, Kandal, Prey Veng, and Svay Rieng. The second area, which yields an average of four-fifths of a ton of rice per hectare, consists of Kampot and Kaoh Kong provinces along the Gulf of Thailand, and some less fertile areas of the central provinces. The third area, with rice yields of less than three-fifths of a ton per hectare, is comprised of the highlands and the mountainous provinces of Preah Vihear, Stoeng Treng, Rotanokiri (Ratanakiri), and Mondol Kiri (Mondolkiri).

Cambodia has two rice crops each year, a monsoon-season crop (long-cycle) and a dry-season crop. The major monsoon crop is planted in late May through July, when the first rains of the monsoon season begin to inundate and soften the land. Rice shoots are transplanted from late June through September. The main harvest is usually gathered six months later, in December. The dry-season crop is smaller, and it takes less time to grow (three months from planting to harvest). It is planted in November in areas that

163

have trapped or retained part of the monsoon rains, and it is harvested in January or February. The dry-season crop seldom exceeds 15 percent of the total annual production.

In addition to these two regular crops, peasants plant floating rice in April and in May in the areas around the Tonle Sap (Great Lake), which floods and expands its banks in September or early October (see Environment, ch. 2). Before the flooding occurs, the seed is spread on the ground without any preparation of the soil, and the floating rice is harvested nine months later, when the stems have grown to three or four meters in response to the peak of the flood (the floating rice has the property of adjusting its rate of growth to the rise of the flood waters so that its grain heads remain above water). It has a low yield, probably less than half that of most other rice types, but it can be grown inexpensively on land for which there is no other use.

The per-hectare rice yield in Cambodia is among the lowest in Asia. The average yield for the wet crop is about 0.95 ton of unmilled rice per hectare. The dry-season crop yield is traditionally higher—1.8 tons of unmilled rice per hectare. New rice varieties (IR36 and IR42) have much higher yields—between five and six tons of unmilled rice per hectare under good conditions. Unlike local strains, however, these varieties require a fair amount of urea and phosphate fertilizer (25,000 tons for 5,000 tons of seed), which the government could not afford to import in the late 1980s.

Other Food and Commercial Crops

The main secondary crops in the late 1980s were maize, cassava, sweet potatoes, groundnuts, soybeans, sesame seeds, dry beans, and rubber (see table 10, Appendix A). According to Phnom Penh, the country produced 92,000 tons of corn (maize), as well as 100,000 tons of cassava, about 34,000 tons of sweet potatoes, and 37,000 tons of dry beans in 1986. In 1987 local officials urged residents of the different agricultural regions of the country to step up the cultivation of subsidiary food crops, particularly of starchy crops, to make up for the rice deficit caused by a severe drought.

The principal commercial crop is rubber. In the 1980s, it was an important primary commodity, second only to rice, and one of the country's few sources of foreign exchange. Rubber plantations were damaged extensively during the war (as much as 20,000 hectares was destroyed), and recovery was very slow. In 1986 rubber production totaled about 24,500 tons (from an area of 36,000 hectares, mostly in Kampong Cham Province), far below the 1969 prewar output of 50,000 tons (produced from an area of 50,000 hectares).

The government began exporting rubber and rubber products in 1985. A major customer was the Soviet Union, which imported slightly more than 10,000 tons of Cambodian natural rubber annually in 1985 and in 1986. In the late 1980s, Vietnam helped Cambodia restore rubber-processing plants. The First Plan made rubber the second economic priority, with production targeted at 50,000 tons—from an expanded cultivated area of 50,000 hectares—by 1990.

Other commercial crops included sugarcane, cotton, and tobacco. Among these secondary crops, the First Plan emphasized the production of jute, which was to reach the target of 15,000 tons in 1990 (see table 11, Appendix A).

Livestock

Animal husbandry has been an essential part of Cambodian economic life, but a part that farmers have carried on mostly as a sideline. Traditionally, draft animals—water buffalo and oxen—have played a crucial role in the preparation of rice fields for cultivation. In 1979 the decreasing number of draft animals hampered agricultural expansion. In 1967 there were 1.2 million head of draft animals; in 1979 there were only 768,000.

In 1987 *Quan Doi Nhan Dan* (People's Armed Forces, the Vietnamese army newspaper) reported a considerable growth in the raising of draft animals in Cambodia. Between 1979 and 1987, the number of cattle and water buffalo tripled, raising the total to 2.2 million head in 1987. In the same year, there were 1.3 million hogs and 10 million domestic fowl.

Fisheries

Cambodia's preferred source of protein is freshwater fish, caught mainly from the Tonle Sap and from the Tonle Sab, the Mekong, and the Basak rivers. Cambodians eat it fresh, salted, smoked, or made into fish sauce and paste. A fishing program, developed with Western assistance, was very successful in that it more than quadrupled the output of inland freshwater fish in three years, from 15,000 tons in 1979 to 68,700 tons in 1982, a peak year. After leveling off, output declined somewhat, dipping to 62,000 tons in 1986. The 1986 total was less than half the prewar figure of some 125,000 tons a year. Saltwater fishing was less developed, and the output was insignificant—less than 10 percent of the total catch (see table 12, Appendix A). According to the First Plan, fisheries were projected to increase their annual output to 130,000 metric tons by 1990.

Industry

Industry accounted for only 5 percent of Cambodia's GDP in 1985, down from 19 percent in 1969. Industrial activity continued to be concentrated in the processing of agricultural commodities, mostly rice, fish, wood, and rubber. Manufacturing plants were small, and they employed an average of fewer than 200 workers. These plants aimed to produce enough consumer goods (soft drinks, cigarettes, and food items) and household products (soap, paper, and utensils) to satisfy local demand.

The extent of Cambodia's industrial rehabilitation could be gauged by a comparison of enterprises in prewar and in postwar times. In 1969 the last year before the country was engulfed in the war sweeping Indochina, a census disclosed 18 large industries countrywide (13 public and 5 mixed public-private sector) and 33,000 small and medium privately owned enterprises. About half the factories operating in 1969 were rice mills, or were otherwise engaged in rice processing. In 1985 the government news agency (Sarpodamean Kampuchea) announced that fifty-six factories had been renovated and had been put back into operation. In the capital itself, about half of Phnom Penh's prewar plants had reopened by 1985. Most industries were producing at far below capacity because of frequent power cuts, shortages of spare parts and of raw materials, and the lack of both skilled workers and experienced managers. Industrial revival continued to be difficult and extremely slow because it was based mainly on the use of limited local resources.

Major Manufacturing Industries

In early 1986, the major industrial plants in Phnom Penh included the Tuol Kok textile factory, the largest of six textile factories in the city (the factory was idle three days a week, however, because of power shortages). There were also four power plants, a soft drink plant, a tobacco factory, a ferro-concrete factory, and some other enterprises that produced consumer goods.

In the municipality of Kampong Saom and in neighboring Kampot Province, rice mills, lumber mills, small brick and tile factories, power plants, an oil refinery, a tractor-assembly plant, cement and phosphate factories, and a refrigeration plant for storing fish were reported to be in operation. In the important industrial center of Ta Khmau, Kampot Province, were a tire factory (possessing its own generator, but lacking rubber and spare parts), several mechanical workshops, and warehouses. Batdambang Province had shops for repairing farm implements, a cotton gin and textile mill, a jute-bag factory, an automobile and tractor repair plant, and a phosphate-fertilizer plant. In Kampong Cham Province, the former center for tobacco growing and for cotton garment making, there were a cotton-spinning textile factory, some silk-weaving operations, and an automobile tire and tube plant.

Village woman weaving
Courtesy Bill Herod

Handicrafts

Small family-run businesses and private enterprises specializing in weaving, tailoring (silk *sampot* and sarongs, the Cambodian national dress), and small manufactured products grew more rapidly than public industries, and they contributed significantly to economic recovery. According to official estimates, the output value of local and of handicraft industries together amounted to 50 percent of the value of production in state industries in 1984. In Phnom Penh alone, there were 1,840 handicraft shops whose output value rose from 14 million riels in 1981 to 50 million riels in 1984.

Domestic Commerce

No information was available in 1987 on the volume of the domestic trade of locally manufactured products or of imported goods. Domestic commerce consisted essentially of contracts between agricultural producers and the state on the one hand, and the private free market on the other hand. Rice was the principal commodity sold to state purchasing agencies in exchange for farm implements, consumer goods, or cash. The state increasingly found itself in competition with private merchants for the procurement of rice. In order to force the peasants to sell rice to the state, the government prohibited private rice traders from transporting rice across provincial borders, a measure that had only limited success. In 1986 state rice procurement amounted to only 154,000 tons, or to just over half of the government's goal of 300,000 tons. Farmers believed that the state purchase price of 2.5 riels per kilogram of unmilled rice was less than the cost of production. In addition, because the government had insufficient supplies of goods such as fertilizer, cloth, and soap to be traded as payment, farmers had little incentive to sell their crops to state buyers. Consequently, in August 1987, the government raised the amount paid to farmers for monsoon-season (long-cycle) unmilled rice from 2.5 to 5.5 riels in an effort to narrow the gap between the official and the free-market prices. At the end of 1987, peasants still complained that the price paid by the state was too low. For example, one kilogram of improved IR rice was priced at between ten and fifteen riels on the free market, but it cost only six riels on the official market.

In contrast to shrinking state domestic trade, private trade continued to grow and to prosper with governmental approval and encouragement. Spouses of high party officials and cadres were actively engaged in petty trade to bring additional incomes to their families. Government workers also moonlighted by working in the private sector to augment low salaries and to make ends meet. Thousands of retail shops, private markets, and restaurants proliferated in Phnom Penh and in other cities. Shops and markets offered a variety of consumer goods, from gold and silver to bicycles and illegally imported consumer items, such as Seiko watches and Heineken beer.

Foreign Trade and Aid

The government controlled all official foreign trade. In July 1979, the Ministry of Local and Foreign Trade set up the Kampuchean Export and Import Corporation (KAMPEXIM, the state trading agency) to handle exports, imports, and foreign aid. In addition, the National Trade Commission was created to be in charge of both internal and external economic coordination. In March 1980, the Foreign Trade Bank was formed to deal with international payments, to expand trade, to provide international loans, and to control foreign exchange. There were reports of special clearing arrangements for trade among the Indochinese countries and with some members of the Council for Mutual Economic Assstance (CMEA, CEMA, or Comecon—see Glossary).

Beginning in 1982, the government made serious efforts to promote foreign trade as a means of accelerating national reconstruction and development. The First Plan emphasized exports as a way to correct imbalances in the national economy, but it did not provide any commodity export target figures. In the late 1980s, Cambodian officials released information revealing the direction and the patterns of trade rather than specific numbers. Most official trade was being conducted with Comecon countries in the form of exchanges of commercial goods. In the absence of authoritative data, unofficial Western sources placed Cambodia's trade deficit at US$100 million to US$200 million annually from 1981 to 1987. According to the Asian Development Bank, the country's total external debt in 1984 was US$491 million, up from US$426 million in 1983, and US$368 million in 1982 (see table 13, Appendix A).

In an attempt to increase foreign exchange earnings, the Heng Samrin regime in 1987 encouraged expatriate Cambodians to remit money to relatives and to friends remaining in the country. Cambodia's Foreign Trade Bank provided the names of sixteen banks in Western Europe, Canada, and Australia that were authorized to handle such transactions. The list included the Moscow Narodny Bank in London and several capitalistic financial institutions, such as the Société Générale in France and the Union des Banques Suisses in Switzerland.

Composition of Trade

Since 1979 Cambodia's major imports have consisted of machinery, tractors, vehicles, fuels and raw materials for light industry, consumer goods, clothing, cement, and chemical fertilizers. According to government information, imports during the first 10 months of 1987 amounted to 97 percent of the plan target, an increase of about 130 percent over the 1986 figure.

The principal exports included natural rubber (latex), resin, maize, tobacco, soybeans, and timber. Private Western sources estimated Cambodia's 1985 export earnings at US$10 million. Other sources reported that they were US$3.2 million just one year later. In 1987 the government news agency reported that the volume of exports handled by the Kampuchean Export and Import Corporation in the first ten months of 1987 had increased tenfold over the corresponding period in 1979.

Major Trading Partners

Cambodia's major trading partners in the 1980s were Vietnam, the Soviet Union, and the countries of Eastern Europe, particularly the German Democratic Republic (East Germany), Czechoslovakia, Poland, Hungary, and Bulgaria. Cambodia also claimed to have trade relations with Japan, one of several countries that had recognized Sihanouk's Coalition Government of Democratic

Table A. *Cambodian and Vietnamese Twin Provinces and Cities, 1986–87*

Cambodian Province/City	Vietnamese Province/City
Batdambang	Quang Nam-Da Nang
Kampot	Kien Giang
Kandal	Ben Tre
Kaoh Kong	Minh Hai
Kampong Cham	Tay Ninh
Kampong Chhnang	Hau Giang
Kampong Saom (C)	Haiphong (C)
Kampong Spoe	Cuu Long
Kampong Thum	Dong Nai
Kracheh	Song Be
Mondol Kiri	Dac Lac
Phnom Penh (C)	Ho Chi Minh City/Hanoi (C)
Preah Vihear	Thuan Hai
Prey Veng	Dong Thap
Pouthisat	Tien Giang
Rotanokiri	Nghia Binh, Gia Lai-Kontum
Siemreab-Otdar Meanchey	Binh Tri Thien
Stoeng Treng	Phu Khanh
Svay Rieng	Long An
Takev	An Giang

(C) = City or independent municipality

Source: Based on information from Michael Vickery, *Kampuchea: Politics, Economics, and Society,* London and Boulder, Colorado, 1986, 149–50.

Kampuchea (CGDK—see Appendix B) and had imposed a trade embargo on the Phnom Penh government of the People's Republic of Kampuchea (PRK—see Appendix B; Foreign Affairs, ch. 4).

Vietnam

In February 1979, Cambodia signed a Treaty of Peace, Friendship and Cooperation with Vietnam that formally strengthened "solidarity and cooperation" between the two countries. As part of the Vietnamese aid program to Cambodia, a joint scheme of pairing Cambodian provinces with Vietnamese "sister provinces" was inaugurated in the same year for the purposes of economic cooperation and of technical, educational and cultural exchange. Cambodia's Rotanokiri Province, however, was linked with two neighboring Vietnamese provinces—Nghia Binh and Gia Lai-Cong Tum. In addition, the municipality of Phnom Penh was paired with two Vietnamese cities—Ho Chi Minh City and Hanoi. Except for the municipalities of Hanoi and Haiphong, all of the Vietnamese participants in the scheme were located in former South Vietnam near their Cambodian counterparts (see fig. 1; table A).

The paired provinces were engaged mostly in barter trade the volume and value of which were unpublicized. Some observers argued that the system facilitated the integration of Cambodia's economy into Vietnam's. They pointed to the case of Batdambang Province, which sent tons of rice to its overpopulated and underfed Vietnamese sister province, Quang Nam-Da Nang, in exchange for bicycles and cement. In another case, Cambodia's Siemreab-Otdar Meanchey Province, supplied Vietnamese counterparts in Binh Tri Thien Province with unmilled rice and other agricultural products; in return, Vietnam supplied workers from Hue and its suburbs to help run the building industry in Siemreab-Otdar Meanchey. This exchange came at the expense of Cambodian workers, who were assigned to find clay, while the new Vietnamese settlers produced bricks and tiles and made a good living. In Siemreab city, the Vietnamese also assumed control of the biggest fish-sauce factory.

According to a Cambodian official's evaluation of foreign cooperation, the pairing system worked successfully. The exchange of goods between the sister provinces and cities helped "meet the needs of the people promptly." Reportedly, the system also helped Cambodia fulfill all of its development targets for 1986. In February 1986, Cambodia and Vietnam signed an agreement to double their trade for that year.

Soviet Union

The first important trade agreement between Cambodia and the Soviet Union was signed in February 1983 and covered three years, 1983 through 1985. According to a Soviet source, Moscow's trade turnover with Cambodia during this period increased from 71.8 to 100.3 million rubles (for value of the ruble, see Glossary). Cambodian exports were mainly rubber, while imports from the Soviet Union consisted of refined petroleum products, textiles, and chemical fertilizers (see table 14, Appendix A).

In July 1984, Cambodia—following the examples of Vietnam, Laos, and the East European countries—set up an Intergovernmental Commission for Trade, Economic, Scientific, and Technical Cooperation to manage its bilateral trade with the Soviet Union. The first session of the commission was held in January 1985. At its fourth meeting, in December 1987, protocols were signed regarding the restoration of rubber plantations and the development of some joint state enterprises.

On March 28, 1986, the two countries signed a five-year trade and aid agreement for the period 1986 to 1990 that would double the level of trade over that of the previous five-year period. The Soviet export package included tractors, fertilizer, petroleum products, machines, and raw materials. In exchange, Cambodia was to export raw rubber, timber, and plant-based industrial products such as lacquer. According to the Phnom Penh Domestic News Service, by the end of 1986 Cambodia had shipped 91 percent of its planned exports to the Soviet Union and had received 104 percent of its planned imports in return. During Cambodian Prime Minister Hun Sen's visit to Moscow in July 1987, the Soviet press reported that the volume of goods sold by the Soviet Union to Cambodia in the 1986 to 1990 period would increase one-and-one-half times over the previous five-year period, whereas goods sold by Cambodia would increase more than four times. In November 1987, the two countries concluded a trade-payments agreement for 1988. Under the terms of this agreement, the Soviet Union was to ship vehicles, tractor equipment, and fertilizer and would receive in exchange "traditional export goods" from Cambodia. Trade turnover between the two countries was projected to reach nearly 80 million rubles in 1988.

East Germany

In 1986 the total trade between Cambodia and East Germany reached about 14 million rubles, a 17 percent increase over the 1985 total of 12 million rubles. Cambodia exported more than 12 million rubles worth of rubber to East Germany and an additional million rubles worth of other goods. Cambodia's imports from East Germany amounted in value to more than 965,000 rubles.

Czechoslovakia

Trade between Cambodia and Czechoslovakia totaled 4.4 million rubles in 1985. In 1986 Cambodia exported 800 tons of rubber, more than 400 cubic meters of timber, and 700 tons of soybeans to Czechoslovakia. Cambodian imports from Czechoslovakia consisted chiefly of medicine and cloth. The two countries signed a protocol in Prague on October 29, 1987, on the exchange of goods planned for 1988. Under the terms of the protocol, total trade would increase by 19 percent over the 1987 level. Cambodia was to export rubber, beans, and timber to Czechoslovakia and was to import tractors, diesel engines, and pharmaceuticals.

Poland

Cambodia's trade with Poland between 1982 and 1985 was estimated at 4.4 million rubles. Cambodia exported rubber, timber, and soybeans and imported Polish textiles, ship engines, and glassware. The two countries set a trade target for 1986 to 1990 amounting to 14.3 million rubles.

In 1986 the trade between Cambodia and Poland amounted to 2.1 million rubles. On February 18, 1987, the two countries negotiated a trade agreement for the year stipulating that Cambodia would export crepe rubber, timber, furniture, soybeans, sesame seeds, and farm products; it would import, in return, antirust paint, soldering rods, sewing machines, boat engines, raw materials for medicine, and consumer goods.

Illicit Trade with Thailand and with Singapore

In addition to official trade with communist states, undeclared, uncontrolled, but government-tolerated trade with Thailand and with Singapore took place among private merchants, despite the trade embargo these two countries had imposed on Cambodia. Prime Minister Hun Sen reportedly declared that, "If the government can't carry out this trade and the people can, we allow them to do it."

Most of Cambodia's trade with Thailand took place in border and in coastal areas, particularly at the southwestern island of Kaoh Kong in the Gulf of Thailand. The illicit barter consisted of exchanging Cambodian dried fish, fresh crabs, shrimp, lobster, animal hides, elephant tusks, baby crocodiles, and gemstones for Thai clothing, sandals, toothpaste and toothbrushes, food, and bicycles. The total value of this growing illicit trade is not known, but some private sources estimated that it amounted to more than US$1 million a month.

Cambodia's illicit trade with Singapore was more visible. Ships registered in Singapore arrived regularly in Phnom Penh to deliver supplies to international relief organizations, operating in the country, as well as to private companies. International agencies estimated the value of undeclared trade with Singapore at US$2 million in 1985.

Foreign Economic and Technical Assistance

In the 1980s, Cambodia's economy relied heavily on multilateral aid and on bilateral economic assistance from Comecon countries. The largest donor was the Soviet Union, followed by Vietnam. East Germany, Czechoslovakia, Poland, Hungary, and Bulgaria sent mostly humanitarian aid, and they offered scientific and cultural assistance. Many Cambodian students received scholarships to study in these countries.

Western countries channeled aid through international organizations, including the International Committee of the Red Cross, the UN Children's Fund, and the Food and Agriculture Organization (FAO), the World Food Program (WFP), and the UN High

Commissioner for Refugees. Private agencies that contributed to the rehabilitation of the Cambodian economy included Oxfam, the American Catholic Relief Services, the American Friends Service Committee, the Church World Service, the World Council of Churches, the Lutheran World Service, CARE, and the Coopération Internationale pour le Développement et la Solidarité (a European Roman Catholic group).

Soviet Aid

Soviet economic assistance to Cambodia was projected to reach 284 million rubles for the 1979 to 1990 period, according to figures made public in November 1987. During the years 1979 to 1980, when the new Cambodian government clung precariously to power, Moscow provided Phnom Penh with a 200 million ruble grant to help fight famine and to restore the Cambodian economy. From 1980 to 1985, Soviet aid, amounting to 44 million rubles, supported the restoration of medical and educational centers and included the provision of tractors, trucks, and road-repair equipment. For Cambodia's First Plan, the Soviet Union provided Phnom Penh with aid worth 40 million rubles, an amount that represented approximately a 10 percent decrease over that given during the previous five years.

During the 1980s, Soviet credits helped to restore thirty facilities in various sectors, including electricity, agriculture, health, education, transport, and communications. Major Soviet-assisted projects included two power plants, one in Phnom Penh (completed in 1984) and the other in Kampong Saom (completed in 1985); the renovation and servicing of the 500-bed Kampuchea-USSR Friendship Hospital (a 200-bed military hospital), the Kampuchea-USSR Friendship Technical Institute, the Pushkin Russian Language Institute, the Institute of Agronomy at Chamka Dong (all established in 1985–86); a seed development center; and a ferroconcrete factory. To assist the rehabilitation of the rubber industry, the Soviet Union helped Cambodia to plant rubber trees on 20,000 hectares of land and to restart a crepe-processing plant that could generate 20,000 tons of natural rubber annually. On April 26, 1986, the Soviet Union signed an agreement to provide assistance for several projects, including the construction of an Intersputnik ground satellite station, a circus, a veterinary center, three tractor-repair workshops, and printers for the semiweekly newspaper *Pracheachon* (The People). Moscow also supplied credits for agricultural and marine projects. Finally, the Soviets provided 1,285 scholarships to Cambodian students for the period 1986 to 1990, many fewer than the 2,364 scholarships that they had awarded from 1980 to 1986.

Vietnamese Aid

Vietnam's economic and technical assistance to Cambodia were difficult to evaluate because neither side chose to disclose the precise monetary value of such aid. For example, the Cambodian Domestic News Service acknowledged that in 1986 the Vietnamese had given Cambodia ''some aid with no strings attached'' for the construction of work sites in Kampong Chhnang and for the Phnom Penh-Hanoi Friendship Kindergarten but did not disclose the amount of money involved in these projects.

Vietnamese officials have indicated vaguely that their friendship treaty with Cambodia committed them to an annual aid package of at least US$25 million. During the first years of the emergency period, Vietnam's aid was estimated by outside sources at US$56 million in 1979 and at US$62 million in 1980.

A large part of Vietnamese aid was assistance in kind, particularly food, medical and school supplies, household commodities, and commercial vehicles, such as passenger buses for Phnom Penh. One important and lasting form of Vietnamese aid consisted of a technical assistance package that included the services of Vietnamese advisers and technical experts as well as training for Cambodian cadres and personnel. According to the Cambodian official news agency, a total of 431 cadres and other personnel received technical training in Vietnam in 1986. In addition, through bilateral agreements, Vietnamese experts conducted short-term, on-the-job training at several Cambodian ministries, general directorates, and offices. The Cambodians reportedly preferred this form of on-site training.

It was reported officially that Cambodian-Vietnamese cooperation had led to the completion of sixty-five projects. Other projects scheduled for the First Plan included consumer-goods enterprises, small industrial and handicraft workshops, animal breeding, and the building of a greenbelt around Phnom Penh.

International and Western Aid

UN relief organizations (the UN Children's Fund, the UN High Commissioner for Refugees, FAO, and WFP) and the International Committee of the Red Cross put together a disaster relief program in 1979 to help the Cambodian people and refugees overcome famine and disease. The cost of the program amounted to US$633.9 million from October 1979 through December 1981. The United States contributed approximately one-third of this total emergency aid. Officials in charge of the program channeled about one-half of the total US$633.9 million (US$334.6 million) to areas under government control. They allocated the other half to relief efforts in border areas and to Cambodian refugees living outside the country. During the same period, private volunteer agencies provided emergency aid amounting to approximately US$100 million.

After the emergency period, the UN aid program to the Heng Samrin government declined drastically. In 1983 an estimated US$4 million was raised against a planned budget of US$16 million; however, the UN Border Relief Operation (UNBRO) continued its aid programs for Cambodian refugees in camps along the Thai-Cambodian border. According to the United States Department of State, UNBRO spent nearly US$35 million on relief efforts in 1985, of which the United States contributed US$12 million. The same year, the United States gave US$800,000 in commodities to the WFP and another US$2 million to the International Committee of the Red Cross for their border relief activities.

Finance

Reliable information on the national budget, on banking, and on the money supply in 1987, was unavailable. However, Cambodia was known to have raised revenues through rental and utility fees, taxes, business registrations, sales of goods by state organizations, and exports. Budgetary financing came largely from the Soviet Union, Vietnam and, to a much smaller extent, from other Comecon members. The government allocated most of the budget to current expenditures, such as those for defense and for state employees' salaries, the latter of which were augmented by allowances of rice, cloth, cigarettes, soap, sugar and other consumer goods (see table 15, Appendix A).

Banking

The creation of the People's National Bank of Kampuchea in 1980 reestablished Cambodia's banking system, which Pol Pot had abolished immediately after the fall of Phnom Penh in 1975. The bank's chairman held ministerial rank in the government (see Government Structure, ch. 4). By 1984 more than thirty branch banks were in operation. The main functions of the bank were to provide funds for state commerce and credits for agriculture.

Currency

The Heng Samrin government reintroduced the country's currency, the riel, in March 1980, at which time the value of one riel equaled the value of one kilogram of rice. The state controlled all foreign exchange, and the official exchange rate for visitors was 4 riels to US$1 in 1980. After five years of relative stability, the government devalued the currency to 30 riels per US$1 in January 1986. A subsequent devaluation, reducing the rate to 100 riels per US$1, took place in October 1987. The move was intended to curb inflation, to stop the growing black market, and to bring in more foreign currency. The free-market rate in Phnom Penh at the time was 125 to 130 riels per US$1. In December 1987, the People's National Bank of Kampuchea issued new five- and ten-riel notes in blue and green and invalidated the country's old red bank notes, in an effort to eliminate the problem of counterfeit currency.

Taxes

The government approved the country's first tax laws in November 1982 and implemented them in 1983. There were three categories of taxes—business, import, and agricultural. In theory, the tax laws stipulated that all private economic enterprises should pay taxes, while tax schedules varied according to income, goods imported, and agricultural productivity. The Ministry of Finance was responsible for tax assessments and for collections on a national level. At subordinate government echelons, provincial and district committees were charged with this duty.

In practice, the government faced many difficulties in collecting taxes. Eventually, it revised assessments to make taxation acceptable to the business community and to the peasantry. For example, the agricultural tax (also called the "patriotic contribution"), introduced during the 1983 to 1984 harvest season, reportedly was suspended in 1985, but was reimposed a year later. Agricultural tax assessments were based on yields and plots, such as lowland paddy, river banks, garden, hillside fields, plantation crop, or highland cropland. The government, however, granted new concessions to some agricultural cooperatives, which previously had been taxed heavily on high-yielding rice harvests, without regard to the high costs of production and the high risks in testing new varieties of rice. Cultivators who grew rice in both the rainy and the dry seasons were subject to tax assessments on each crop. Partial and full tax exemptions were granted to peasants who brought vacant land into production, to families of soldiers, to the war handicapped, and to victims of natural calamities.

Transportation and Communications

War and continuing fighting severely damaged Cambodia's transportation system—a system that had been inadequately developed in peacetime. The country's weak infrastructure hindered emergency relief efforts and created tremendous problems of procurement of supplies in general and of distribution. Cambodia received Soviet technical assistance and equipment to support the maintenance of the transportation network.

Roads and Highways

In the late 1980s, Cambodia had about 13,350 kilometers of roads, compared with 19,480 kilometers in 1969. Of the current total, only about 20 percent of the roads and highways were covered with asphalt and were in passable condition; about 50 percent of the roads were made of crushed stone, gravel, or improved earth; and the remaining approximately 30 percent were unimproved earth or were little more than tracks. In 1981 Cambodia opened a newly repaired section of National Route 1, which runs southeast from Phnom Penh to the Vietnamese border. The road, which suffered damage during the war years, was restored most probably by Vietnamese army engineers. In the late 1980s, Cambodia's road network was both underutilized and unable to meet even the modest demands placed upon it by an unindustrialized and agrarian society (see fig. 8). Commercial vehicles, such as trucks and buses, were insufficient in number and lacked spare parts necessary to keep them running. Road construction and maintenance were ignored by a financially hard-pressed government, while insurgents regularly destroyed bridges and rendered some routes unsafe for travel.

Railroads

Cambodia had two rail lines, both originating in Phnom Penh, totaling about 612 kilometers of single, one-meter-gauge track. The French built the first line, which runs from Phnom Penh to Paoy Pet on the Thai border, between 1930 and 1940. Assistance from France, West Germany, and China, between 1960 and 1969, supported the construction of the second line, which runs from Phnom Penh to Kampong Saom. Rail service ceased during the war, but resumed in the early 1980s. Guerrilla activities, however, continued to disrupt service.

Water Transportation

The nation's extensive inland waterways were important historically in domestic trade. The Mekong and the Tonle Sab rivers, their numerous tributaries, and the Tonle Sap provided avenues of considerable length, including 3,700 kilometers navigable all year by craft drawing 0.6 meters and another 282 kilometers navigable

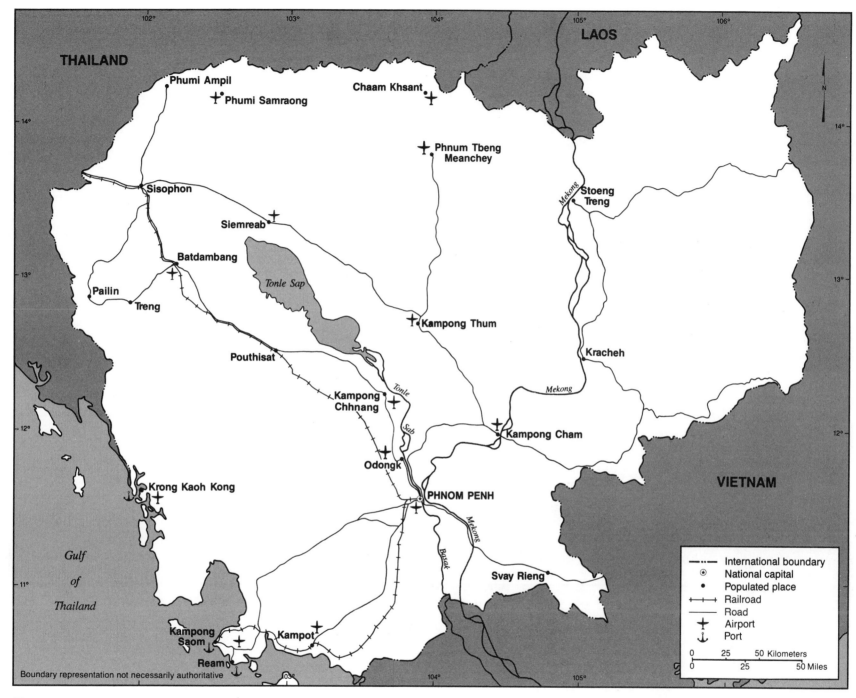

Figure 8. Transportation System, 1987

180

to craft drawing 1.8 meters. In some areas, especially west of the Mekong River and north of the Tonle Sab River, the villages were completely dependent on waterways for communications. Launches, junks, or barges transported passengers, rice, and other food in the absence of roads and railways.

According to the Ministry of Communications, Transport, and Posts, Cambodia's main ferry services crossing the Basak River and the middle Mekong River at Neak Luong (Phumi Prek Khsay), Tonle Bet, Sre Ambel, Kampong Cham, and Stoeng Treng were restored in 1985. The major Mekong River navigation routes also were cleared for traffic.

Ports

Cambodia has two major ports, Phnom Penh and Kampong Saom, and five minor ones. Phnom Penh, located at the junction of the Basak, the Mekong, and the Tonle Sab rivers, is the only river port capable of receiving 8,000-ton ships during the wet season and 5,000-ton ships during the dry season. It remains an important port for international commerce as well as for domestic communications.

Kampong Saom, Cambodia's only seaport, reopened in late 1979. It had been built in 1960 with French assistance. In 1980 some 180 Soviet dockworkers, having brought with them forklifts and trucks, were reportedly working at Kampong Saom as longshoremen or as instructors of unskilled Cambodian port workers. By 1984 approximately 1,500 Cambodian port workers were handling 2.5 tons of cargo per day. According to official statistics, Kampong Saom had handled only 769,500 tons in the four prior years (1979 to 1983), a level that contrasted sharply with the port's peacetime capacity of about 1 million tons of cargo per year.

Airports

The country possesses twenty-six airfields, of which only thirteen were usable in the mid-1980s. Eight airfields had permanent-surface runways. Pochentong International Airport near Phnom Penh is the largest airport; it also serves as the main base for the renascent Cambodian Air Force (see Kampuchean, or Khmer, People's Revolutionary Armed Forces, ch. 5). Cambodia opened a new Soviet-built airfield at Ream near Kampong Saom in late 1983. There are additional secondary airports in Siemreab and in Batdambang.

Air Kampuchea was established in 1982 and flew only one route—from Phnom Penh to Ho Chi Minh City in Vietnam. In 1984 commercial air service was inaugurated between Phnom Penh and Hanoi with the arrival at Hanoi International Airport of the Kampuchean Civil Aviation Company's (AKASCHOR) first flight. Since then, there has been regular air service from Phnom Penh to Hanoi, Vientiane, and Moscow.

Telecommunications

Postal, telegraph, and telegram services under the Ministry of Communications, Transport, and Posts were restored throughout most of the country in the early 1980s. Radio communications were frequent; the Voice of the Kampuchean People broadcasted ten hours daily from Phnom Penh in the late 1980s. An estimated 171,000 radio sets existed in the country in 1984 (the last year for which data were available). Cambodia's only television station began broadcasting, with Vietnamese assistance, in December 1984. Color transmissions began in July 1986.

In January 1987, the Soviet-aided Intersputnik space communications station began operation in Phnom Penh and established two-way telecommunication links between the Cambodian capital and the cities of Moscow, Hanoi, Vientiane, and Paris. The completion of the earth satellite station (built on the grounds of Phnom Penh's old Roman Catholic cathedral), restored the telephone and telex links among Phnom Penh, Hanoi, and other socialist countries for the first time since 1975. Although telecommunications services were limited to the government, these advances in communications helped break down the country's isolation, both internally and internationally.

* * *

The major publications on statistical data and key indicators of Cambodia's economy are the *UN Statistical Yearbook for Asia and the Pacific,* the *FAO Production Yearbook,* the ADB *Key Indicators,* the *EIU Quarterly Economic Review of Indochina,* the *Far East and Australasia,* and the *Asian Economic Handbook.*

First-hand observations and field reports from Cambodia are found in various issues of the *Far Eastern Economic Review* and *Keesing's Records of World Events.* Cambodian official statements, news, and radio broadcasts are monitored and translated into English in the Foreign Broadcast Information Service's *Daily Report: East Asia* and the Joint Publications Research Service's *Southeast Asia Report,* two important sources of information.

Scholarly studies and analytical essays on the Cambodian economy are scarce. Among the most useful is Khieu Samphan's doctoral dissertation, *Cambodia's Economy and Industrial Development,* a helpful guide to understanding the Pol Pot regime's economic policy and thinking. Ben Kiernan's "Kampuchea 1979–81: National Rehabilitation in the Eye of an International Storm" and Michael Vickery's *Kampuchea* offer good analyses of the economic system and its problems, particularly in agriculture and in industry. Two studies on the serious food problem in Cambodia are *The Quality of Mercy* by William Shawcross, who focused his study on the Emergency Food Aid Program to Cambodia during the critical 1979–83 period, and D. Mosyakov's "Solving the Food Problem in Kampuchea." (For further information and complete citations, see Bibliography.)

Chapter 4. Government and Politics

The Independence Monument in Phnom Penh

THE 1970S WERE cruel years for the Khmer people, and their impact was still being felt in the late 1980s. The decade opened turbulently, with the deposition of ruler Prince Norodom Sihanouk, who had been in power from 1941, during the period when the war in Vietnam boiled over into Cambodia. The country, militarily feeble and putatively neutral, soon plunged into a succession of upheavals, punctuated by foreign incursions, civil war, and famine. The Khmer Rouge (see Appendix B), under Pol Pot (also known as Saloth Sar) and aided initially by the Democratic Republic of Vietnam (North Vietnam), overran in 1975 the pro-Western Khmer Republic (see Appendix B) led by the president, General Lon Nol. At least 1 million Cambodians either were murdered or starved to death under the Pol Pot regime. In 1979, however, Vietnam ousted the Khmer Rouge regime and installed a puppet regime headed by Heng Samrin, a former Khmer Rouge military commander (see fig. 9).

The Vietnamese set out to tighten their grip on the country by occupying and colonizing it. Meanwhile, the deposed Khmer Rouge regime regrouped in remote enclaves near the Thai border to give armed resistance to Vietnamese forces and the puppet government in Phnom Penh, the nation's capital.

At the end of the 1970s, Cambodia was divided politically and territorially under two regimes, each claiming to be the sole legitimate government of the nation. Since then, the competing regimes have been locked in an armed struggle in Cambodia, as one side contested the Vietnamese presence and the other acquiesced more or less grudgingly to its role as Hanoi's surrogate.

Vietnam promised repeatedly to leave Cambodia by 1990, and by the end of 1987, Hanoi had staged six partial troop withdrawals. Officials in Hanoi indicated, however, that phased withdrawals would end and that Vietnamese forces would return to Cambodia if there were a threat to Vietnam's national security. Members of the Association of Southeast Asian Nations (ASEAN) and most Western nations were skeptical of the moves and viewed them as merely disguised troop rotations. Among Cambodia's noncommunist neighbors, Thailand especially was concerned about the threat posed to its own security by a large, well-armed Vietnamese army just to the east of its borders. On the diplomatic front, the United Nations (UN) routinely condemned the Vietnamese military presence in Cambodia on an annual basis, and most countries

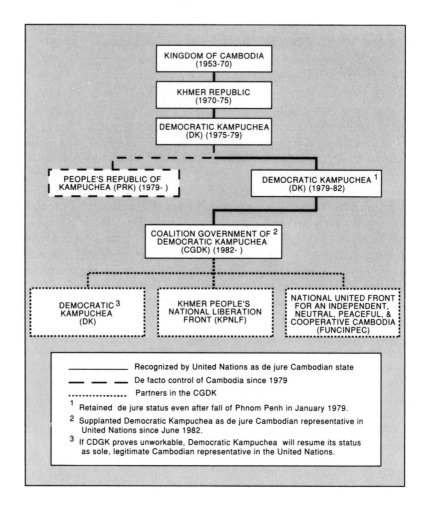

Figure 9. Successive Governments in Cambodia (since Independence)

withheld diplomatic recognition from the pro-Vietnamese Heng Samrin regime in Phnom Penh.

In 1987 uncertain prospects for peace continued to vex Cambodian nationalists. Differences—among warring Cambodian factions and their respective foreign sponsors over the projected terms of a possible settlement—were likely to remain unresolved in the foreseeable future. Meanwhile, the Cambodian people continued to suffer from the war between anti-Vietnamese guerrillas on the one side and the Vietnamese and the Heng Samrin forces on the other side. The Cambodian search for reconciliation among contending parties can be understood only when the perspectives of foreign powers are taken into account.

In the late 1980s, the ruling political organization in Phnom Penh was the Marxist-Leninist Kampuchean (or Khmer) People's Revolutionary Party (KPRP—see Appendix B), a political offshoot of the Indochinese Communist Party (ICP—see Appendix B), founded by Ho Chi Minh in 1930. Heng Samrin headed both the state bureaucracy and the party apparatus in late 1987. Hun Sen, prime minister since January 1985, chaired the single-party, KPRP-run government, that was administered by the Council of Ministers. In seeking to enlist mass support for its regime, the KPRP depended on an umbrella popular front organization, affiliated with numerous social and political groups, that was called the Kampuchean (or Khmer) United Front for National Construction and Defense (KUFNCD—see Appendix B). The KPRP, in exercising power in Phnom Penh under Vietnamese mentorship, pursued three main objectives: to combat the enemy (anti-Vietnamese resistance groups); to intensify production for the fulfillment of targets set in the First Five-Year Program of Socioeconomic Restoration and Development (1986–90), hereafter known as the First Plan; and to build up the party's revolutionary forces by strengthening the regime's political and administrative infrastructure and its national security establishment. The party's foreign policy goals were to reinforce solidarity with Vietnam and to develop cooperation with the Soviet Union, the principal source of economic assistance to the government in Phnom Penh.

The other regime competing for legitimacy in the 1980s was an unlikely partnership of feuding communist and noncommunist factions, the Coalition Government of Democratic Kampuchea (CGDK—see Appendix B). The coalition government, with Sihanouk serving on and off as president, was formed in 1982 under the sponsorship of China and the ASEAN states. The coalition comprised the Khmer Rouge and two noncommunist groups led by Sihanouk and Son Sann. Son Sann, a former prime minister under Sihanouk, was known for his dislike of Sihanouk and of the Khmer Rouge.

Despite its claim that it was based inside Cambodia, the CGDK was a government in exile. It operated out of Beijing, Pyongyang, or Bangkok, or wherever its three leaders—Sihanouk, Khieu Samphan, and Son Sann—happened to be, whether or not they were together. In the 1984 to 1985 Vietnamese dry-season offensive, the coalition lost nearly all of its fixed guerrilla bases along the Thai border. Nonetheless, its fighters continued to operate in small bands in many Cambodian provinces. The CGDK's forces sought to drive

189

the Vietnamese out of the country, to win over the Cambodians who were resentful of the Vietnamese, to destabilize the Heng Samrin regime, and to seek international aid for continued resistance. The coalition government had a distinct asset that its rival lacked—it was recognized by the United Nations as the lawful representative of the state of Cambodia.

Major Political Developments, 1977–81

Background

The communist conquest of Phnom Penh and of Saigon (renamed Ho Chi Minh City) in April 1975 seemed to presage realization of Ho Chi Minh's long-cherished political dream—stated in a 1935 resolution of the ICP—an Indochinese federation comprising Vietnam, Laos, and Cambodia. Many observers believed—because of Vietnam's efforts to nurture a Cambodian communist party that was tied closely to Hanoi—that the Indochinese federation that emerged would be controlled by Hanoi. The Khmer Rouge victory of 1975, however, won by Pol Pot's chauvinistic and hardline party faction with its abiding distrust of Vietnam, doomed this prospect for the time being.

In mid-1975, a series of border clashes erupted between Cambodian and Vietnamese forces. Each side blamed the other for initiating the conflicts, which occurred even as Hanoi defended the Pol Pot regime against international criticism of atrocities inside Cambodia. Border fighting increased in 1977, according to some reports. In June of that year, Vietnam proposed negotiations to settle the border dispute, but the Khmer Rouge said negotiations would be premature. In December, Cambodia accused Vietnam of aggression, demanded withdrawal of its troops from the country, and severed diplomatic ties. In February 1978, Hanoi called for an immediate end to all hostile military activities in the border region and for the conclusion of a peace treaty. At the same time, Hanoi denied the allegations that it had been trying to incorporate Cambodia into an Indochinese federation, adding that Vietnam had not entertained the idea of federation since the ICP was dissolved in 1951. The Pol Pot regime continued to claim, however, that Vietnam had never abandoned the idea of a federation, and the regime called on Hanoi to cease activities aimed at overthrowing the Government of Democratic Kampuchea.

Cambodia in Turmoil

On December 25, 1978, Vietnam launched a full-scale invasion of Cambodia (see Vietnamese Invasion of Cambodia, ch. 5). Phnom Penh fell, after minimal resistance, on January 7, 1979, and on the following day an anti-Khmer Rouge faction announced the formation of the Kampuchean People's Revolutionary Council (KPRC), with Heng Samrin as president of the new ruling body. On January 10, the KPRC proclaimed that the new official name of Cambodia was the People's Republic of Kampuchea (PRK—see Appendix B). Within a week, the PRK notified the United Nations Security Council that it was the sole legitimate government of the Cambodian people.

Vietnam was the first country to recognize the new regime, and Phnom Penh lost no time in restoring diplomatic relations with Hanoi. From February 16 to February 19, the PRK and Vietnam held their first summit meeting in Phnom Penh and cemented their relationship by signing a twenty-five-year Treaty of Peace, Friendship and Cooperation. The treaty declared that the "peace and security of the two countries are closely interrelated and that the two Parties are duty-bound to help each other. . . ." Article 2 of the treaty dealt specifically with mutual security assistance to help each defend against "all schemes and acts of sabotage by the imperialist and international reactionary forces." The two governments also signed agreements for cooperation on economic, cultural, educational, public health, and scientific and technological issues.

In rapid succession, the Soviet Union, other Marxist-Leninist states, and a number of pro-Moscow developing countries had also recognized the new regime. By January 1980, twenty-nine countries had recognized the PRK, yet nearly eighty countries continued to recognize the Khmer Rouge.

More countries voiced opposition to Vietnam's involvement in Cambodia. Most vocal was Thailand, the security of which was threatened directly by the turn of events in Cambodia. (Thailand shares an 800-kilometer border with Cambodia, and historically it has regarded the country as a buffer against Vietnamese expansion—see Regional Divisions, ch. 2.) The Thai government demanded Vietnam's immediate withdrawal from Cambodia so that the Cambodians would be able to choose their own government without foreign interference. Thailand's allies in ASEAN—Indonesia, Malaysia, the Philippines, and Singapore—agreed with Bangkok's position.

The United States also agreed with Thailand's position. Although it had never recognized Democratic Kampuchea and disapproved of the human rights violations perpetrated by the Khmer Rouge, the United States nonetheless supported Democratic Kampuchea's request for an emergency session of the UN Security Council. China expressed its support for the Khmer Rouge and even accused Vietnam of attempting to force Cambodia into an Indochinese federation and of serving as an ''Asian Cuba''—a surrogate for the Soviet policy of global hegemony.

Soviet leaders hailed the PRK's ''remarkable victory'' and expressed their full support for a peaceful, independent, democratic, and nonaligned Cambodia that would advance toward socialism. Moscow also accused Pol Pot's Khmer Rouge regime of genocide and implied that China had imposed the regime on Cambodia.

Despite objections from the Soviet Union and from Czechoslovakia, the UN Security Council allowed Prince Sihanouk to argue the case for Democratic Kampuchea in early January 1979. Sihanouk—who had distanced himself from Khmer Rouge brutality, charged that Vietnam had committed flagrant acts of aggression against Cambodia, and he asked the council to demand an end to Hanoi's interference in Cambodian affairs. He also urged that the council not recognize the puppet regime in Phnom Penh, and he appealed to all nations to suspend aid to Vietnam.

In the UN Security Council debate, Vietnam unsuccessfully challenged Sihanouk's claim to represent Cambodia, asserting that he spoke for a regime that no longer existed. Vietnam also charged that the Pol Pot regime had provoked the border war and that Hanoi's presence in Cambodia was necessary and was strictly an issue between Vietnam and the PRK. Hanoi argued, moreover, that the Cambodian crisis was a matter of internal strife among rival groups that was brought on by Pol Pot's atrocities against his own countrymen. Hanoi actually asserted that there was no ''Cambodian problem'' that warranted a debate in the UN or anywhere else in the international political arena.

The fifteen-member UN Security Council, however, failed to adopt a resolution on Cambodia. Seven nonaligned members on the council had submitted a draft resolution, which was endorsed by Britain, China, France, Norway, Portugal, and the United States. But the draft, which called for a cease-fire in Cambodia and for the withdrawal of all foreign forces from that country, was not approved because of objections from the Soviet Union and from Czechoslovakia.

The fate of Cambodia was interwoven with the security interests of its Asian neighbors. For example, on February 17, 1979, China attacked Vietnam, apparently to ease Vietnamese pressure against Thailand and against Chinese-supported Khmer Rouge guerrillas. The Cambodian question surfaced again in the UN Security Council session that was convened on February 23 to consider ending the hostilities along the Vietnamese-Chinese border and in Cambodia. This time the focus was on regional power politics; China demanded that the UN Security Council censure Vietnam for its invasion of Cambodia, and the Soviet Union asked that the council condemn China for its "aggression" against Vietnam. The United States called for the withdrawal of Chinese forces from Vietnam and of Vietnamese forces from Cambodia.

In late 1979, the stage was set for an international political showdown over Cambodia. In September of that year, the UN General Assembly rejected the efforts of the Soviet Union, the Congo, and Panama to challenge the legality of Democratic Kampuchea and decided that it should continue to be represented at the United Nations. The vote was seventy-one to thirty-five in support of the decision, with thirty-four abstentions. (Sihanouk, who no longer represented the Khmer Rouge regime, argued that the Cambodian seat should be left vacant because neither of the two Cambodian claimants had the mandate of the Cambodian people.) In November, the UN General Assembly adopted an ASEAN-sponsored resolution by a vote of eighty-one to twenty-one, with twenty-nine abstentions, calling for immediate Vietnamese disengagement from Cambodia. The resolution also called on all states to refrain from interference in, and acts of aggression against, Cambodia and its Southeast Asian neighbors. The assembly mandated the UN secretary general to explore the possibility of an international conference on Cambodia and appealed for international humanitarian aid for the country's population and for its refugees who had fled to neighboring countries.

Cambodia's PRK regime, under the leadership of Heng Samrin, set out to restore the country's social and economic life, which had been racked by a decade of political turmoil. During 1979 the country was still reeling from the horrors of the Khmer Rouge, and the lack of educated and qualified personnel to staff administrative posts was hampering efforts to reestablish a civil government. Most of the country's educated elite had been murdered during the Pol Pot era, while others had fled to safety in Vietnam. (In August 1979, a Phnom Penh "people's revolutionary tribunal" tried Pol Pot and his closest confidant, Foreign Minister Ieng Sary, in absentia, on charges of genocidal crimes and then sentenced them to death.) Another complication for the Heng Samrin regime was the growing Khmer Rouge guerrilla resistance in the western and the northwestern border areas.

By mid-1980, life in villages and in towns had stabilized somewhat, and relief aid from the Soviet Union, Vietnam, and some Western countries had helped to prevent mass starvation. Meanwhile, the regime had managed gradually to extend its administrative control to outlying areas close to the Thai border and had initiated the drafting of a constitution in January 1980. The

National Assembly, which had been elected in May 1981, formally adopted and promulgated the Constitution in June.

But opposition to the Heng Samrin regime had been growing since 1979. The most prominent opposition group was the Khmer Rouge, which sought to reestablish its political legitimacy and to mobilize the Cambodian people against the Vietnamese. In January 1979, Khmer Rouge leaders announced the formation of the Patriotic and Democratic Front of the Great National Union of Kampuchea (PDFGNUK—see Appendix B), a popular front organization in which the Kampuchean (or Khmer) Communist Party (KCP—see Appendix B), under Pol Pot planned to play a dominant role.

As part of an image-rebuilding effort, the Khmer Rouge announced the replacement, in December 1979, of Prime Minister Pol Pot with the politically moderate Khieu Samphan. The replacement did not affect Pol Pot's position as leader of the KCP or his control of the Khmer Rouge armed forces, officially called the National Army of Democratic Kampuchea (NADK—see Appendix B; National Army of Democratic Kampuchea, ch. 5). Khieu Samphan retained his position as president of the State Presidium of Democratic Kampuchea, a post equivalent to head of state under the 1975 constitution of Democratic Kampuchea. At about the same time, it also was disclosed that the political program of the PDFGNUK, adopted in December, would serve as the provisional fundamental law of Democratic Kampuchea until free elections could be held. Sihanouk described the episode as a ploy designed to give the Khmer Rouge's "odious face" a mask of respectability.

The first and principal noncommunist resistance group was the Khmer People's National Liberation Front (KPNLF—see Appendix B) led by Son Sann. The front's military arm was the Khmer People's National Liberation Armed Forces (KPNLAF—see Appendix B). It was originally formed, in March 1979, by General Dien Del, a former army officer under Lon Non's Khmer Republic (see Coalition Government Resistance Forces, ch. 5). Son Sann's formation of the KPNLF on October 9, 1979, coincided with the ninth anniversary of the founding of the Khmer Republic and therefore symbolized rejection of "Sihanoukism." After 1979 Son Sann and Sihanouk often clashed over the issue of coalition-building and national reconciliation, despite their common distaste for the Khmer Rouge and for the Vietnamese occupation. After 1985 the KPNLF fell into disarray as a result of leadership disputes in the movement's top echelon. By late 1987, it still had not regained its former stature or fighting strength.

The second noncommunist, nationalist resistance faction was the Sihanouk group called initially the Movement for the National Liberation of Kampuchea (Mouvement pour la Libération Nationale du Kampuchéa—MOULINAKA—see Appendix B), formed in August 1979 by Kong Sileah after his split with General Dien Del. In September, Sihanouk set up the Confederation of Khmer Nationalists from his base in Pyongyang, Democratic People's Republic of Korea (North Korea). The confederation lacked support because key actors in the Cambodian situation perceived it to be merely a forum, and that only for "committed Sihanoukists." Around March 1981, the MOULINAKA group joined with other small pro-Sihanouk factions to establish a political organization called the National United Front for an Independent, Neutral, Peaceful, and Cooperative Cambodia (Front Uni National pour un Cambodge Indépendant, Neutre, Pacifique, et Coopératif—FUNCINPEC—see Appendix B). The movement soon formed its own armed wing, the Sihanouk National Army (Armée Nationale Sihanoukiste—ANS—see Appendix B), which began minor incursions into Cambodia (see Coalition Government Resistance Forces, ch. 5). As a political movement, FUNCINPEC quickly acquired a legitimacy beyond its numbers, because of the impeccable nationalist credentials of its head, Sihanouk. Moreover, although it remained the smallest of the Khmer resistance groups until 1985, its quest for stature was abetted by its having neither the opprobrious human rights record of the Khmer Rouge to live down, nor the debilitating leadership disputes of the KPNLF with which to contend.

Coalition Government of Democratic Kampuchea

The establishment of the tripartite Coalition Government of Democratic Kampuchea (CGDK—see Appendix B) in June 1982 was a significant achievement for the resistance groups, which had quarreled bitterly throughout the negotiations that led to unity. Following its founding, the CGDK became the center of the anti-Vietnamese cause, served as the country's lawful spokesman in international forums, and demonstrated a credible capacity for bringing the Cambodian conflict to a political and military stalemate. In the late 1980s, this stalemate renewed multilateral interest in a settlement of the Cambodian question.

Origins of the Coalition

In the aftermath of the 1978 Vietnamese invasion, many Cambodians clamored for national unity, but only a few responded to the Khmer Rouge's appeal for unity under the PDFGNUK (see

Major Political Developments, 1977–81, this ch.). Their reluctance to rally behind the Khmer Rouge was understandable because they envisioned a new Cambodia that was neither ruled by the Khmer Rouge nor controlled by the Vietnamese. Many Cambodians believed that an essential condition of any movement aimed at restoring national freedom should be opposition to the Khmer Rouge and the Vietnamese. Sihanouk and Son Sann were both uneasy about reconciliation with the Khmer Rouge. Still, Cambodian solidarity against Hanoi would be fragile at best without the participation of the Khmer Rouge, the strongest of all the resistance groups.

Then in January 1979, Sihanouk, charged by the Democratic Kampuchea leadership with presenting Cambodia's case before the United Nations, broke with his sponsors and demanded that the Khmer Rouge be expelled from the United Nations for their mass murders. And in early 1980, he deplored ASEAN's continued recognition of Democratic Kampuchea, criticized China's military aid to the Khmer Rouge, and accused Thai authorities of closing their eyes to Chinese arm shipments through Thailand to Khmer Rouge rebels. In June 1980, Sihanouk, frustrated, announced his permanent retirement from all political activities.

Meanwhile, Son Sann, who had been indirectly in touch with Pol Pot since November 1979, announced in January 1980 that he would form an anti-Vietnamese united front with the Khmer Rouge if the group's leaders agreed to step down and to relinquish their power to his new organization. He also raised the possibility of forming his own provisional government to rival the Khmer Rouge. Cooperation with Sihanouk seemed unlikely.

Khieu Samphan, president of the State Presidium of the defunct regime of Democratic Kampuchea, proposed that Son Sann join forces with the Khmer Rouge on a common political platform. In 1979 and in 1980, the Khmer Rouge reportedly came under pressure from China to forge a united front under Sihanouk or Son Sann. The ASEAN countries also urged the Khmer Rouge to put its blood-stained image behind it and to mend its political fences with the noncommunist resistance groups. The United Nations informed the Khmer Rouge that a new mode of behavior would be necessary if its deposed regime were to retain its seat in the organization.

The united front idea got off to a slow start in 1981. In February Sihanouk, reversing his retirement from politics, indicated his willingness to lead the front if China and the Khmer Rouge supported his preconditions of Chinese military and financial assistance to all Cambodian resistance factions, not just the Khmer Rouge,

(Top) Prince Norodom Sihanouk,
President of the Coalition
Government of Democratic
Kampuchea, addresses a
session of the General
Assembly of the
United Nations.
Courtesy
United Nations Photo

(Bottom) Prince Norodom
Ranariddh reviews combatants of
the Armée Nationale
Sihanoukiste on Thai-
Cambodian border.
Courtesy Frank Tatu

and of the disarming of all resistance groups after the Vietnamese disengagement from Cambodia. The disarming was essential, he asserted, to prevent the Khmer Rouge from inaugurating a new round of terror and a new civil war. As a safeguard, Sihanouk also wanted an international peace-keeping force after the Vietnamese departure, an internationally guaranteed neutralization of Cambodia, and a trusteeship under which the country would be a ward of the United Nations for five to ten years. Furthermore, he requested that the country's official name be Cambodia instead of Democratic Kampuchea. The name change was a bid to undermine the legal status of the Pol Pot regime as de jure representative of Democratic Kampuchea because the latter designation had been that of the Khmer Rouge exclusively.

Son Sann was indifferent to Sihanouk's willingness to lead the front. Khieu Samphan, on the other hand, was conciliatory and stated that the KCP would be disbanded if necessary. He acknowledged at the same time that Democratic Kampuchea had blundered by trying to develop the country "much too fast," adding that this haste had "affected the health of people" and had cost the lives of nearly 1 million Cambodians. He also blamed Vietnam's "special warfare of genocide" for the deaths of "2.5 million" Cambodians. In addition, he claimed that a new Cambodia would not be socialist, would honor private property, and would cooperate on a "large-scale" with the West. He even said that Democratic Kampuchea was ready to join ASEAN as a member "at any time."

Sihanouk and Khieu Samphan held their first exploratory unity talks in Pyongyang on March 10 and 11, 1981, without Son Sann, who claimed that neither of the two spoke for the Cambodian people. The talks foundered because Khieu Samphan objected to Sihanouk's demand that all resistance factions be disarmed in the future.

Sihanouk sought to enlist the cooperation of Son Sann, especially in securing arms from China and from the United States. Sihanouk realized, however, that China would not back his 2,000-strong force unless he collaborated with the Khmer Rouge on its terms. Then in April, Sihanouk said he was willing to drop his demand for the disarmament of Khmer Rouge forces in exchange for Chinese aid to the ANS.

Son Sann reacted cautiously to the Sihanouk-Khieu Samphan talks, distrusting collaboration with the Khmer Rouge at least until after the KPNLF's military strength matched that of the communist faction. However, he left open the possibility of future cooperation, citing a KPNLF-Khmer Rouge cease-fire accord in early 1980.

Son Sann also disclosed that he had ignored Sihanouk's four attempts at tactical cooperation since 1979.

By August 1981, unity talks seemed to have collapsed because of unacceptable preconditions advanced by the KPNLF and by the Khmer Rouge. Son Sann was adamant that Khmer Rouge leaders "most compromised" by their atrocities be exiled to China and that the proposed united front be led by the KPNLF. Meanwhile, Khieu Samphan urged his rivals not to undermine the autonomy of the Khmer Rouge or to undo the legal status of Democratic Kampuchea.

The three leaders broke their deadlock, with encouragement from ASEAN, and held their first summit in Singapore from September 2 to 4. They reached a four-point accord that included the creation of "a coalition government of Democratic Kampuchea"; the establishment of an ad hoc committee to draw up a blueprint for the coalition government; an expression of support for the resolution of the first International Conference on Kampuchea (held in New York, July 13 to July 17, 1981) as well as for other relevant UN General Assembly resolutions on Cambodia; and an appeal for international support of their common cause. They also decided not to air their internal differences publicly "during the whole period of the agreement" and not to attack one another on the battlefield. Most observers regarded the agreement as a breakthrough that would enable the Khmer Rouge regime to hold onto its seat in the United Nations and that would enhance the prospect of increased access to foreign military assistance for the KPNLF and FUNCINPEC.

At a joint press conference on September 4, all sides sought to paper over their differences. Son Sann muted his demand for the removal of the Khmer Rouge leadership, and Khieu Samphan portrayed Democratic Kampuchea in a new, moderate light, maintaining that it would respect individual rights and private ownership of property. Sihanouk noted that the three resistance groups would maintain their separate military units, but under a joint general staff and a military council that soon would be established.

But in a separate press interview the following day, Sihanouk provided a glimpse of those differences that persisted among the resistance leaders. He revealed his reluctance to join what he called "war-mongering" leaders, possibly alluding to Khieu Samphan or to Son Sann. Sihanouk held out little hope for a military solution to the unrest in Cambodia and emphasized that China, the Soviet Union, and the United States would have to lend assistance if the crisis were to be solved peacefully. Sihanouk also struck a prophetic note, saying that Cambodians must not only reach "an honorable compromise'' with the Vietnamese, but they should also work out a comprehensive reconciliation among themselves and should include the Vietnamese-installed puppet regime in Phnom Penh.

Between September 13 and November 14, 1981, the ad hoc committee established under the accord met nine times in Bangkok and agreed on principles of equal power sharing among the three factions, on decision making by consensus, and on use of Democratic Kampuchea's legal framework as the basis for the proposed coalition government. To no one's surprise, these principles were subject to conflicting self-serving interpretations. Sihanouk and Son Sann feared that the Khmer Rouge group would somehow exploit the coalition scheme at their expense. Their fear was well-founded in that Khieu Samphan wanted the coalition government to be an integral part of Democratic Kampuchea. In an apparent effort to offset the perceived Khmer Rouge advantage, Son Sann resurrected his demand that Khmer Rouge leaders be excluded from the coalition government and that the KPNLF be guaranteed control of a majority of key ministerial posts. The Khmer Rouge called Son Sann's demands ''unreasonable.'' By mid-November, Son Sann had announced his dissociation from the coalition scheme.

On November 22 and 23, Singapore intervened, with backing from Thailand and the other ASEAN countries, and proposed the formation of ''a loose coalition government'' in which Democratic Kampuchea would become one of three equal partners of the alliance, not the all-important constitutional anchor for the tripartite government. Sihanouk praised the Singapore formula as ''a much better deal'' for the noncommunist groups. The Khmer Rouge rejected the formula, asserted that the loose coalition arrangement would not have any legal status as ''the Democratic Kampuchean Government,'' and, on December 7, criticized Sihanouk and Son Sann for attempting to ''isolate and weaken'' the Khmer Rouge, which was the only force both fighting and stalemating the Vietnamese.

In February 1982, Sihanouk and Khieu Samphan met in Beijing without Son Sann to clarify several ambiguities. One notable result of the meeting was a shift in the Khmer Rouge insistence on constitutional linkage between Democratic Kampuchea and the proposed coalition government. In what was described as ''another concession,'' Khieu Samphan elaborated the position that his side would not attempt to integrate the other resistance groups into ''the Democratic Kampuchean institutions.'' He emphasized, however, that the others must accept and defend the ''legal status'' of Democratic Kampuchea as a UN member state. Sihanouk asked

Son Sann to resolve his differences with Khieu Samphan and to join the coalition. By May, Son Sann had softened his anti-Khmer Rouge posture and had expressed readiness to cooperate with the others under a Thai-proposed plan that would have Sihanouk as head of state, Son Sann as prime minister, and Khieu Samphan as deputy prime minister. In talks with Khieu Samphan in mid-June, Son Sann agreed on the principle of tripartite rule.

Coalition Structure

The three leaders finally signed an agreement on the long-sought coalition on June 22, 1982, in Kuala Lumpur. Sihanouk pledged to be "a loyal partner" and to respect the accord; Son Sann praised the CGDK as "an authentic and legal government"; and Khieu Samphan voiced hope that the CGDK would last a long time, even after the eventual Vietnamese departure. The three signed the coalition agreement without identifying their organizations because Son Sann had refused to recognize Sihanouk's FUNCINPEC.

The June agreement failed to mitigate substantially suspicion of the Khmer Rouge. Sihanouk and Son Sann, for instance, refused to allow CGDK headquarters to be located on Khmer Rouge-controlled territory. Within only a few days of the signing, Sihanouk proposed—at the urging of Singapore and Malaysia—that the two noncommunist groups merge in an effort to improve their standing vis-à-vis the Khmer Rouge. But Son Sann, wanting to maintain a separate identity, rejected the idea. In addition, Sihanouk had planned to announce, in Bangkok on July 12, that the agreement had been signed, but the Voice of Democratic Kampuchea—the Khmer Rouge's clandestine radio station, aired the text of the accord on July 11 and upstaged Sihanouk. Animosity between Sihanouk and Khieu Samphan grew because of the incident.

The purpose of the CGDK, as stated in the June accord, was "to mobilize all efforts in the common struggle to liberate Kampuchea from the Vietnamese aggressors" and "to bring about the implementation of the declaration of the International Conference on Kampuchea and other relevant UN General Assembly resolutions." After the Vietnamese withdrawal, the Cambodians were to determine their own future through a general, free, and secret election under UN supervision.

The CGDK was to function within the "legitimacy and framework of the State of Democratic Kampuchea," and its three partners were to share power equally and to make decisions by consensus. Each partner would have a certain degree of freedom and would maintain organizational and political autonomy. The autonomy would be needed should the CGDK prove unworkable,

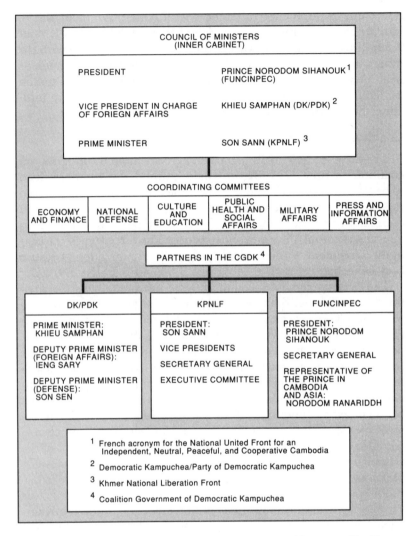

COUNCIL OF MINISTERS
(INNER CABINET)

| PRESIDENT | PRINCE NORODOM SIHANOUK[1]
(FUNCINPEC) |
| VICE PRESIDENT IN CHARGE OF FORIEGN AFFAIRS | KHIEU SAMPHAN (DK/PDK)[2] |
| PRIME MINISTER | SON SANN (KPNLF)[3] |

COORDINATING COMMITTEES

| ECONOMY AND FINANCE | NATIONAL DEFENSE | CULTURE AND EDUCATION | PUBLIC HEALTH AND SOCIAL AFFAIRS | MILITARY AFFAIRS | PRESS AND INFORMATION AFFAIRS |

PARTNERS IN THE CGDK[4]

DK/PDK	KPNLF	FUNCINPEC
PRIME MINISTER: KHIEU SAMPHAN

DEPUTY PRIME MINISTER (FOREIGN AFFAIRS): IENG SARY

DEPUTY PRIME MINISTER (DEFENSE): SON SEN | PRESIDENT: SON SANN

VICE PRESIDENTS

SECRETARY GENERAL

EXECUTIVE COMMITTEE | PRESIDENT: PRINCE NORODOM SIHANOUK

SECRETARY GENERAL

REPRESENTATIVE OF THE PRINCE IN CAMBODIA AND ASIA: NORODOM RANARIDDH |

[1] French acronym for the National United Front for an Independent, Neutral, Peaceful, and Cooperative Cambodia

[2] Democratic Kampuchea/Party of Democratic Kampuchea

[3] Khmer National Liberation Front

[4] Coalition Government of Democratic Kampuchea

Source: Based on information from Central Intelligence Agency, Directorate of Intelligence, *Who's Who in Cambodia: A Reference Aid,* CR 85–10626, March 1985 (Chart, no pagination).

Figure 10. Coalition Government of Democratic Kampuchea, 1987

in which case the right to represent Cambodia would revert to the Khmer Rouge ''in order to ensure the continuity of the state of Democratic Kampuchea'' as a member of the United Nations.

The coalition's top governing body was the ''inner cabinet,'' formally called the Council of Ministers (see fig. 10). The three-member inner cabinet consisted of Sihanouk as president of Democratic Kampuchea, Khieu Samphan as vice president in charge of foreign affairs, and Son Sann as prime minister. The cabinet was to meet regularly inside Cambodia—to demonstrate the viability of the CGDK—for the purposes of discussing domestic and foreign policy matters and of resolving differences within the coalition. Below the inner cabinet were six coordinating committees, each with one representative from each of the coalition's three factions. The six committees, or ministries, were in charge of economy and finance; national defense; culture and education; public health and social affairs; military affairs, and press and information affairs.

In the late 1980s, the CGDK claimed to have held an inner cabinet session inside Cambodia at least once a year since its formation. According to unconfirmed reports, much of the time in these sessions was devoted to charges made by Sihanouk that Khmer Rouge soldiers had attacked his troops. The Khmer Rouge denied the charges, blaming "Vietnamese agents" for such incidents if, indeed, they had occurred at all.

In 1987 Sihanouk engaged in considerable maneuvering as he sought to restore some momentum to the search for a negotiated solution to the situation in Cambodia. Adopting the tactic of temporary abdication of responsibility that he had employed before in his long political career, he began a one-year leave of absence from his duties as president of the CGDK in May 1987. Sihanouk cited several reasons for his decision. The first was his displeasure with continued Khmer Rouge attacks on his troops and the human rights violations by the Khmer Rouge and by the KPNLF against displaced persons in refugee camps controlled by these groups (see Migration and Refugees, ch. 2). The second reason was the alleged "duplicity" of unnamed foreign governments, which, Sihanouk said, were exploiting Cambodia as a pawn in their power struggle. He also claimed that an unidentified foreign sponsor—probably an allusion to China—was deliberately holding back "the rebirth of Sihanoukism" for the benefit of the Khmer Rouge. Finally, Sihanouk added that he was leaving to explore the prospect of reconciliation with leaders of Hanoi and Phnom Penh. Sihanouk's temporary dissociation from the CGDK, some observers believed, would free him from the burden of consulting with Son Sann and Khieu Samphan.

Democratic Kampuchea

In 1987 the United Nations continued to recognize Democratic Kampuchea as the legal representative of Cambodia in the General Assembly, in spite of objections by the People's Republic of

Kampuchea (PRK), the Vietnamese-installed regime in Phnom Penh; thus, under international law, Democratic Kampuchea continued to exist as an entity with full sovereignty even though it did not possess all four of the conventional criteria of statehood: people, territory, government, and supreme authority within the borders of a given country. Under the 1982 tripartite agreement, the CGDK had replaced the Khmer Rouge regime as de jure representative of Democratic Kampuchea. Nevertheless, the Khmer Rouge continued to identify itself as Democratic Kampuchea even after the accord was signed. As a result, the terms Democratic Kampuchea and the Khmer Rouge became virtually synonymous and in fact were used interchangeably (see fig. 10).

In late 1987 Democratic Kampuchea was being governed under the political program of the PDFGNUK that had been adopted formally in December 1979 as "the provisional fundamental law . . . at the current stage of our people's war against the Vietnamese aggressors" (see Major Political Developments, 1977–81, this ch.). It guaranteed "democratic freedoms" in political, religious, and economic life; a parliamentary system based on a popularly elected national assembly under UN supervision; a national army; and a national economy respecting "individual or family productive activity." The program reflected the Khmer Rouge's attempt to create a new image attuned to moderation, nationalism, and patriotism.

The KCP, synonymous with the Khmer Rouge, was the largest and strongest component of the CGDK in 1987. In December 1981, however, the party had announced its dissolution, citing the incompatibility of communism with Democratic Kampuchea's anti-Vietnamese united front line. It is difficult to ascertain whether the KCP was indeed disbanded because the Khmer Rouge always were secretive. The change of name to the Party of Democratic Kampuchea (PDK—see Appendix B) probably was a cosmetic gesture aimed at regaining international respectability following the party's imposition of a brutal regime on Cambodia from 1975 to 1978. The party's essential continuity was probable because the PDK leadership remained identical to that of its predecessor, the KCP, and the most important party leader—Pol Pot—exercised a shadowy, but powerful, influence behind the scenes in 1987 just as he had in the 1970s. Fragmentary accounts that reached the outside world hinted that, despite the name change, the party continued to treat refugees and peasants under its control with a arshness and an arbitrariness that showed little more concern for human rights than that of the former communist government of Cambodia.

In the name of Democratic Kampuchea, the Khmer Rouge issued a comprehensive conciliatory policy statement on July 6, 1985. It noted that the "Democratic Kampuchea side" expressed readiness to hold peace talks with Vietnam—but only after Vietnam's complete withdrawal from Cambodia—and indicated willingness to welcome "other Cambodians, including Heng Samrin and his group" as long as they no longer served the Vietnamese. Referring to the future of Cambodia, the Khmer Rouge side hinted for the first time that it might accept exclusion from a postwar government that might include the Heng Samrin regime. The Khmer Rouge also expressed greater openness to the establishment of a new Cambodia with a parliamentary and liberal capitalist system.

The Khmer Rouge's principal leaders, from July 1985, were Khieu Samphan, Ieng Sary, and Son Sen, in addition to Pol Pot who operated behind the scenes. Khieu Samphan was concurrently chairman of the State Presidium, prime minister of Democratic Kampuchea, provisional chairman of the PDFGNUK, and vice president in charge of foreign affairs of the CGDK. Son Sen served as commander in chief of the National Army of Democratic Kampuchea (NADK) and, in that capacity, as the Khmer Rouge chairman on the Coordinating Committee for National Defense. Ieng Sary served as Democratic Kampuchea's deputy prime minister in charge of foreign affairs and as its chairman on the Coordinating Committee for Economy and Finance. Other key figures included Ieng Thirith (also known as Khieu Thirith, reportedly related to Khieu Samphan), wife of Ieng Sary and head of Democratic Kampuchea's Red Cross Society; Ta Mok (also known as Chhet Choeun), vice chairman and chief of the general staff of the NADK and reportedly Pol Pot's right-hand man; and Nuon Chea (also known as Long Reth)—a political hardliner loyal to Pol Pot—chairman of the Standing Committee of the People's Representative Assembly of Democratic Kampuchea. Pol Pot, formerly prime minister, the KCP's general secretary, and commander in chief of the NADK, headed the Higher Institute for National Defense from September 1985 onward. Although reportedly in failing health and in Beijing-induced retirement in China in 1987, Pol Pot was still the power behind the scenes, according to some observers.

Ieng Sary's status in 1987 was unclear because he had not been seen in public since August 1985. For years Ieng Sary and Pol Pot were named by their adversaries as the two figures most responsible for mass murders in Cambodia, and Hanoi and the Heng Samrin regime insisted on their exclusion from any future political accommodation with the CGDK.

The Khmer People's National Liberation Front

From its inception in October 1979, the right-wing, pro-Western, former prime minister Son Sann, noted for his integrity and for his unyielding personality, led the Khmer People's National Liberation Front (KPNLF—see Appendix B). The organization was the strongest of the country's noncommunist resistance forces. Its key figures were formerly prominent in the administrations of Sihanouk and of republican leader Lon Nol. A number of displaced Cambodians sheltered in temporary camps on Thai soil near the Thai-Cambodian border backed the KPNLF, which had originated in the anti-Khmer Rouge movement of the 1960s. It controlled about 160,000 civilians confined at "Site 2," a camp in Thailand barely a kilometer from the Cambodian border. Most of the people in the camp were toughened survivors of the Pol Pot era, and they were therefore a potential pool from which to recruit armed rebels for the KPNLF.

In the 1984 to 1985 Vietnamese dry-season offensive, the KPNLF reportedly lost nearly a third of its 12,000 to 15,000 troops in battle and through desertions (see Khmer People's National Liberation Armed Forces, ch. 5). This setback, which was blamed on Son Sann for his alleged meddling in military matters, aggravated the long-standing personality conflicts within the KPNLF. Some KPNLF members criticized Son Sann's alleged tendency toward being dictatorial and unbending, and they questioned his lukewarm attitude toward the idea of a unified military command that included Sihanouk's ANS. Criticism mounted after reports that some of the organization's field commanders were involved in the black market and in other forms of corruption. Charges of human rights violations in the KPNLF-run camps for displaced persons further fueled internal dissension.

In December 1985, a dissident faction, wanting to limit Son Sann's role to ceremonial duties, announced the formation of a Provisional Central Committee of Salvation, which would be the new executive body of the KPNLF. The new group asserted that it had seized power from Son Sann in order to put an end to the internal problems of the KPNLF. Key members of the group included two KPNLF vice presidents: General Sak Sutsakhan, formerly Lon Nol's chief of staff; and General Dien Del, commander in chief and chief of staff of the KPNLF armed forces. Other notables were Abdul Gaffar Peangmeth and Hing Kunthon, two executive committee members whom Son Sann had dismissed earlier, and Huy Kanthoul, a former prime minister.

Son Sann countered with the formation of a new military command committee under General Prum Vith. He said, however, that General Sak would remain as commander in chief of the Joint Military Command (that now included the ANS), which was launched in January 1986, reportedly as a concession to the dissident group. Under a compromise worked out through a third party, General Sak regained his control of the armed forces in March 1986. Son Sann, then seventy-four years old, withdrew a previous threat to resign as CGDK prime minister. By early 1987, unity in the KPNLF had been restored, and Son Sann retained his presidency, while General Sak remained in full control of the military.

In a major reshuffle of the military high command in March, General Sak placed his deputy, Dien Del, in charge of anticorruption measures. The need for sweeping internal reform already had become a pressing issue in January 1987, when morale was so low that several hundred KPNLF soldiers defected to Sihanouk's ANS.

National United Front for an Independent, Peaceful, Neutral, and Cooperative Cambodia

Sihanouk's political organization, the National United Front for an Independent, Peaceful, Neutral, and Cooperative Cambodia (Front Uni National pour un Cambodge Indépendant Neutre, Pacifique, et Coopératif—FUNCINPEC—see Appendix B), emerged in 1987 as an increasingly popular resistance group, that drew support from a broad range of Cambodians. FUNCINPEC's indispensable asset was Sihanouk himself. He maintained residences in Pyongyang, in Mougins (located in southern France), and in Beijing. His son, Prince Norodom Ranariddh, was Sihanouk's sole authorized spokesman and was the head of FUNCINPEC's office in Bangkok. Among his confidants were Nhek Tioulong, a former cabinet minister under Sihanouk; Buor Hel, a cousin of Sihanouk's; and Chak Saroeun, FUNCINPEC secretary general. As vice president of the organization's Executive Committee and commander in chief of the ANS, former prime minister In Tam was also a key FUNCINPEC loyalist, but he resigned in March 1985 as the result of a feud with Prince Ranariddh.

FUNCINPEC had its share of internal problems. After In Tam's departure, Ranariddh, to the dismay of In Tam's supporters, became the ANS's temporary commander in chief. In January 1986, Sihanouk reshuffled the ANS high command, formally appointing his son commander in chief and, in addition, ANS chief of staff. Sihanouk also dismissed General Teap Ben, who had been chief of staff since 1981, for alleged embezzlement of refugee funds and for disloyalty; Teap Ben was relegated to the nominal post of deputy commander in chief of the Joint Military Command. In May 1986, Sihanouk, citing Ranariddh's heavy workload, was reported to be considering the appointment of General Toal Chay as the new ANS chief of staff. At the end of 1987, however, Sihanouk's son continued to hold the two key military posts.

The People's Republic of Kampuchea

The People's Republic of Kampuchea (PRK—see Appendix B) has "its ultimate origin," according to Cambodia expert Michael Vickery, "in the same revolutionary victory of 17 April 1975 as does the rival Pol Pot [Democratic Kampuchea] group." The PRK's patron since 1979 has been Vietnam, and in late 1987, many observers believed that the survival of the Phnom Penh regime depended on Vietnam's continued occupation of the country.

The PRK was established in January 1979 in line with the broad revolutionary program set forth by the Kampuchean (or Khmer) National United Front for National Salvation (KNUFNS—see Appendix B), which was formed on December 2, 1978, in a zone liberated from the Khmer Rouge. Of the front's fourteen central committee members, the top two leaders—Heng Samrin, president, and Chea Sim, vice president—were identified as "former" KCP officials. Ros Samay, secretary general of the KNUFNS, was a former KCP "staff assistant" in a military unit. The government of Democratic Kampuchea denounced the KNUFNS, as "a Vietnamese political organization with a Khmer name," because several of its key members had been affiliated with the KCP.

The initial objectives of the KNUFNS were to rally the people under its banner, to topple the Pol Pot regime, to adopt a new constitution for a "democratic state advancing toward socialism," to build mass organizations, and to develop a revolutionary army. Its foreign policy objectives included pursuing nonalignment, settling disputes with neighbors through negotiations, putting an end to "the border war with Vietnam" provoked by the Pol Pot regime, and opposing foreign military bases on Cambodian soil. On December 26, 1978, the day after the Vietnamese invasion, the KNUFNS reiterated its opposition to foreign military bases.

On January 1, 1979, the front's central committee proclaimed a set of "immediate policies" to be applied in the "liberated areas." One of these policies was to establish "people's self-management committees" in all localities. These committees would form the basic administrative structure for the Kampuchean People's Revolutionary Council (KPRC), decreed on January 8, 1979, as the central administrative body for the PRK. The KPRC served as the ruling body of the Heng Samrin regime until June 27, 1981, when a new Constitution required that it be replaced by a newly elected Council of Ministers. Pen Sovan became the new prime minister.

He was assisted by three deputy prime ministers—Hun Sen, Chan Si, and Chea Soth.

The Constitution

The Constitution of the PRK, promulgated on June 27, 1981, defines Cambodia as "a democratic state . . . gradually advancing toward socialism." The transition to socialism was to take place under the leadership of the Kampuchean (or Khmer) People's Revolutionary Party (KPRP—see Appendix B), a Marxist-Leninist party founded in June 1951 (see The Emergence of Nationalism, ch. 1). The Constitution explicitly defines the country's position in international relations. It places Cambodia within the Soviet Union's orbit. The country's primary enemies, according to the Constitution, are "the Chinese expansionists and hegemonists in Beijing, acting in collusion with United States imperialism and other powers."

The Constitution guarantees a broad range of civil liberties and fundamental rights. Citizens are to be equal before the law and are entitled to enjoy the same rights and duties regardless of sex, religion, or race. They have the right to participate in the political, economic, social, and cultural life of the country and to be paid according to the amount and quality of work they perform. Men and women are entitled to equal pay for equal work. All individuals—including monks and soldiers—over the age of eighteen may vote, and citizens over twenty-one may run for election. The Constitution also guarantees the inviolability of people and of their homes; privacy of correspondence; freedom from illegal search and arrest; the right to claim reparation for damages caused by illegal actions of the state, social organizations, and their personnel; and freedom of speech, of the press, and of assembly. The exercise of fundamental rights, however, is subject to certain restrictions. For example, an act may not injure the honor of other persons, nor should it adversely affect the mores and customs of society, or public order, or national security. In line with the principle of socialist collectivism, citizens are obligated to carry out "the state's political line and defend collective property."

The Constitution also addresses principles governing culture, education, social welfare, and public health. Development of language, literature, the arts, and science and technology is stressed, along with the need for cultural preservation, tourist promotion, and cultural cooperation with foreign countries.

Provisions for state organs are in the constitutional chapters dealing with the National Assembly, the Council of State, the Council of Ministers, the local people's revolutionary committees, and the judiciary. Fundamental to the operation of all public bodies is the principle that the KPRP serves as the most important political institution of the state. Intermediary linkages between the state bureaucracy and grass-roots activities are provided by numerous organizations affiliated with the KUFNCD (see The Kampuchean (or Khmer) United Front for National Construction and Defense, this ch.).

Government Structure

An administrative infrastructure, functioning under the KPRC, was more or less in place between 1979 and 1980. With the promulgation of the Constitution in June 1981, new organs, such as the National Assembly, the Council of State, and the Council of Ministers, assumed KPRC functions (see fig. 11). These new bodies evolved slowly. It was not until February 1982 that the National Assembly enacted specific laws for these bodies.

The National Assembly

The ''supreme organ of state power'' is the National Assembly, whose deputies are directly elected for five-year terms. The assembly's 117 seats were filled on May 1, 1981, the date of the PRK's first elections. (The KNUFNS had nominated 148 candidates.) The voter turnout was reported as 99.17 percent of the electorate, which was divided into 20 electoral districts.

During its first session, held from June 24 to June 27, the assembly adopted the new Constitution and elected members of the state organs set up under the Constitution. The assembly had been empowered to adopt or to amend the Constitution and the laws and to oversee their implementation; to determine domestic and foreign policies; to adopt economic and cultural programs and the state budget; and to elect or to remove its own officers and members of the Council of State and of the Council of Ministers. The assembly also was authorized to levy, revise, or abolish taxes; to decide on amnesties; and to ratify or to abrogate international treaties. As in other socialist states, the assembly's real function is to endorse the legislative and administrative measures initiated by the Council of State and by the Council of Ministers, both of which serve as agents of the ruling KPRP.

The National Assembly meets twice a year and may hold additional sessions if needed. During the periods between its sessions, legislative functions are handled by the Council of State. Bills are introduced by the Council of State, the Council of Ministers, the assembly's several commissions (legislative committees), chairman of the KUFNCD, and heads of other organizations. Individual deputies are not entitled to introduce bills.

Once bills, state plans and budgets, and other measures are introduced, they are studied first by the assembly's commissions, which deal with legislation, economic planning, budgetary matters, and cultural and social affairs. Then they go to the assembly for adoption. Ordinary bills are passed by a simple majority (by a show of hands). Constitutional amendments require a two-thirds majority. The Council of State must promulgate an adopted bill within thirty days of its passage. Another function of the assembly is to oversee the affairs of the Council of Ministers, which functions as the cabinet. Assembly members may make inquiries of cabinet officials, but they are not entitled to call for votes of confidence in the cabinet. Conversely, the Council of Ministers is not empowered to dissolve the National Assembly.

The Constitution states that in case of war or under "other exceptional circumstances," the five-year life of the Assembly may be extended by decree. In 1986 the assembly's term was extended for another five years, until 1991.

The Council of State

The National Assembly elects seven of its members to the Council of State. After the assembly's five-year term, council members remain in office until a new assembly elects a new council. The chairman of the council serves as the head of state, but the power to serve as ex officio supreme commander of the armed forces was deleted from the final draft of the Constitution.

The council's seven members are among the most influential leaders of the PRK. Between sessions of the National Assembly, the Council of State carries out the assembly's duties. It may appoint or remove—on the recommendation of the Council of Ministers—cabinet ministers, ambassadors, and envoys accredited to foreign governments. In addition, the Council of State organizes elections to the National Assembly, convenes regular and special sessions of the assembly, promulgates and interprets the Constitution and the laws, reviews judicial decisions, rules on pardons and on commutations of sentences, and ratifies or abrogates treaties. Foreign diplomatic envoys present their letters of accreditation to the Council of State.

The Council of Ministers

The government's top executive organ is the Council of Ministers, or cabinet, which in late 1987 was headed by Hun Sen (as it had been since January 1985). Apart from the prime minister

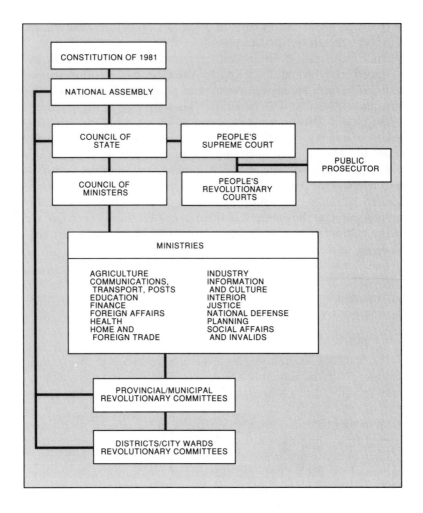

Figure 11. Government of the People's Republic of Kampuchea, 1987

(formally called chairman), the Council of Ministers has two deputy prime ministers (vice chairmen) and twenty ministers. The National Assembly elects the council's ministers for five-year terms. They are responsible collectively to the assembly. When the assembly is not in session, they are responsible to the Council of State. The prime minister must be a member of the assembly; other council members, however, need not be. The council's five-year term continues without hiatus until a new cabinet is formed after general elections.

The Council of Ministers meets weekly in an executive session, which is attended by the prime minister, the deputy prime ministers, and a chief of staff who is called the Minister in Charge of the Office of the Council of Ministers. The executive group prepares an agenda for deliberation and adoption by the council's monthly plenary session. (A secretary general of the Council of Ministers provides administrative support for the cabinet.) The executive group also addresses measures for implementing the plenary session's decisions, and it reviews and coordinates the work of government agencies at all levels. Decisions made in the executive sessions are "collective," whereas those in the plenary sessions are by a majority. Representatives of KUFNCD and other mass organizations, to which all citizens may belong, may be invited to attend plenary sessions of the council "when [it is] discussing important issues." These representatives may express their views but they are not allowed to vote.

Government ministries are in charge of agriculture; communications, transport, and posts; education; finance; foreign affairs; health; home and foreign trade; industry; information and culture; interior; justice; national defense; planning; and social affairs and invalids. In addition, the cabinet includes a minister for agricultural affairs and rubber plantations, who is attached to the Office of the Council of Ministers; a minister in charge of the Office of the Council of Ministers; a secretary general of the Office of the Council of Ministers, who is also in charge of transport and of Khmer-Thai border defense networks; a director of the State Affairs Inspectorate; and the president-director general of the People's National Bank of Kampuchea.

The Office of the Council of Ministers serves as the administrative nerve center of the government. Directed by its cabinet-rank minister, this office is supposed "to prepare, facilitate, coordinate, unify, and guide all activities of individual ministries and localities." Fiscal inspection of public institutions is the responsibility of the State Affairs Inspectorate, which has branch offices in all provinces.

The Judiciary

The restoration of law and order has been one of the more pressing tasks of the Heng Samrin regime. Since 1979 the administration of justice has been in the hands of people's revolutionary courts that were set up hastily in Phnom Penh and in other major provincial cities. A new law dealing with the organization of courts and with the Office of Public Prosecutor was promulgated in February 1982. Under this law, the People's Supreme Court became the highest court of the land.

The judicial system comprises the people's revolutionary courts, the military tribunals, and the public prosecutors' offices. The Council of State may establish additional courts to deal with special cases. The Council of Ministers, on the recommendations of local administrative bodies called people's revolutionary committees, appoints judges and public prosecutors. Two or three people's councillors (the equivalents of jurors or of assessors) assist the judges, and they have the same power as the judges in passing sentence (see Protection Under the Law, ch. 5).

Local People's Revolutionary Committees

In late 1987, the country was divided into eighteen provinces (*khet*) and two special municipalities (*krong*), Phnom Penh and Kampong Saom, which are under direct central government control. The provinces were subdivided into about 122 districts (*srok*), 1,325 communes (*khum*), and 9,386 villages (*phum*). The subdivisions of the municipalities were wards (*sangkat*).

An elective body, consisting of a chairman (president), one or more vice chairmen, and a number of committee members, runs each people's revolutionary committee. These elective bodies are chosen by representatives of the next lower level people's revolutionary committees at the provincial and district levels. At the provincial and district levels, where the term of office is five years, committee members need the additional endorsement of officials representing the KUFNCD and other affiliated mass organizations. At the commune and ward level, the members of the people's revolutionary committees are elected directly by local inhabitants for a three-year term.

Before the first local elections, which were held in February and March 1981, the central government appointed local committee officials. In late 1987, it was unclear whether the chairpersons of the local revolutionary committees reported to the Office of the Council of Ministers or to the Ministry of Interior.

The Media

The state controls printed and electronic communications media and regulates their content. The most authoritative print medium in 1987 was the ruling KPRP's biweekly journal, *Pracheachon* (The People), which was inaugurated in October 1985 to express the party's stand on domestic and international affairs. Almost as important, however, was the weekly of the KUFNCD, *Kampuchea*. The principal publication of the armed forces was the weekly *Kangtap Padevat* (Revolutionary Army). As of late 1987, Cambodia still had no daily newspaper.

Radio and television were under the direction of the Kampuchean Radio and Television Commission, created in 1983. In 1986 there were about 200,000 radio receivers in the country. The Voice of the Kampuchean People (VOKP) radio programs were broadcast in Khmer, Vietnamese, French, English, Lao, and Thai. With Vietnamese assistance, television broadcasting was instituted on a trial basis in December 1983 and then regularly at the end of 1984. As of March 1986, Television Kampuchea (TVK) operated two hours an evening, four days a week in the Phnom Penh area only. There were an estimated 52,000 television sets as of early 1986. In December 1986, Vietnam agreed to train Cambodian television technicians. The following month, the Soviet Union agreed to cooperate with Phnom Penh in the development of electronic media. Cambodian viewers began to receive Soviet television programs after March 1987, through a satellite ground station that the Soviet Union had built in Phnom Penh (see Telecommunications, ch. 3).

Beginning in 1979, the Heng Samrin regime encouraged people to read official journals and to listen to the radio every day. Widespread illiteracy and a scarcity of both print media and radio receivers, however, meant that few Cambodians could follow the government's suggestion. But even when these media were available, "cadres and combatants" in the armed forces, for example, were more interested in listening to music programs than in reading about "the situation and developments in the country and the world or articles on good models of good people."

The Kampuchean (or Khmer) People's Revolutionary Party

In late 1987, the Kampuchean (or Khmer) People's Revolutionary Party (KPRP—see Appendix B) continued to be the ruling Marxist-Leninist party of the PRK (see fig. 12). It is an offshoot of the Indochinese Communist Party (ICP—see Appendix B), which played a dominant role in Cambodian resistance against the French and the Japanese (see The French Colonial Period, ch. 1). Some leaders of the anticolonial Cambodian resistance, or Khmer Issarak (see Appendix B), had been members of the ICP, and they had helped found the KPRP in 1951. The party was formed after the decision by the ICP's Second Party Congress in February 1951 to dissolve itself and to establish three independent parties for Vietnam, Cambodia, and Laos. On September 30, 1960, the KPRP party was renamed the Workers' Party of Kampuchea (WPK—see Appendix B). Pol Pot emerged as the key figure. In 1966, shortly after Pol Pot returned from talks with Chinese leaders in Beijing, the party's name was changed to the KCP.

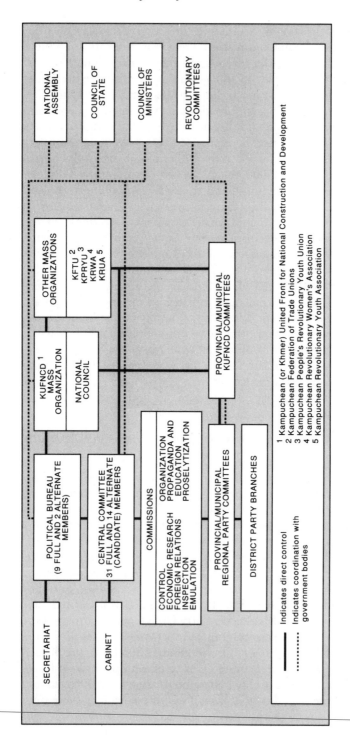

NATIONAL ASSEMBLY

COUNCIL OF STATE

COUNCIL OF MINISTERS

REVOLUTIONARY COMMITTEES

OTHER MASS ORGANIZATIONS

KFTU [2]
KPRYU [3]
KRWA [4]
KRUA [5]

KUFNCD [1] MASS ORGANIZATION

NATIONAL COUNCIL

PROVINCIAL/MUNICIPAL KUFNCD COMMITTEES

POLITICAL BUREAU (9 FULL AND 2 ALTERNATE MEMBERS)

CENTRAL COMMITTEE 31 FULL AND 14 ALTERNATE (CANDIDATE) MEMBERS

COMMISSIONS

CONTROL
ECONOMIC RESEARCH
FOREIGN RELATIONS
INSPECTION
EMULATION

ORGANIZATION
PROPAGANDA AND EDUCATION
PROSELYTIZATION

PROVINCIAL/MUNICIPAL REGIONAL PARTY COMMITTEES

DISTRICT PARTY BRANCHES

SECRETARIAT

CABINET

Indicates direct control

Indicates coordination with government bodies

1 Kampuchean (or Khmer) United Front for National Construction and Development
2 Kampuchean Federation of Trade Unions
3 Kampuchean People's Revolutionary Youth Union
4 Kampuchean Revolutionary Women's Association
5 Kampuchean Revolutionary Youth Association

Source: Based on information from Joint Publications Research Service (JPRS), *Southeast Asia Report*, JPRS–SEA–87–051, 10 April 1987, 1–150.

Figure 12. Organization of the Kampuchean (or Khmer) People's Revolutionary Party, 1987

The communist party in Cambodia has a history of bitter factional feuds. After the Second Party Congress in 1960 and the disappearance of party General Secretary Tou Samouth in 1962, the party split into pro-Soviet and pro-Chinese factions. The dominant faction, led by Pol Pot, adopted a position that was pro-Chinese and anti-Soviet. In January 1979, the split became irreversible as the pro-Vietnamese/pro-Soviet faction under Pen Sovan replaced the Pol Pot faction as the de facto ruler in Phnom Penh. The rival factions even disagreed on the founding date of the communist party in Cambodia: the Pol Pot faction, under Khieu Samphan, in late 1987, claimed September 30, 1960; however, the other group, the mainstream KPRP under Heng Samrin, continued to honor 1951 as the founding year.

The Heng Samrin faction held the Third Party Congress of what would later become the KPRP between January 5 and 8, 1979. Heng Samrin's faction claimed that it alone was the legitimate descendant of the communist party founded in 1951. Very little is known about the Third Party Congress (also known as the Congress for Party Reconstruction) except that Pen Sovan was elected first secretary of the Central Committee and that the party then had between sixty-two and sixty-six regular members.

Some key figures in the Pen Sovan leadership were former collaborators with Pol Pot, but this information, and the communist ideological convictions of the new leadership were not publicized because the leadership feared backlash from people who had been brutalized by the Pol Pot regime. Such concern was implicit in Pen Sovan's political report to the Fourth Party Congress held from May 26 to May 29, 1981. In the report, he was careful to distance the KPRP from Pol Pot's KCP, and he denounced the KCP as a traitor to the party and to the nation.

The KPRP decided at the Fourth Party Congress to operate "openly." This move seemed to reflect the leadership's growing confidence in its ability to stay in power. The move may have had a practical dimension as well because it involved the people more actively in the regime's effort to build the country's political and administrative infrastructure.

The Fourth Party Congress reviewed Pen Sovan's political report and defined the party's strategy for the next several years. The Congress adopted five "basic principles of the party line," which were to uphold the banners of patriotism and of international proletarian solidarity; to defend the country (the primary and sacred task of all people); to restore and to develop the economy and the culture in the course of gradual transition toward socialism; to strengthen military solidarity with Vietnam, Laos, the Soviet Union, and other socialist nations; and to develop "a firm Marxist-Leninist party." At the Congress it was decided that henceforth the party would be known as the KPRP, in order to distinguish it from "the reactionary Pol Pot party and to underline and reassert the community of the party's best traditions." The Fourth Party Congress also proclaimed its resolve to stamp out the "reactionary ultra-nationalist doctrine of Pol Pot," to emphasize a centralized government and collective leadership, and to reject personality cults. The "ultranationalist doctrine" issue was an allusion to Pol Pot's racist, anti-Vietnamese stance. The Congress, attended by 162 delegates, elected twenty-one members of the party Central Committee, who in turn elected Pen Sovan as general secretary and the seven members of the party inner circle to the Political Bureau. It also adopted a new statute for the party, but did not release the text.

According to Michael Vickery, veterans of the independence struggle of the 1946 to 1954 period dominated the party Central Committee. A majority of the Central Committee members had spent all or part of the years 1954 to 1970 in exile in Vietnam or in the performance of "duties abroad."

The KPRP's pro-Vietnamese position did not change when Heng Samrin suddenly replaced Pen Sovan as party leader on December 4, 1981. Pen Sovan, who was reportedly flown to Hanoi under Vietnamese guard, was "permitted to take a long rest," but observers believed that he was purged for not being sufficiently pro-Vietnamese. In any case, the new general secretary won Hanoi's endorsement by acknowledging Vietnam's role as senior partner in the Cambodian-Vietnamese relationship. The party recognized the change in leadership symbolically by changing the official founding date of the KPRP from February 19, 1951, to June 28, 1951, in deference to the Vietnam Workers' Party (Dang Lao Dong Viet Nam), which was established in March 1951.

In mid-1981, the KPRP was essentially a skeletal organization. It had few party branches except for those in Phnom Penh, in Kampong Saom, and in the eighteen provincial capitals. Party membership was estimated at between 600 and 1,000, a considerable increase over 1979 but still only a fraction of the number of cadres needed to run the party and the government. In 1981 several of the 18 provinces had only 1 party member each, and Kampong Cham, the largest province with a population of more than 1 million, had only 30 regular members, according to Cambodia specialist Ben Kiernan.

The party held its Fifth Party Congress from October 13 to October 16, 1985, to reflect on the previous five years and to chart a new course for the next several years. The party's membership had increased to 7,500 regulars (4,000 new members joined in 1985 alone). The party had an additional pool of 37,000 "core" members from which it could recruit tested party regulars. There were only 4,000 core members in mid-1981. According to General Secretary Heng Samrin's political report, the KPRP had twenty-two regional committees and an undisclosed number of branches, circles, and cells in government agencies, armed forces units, internal security organs, mass organizations, enterprises, factories, and farms. The report expressed satisfaction with party reconstruction since 1981, especially with the removal of the "danger of authoritarianism" and the restoration of the principles of democratic centralism and of collective leadership. It pointed out "some weaknesses" that had to be overcome, however. For example, the party was "still too thin and weak" at the district and the grass-roots levels. Ideological work lagged and lacked depth and consistency; party policies were implemented very slowly, if at all, with few, if any, timely steps to rectify failings; and party cadres, because of their propensities for narrow-mindedness, arrogance, and bureaucratism, were unable to win popular trust and support. Another major problem was the serious shortage of political cadres, economic and managerial cadres, and technical cadres. Still another problem that had to be addressed "in the years to come" was the lack of a documented history of the KPRP. Heng Samrin's political report stressed the importance of party history for understanding "the good traditions of the party."

The report to the Fifth Congress noted that Heng Samrin's administration, in coordination with "Vietnamese volunteers," had destroyed "all types" of resistance guerrilla bases. The report also struck a sobering note: the economy remained backward and unbalanced, with its material and technical bases still below pre-war levels, and the country's industries were languishing from lack of fuel, spare parts, and raw materials. Transition toward socialism, the report warned, would take "dozens of years."

To hasten the transition to socialism, the Fifth Congress unveiled the PRK's First Plan, covering the years 1986 to 1990 (see Economic Role of the KPRP, ch. 3). The program included the addition of the "private economy" to the three sectors of the economy mentioned in the Constitution (the state sector, collective sector, and the family sector). Including the private economy was necessary because of the "very heavy and very complex task" that lay ahead in order to transform the "nonsocialist components" of the economy to an advanced stage. According to the political report submitted to the congress, mass mobilization of the population was considered crucial to the successful outcome of the First Plan. The report also noted the need to cultivate "new socialist men" if Cambodia were to succeed in its nation-building. These men were supposed to be loyal to the fatherland and to socialism; to respect manual labor, production, public property, and discipline; and to possess "scientific knowledge."

Heng Samrin's political report also focused on foreign affairs. He recommended that Phnom Penh strengthen its policy of alliance with Vietnam, Laos, the Soviet Union, and other socialist countries. He stressed—as Pen Sovan had in May 1981—that such an alliance was, in effect, "a law" that guaranteed the success of the Cambodian revolution. At the same time, he urged the congress and the Cambodian people to spurn "narrow-minded chauvinism, every opportunistic tendency, and every act and attitude infringing on the friendship" between Cambodia and its Indochinese neighbors. (He was apparently alluding to the continued Cambodian sensitivity to the presence of Vietnamese troops and of about 60,000 Vietnamese settlers in Cambodia. CGDK sources maintained that there were really about 700,000 Vietnamese settlers in the country.) The KPRP's three objectives for the period 1986 to 1990 were to demonstrate military superiority "along the border and inside the country" for complete elimination of all anti-PRK activities; to develop political, military, and economic capabilities; and to strengthen special relations with Vietnam as well as mutual cooperation with other fraternal countries. Before Heng Samrin's closing address on October 16, the 250 party delegates to the congress elected a new Central Committee of 45 members (31 full members and 14 alternates). The Central Committee in turn elected Heng Samrin as general secretary, a new Political Bureau (nine full members and two alternates), a five-member Secretariat, and seven members of the Central Committee Control Commission.

After the Fifth Congress, the party's organizational work was intensified substantially. The KPRP claimed that by the end of 1986 it had more than 10,000 regular members and 40,000 candidate members who were being groomed for regular status.

The Kampuchean (or Khmer) United Front for National Construction and Defense

The ruling KPRP grew slowly in membership over the years and was supported by a mass organization from which it drew its applicants and support. This organization, known as the KNUFNS, had been formed in late 1978 with Vietnamese backing, as a common front against the Pol Pot regime in Phnom Penh. The organization underwent various name changes, emerging eventually in late 1981 as the Kampuchean (or Khmer) United Front for National Construction and Defense (KUFNCD—see Appendix B). In the meantime, its role in the political life of the nation had been officially established in the Constitution, which states in Article 3 that "The Kampuchean Front for National Construction and the revolutionary mass organizations constitute a solid support base of the state, encouraging the people to fulfill their revolutionary tasks."

The KUFNCD's specific missions were to transmit party policies to the masses, to act as an ombudsman, and to mobilize the people around the regime's efforts to consolidate the so-called "worker-peasant alliance." The front's cadres were required to stay in close touch with the people, to report their needs and problems to authorities, and to conduct mass campaigns to generate support for the regime, or to lead "emulation" drives to spur the population to greater efforts in pursuit of specific goals. The cadres were also responsible for organizing networks of KUFNCD activists in villages and in communes and for coordinating their functions with cadres of various mass organizations.

The KUFNCD also was responsible for conducting "activities of friendship," which were aimed at improving the climate for close cooperation with "the Vietnamese people and the Vietnamese army and experts." Another major function of the front was to reeducate Buddhist monks so that they would "discard the narrow-minded views of dividing themselves into groups and factions" and would participate more actively in the revolutionary endeavors of the KUFNCD.

Among the more important mass organizations affiliated with the KUFNCD were the Kampuchean Federation of Trade Unions (KFTU—62,000 members in December 1983), officially described as "the training school of the working class for economic and administrative management"; and the Kampuchean People's Revolutionary Youth Union (KPRYU), an important reservoir of candidate members for the KPRP and "a school of Marxism" for people between the ages of fifteen and twenty-six. As of March 1987, when the Youth Union held its Second National Congress, there were more than 50,000 members in villages, factories, enterprises, hospitals, schools, public offices, and the armed forces. Other mass organizations included the Kampuchean Revolutionary Youth Association (KRYA), an 800,000-member group for children (aged 9 to 16); the Kampuchean Young Pioneers Organization (KYPO), a 450,000-member group for pre-schoolers under the general guidance of the KPRYU and the KRYA; and the Kampuchean Revolutionary Women's Association (KRWA), which claimed 923,000 members as of October 1983. All these organizations held rallies to arouse public awareness on national commemorative occasions such as the Kampuchea-Vietnam Solidarity Day on February 18, the Day of Hatred ("against the genocidal Pol Pot-Ieng Sary-Khieu Samphan clique and the Sihanouk-Son Sann reactionary groups") observed on May 20, and the day of solidarity between the people and the army on June 19.

Foreign Affairs

In 1987 the two Cambodian regimes continued to compete for respect and for legitimacy, and they both continued to proclaim a foreign policy based on peaceful coexistence, neutrality, and nonalignment. The CGDK, however, had the major share of international recognition as de jure representative of Cambodia, even though it did not possess supreme authority within the borders of Cambodia. De facto control of national territory was in the hands of the PRK, but, because the PRK had originated during the Vietnamese invasion and occupation of Cambodia, it was unable to gain legitimacy in the eyes of the United Nations. The United Nations would not validate an illegal act consummated by force of arms (see Cambodia in Turmoil, this ch.). Recognizing the PRK regime would be contrary to the UN Charter, which calls for peaceful settlement of all conflicts and for nonintervention in the internal affairs of sovereign and independent nations. In July 1982, the Phnom Penh regime, recognizing the futility of challenging the legality of the CGDK, announced that "in the immediate future" it would not seek "to reclaim the Kampuchean seat at the United Nations."

The Coalition's Strategy

The CGDK had formal diplomatic relations at the ambassadorial level with Bangladesh, China, Egypt, Malaysia, North Korea, Pakistan, Senegal, Somalia, Sudan, and Yugoslavia (as of late 1987). Chinese and North Korean relations with the coalition occasionally were in the limelight in the 1980s—Chinese relations because of China's role as the principal donor of material and military assistance to the CGDK, and North Korean relations because Sihanouk maintained his "private" residence in Pyongyang (a palace built for him by the president of North Korea, Kim Il Sung, in the early 1970s). Bangkok also was mentioned frequently in Cambodian foreign affairs because it had hosted meetings of CGDK leaders with Chinese and Thai officials regarding events in Indochina. Bangkok was also the site for the Office of Samdech Norodom Sihanouk's Personal Representative for Cambodia and Asia, which

Former royal palace, Phnom Penh
Courtesy Bill Herod

was headed by Sihanouk's son Prince Norodom Ranariddh. This office was Sihanouk's informal embassy.

The CGDK had a permanent mission—consisting of representatives from all three of the CGDK partners—to the United Nations in New York. In formal debates in the UN General Assembly, however, the chief delegate of the Khmer Rouge group represented the CGDK because the coalition's June 1982 agreement said that the diplomatic envoys of Democratic Kampuchea who were in office at that time would remain in their posts. The permanent mission became active each September during the UN General Assembly's opening session. Mission representatives sought to obtain reaffirmation of the General Assembly's September 1979 resolution calling for an unconditional withdrawal of "foreign" (Vietnamese) troops from Cambodia and for Cambodian self-determination free of external constraints. In 1979 ninety-one nations backed the resolution, twenty-one nations opposed it, and twenty-nine abstained. In 1987, although 117 nations reaffirmed the same resolution, the number of countries which opposed it remained essentially unchanged. Some countries, such as the United States, supported resolutions but did not recognize Democratic Kampuchea, the CGDK, or the PRK. Britain and Australia withdrew recognition of Democratic Kampuchea in December 1979, and in October 1980, respectively, but both supported the CGDK's effort to get the Vietnamese

223

troops out of Cambodia and to determine its future freely under UN supervision.

Phnom Penh and Its Allies

Following its establishment, the primary foreign relationships of the PRK were those with Vietnam, Laos, the Soviet Union, and the countries of Eastern Europe. The PRK had only one resident mission in a noncommunist state, the one in India. The PRK also maintained diplomatic relations with about twenty other Third World nations, including Afghanistan, Angola, the Congo, Ethiopia, Libya, Madagascar, Mozambique, Nicaragua, and Panama. In 1980 about thirty countries recognized the PRK; seven years later, that number had not changed. In 1987 nearly eighty countries recognized Democratic Kampuchea.

The Search for Peace

The most intractable foreign policy question facing the rival Cambodian regimes in the 1980s was that of how to establish an independent, neutral, and nonaligned Cambodia under a set of terms agreeable to all those, both at home and abroad, who were interested. Despite differing perceptions of potential gains and losses, all parties to the Cambodian dispute were striving for reconciliation. This was a positive sign, especially because in 1979 and in 1980, no one, except perhaps Sihanouk, believed that reconciliation was possible.

In the first two years of the Cambodian crisis, the rival Cambodian regimes had different priorities. The Heng Samrin regime's overriding concern was to consolidate its political and its territorial gains, while relying on the Vietnamese to take the lead in foreign affairs and in national security. The political price of this external dependence was high because it contributed to Phnom Penh's image as a Vietnamese puppet. Vietnam also paid a price for its assertion that it had intervened only "at the invitation" of Heng Samrin "to defend the gains of the revolution they have won . . . at a time when the Beijing expansionists are colluding with the United States." Phnom Penh and Hanoi also asserted speciously that political turmoil inside Cambodia constituted a civil war and was, therefore, of no concern to outsiders. Vietnam's attempts to shield the Cambodian crisis from external scrutiny led its noncommunist neighbors to suspect that Hanoi was finally moving to fulfill its historical ambition of dominating all of Indochina.

Anti-Heng Samrin resistance groups pursued an opposite course. Their strategy was to internationalize the Cambodian question—with political support from China and from the ASEAN nations—as a case of unprovoked Vietnamese aggression, in order to put pressure on Vietnam and to undermine the legitimacy of the Heng Samrin administration. At the same time, the resistance groups sought to destabilize the Heng Samrin regime by challenging the Vietnamese occupation forces. The regime in Phnom Penh, with support from Vietnam and from the Soviet Union, nevertheless continued to consolidate its gains.

In 1981 the rival camps pressed on with their confrontational tactics. The anti-Vietnamese resistance factions, despite their long-standing, internal feuds, began to negotiate among themselves for unity against their common enemy. On the diplomatic front, they worked closely with ASEAN to convene the UN-sponsored International Conference on Kampuchea, which took place from July 13 to July 17, 1981, in New York. The conference, attended by representatives from seventy-nine countries and by observers from fifteen countries, adopted a declaration of principles for settling the Cambodian crisis. The central elements of the declaration were those contained in the UN General Assembly resolution of 1979 and in the proposals for Cambodian peace announced by the ASEAN countries in October 1980. The declaration called for the withdrawal of all foreign forces in the shortest possible time under the supervision and the verification of a UN peacekeeping-observer group; for arrangements to ensure that armed Cambodian factions would not prevent or disrupt free elections; for measures to maintain law and order during the interim before free elections could be held and a new government established; for free elections under UN auspices; for the continuation of Cambodia's status as a neutral and nonaligned state; and for a declaration by the future elected government that Cambodia would not pose a threat to other countries, especially to neighboring states. The declaration also called on the five permanent members of the UN Security Council (China, France, the Soviet Union, Britain, and the United States) and on all other states to pledge to respect Cambodia's independence, its territorial integrity, and its neutral status and to declare that they would neither draw Cambodia into any military alliance, nor introduce foreign troops into the country, nor establish any military bases there. The declaration's principles were reaffirmed in successive UN General Assembly resolutions, and they formed the basis of the ASEAN-sponsored framework for resolving the Cambodian question in the 1980s.

Since 1979 the ASEAN countries have played a significant role on behalf of the Cambodian resistance factions. Individually and collectively, through the annual conferences of their foreign ministers, these countries consistently have stressed the importance of Vietnam's withdrawal as a precondition for a comprehensive political settlement of the Cambodian question. They have rejected all moves by Hanoi and Phnom Penh that were aimed at legitimizing the Vietnamese occupation of Cambodia and the Heng Samrin regime. Together with China, they also were architects of the Coalition Government of Democratic Kampuchea.

Phnom Penh's principal foreign policy spokesman has been Vietnam, and its major diplomatic moves have been coordinated by and proclaimed by the annual conference of foreign ministers of the three Indochinese states meeting consecutively in Hanoi (or Ho Chi Minh City), in Phnom Penh, and in Vientiane. Hanoi's position on Cambodia has been that the "so-called Kampuchean problem is but the consequence of Chinese expansionism and hegemonism," that Vietnam's military presence in Cambodia was defensive because it was meeting the Chinese threat to Cambodia and to Vietnam, and that Hanoi would withdraw from Cambodia when the Chinese threat no longer existed.

Thailand's stance on the Cambodian issue has been of particular concern to Phnom Penh and to Hanoi. ASEAN initially maintained the position that Thailand was not a party to the Cambodian conflict but an "affected bystander" entitled to adopt a policy of neutrality. Hanoi and Phnom Penh denounced that posture as "sham neutrality" and accused Thailand of colluding with China; they alleged that Thailand allowed shipment of Chinese arms through its territory to the "remnants of [the] Pol Pot-Ieng Sary clique," which was operating inside the Thai border. They also claimed that Bangkok sheltered and armed Pol Pot's guerrillas and other Cambodian "reactionaries."

Nevertheless, the Heng Samrin regime made friendly overtures to Bangkok. In June 1980, for example, it proposed a meeting to discuss resuming "normal relations" and turning their common border into "a border of friendship and peace." The Heng Samrin regime stated that its primary concern was the elimination of "all hostile acts" between the two countries and that it was willing to forget the past and "all the provocations launched by Thailand against Cambodia." Thailand replied that talks with the Heng Samrin regime would solve nothing. Besides, Thai officials said, such talks would lend an inappropriate appearance of recognition to the Phnom Penh regime. They also stressed that Vietnam had to withdraw from Cambodia before constructive talks could take place.

In July 1980, the three Indochinese states proposed the signing of multilateral or bilateral treaties of peaceful coexistence, non-aggression, and noninterference among themselves and Thailand.

*Independence monument
in Phnom Penh
Courtesy Mr. and Mrs.
Robert E. Hammerquist*

They added that the treaties should also be signed by "other Southeast Asian countries." The proposal also called for the creation of a Southeast Asian zone of peace and stability and for a demilitarized border zone between Cambodia and Thailand. Bangkok, however, viewed the proposal as an attempt to divert international attention from the fundamental question of Vietnamese occupation and as a gambit to get indirect or "back-door" recognition for the Heng Samrin regime.

The Indochinese states sought to open a dialogue with the ASEAN countries in 1981 by proposing a regional conference, which was to be attended also by observers such as the UN secretary general and by representatives from several countries. The proposal was Hanoi's way of internationalizing the Cambodian issue: Vietnam would be able to link its role in Cambodia to the roles of Thailand and of China in aiding the anti-Vietnamese resistance groups. To highlight the linkage, Hanoi made two suggestions: first, the regional conference could address "the Cambodian question" if the Thai and Chinese connections also were discussed; and second, Vietnam would immediately withdraw some of its troops if and when Thailand stopped aiding the resistance groups and if the UN withdrew its recognition of Democratic Kampuchea.

In July 1982, Hanoi, aware that no one was taking it seriously, departed from its previous position. It announced that it had gone

227

ahead with a partial withdrawal and now demanded only that Thailand promise to stop aiding Khmer insurgents. At that time, the Indochinese foreign ministers revealed that "in the immediate future," the PRK would not plan to reclaim the Cambodian seat at the United Nations if the Pol Pot clique were expelled from that organization. The Thai government dismissed Hanoi's statement as a rhetorical concession designed only to mislead the world and characterized the partial withdrawal as nothing more than a disguised troop rotation.

At the first Indochinese summit held on February 22 and February 23, 1983, in Vientiane, the participants declared that all Vietnamese "volunteers" would be withdrawn when external threats to Cambodia no longer existed, but that Hanoi, would reassess its option to return to Cambodia if a new threat emerged after it had withdrawn from the country.

Hanoi contended that its partial withdrawal was a positive first step toward eventual restoration of peace in Cambodia, but some observers felt that the real reason for the withdrawal was Hanoi's realization that a deadlock over the Cambodian issue would create too much of a drain on its limited resources. Another likely reason for the withdrawal was the growing Cambodian irritation with the movement of Vietnamese nationals into Cambodia's fertile lands around the Tonle Sap (see Migration and Refugees, ch. 2). This population migration was a potential source of renewed ethnic conflict.

In July 1983, the Indochinese foreign ministers denied "the slanderous allegation of China, the United States, and a number of reactionary circles within the ASEAN countries" that Vietnam was aiding and abetting Vietnamese emigration to Cambodia. (Khmer Rouge sources claimed that as of 1987, between 600,000 and 700,000 Vietnamese immigrants were in Cambodia; the Heng Samrin regime put the number at about 60,000.)

In September 1983, ASEAN foreign ministers issued a joint "Appeal for Kampuchean Independence," proposing a phased Vietnamese withdrawal, coupled with an international peacekeeping force and with assistance in rebuilding areas vacated by the Vietnamese. Hanoi rejected the appeal, however, seeking instead a position of strength from which it could dictate terms for a settlement. Vietnam launched a major dry-season offensive in 1984 in an attempt to crush all resistance forces permanently. The offensive destroyed most, if not all, resistance bases.

In January 1985, the Indochinese foreign ministers claimed that the Cambodian situation was unfolding to their advantage and that the Cambodian question would be settled in five to ten years with or without negotiations. At that time, PRK Prime Minister Hun Sen revealed Phnom Penh's readiness to hold peace talks with Sihanouk and with Son Sann, but only if they agreed to dissociate themselves from Pol Pot. On March 12, Hun Sen proposed a dialogue with rival factions under a six-point plan. The proposal called for the removal of the Pol Pot clique from all political and military activities; for a complete Vietnamese withdrawal; for national reconciliation and for free elections under UN supervision; for peaceful coexistence in Southeast Asia; for cessation of external interference in Cambodian affairs; and for the establishment of an international supervisory and control commission to oversee the implementation of agreements. Shortly afterward, Hanoi stressed that the question of foreign military bases in Cambodia was an issue that could be negotiated only between Vietnam and Cambodia. Hanoi also signaled that the Khmer Rouge regime could participate in the process of Cambodian self-determination only if it disarmed itself and broke away from the Pol Pot clique.

From "Proximity Talks" to a "Cocktail Party"

The conciliatory gestures of Hanoi and of Phnom Penh were part of a spate of proposals and counterproposals made in 1985. On April 9, Malaysia suggested "proximity," or indirect, talks between the CGDK and the Heng Samrin regime. Vietnam, the PRK, and the Soviet Union reacted favorably. Sihanouk voiced "personal" support for indirect negotiations. He was, however, uncertain whether his CGDK partners and unnamed foreign powers would go along with the Malaysian proposal because such talks, indirect as they might be, not only would imply de facto recognition of the Phnom Penh regime but also would obscure the question of Vietnamese occupation. ASEAN's deputy foreign ministers met in Bangkok in May, nevertheless; they endorsed the Malaysian plan and referred the matter to CGDK's representatives in Bangkok. At the time of the ASEAN meeting, Sihanouk released a memorandum that called for unconditional peace talks among all Cambodian factions and for the formation of a reconciliation government comprising both the CGDK and the Heng Samrin regime.

During the ensuing diplomatic exchanges, the Malaysian plan was discarded. The ASEAN foreign ministers, who met in Kuala Lumpur from July 8 to July 9, 1985, adopted a Thai compromise proposal that called for "a form of indirect or proximity talks" between the CGDK and Vietnam. The proposal noted that the Heng Samrin regime could attend the talks only as part of the Vietnamese delegation. The CGDK, China, and the United States backed the

Thai proposal, but Phnom Penh and Hanoi rejected it as a scheme to restore the Pol Pot faction to power.

In yet another attempt to break the Cambodian impasse, Indonesia offered in November 1985 to host an informal "cocktail party" for all warring Cambodian factions. (At that time Indonesia served as ASEAN's official "interlocutor" with Vietnam.) Indonesia apparently had concluded that such an informal gathering was timely in view of two recent developments: the Khmer Rouge announcement in July that it would acquiesce, if necessary, to being excluded from a future Cambodian coalition government; and Hanoi's disclosure in August that it would complete its withdrawal from Cambodia by 1990 (five years sooner than had been indicated in its April 1985 announcement), even in the absence of a political settlement on the Cambodian issue at that time. Another notable development was the Khmer Rouge disclosure in September that Pol Pot had stepped down from his post as commander in chief of the armed forces to take up a lesser military post. On December 30, Khieu Samphan stated that Pol Pot's political-military role would cease permanently upon Hanoi's consenting to complete its withdrawal by the end of 1990. Hanoi, in an apparent departure from its previous stand, pledged that its pullout would be completed as soon as the Khmer Rouge forces disarmed.

In 1986 the Cambodian stalemate continued amid further recriminations and new conciliatory gestures. On March 17, the CGDK issued an eight-point peace plan that included the Heng Samrin regime in a projected four-party Cambodian government. The plan called for a two-phase Vietnamese withdrawal; for a cease-fire to allow an orderly withdrawal—both the cease-fire and the withdrawal to be supervised by a UN observer group, for the initiation of negotiations, following the first phase of the withdrawal, and for the formation of an interim four-party coalition government with Sihanouk as president and Son Sann as prime minister. According to the plan, the coalition government would then hold free elections under UN supervision to set up a liberal, democratic, and nonaligned Cambodia, the neutrality of which would be guaranteed by the UN for the first two or three years. The new Cambodia would welcome aid from all countries for economic reconstruction and would sign a nonaggression and peaceful coexistence treaty with Vietnam. Hanoi and Phnom Penh denounced the plan and labeled it as a vain attempt by China to counter the PRK's "rapid advance." Sihanouk shared some of the misgivings about the plan, fearing that, without sufficient safeguards, the Khmer Rouge would dominate the quadripartite government that emerged. Perhaps to allay such misgivings, China signaled the possibility of ending its aid to the Khmer Rouge if Vietnam withdrew from Cambodia.

In late October 1986, Hanoi, through an Austrian intermediary, suggested two-stage peace negotiations to Sihanouk. In the first stage, there were to be preliminary talks in Vienna among all Cambodian parties, including the Khmer Rouge (Pol Pot, however, was to be excluded). The second phase was to be an international conference that included the contending Cambodian factions, as well as Vietnam, and other interested countries. Sihanouk responded with a counterproposal that called for his meeting with a top-level Vietnamese leader. This meeting was to be followed by an all-Cambodian session and then by an international conference. According to unconfirmed reports, Pol Pot, now gravely ill, had been transferred to Beijing shortly after Hanoi's offer to Sihanouk. If these reports were true, Pol Pot's role within the Khmer Rouge camp may have ended with his illness.

A new phase in the Cambodian peace strategies began in 1987. At the beginning of the year Hanoi renewed its October bid to Sihanouk. Hanoi appeared eager to seek a way out of the Cambodian imbroglio, but continued to argue that Vietnam had "security interests" in Cambodia and that China was the main threat to Southeast Asia. It also was evident that Hanoi was attempting to split ASEAN's consensus on Cambodia by claiming that Indonesia and Malaysia had a correct view of the Chinese threat while rejecting the view of Thailand and Singapore that Vietnam was ASEAN's principal nemesis in the region.

In addition, as Soviet interest in Cambodia grew, there was speculation among observers that Moscow might involve itself in the quest for a negotiated settlement. A visit to Phnom Penh in March 1987 by Soviet foreign minister Eduard Shevardnadze signaled a departure from Moscow's long-standing position that it was only "a third party" to the Cambodian conflict. It also constituted tacit acknowledgment that the Soviet Union had been supporting—at least indirectly—Vietnam's presence in Cambodia through economic and military aid, which totaled the equivalent of US$2 billion per year (see Foreign Trade and Aid, ch. 3; Military Developments in Postwar Cambodia, ch. 5).

The Heng Samrin regime became more assertive in articulating its policy options than it had been before. It became known in early April that Hun Sen had sent word to Sihanouk suggesting a meeting in Canberra, or Paris, or Stockholm at the prince's convenience. (It was Hun Sen's second effort to initiate such a dialogue. In 1984 he had proposed a similar meeting, but Sihanouk had declined because of objections by China and by his CGDK partners.)

Sihanouk's one-year leave of absence from the CGDK, effective May 7, 1987, was a good sign for Cambodia because he could now freely explore possibilities for a settlement without squabbling with his coalition partners. On June 23, Sihanouk agreed to see Hun Sen in Pyongyang, but two days later, hours after Chinese acting premier Wan Li had met with Sihanouk's wife, Princess Monique, Sihanouk abruptly canceled the meeting. China apparently objected to any negotiations as long as Vietnam kept troops in Cambodia. Sihanouk said in July that he preferred to talk first with a Vietnamese leader because the Cambodian conflict was between the Khmer and the Vietnamese and not among the Cambodian factions. He said that he would not mind meeting with Hun Sen, however, as long as the initiative for such a meeting came from Hun Sen or his regime and not from Hanoi.

Events occurred rapidly in the summer of 1987. In June UN secretary general Javier Perez de Cuellar issued a compromise plan that called for a phased Vietnamese withdrawal; for national reconciliation leading to the formation of a new coalition government with Sihanouk as president; for a complete Vietnamese pullout and for free elections; and for special provisions to deal with the armed Cambodian factions. On July 1, while ostensibly on vacation in the Soviet Union, Hun Sen had talks with Foreign Minister Eduard Shevardnadze. The two agreed that "the realities which prevail in the region" must not be ignored in any plan for Cambodian settlement. On July 25, the Khmer Rouge faction publicly disavowed any intention to return to power at the expense of other factions and stated that to do so would jeopardize its national union policy and would alienate "friends in the world."

Hanoi, meanwhile, continued to put off discussions about its presence in Cambodia, thereby forcing the resistance to deal directly with the Heng Samrin regime. Between July 27 and July 29, Vietnam's foreign minister, Nguyen Co Thach, conferred with his Indonesian counterpart in Ho Chi Minh City and called for "an informal meeting" or cocktail party of all Cambodian factions without any preconditions. The cocktail party, to be held in Jakarta, was to be followed by a conference of all concerned countries, including Vietnam. On July 30, Heng Samrin journeyed to Moscow to consult with Soviet leader Mikhail S. Gorbachev. Then in an interview published in the Italian Communist Party daily *L'Unita* on August 12, Hun Sen sought to exonerate the Soviet Union from blame for Cambodia's plight and instead blamed China for the country's difficulties. Referring to the proposed meeting with

*Phnom Penh Hill
Courtesy Mr. and Mrs.
Robert E. Hammerquist*

Sihanouk, Hun Sen insinuated that Sihanouk had "bosses" who would not let him engage freely in a dialogue. On August 13, the Indochinese governments endorsed "the Ho Chi Minh formula" (Hanoi's term for Indonesia's original cocktail party idea) as a significant "breakthrough" toward a peaceful settlement in Cambodia.

The ASEAN foreign ministers met informally on August 16 to discuss the cocktail party idea, and they forged a compromise that papered over some of the differences among the six member states concerning the Cambodia situation. Even this attempt to achieve unanimity proved fruitless, however, as Hanoi rejected the ASEAN suggestion.

The Sihanouk-Hun Sen Meeting

Hun Sen's April 1987 proposal for a talk with Sihanouk was resurrected in August when the prince sent a message to Hun Sen through the Palestine Liberation Organization's ambassador in Pyongyang. Sihanouk was hopeful that his encounter with Hun Sen would lead to another UN-sponsored Geneva conference on Indochina, which, he believed, would assure a political settlement that would allow Vietnam and the Soviet Union to save face. Such a conference, Sihanouk maintained, should include the UN secretary general, representatives of the five permanent members of the UN Security Council, Laos, Vietnam, and the four Cambodian factions. He also suggested the inclusion of ASEAN countries,

233

members of the defunct International Control Commission (India, Canada, and Poland), and other concerned parties.

The Heng Samrin regime had apparently envisioned a meeting between Sihanouk and Hun Sen when it announced on August 27 a "policy on national reconciliation." While artfully avoiding the mention of Vietnam, the policy statement called for talks with the three resistance leaders but not with "Pol Pot and his close associates." An appeal to overseas Cambodians to support Phnom Penh's economic and national defense efforts and assurances that Cambodians who had served the insurgent factions would be welcomed home and would be assisted in resuming a normal life and in participating in the political process were key features of the policy. The regime also expressed for the first time its readiness to negotiate the issue of Cambodian refugees in Thailand. The offer to negotiate undercut the resistance factions, which, Phnom Penh contended, were exploiting displaced Cambodians by using them against the Heng Samrin regime for military and political purposes.

Resistance leaders questioned Phnom Penh's sincerity in promulgating its policy of reconciliation and were uncertain how to respond. At their annual consultation in Beijing, they and their Chinese hosts predictably called for a Vietnamese pullout as a precondition to a negotiated settlement. Sihanouk, however, launching a gambit of his own through Cambodian émigrés in Paris, called for reconciliation among all Khmer factions. The initiative met with a favorable, but qualified, response from PRK Prime Minister Hun Sen and, in early October, the Phnom Penh government unveiled its own five-point plan for a political settlement. The PRK proposals envisioned peace talks between the rival Cambodian camps and "a high position [for Sihanouk] in the leading state organ" of the PRK, Vietnamese withdrawal in conjunction with the cutoff of outside aid to the resistance, general elections (organized by the Heng Samrin regime) held after the Vietnamese withdrawal, and the formation of a new four-party coalition. The October 8 plan also proposed negotiations with Thailand for the creation of a zone of peace and friendship along the Cambodian-Thai border, for discussions on an "orderly repatriation" of Cambodian refugees from Thailand, and for the convening of an international conference. The conference was to be attended by the rival Cambodian camps, the Indochinese states, the ASEAN states, the Soviet Union, China, India, France, Britain, the United States, and other interested countries. The CGDK, however, rejected the plan as an attempt to control the dynamics of national reconciliation while Cambodia was still occupied by Vietnam.

Sihanouk and the PRK continued their exploratory moves. On October 19, Hun Sen agreed to meet with Sihanouk, even though Sihanouk had cancelled similar meetings scheduled for late 1984 and for June 1987. At the end of October, Hun Sen flew to Moscow for diplomatic coordination. The CGDK announced on October 31 that a "clarification on national reconciliation policy" had been signed by all three resistance leaders. It was likely that the two main goals of the clarification, which was dated October 1, were to restate the CGDK's position on peace talks and to underline the unity among the resistance leaders. The statement said that "the first phase" of Vietnamese withdrawal must be completed before a four-party coalition government could be set up, not within the framework of the PRK but under the premises of a "neutral and noncommunist" Cambodia.

Sihanouk was clearly in the spotlight at this point. It was possible that his personal diplomacy would stir suspicion among his coalition partners, as well as among Chinese and ASEAN leaders. It was also possible that he might strike a deal with Phnom Penh and Hanoi and exclude the Khmer Rouge faction and its patron, China. Mindful of such potential misgivings, Sihanouk went to great lengths to clarify his own stand. He said that he would not accept any "high position" in the illegal PRK regime, that he would disclose fully the minutes of his talks with Hun Sen, and that he would not waver from his commitment to a "neutral and noncommunist" Cambodia free of Vietnamese troops.

Sihanouk and Hun Sen met at Fère-en-Tardenois, a village northeast of Paris, from December 2 to December 4, 1987. The communiqué they issued at the end of their talks mentioned their agreement to work for a political solution to the nine-year-old conflict and to call for an international conference. The conference, to be convened only after all Cambodian factions reached an agreement on a coalition arrangement, would support the new coalition accord and would guarantee the country's independence, neutrality, and nonalignment. The two leaders also agreed to meet again at Fère-en-Tardenois in January 1988 and in Pyongyang at a later date. The communiqué ended with a plea to the other Cambodian parties—Sihanouk's coalition partners—to join the next rounds of talks.

The communiqué offered no practical solution. In fact, it did not mention Vietnam, despite Sihanouk's demand that the communiqué include a clause on Vietnamese withdrawal. At a December 4 press conference, Hun Sen disclosed an understanding with Sihanouk that "concrete questions" would be discussed at later meetings. Included in the concrete questions were "the withdrawal of Vietnamese troops, Cambodia's future government, and Norodom Sihanouk's position.'' Hun Sen also revealed that during the meeting Sihanouk had told him that ''the future political regime of Cambodia'' should be a French-style democracy with a multiparty system and free radio and television. In an official commentary the following day, Hanoi was deliberately vague on Hun Sen's concrete questions, which, it said, would be dealt with ''at the next meetings.''

In foreign capitals, there were mixed reactions to what Hun Sen called the ''historic meeting.'' Officials in Phnom Penh, Hanoi, Vientiane, and Moscow were enthusiastic. Thai officials, however, were cautious, if not disappointed, and they stressed the need for Vietnamese withdrawal and for Thailand's participation in peace talks with the Cambodians. Kuala Lumpur and Jakarta both welcomed the unofficial, or indirect, talks as a promising start toward a political solution. They agreed with Bangkok on the necessity of Vietnamese withdrawal. Officials in Pyongyang said the meeting was ''a good thing,'' but declined to accept the suggestion of Hun Sen and Sihanouk that they mediate between China and the Soviet Union on the Cambodian issue. China stressed that it supported Sihanouk's efforts to seek ''a fair and reasonable political settlement of the Kampuchean question.'' Such a settlement was said to be possible only when Vietnam withdrew all its troops from Cambodia.

On December 10, Sihanouk abruptly announced the cancellation of the second meeting with Hun Sen. He said that such a meeting would be useless because Son Sann and Khieu Samphan refused to participate in it and because they also refused to support the joint communiqué. He added that—out of fear that the governments in Phnom Penh, Hanoi, and Moscow might realize an unwarranted propaganda advantage from the meeting—he would not meet Hun Sen. But on December 15, Sihanouk announced abruptly that he would resume talks with Hun Sen because ASEAN members saw the cancellation as ''a new complication'' in their efforts to pressure the Vietnamese into leaving Cambodia. By December 20, Sihanouk and Hun Sen had agreed to resume talks on January 27, 1988. On December 21, Son Sann expressed his readiness to join the talks in a personal capacity, provided that Vietnam agreed to attend the talks or, if this was not possible, provided that Vietnam informed the UN secretary general and the five permanent members of the UN Security Council of its plan to vacate Cambodia as quickly as possible after all Cambodian factions had embarked on the process of internal reconciliation.

As 1987 drew to a close, talking and fighting continued amid hopes and uncertainties about the future of Cambodia. It was equally clear that progress toward a political settlement hinged chiefly on the credibility of Vietnam's announced intention to withdraw from Cambodia by 1990 and that this withdrawal alone was insufficient to guarantee a peaceful solution to Cambodia's problems. At least three more critical issues were at stake: an equitable power-sharing arrangement among these four warring factions, an agreement among the factions to disarm in order to ensure that civil war would not recur, and an effective international guarantee of supervision for the implementation of any agreements reached by the Cambodian factions. Still another critical question was whether or not an eventual political settlement was sufficient to assure a new Cambodia that was neutral, nonaligned, and non-communist.

* * *

Cambodia: 1975-1982 by Michael Vickery provides an instructive discussion on the throes of transition from Pol Pot's Democratic Kampuchea to Heng Samrin's People's Republic of Kampuchea. *Kampuchea: Politics, Economics and Society,* also by Michael Vickery, presents a wide-ranging treatment of the People's Republic of Kampuchea. Other studies include Ben Kiernan's *How Pol Pot Came to Power;* Craig Etcheson's *The Rise and Demise of Democratic Kampuchea; Revolution and Its Aftermath in Kampuchea: Eight Essays,* edited by David P. Chandler and Ben Kiernan; Milton Osborne's *Before Kampuchea: Preludes to Tragedy;* and *Kampuchea: Decade of the Genocide—Report of a Finnish Inquiry Commission,* edited by Kimmo Kiljunen.

External factors impinging on Cambodia in the 1970s and the 1980s are analyzed from various perspectives in William Shawcross's *Sideshow: Kissinger, Nixon, and the Destruction of Cambodia; The Third Indochina Conflict,* a collection of essays edited by David Elliot; Chang Pao-min's *Kampuchea Between China and Vietnam,* which describes Cambodia as a pawn in Sino-Vietnamese rivalry for influence in Southeast Asia in general and Indochina in particular; and Henry Kissinger's *White House Years* and *Years of Upheaval.* Kishore Mahbubani's "The Kampuchean Problem: A Southeast Asian Perspective," in the Winter 1983–84 issue of *Foreign Affairs,* analyzes the complexity of the Cambodian problem, a topic also covered in Justus van der Kroef's " 'Proximity Cocktails' and 'Provisional Salvation': Cambodia's Tortuous Course," in the April 1986 issue of *Issues & Studies.* The Fall 1986 issue of the

International Journal of Politics is a special edition of six essays devoted entirely to the subject of "Cambodia: Politics and International Relations."

Further insights into the politics of warring Cambodian factions are offered in the following publications: *Indochina Chronology*, a quarterly publication of the Institute of East Asian Studies, University of California at Berkeley, which contains a section on Kampuchea; *Southeast Asian Affairs*, an annual publication of the Institute of Southeast Asian Studies, Singapore; the *Far Eastern Economic Review's* annual *Asia Yearbook;* "Kampuchea" in the *Yearbook on International Communist Affairs*, of the Hoover Institution on War, Revolution and Peace; and the occasional "Kampuchea Diary" columns by Jacques Bekaert, in the *Bangkok Post*. (For further information and complete citations, see Bibliography.)

Chapter 5. National Security

*(Top) Male officers and female militia member of the Kampuchean (or Khmer)
People's Revolutionary Armed Forces
(Bottom) Guerrillas of the Khmer People's
National Liberation Front*

HISTORY ATTESTS TO CAMBODIA'S martial origins. In antiquity Cambodia, having conquered Laos, parts of Thailand, and the Malay Peninsula, held sway over a vast area of Southeast Asia. Khmer martial prowess waned in the early fifteenth century, however, and Cambodia subsequently endured periods of colonization, occupation, and vassalage by its more militarily powerful neighbors, Thailand and Vietnam. This long period of decline reached its nadir in the early nineteenth century, when Cambodia nearly ceased to exist as a sovereign state as the result of encroachments by its neighbors. In 1863 the Cambodian king acquiesced in the establishment of a French protectorate over his nation, in order to preserve it from extinction. The protectorate's authority was extended often by force of arms, and ultimately Cambodia became a de facto colony that eventually gave birth to a modern state with its own armed forces and military doctrine.

Since World War II, Cambodia has enjoyed few strife-free periods. Its people have suffered colonization, prolonged civil war, and occupation by a foreign power almost continuously. During this time, it has been ruled by three authoritarian governments of differing ideological orientations and varying degrees of repression.

American military aid to Cambodia began indirectly in 1950 in the form of a security assistance program for the French forces in Indochina, that enabled them to expand a recently created indigenous army. In 1955 the United States agreed to continue this aid to the independent kingdom of Cambodia. The program, which included military training and a resident Military Assistance Advisory Group (MAAG), lasted until terminated by the Cambodian government. Security assistance was again extended to the Khmer Republic (see Appendix B) from 1970 until that government fell in 1975 to the Khmer Rouge (see Appendix B). After 1975 the United States extended humanitarian assistance through United Nations (UN) agencies to Cambodian refugees on the Thai border and gave nonlethal aid, only, to the two noncommunist components of the Coalition Government of Democratic Kampuchea (CGDK—see Appendix).

In 1987 Cambodia was the reluctant host to a substantial Vietnamese military presence, reinforced by its Cambodian surrogate army. History thus appeared to be repeating itself, and foreign observers and Cambodian nationalists feared that the country eventually might become part of a Hanoi-dominated Indochinese federation. The UN recognized the tripartite CGDK as the legitimate government of Cambodia. The insurgent forces of the coalition were capable only of conducting guerrilla raids and sabotage missions within Cambodian territory, against the Vietnamese occupation forces and the Kampuchean (or Khmer) People's Revolutionary Armed Forces (KPRAF—see Appendix B) of the Phnom Penh government, the People's Republic of Kampuchea (PRK—see Appendix B). A number of foreign observers assessed the military situation as a stalemate and doubted that Hanoi would, or could, fulfill its public commitment to withdraw its forces by 1990 from a Cambodia that was becoming a "strategic appendage" of the "indivisible strategic unit of Indochina" claimed by Vietnamese military doctrine.

Historical Background

The Time of Greatness, A.D. 802–1431

Bas-relief friezes in galleries of the vast Angkor Wat complex in Siemreab depict Cambodia's land and naval conquests during its "time of greatness," the Angkorian Period, which spanned the years from A.D. 802 to 1431 (see The Angkorian Period, ch. 1). During this time, the Khmer Empire, by force of arms, extended its dominions to encompass much of Southeast Asia. The warrior kings, who actually led troops in battle, did not customarily maintain standing armies but raised troops as necessity required. Historian David P. Chandler has described the relationship between the monarch and the military:

> Though the king, who led his country into battle, sometimes engaged his chief enemy in single combat, Khmer military strength rested on the junior officers, the captains of militia. These men commanded the loyalty of peasant groups in their particular locality. If the king conquered a region, a new captain of militia would be enrolled and put under an oath of allegiance. The captains were simply headmen of the outlying regions, but their connection with the king enhanced their status. In time of war they were expected to conscript the peasants in their district and to lead them to Angkor to join the Khmer army. If the captains disobeyed the king they were put to death. The vast majority of the Khmer population were of the farmer-builder-soldier class.

Little is known conclusively about warfare in early Cambodia, but much can be assumed from the environment or deduced from epigraphic and sculptural evidence. The army was made up of peasant levies, and because the society relied on rice cultivation, Khmer military campaigns were probably confined to the dry season when peasant-soldiers could be spared from the rice fields. Battles were fought on hard-baked plains from which the padi (or rice) had been harvested. Tactics were uncomplicated. The Khmer engaged their foes in pitched frontal assaults, while trying to keep the sun at their backs. War elephants were widely employed, for both tactical and logistical purposes. Late in the Khmer Empire, the ballista (a kind of catapult, often shaped like a giant crossbow) took its place in regional warfare. It probably was introduced to the Cambodians by Cham (see Glossary) mercenaries, who had copied it earlier from Chinese models.

The Khmer Empire's principal adversaries were the Thai, the Vietnamese, and the Cham from the powerful kingdom of Champa in central Vietnam. Warfare, seemingly, was endemic, and military campaigns occurred continuously. The Cham—attacking by land in 1177 and again by water in 1178—sacked Angkor twice. In 1181 a young nobleman who was shortly to become Jayavarman VII, and to emerge as one of the greatest of the ancient Khmer kings, raised an army and defeated the Cham in a naval battle. After his death, ca. 1218, Kambuja entered a long decline, resulting in eventual disintegration.

Period of Decline, 1431-1863

Scholars frequently assert that the decline of the Khmer Empire was precipitated by the drain on its economy, and on the morale and energy of its people, caused by the continual and monumental construction program at Angkor. Dynastic rivalries took their toll, and slave rebellions are also thought to have hastened the demise of the empire.

Over the centuries, the Khmer kings never completely pacified the countryside. Khmer martial spirit survived, as was demonstrated by uprisings and rebellions, either spontaneous or contrived, throughout periods of foreign encroachment and domination. Among the significant rebellions was one that occurred beginning in 1840 which resulted in Cambodia's being placed under the joint suzerainty of Thailand and Vietnam (see Domination by Thailand and Vietnam, ch. 1).

The French Protectorate, 1863-1954

Following entreaties that had been made a decade earlier by Cambodian King Ang Duong to Napoleon III for protection from the Vietnamese, his "traditional enemies," a delegation of French naval officers in 1863 proceeded to Phnom Penh from Saigon to conclude a treaty with Duong's son, now King Norodom (1859-1904), that created a French protectorate (see The French Protectorate, ch. 1). It is generally accepted by historians that only the intervention of the French prevented the extinction of Cambodia.

Heavy taxation as well as resentment against foreign domination and the puppet rulers who sat on the throne in Phnom Penh were the causes of the intermittent rebellions that marked the colonial period. Revolts erupted in 1866 and in 1870 that attracted considerable support in the countryside. They were quelled by the French, assisted by Norodom's half brother (the future king), Sisowath, who led his troops alongside the French in the suppression of both rebellions.

Another serious rebellion occurred in 1884, when the French forced upon King Norodom a new treaty that tightened their control over Cambodia. The reforms stipulated in the new accord, such as the abolition of slavery and the institutionalization of land ownership, struck at the very heart of the privileged status enjoyed by the Cambodian elite in the countryside. The result was a widespread insurrection evoking such support that a local French official in Kampong Cham noted in 1886 that ''. . . the entire Cambodian population acquiesces in the revolt.'' Quelling the rebellion took one and one-half years, and it tied down some 4,000 French and Vietnamese troops that had been brought in from Cochinchina (the southern part of Vietnam).

Unrest surfaced periodically before World War II, and various episodes of Cambodians' defying colonial rule were recorded. Reports by French officials also hinted at widespread insecurity in the countryside, where peasants frequently were at the mercy of bandit gangs. The colonial military forces in Cambodia, which were available to quell potential insurrections during this period, consisted of a light infantry battalion (Bataillon Tirailleurs Cambodgiens) and a national or native constabulary (Garde Nationale, also called Garde Indigène).

The light infantry battalion, a Khmer unit with French officers, was part of a larger force, the third brigade, which had responsibility for Cambodia and for Cochinchina. In addition to the Cambodian battalion, the brigade was composed of French colonial and Vietnamese light infantry regiments and support elements. The brigade, headquartered in Saigon, was ultimately responsible to a supreme military command for Indochina located in Hanoi.

Under the French pre-World War II colonial regime, the constabulary consisted of a force of about 2,500 men and a mixed Franco-Khmer headquarters element of about forty to fifty officers, technicians, and support personnel. The force was divided into about fifteen companies deployed in the provinces. Control of the constabulary was vested in the colonial civil administration, but in times of crisis, command could pass quickly to military authorities in Saigon or in Hanoi. Service in the constabulary theoretically was voluntary, and personnel received a cash salary. Enlistments, however, were rarely sufficient to keep pace with personnel requirements, and villages occasionally were tasked to provide recruits.

The Japanese Occupation, 1941–45

In 1940 the Japanese government, after negotiating a treaty of friendship with Thailand, sought special concessions in Indochina from the French colonial authorities. The Vichy administration in Hanoi, under pressure from the German government, signed an agreement with Tokyo that permitted the movement of Japanese troops through the transportation hubs of Indochina.

Thailand subsequently sought to take advantage of both its friendship with Tokyo and French military weakness in the region by launching an invasion of Cambodia's western provinces. Although the French suffered a series of land defeats in the skirmishes that followed, a unique twist in the confrontation came from a naval battle that ensued near the Thai island of Ko Chang. A small French naval force intercepted a Thai battle fleet, en route to attack Saigon, and sank two battleships and other light craft. The Japanese then intervened and arranged a treaty, signed in Tokyo in March 1941, compelling the French to concede to Thailand the provinces of Battambang, Siemreab, and parts of Kampong Thum and Stoeng Treng. Cambodia thus lost one-third of its territory and nearly half a million citizens.

The Japanese, while leaving the Vichy colonial government nominally in charge throughout Indochina, established in Cambodia a garrison that numbered 8,000 troops by August 1941. Preservation of order on a day-to-day basis, however, continued to be the responsibility of the colonial authorities, who were permitted to retain the constabulary and the light infantry battalion. These forces were sufficient to quell the first stirrings of nationalistic unrest in 1941 and in 1942.

Anti-French agitation assumed a more overt form, in July 1942, when early nationalist leaders Pach Chhoeun and Son Ngoc Thanh organized a demonstration in Phnom Penh over an obscure incident involving Cambodian military personnel. In this occurrence, a monk named Hem Chieu attempted to subvert some Khmer military personnel by involving them in vague coup plotting against the colonial administration. The plot was discovered, and the monk was arrested; Chhoeun and Thanh, believing they had tacit Japanese support, staged a march on the French residency by some 2,000 people, many of them monks. The repressive reaction by

245

the colonial authorities resulted in many injuries and in mass arrests. Although the Japanese failed to support Thanh as he had expected, they spirited him away to Japan, where he was trained for the next three years and was commissioned a captain in the Japanese army. Chhoeun was arrested and sentenced to life imprisonment.

On March 9, 1945, Japanese forces in Indochina, including those in Cambodia, overthrew the French colonial administration; and, in a bid to revive the flagging support of local populations for Tokyo's war effort, they encouraged indigenous rulers to proclaim independence (see The Emergence of Nationalism, ch. 1). During this period of Japanese-sponsored independence, the fate of the constabulary and of the light infantry battalion remained uncertain. The battalion apparently was demobilized for the most part, while the constabulary remained in place but was reduced to ineffectuality. Presumably both forces were leaderless because their French officers were interned by the Japanese for the remainder of the war.

Tokyo, however, did not plan to leave the Indochinese countries without a military force following the March 9 coup. Plans had been prepared for the creation of 5 volunteer units of 1,000 troops each. There was no thought that such a native force would fight alongside Japanese troops, but rather that it would be used to preserve public order and internal security. It was intended that recruitment of indigenous personnel for the volunteer units would be through physical and written exams. Before the plan could be implemented in Cambodia, however, the war ended, and the concept died without further action.

The conclusion of World War II caused considerable turmoil in Cambodia: a defeated Japanese military contingent waited to be disarmed and repatriated; French nationals newly released from internment sought to resume their prewar existence; diverse Allied military units returned to Phnom Penh to reimpose a colonial administration. In the countryside there were two sources of unrest. On the western fringes of the country, the Khmer Issarak (see Appendix B), nationalist insurgents with Thai backing, declared their opposition to a French return to power in Cambodia, proclaimed a government-in-exile, and established a base in Batdambang Province (see fig. 1). On the eastern frontier, the Vietnamese communist forces, or Viet Minh (see Appendix B) infiltrated the Cambodian border provinces, organized a "Khmer People's Liberation Army" (not to be confused with the later Cambodian force, the Kampuchean (or Khmer) People's National Liberation Armed Forces [KPNLAF—see Appendix B], which is

*A sub-lieutenant of the
Cambodian national army,
ca. 1952
Courtesy National Archives*

sometimes called the Khmer People's National Liberation Army),
and began seeking a united front with the Khmer Issarak.

The First Indochina War, 1945–54

It was under such exigencies that a Cambodian army was created,
primarily by Prince Monireth, the heir to the throne, who earlier
had been passed over by the French in favor of Prince Norodom
Sihanouk, who was considered more pliable. In the fall of 1945,
Monireth gained the concurrence of returning French authorities
in his plan to raise an indigenous military force to fill the vacuum
left by the defeated Japanese and to counter mounting internal dis-
order. On November 23, in his capacity as defense minister, he
made public two decisions concerning this issue. The first was to
form the first battalion of a nascent Cambodian army, and he invited former noncommissioned officers (NCOs) of the demobilized
colonial light infantry battalion to join the new unit. The second
was to open an officer-candidate school, and he extended an invitation to young men between the ages of eighteen and twenty-five
with a junior high-school education to apply for admission. The
school duly opened on January 1, 1946, and part of it was reserved
for NCO training.

Two important agreements between Phnom Penh and Paris gave
the Cambodian military forces a firmer official footing in 1946.
The first, the Franco-Cambodian Modus Vivendi of January 7,

247

1946, for the most part concerned political matters. In military affairs, however, it gave official recognition to the existence of a Cambodian army, although it placed French advisers in the Cambodian Ministry of Defense and declared that French authorities had responsibility for maintaining order in Cambodia.

The second agreement, the Franco-Khmer Military Convention of November 20, 1946, was more significant in Cambodian military history because it established the organization and the mission of the nation's armed forces. The pact affirmed that Cambodia, as an autonomous state within the French Union, would have at its disposal indigenous forces, the missions of which were to uphold the sovereignty of the king, to preserve internal security, and to defend the frontiers of the country. The accord also noted that Cambodia participated in the defense of the French Union by placing its military units at the disposal of the French High Commissioner for Indochina, and that, reciprocally, other French Union forces helped to defend Cambodia. The Cambodian forces were to be composed of units with a territorial responsibility and a mobile reserve. The supreme commander would be the king, who would exercise his powers through a Ministry of Defense assisted by a Franco-Khmer general staff. The Cambodians also were granted the responsibilities of recruiting, of determining obligatory military service, of designating unit tables of organization and equipment, and of deploying troops internally. The stationing of Cambodian units outside the country, however, was to be based on mutual understanding between the king and the French High Commissioner for Indochina (see The Struggle for Independence, ch. 1).

In 1947 the Cambodian government faced a mounting threat from several thousand Khmer Issarak combatants, whose numbers would swell to around 10,000 by 1949. In an effort to keep pace with their domestic adversaries, the Cambodian military forces slowly but inexorably grew in numbers as the months and years passed. In January 1947, the effective strength of the Cambodian military stood at about 4,000 personnel, of which 3,000 served in the constabulary. The remainder were in a mobile reserve of two battalion-sized units (one of them newly formed) named, respectively, the First Cambodian Rifle Battalion and the Second Cambodian Rifle Battalion (Bataillon de Chasseurs Cambodgiens). These first Cambodian military units went into action in 1947 against the Khmer Issarak. During the next two years, two more rifle battalions were added, bringing total strength up to 6,000 personnel, with about half serving in the Garde Nationale and half in the mobile reserve. The latter at this time comprised three rifle battalions (one battalion had been allocated to French Union forces elsewhere in Indochina).

In July 1949, in another military agreement with France, Cambodian forces were granted autonomy within operational sectors in the provinces of Siemreab and Kampong Thum, which had been part of the territory returned to Cambodia by Thailand in early 1947. Under an additional protocol signed in June 1950, provincial governors were assigned the responsibility for the pacification of the territories under their jurisdictions; to accomplish this mission they were each given a counterinsurgency force consisting of one independent infantry company.

The early 1950s were marked by further milestones in the development of the Cambodian military forces. In the fall of 1950, a military assistance agreement between the United States and France provided for an expansion of indigenous forces in Indochina, and by 1952 Cambodian troop strength had reached 13,000 personnel, greater than that of French forces in the country. In the meantime, more rifle battalions were formed, combat-support units were established, and a framework for logistical support was set up. Cambodian units were given wider responsibility: protection of the rubber plantations in the area of the middle Mekong, and, to prevent infiltration by the Viet Minh, surveillance of the coastal areas of the southern provinces and of the eastern frontier with Cochinchina.

In June 1952, Prince Sihanouk—determined to transcend his figurehead role—seized power, staging what was termed a "royal coup d'état." He suspended the constitution "to restore . . . order and security throughout the country." Taking command of army operations, he led his troops against Son Ngoc Thanh's Khmer Issarak forces in Siemreab Province, where he announced that he had driven "700 red guerrillas" across the border into Thailand. As the year wore on, the French returned to Cambodian control the battalion that had been assigned to the French Union forces since the late 1940s. The unit returned ceremoniously to Phnom Penh in October. In December the Cambodian operational sector of Siemreab was enlarged by the addition of Batdambang Province, and the subsector of Batdambang City came under the command of a previously obscure lieutenant colonel, Lon Nol. The operational sector of Kampong Thum was given its own combat element, the Third Cambodian Rifle Battalion, an elite unit that was subject to the direct orders of the monarch.

In early 1953, Sihanouk embarked on a world tour to publicize his campaign for independence, contending that he could "checkmate communism by opposing it with the force of nationalism."

Following his tour, he "retired" to Batdambang Province, which was declared a "free zone of independence" and where he was joined by 30,000 Cambodian troops and police in a show of support and strength. Elsewhere, Cambodian troops under French officers staged slowdowns or refused the commands of their superiors, as a demonstration of solidarity with Sihanouk. Full independence was granted by France in November 1953, and Sihanouk, returning to Phnom Penh, took command of the army of 17,000 troops, which had been renamed the Royal Khmer Armed Forces (Forces Armées Royales Khmères—FARK—see Appendix B).

In March 1954, combined Viet Minh and Khmer Issarak forces launched attacks from Vietnam into northeastern Cambodia. Sihanouk personally directed a sustained counterattack. Conscription was instituted for men between fifteen and thirty-five years of age, and national mobilization was declared. Following the conclusion of the Geneva Conference on Indochina in July, Viet Minh representatives agreed to withdraw their troops from Cambodia. After a brief rebellion by the Khmer Issarak in late 1954, one of its principal leaders, Son Ngoc Thanh, surrendered in response to an amnesty decree, but, upon denial of an audience with Sihanouk, he departed for Thailand. FARK force levels were 47,000, but, with demobilization after Geneva, this dropped to 36,000, the approximate level at which it was to be maintained for the next fifteen years except during periods of emergency.

The Second Indochina War, 1954–75

In May 1955, the United States and Cambodia signed an agreement providing for security assistance and for the establishment of a thirty-person MAAG. During the next eight years, until the assistance program was discontinued at Cambodian request in November 1963, FARK received from the United States supplies and equipment worth approximately US$83.7 million, in addition to military budget support. In the meantime, the French also retained a military training mission in Cambodia that was to remain until 1971. FARK traditions and doctrine remained French, and there was some incompatibility with United States military doctrine and outlook.

Although the United States undertook a substantial security-assistance program in Cambodia, and the kingdom was included as a "protocol state" in the Southeast Asia Treaty Organization (SEATO), failure to obtain more concrete assurances of defense assistance motivated Cambodia to adopt a neutralist foreign policy. Subsequently adopted as law, this policy declared that Cambodia would "abstain from military or ideological alliances" but

King Norodom Suramarit troops the line of
FARK military units at his coronation in March 1955.
Courtesy National Archives

would retain the right to self-defense. Cambodia continued to be aware of the serious threat to its independence posed by the Democratic Republic of Vietnam (North Vietnam).

FARK's mission thus became a defensive one, that is, to insure Cambodia's territorial integrity within the framework of neutrality. The FARK high command remained fairly stable, staffed by a limited number of well-trained personnel, many of whom had been educated abroad. Ranking officers, however, became highly politicized, if not subservient, because they were more or less compelled by Sihanouk at his whim to perform active roles in national political life. Throughout the years that followed the Geneva Conference, Sihanouk, supreme commander of FARK, controlled national policies affecting the military establishment, and FARK's operational parameters were circumscribed by his frequent policy vacillations. Because of this, FARK never developed as an effective or viable military organization.

In addition to the Vietnamese threat, the Cambodian government perceived a menace to internal stability from Son Ngoc Thanh's resurgent antimonarchist Khmer Serei (see Appendix B). Although contemporary observers suggested that the Khmer Serei seemed "to be more of a nuisance . . . than a genuine threat," the group's insurgent activities and subversive efforts were viewed with increasing alarm by Phnom Penh. In March 1959, for example, the provincial governor of Siemreab, General Dap Chhuon, a former Khmer Issarak leader who once had fought alongside Sihanouk, was implicated in an attempted Khmer Serei uprising (known at the time as the Bangkok Plot) and was executed. Sihanouk believed the United States had been behind the plot, and his proclivity for assuming complicity between Washington and the Khmer Serei became a particularly significant factor a few years later. In approximately 1965 to 1966, the United States Military Assistance Command—Vietnam (MACV) began recruitment for the Studies and Operations Group and civilian irregular defense groups of Khmer Krom (see Appendix B) living in the Mekong Delta, many of whom were Khmer Serei members. In his public pronouncements regarding Khmer Serei activity, Sihanouk charged that the group had originated in South Vietnam and Thailand, and had the backing of both governments. Over the years, there were countless Khmer Serei incidents, followed by amnesties, surrenders, executions, and acrimonious Cambodian charges against South Vietnam, Thailand, and the United States. After Sihanouk was deposed in 1970, the Lon Nol government pardoned some 500 political prisoners, the majority of whom were Khmer Serei. Charges surfaced in 1987 that during his rule Sihanouk had executed as many as 1,000 Khmer Serei suspects.

In the uneasy peace between the First Indochina War and the Second Indochina War, a number of incidents occurred on Cambodia's border with South Vietnam. In June 1958, two South Vietnamese battalions briefly occupied a village in Stoeng Treng Province, and Sihanouk appealed for United States intervention. Receiving no response that satisfied him, Sihanouk established diplomatic relations with China and announced that this action was a direct consequence of South Vietnam's violation of Cambodian territory. Cambodia was also not silent during the early stages of border violations by North Vietnam. In 1959 Phnom Penh complained that North Vietnamese regulars were using northeastern Cambodia to infiltrate South Vietnam. Cambodia made concerted efforts to demonstrate that it was policing its eastern borders, but, although the incursions were publicly admitted, the existence of base areas was not. By the mid-1960s, sites along Cambodia's eastern borders were serving as bases for North Vietnamese and for South Vietnamese communist, or Viet Cong (see Appendix B) forces fighting the South Vietnamese government. FARK, restrained by Sihanouk's policies, which, in effect, constituted a modus vivendi with the intruders, could do little more than monitor these activities. The continuation of border incidents, and

*Armored cars pass in review during coronation
parade of King Norodom Suramarit in March 1955
Courtesy National Archives*

Sihanouk's repeated charges of United States complicity with the
Khmer Serei, led to a steady deterioration in Cambodian-American
relations.

In November 1963, after the clandestine Khmer Serei radio
resumed anti-Sihanouk broadcasts that the Cambodian government
alleged were beamed from Thailand and from South Vietnam with
transmitters supplied by the United States, Sihanouk terminated
the economic and security assistance agreements with Washington. He also demanded the departure from Cambodia of all non-
diplomatic United States government personnel. The final rupture
in diplomatic relations came two years later, after Cambodia
filed a complaint in the UN Security Council against the United
States and South Vietnam for their ''repeated acts of aggression
against Cambodia.'' Relations were formally terminated May 3,
1965.

Although still receiving French military assistance and training
(a program that was to continue until 1972), Cambodia began
soliciting and accepting military assistance from communist countries as well, after the termination of United States aid. In 1963
FARK received four Soviet MiG aircraft at the beginning of a program in which China also joined. The inevitable results of a variety
of suppliers were mixed equipment inventories.

In 1966 Sihanouk secretly granted access to the deep-water port of Sihanoukville (later called Kampong Saom), in western Kampot Province, to the North Vietnamese. With the complicity of ranking FARK officers, Sihanoukville became a main entrepôt for North Vietnamese military supplies from China and from the Soviet Union. Armaments were then transported to North Vietnamese and Viet Cong sanctuaries on the border with South Vietnam, ironically over the ''Friendship Highway'' built with United States aid and sometimes in FARK trucks supplied as part of the United States security-assistance program. This effective supply route enabled the North Vietnamese and the Viet Cong to stockpile substantial amounts of armaments and equipment for the 1968 Tet Offensive against the Saigon government. FARK profited from armaments pilfered from the Vietnamese shipments, and suborned FARK officers derived personal advantage from the Sihanoukville traffic through fees, bribes, and other special arrangements.

In 1967 a peasant uprising broke out in the Samlot district of Batdambang Province. Its significance was not appreciated immediately. At the time, Sihanouk attributed the attacks, which first occurred in about January, to ''the Khmer Viet Minh'' (see Appendix B), whom he also labeled ''Khmer Rouge'' (see Appendix B) to distinguish them from the ''Khmer Bleu'' (see Appendix B). Sihanouk vacillated in placing the blame for the unrest, however, and later charged the ''Thai patriotic front'' with being its instigators. Acting on his orders, FARK harshly suppressed the Batdambang insurgents, who had acted spontaneously, and not at Khmer Rouge direction. Although Sihanouk announced two months later that the Batdambang rebellion was ''completely at an end,'' there were subsequent references to continuing Khmer Rouge activity in the countryside.

The uprising convinced the Khmer communists (including a former school teacher named Saloth Sar, later to emerge under the alias Pol Pot) who earlier had gone underground, that the time was at hand to escalate the armed struggle against the Phnom Penh government. Shortly thereafter, the Revolutionary Army of Kampuchea (RAK—see Appendix B) came into being. The Khmer Rouge dated its own founding from January 17, 1968. RAK leaders, including Pol Pot, who had just returned from a prolonged visit to China, retreated to the jungle and mountains of Rotanokiri Province (Ratanakiri) in northeastern Cambodia. There they hoped to exploit the disaffection of the Khmer Loeu (see Appendix B) over the policies of the Phnom Penh government concerning taxation, forced labor, and the resettlement of lowland Khmers in the Khmer Loeu areas. For the next two and one-half years, the newly formed RAK remained small (estimates varied from 400 to 2,000 personnel), and poorly equipped with captured weapons. The Khmer Rouge found that, in spite of the Samlot rebellion, discontent against the government in Phnom Penh was then insufficient to attract large numbers of people to the rigors of an armed insurgency. As for external support, there was no move on the part of Hanoi to provide military assistance to the Khmer Rouge because such action would have alienated Sihanouk's government and would have imperiled continued North Vietnamese and Viet Cong access to Cambodian territory as well as their use of the port of Sihanoukville.

In 1969 the United States undertook the first of two bombing campaigns against enemy targets in Cambodian territory. Code-named the Menu series, these air operations consisted of tactical strikes against North Vietnamese and Viet Cong base areas on the Cambodian-Vietnamese border. They partially dislodged the North Vietnamese and the Viet Cong and drove them more deeply into Cambodia in quest of safer havens. This brought FARK elements into more frequent hostile contact with the communists, and there were reports of FARK forces' being involved in joint operations with South Vietnamese forces against the North Vietnamese and the Viet Cong. Sihanouk became increasingly distressed with these developments; his attitude toward the communist Vietnamese changed, and authorization for continued use of Sihanoukville was terminated. In April, speaking in Rotanokiri Province, Sihanouk stated that "to deal with the Viet Cong and Viet Minh," he had ordered General Lon Nol "to give up the defensive spirit and adopt an offensive spirit." Sihanouk announced during a press conference on June 11, 1969 that ". . . at present there is war in Rotanokiri [province] between Cambodia and Vietnam."

Sihanouk left Cambodia for medical treatment in France in January 1970. Citing disagreement over economic and administrative matters, after week-long anticommunist rioting in Phnom Penh, the Cambodian National Assembly on March 18 passed a unanimous vote of nonconfidence in Sihanouk and replaced him as chief of state (see The March 1970 Coup d'Etat, ch. 1). Although Sihanouk's deposition was nominally a parliamentary action, the leaders of the participants consisted primarily of FARK officers, headed by Lon Nol, who had been the prime minister since the previous August (and who, Sihanouk had once suggested, would be his likeliest successor). The coup was bloodless, although FARK contingents were on the alert in Phnom Penh and took control of key installations, such as the airport and the radio station.

At the time Sihanouk was deposed, FARK, soon to be renamed the Khmer National Armed Forces (Forces Armées Nationales Khmères—FANK—see Appendix B), had 35,000 to 40,000 personnel, organized for the most part as ground forces. The Lon Nol government repeatedly sought negotiations for a peaceful withdrawal of the North Vietnamese and the Viet Cong forces from its territory. These overtures were rejected, and in April the Vietnamese communists began moving out of their sanctuaries and deeper into Cambodia, in efforts to preserve their lines of communication and to maintain the corridor to the port of Sihanoukville. President Richard M. Nixon spoke on April 30, 1970 to the American nation, and said that "thousands of their [North Vietnamese and Viet Cong] soldiers are invading the country from the sanctuaries and they are encircling the capital." Lon Nol, in the meantime, had called up military reserves, had requested UN intervention, and, while reiterating Cambodia's position of neutrality, had issued a call for international assistance.

Between April 29 and May 1, 1970, South Vietnamese and United States ground forces drove into Cambodia's border areas in a determined bid to overrun and to destroy North Vietnamese and Viet Cong logistical depots and sanctuaries. There also was hope at United States MACV headquarters that the offensive would result in the capture of the Central Office for South Vietnam, the Viet Cong headquarters for directing the war against the Saigon government. The operation resulted in the capture of vast quantities of enemy matériel and it bought time for Washington and Saigon to proceed with "Vietnamization," the process of turning over the conduct of the war to the South Vietnamese government. For the shaky Lon Nol government in Phnom Penh, however, the results of the incursion were destabilizing and far-reaching. In retreating before United States and South Vietnamese troops, North Vietnamese and Viet Cong forces penetrated farther west into Cambodian territory, overrunning government outposts as they went. Soon all of northeastern Cambodia had fallen to the North Vietnamese or to the Viet Cong, who then proceeded to turn the captured areas over to the Khmer insurgents and to forge them into a full-fledged revolutionary army.

To help hard-pressed FANK, Nixon laid down guidelines for United States assistance to Cambodia, promising, among other things, to turn over to the government in Phnom Penh equipment captured during the incursion, and to "provide military assistance . . . in the form of small arms and relatively unsophisticated equipment in types and quantities suitable for their army." Thus began a structured military assistance program, supplementing the ad hoc support begun shortly before the incursion, that was to total US$1.18 billion by the fall of the Lon Nol government in April 1975. Although all United States troops were withdrawn from Cambodian territory, South Vietnamese forces were accorded ''automatic authority'' to operate in Cambodia in a sixteen-kilometer corridor along the frontier.

The Lon Nol government very shortly afterwards declared martial law and total mobilization, and it began expansion of its army. United States government studies conducted shortly before Sihanouk's deposition had expressed serious reservations about the capabilities of the government forces, noting the ''lack of combat experience, equipment deficiencies, ... lack of mobility,'' and citing ''incompetent and corrupt officers'' as the ''greatest shortcoming.''

The same officers were, however, retained by FANK and their inadequacy rapidly became apparent as military rosters were padded with non-existent ''phantom troops.'' United States advisers attempting to keep track of FANK's development were constantly hampered by the difficulty of accurately estimating the number of Cambodian troops. (Accurate numbers were important because the United States was then providing assistance for FANK's military pay and allowances.) United States Senate staff investigators reported that United States officials acknowledged in January 1972 that the Khmer Republic's military strength figures were ''grossly exaggerated'' by at least 10 percent. The Senate report concluded there was ''no greater mystery in Cambodia than the size of the Cambodian Government's armed forces.'' In December 1972, the information minister of the newly proclaimed Khmer Republic announced that 100,000 troops were found to be ''nonexistent.'' According to the United States secretary of state's report to the Congress for the years 1969 and 1970, FANK grew ''from under 40,000 in March 1970 to some 200,000 in January 1971.'' In reality, FANK levels probably never reached such a high number, and many of its new soldiers were youthful and inexperienced.

Limited basic training of the inductees, some of it in Thailand and in South Vietnam, began almost immediately after the introduction of martial law. Such training, however, could not satisfy FANK's pressing need to teach peasant farmers to man the equipment provided by the United States, to fight effectively in sizable units, and to comprehend modern military doctrine.

In spite of a steady infusion of United States security assistance and the influx of new FANK personnel, the government forces were unable to hold their own against their adversaries. Because much of the country remained under North Vietnamese control after the withdrawal of United States and South Vietnamese troops, initial FANK strategy focused on holding the heartland of Cambodia south of a line of demarcation dubbed the "Lon Nol Line." This strategy conceded about half the country to the enemy, but it was the heavily forested, sparsely populated, northern half. If the Lon Nol Line could be held, the government would control the southern half with most of the population and all of the rich, rice-growing areas.

To defend this territory, FANK unleashed its two most ambitious offensives: Chenla I, in August 1970, and Chenla II, in August 1971. Both had as their objectives the reopening of Route 6 to Kampong Thum and the reassertion of government control over this fertile agricultural area. Both operations failed. Chenla I stalled short of its objective in the face of fierce resistance from the North Vietnamese Ninth Division. FANK units were then withdrawn to protect the capital from enemy commando teams. Chenla II was successful in securing its initial goals, and FANK columns from north and south met jubilantly on Route 6 along the way to Kampong Thum. As the government forces celebrated, however, their old nemesis, the North Vietnamese Ninth Division, tore into the extended FANK lines with ferocity, slaughtering many of them and leaving the rest cut off and compelled to fight their way back to their own lines as best they could. Former FANK commander General Sat Sutsakhan noted ruefully about Chenla II after the war that, "In this operation FANK lost some of its best units of infantry as well as a good part of its armor and a great deal of transport, both military and civil."

The North Vietnamese, however, were neither the only, nor the most determined adversary with whom FANK had to deal. A far more lethal threat was soon posed by a revitalized Khmer Rouge-dominated force that had evolved considerably since its days as the ragtag, poorly armed band of irregulars known then as the RAK. The development of the RAK had owed much to the opportunism of the Khmer Rouge leaders, who had been able to transform a forlorn communist insurgency with no chance of succeeding in the late 1960s, into a war of national liberation headed by the country's most eminent nationalist, Sihanouk.

From Beijing, where he had been stranded by the coup that deposed him, Sihanouk in 1970 announced the formation of a Royal Government of National Union of Kampuchea (Gouvernement Royal d'Union Nationale du Kampuchéa—GRUNK—see Appendix B). This government, he said, would be under the leadership of a broad umbrella organization, the National United Front of Kampuchea (Front Uni National du Kampuchéa—FUNK—see

Insurgents of the KPNLAF on patrol
near the Thai-Cambodian border
Courtesy Frank Tatu

Appendix B). The prestige of Sihanouk's name thus helped the Khmer Rouge in their recruitment effort. Rural peasant volunteers believed they were joining a broad-based national resistance movement, headed by the prince, against an ineffectual puppet regime in Phnom Penh. Several groups also rallied to the broad appeal of the GRUNK/FUNK. Such groups included the pro-Sihanouk Khmer Rumdo (see Appendix B), the Khmer Viet Minh, and the Khmer Loeu.

To accommodate the disparate elements that were rallying to the resistance cause, the RAK was renamed the Cambodian People's National Liberation Armed Forces (CPNLAF—see Appendix B). As this force grew in size and in proficiency, it was able to relieve North Vietnamese units of their combat burden in Cambodia. By 1973 there were reportedly no more than 5,000 North Vietnamese combat troops in Cambodia, and of this number only 2,000 to 3,000 were deployed against FANK units.

After the Chenla campaigns, FANK was unable to regain the offensive, and its operations became a series of hard-fought defensive actions against an enemy whose momentum could not be stayed. Individual unit valor and fleeting tactical successes did little to relieve the unbroken string of FANK setbacks—overrun outposts, annihilated battalions, cut-off columns, plummeting morale, exhausted supplies, steadily shrinking government territory, and enemy units that were drawing ever closer around Phnom Penh. A harbinger of future trends was discernible as early as November 1972, two-and-one-half years before the final defeat. FANK strategists at that time acknowledged the waning capability of their armed forces and redrew the Lon Nol Line. The new line of demarcation signified a profound strategic realignment because it conceded most of the country, including the rich rice-growing areas around the Tonle Sap, to the enemy. In accordance with the redrawn Lon Nol line, FANK was committed to defend no more than the triangular corner of southeastern Cambodia, which held a majority of the population and was bounded generally by Route 4 from Phnom Penh to Kampong Saom on the west, and by Route 1 from Phnom Penh to the Vietnamese border on the east. The apex of the triangle passed just north of Odongk, the former royal capital that was to be the scene of heavy fighting later in the war. Even this retrenchment, however, turned out to be impractical, as successive engagements failed to dislodge the enemy troops south of the new defense line, and FANK increasingly found itself hard pressed from that direction as well.

By 1973 United States Department of State sources, possibly underestimating, noted that the Khmer Rouge-dominated CPNLAF controlled about 60 percent of Cambodia's territory and 25 percent of the population. Despite a sustained United States bombing campaign that year to blunt the steady advance of the CPNLAF and to relieve pressure on FANK, the Khmer Rouge insurgent forces were able to absorb their losses, to maintain the initiative, and to subject an increasingly demoralized and cornered FANK to unremitting pressure.

The denouement for FANK and for the Khmer Republic began on New Year's Day 1975 when the CPNLAF unleashed its final offensive. As winter turned into spring, the enemy battered the defenses of Phnom Penh from every direction. Routes into the city were cut, reopened, and cut again; river convoys were forced to run a gauntlet of hostile fire to reach the beleaguered capital and finally could no longer break through; United States aircraft, in a forlorn attempt to maintain a lifeline into the city, set up an airlift from bases in Thailand. The effort worked briefly, until the airport itself was interdicted by hostile rocket fire. By early April, Phnom Penh was surrounded on all sides, and its defenses were crumbling. FANK attempts to break out of the encircled city stalled in the face of intense Khmer Rouge firepower. Government units were decimated, exhausted, and out of supplies; finally, they were unable to hold out any longer. The fall of the capital on April 17 marked the demise of the Khmer Republic and the total defeat of FANK, which in the end had been totally outclassed and outfought, not by an army of guerrillas—that phenomenon so intensively studied during the period, but by a tough, disciplined, regular force in a conventional war of movement, by fire and by maneuver.

Military Developments under the Khmer Rouge

Khmer Rouge Armed Forces

The 68,000-member Khmer Rouge-dominated CPNLAF force that completed its conquest of Cambodia in April 1975 was a highly dedicated and disciplined peasant army, trained in the rigors of guerrilla warfare as well as in full-scale combat. Its shadowy intellectual leaders, adhering to the Maoist principles of guerrilla warfare, had taken their core "fish" from only three scattered companies, when optimum conditions had been presented to them in 1970, and had propelled them through the "water" of the people in the countryside, while collecting thousands of proselytes on the way. These leaders were fiercely independent, at first grudgingly accepting training and arms from the Vietnamese—the hated traditional enemy—while on occasion violently turning on these nominal allies, behavior that presaged the fatal conflict that was to come. When most North Vietnamese and Viet Cong combat divisions had withdrawn from the field in Cambodia at the end of 1972, the RAK had experienced phenomenal growth, reaching an estimated 50,000. Its personnel continued to arm themselves by capturing or purchasing weaponry from FANK. The insurgents marched under the banners of nationalism, of legitimacy, and of national preservation—the escutcheon of Sihanouk. In the end, they defeated an army which had a strength on paper of 230,000, but which possibly numbered as few as 150,000. FANK had been armed by the United States with military weaponry and equipment worth US$1.18 billion, an abundance of matériel that now fell into the hands of the CPNLAF.

At the beginning of the regime of Democratic Kampuchea, the CPNLAF—now renamed the RAK once again, under its long-time commander and then Minister of Defense Son Sen, had 230 battalions in 35 to 40 regiments and in 12 to 14 brigades. The command structure in units was based on three-person committees in which the political commissar ranked higher than the military commander and his deputy. The country was divided into zones and special sectors, the boundaries of which changed slightly over the years. Within these areas, the RAK's first task upon "liberation," as a calculated policy, was the peremptory execution of former FANK officers and of their families, without trial or fanfare.

The next priority was to consolidate into a national army the separate forces that were operating more or less autonomously in the various zones. The Khmer Rouge units were commanded by zonal secretaries who were simultaneously party and military officers, some of whom were said to have manifested "warlord characteristics." Troops from one zone frequently were sent to another zone to enforce discipline. It was such efforts to discipline zonal secretaries and their dissident or ideologically impure cadres that gave rise to the purges that were to decimate RAK ranks, to undermine the morale of the victorious army, and to generate the seeds of rebellion. As journalist Elizabeth Becker noted, "in the end paranoia, not enemies, was responsible for bringing down the regime."

Khmer-Vietnamese Border Tensions

Border tensions between Cambodia and Vietnam (aside from traditional Khmer fear and hatred of the Vietnamese) goes back to the controversy over the Brévié Line, drawn in 1939 by French colonial administrators and considered by Vietnam to be the official international boundary between the two countries. For years after the French departure, various Cambodian governments attempted to negotiate the return of Cochinchina—known in Cambodia as Kampuchea Krom, which they maintained was a French colony, not a protectorate, that had been promised to Cambodia by early French colonial authorities. Negotiations to solve the border dispute were held between 1975 and 1977, but they made no progress and were suspended. The Khmer Rouge also felt an abiding distrust of the Vietnamese, who, they believed, had never renounced their determination to incorporate Cambodia into a larger, Hanoi-dominated Indochina federation.

Clashes between the RAK and Vietnamese communist forces began in Cambodia as early as 1970, when there were reported incidents of Khmer Rouge units firing on North Vietnamese. Reports continued of engagements of growing intensity, particularly after 1973. The North Vietnamese, because they urgently needed sanctuaries in Cambodia in order to pursue their war in South Vietnam, chose to ignore the incidents and were still prepared, at the end of Cambodia's long civil war, to send sapper and artillery groups to help the CPNLAF take Phnom Penh. After the communist victories of April and May 1975, clashes between Vietnamese and Khmer Rouge units centered on the border. Skirmishing began about a month after the fall of Phnom Penh, when Hanoi accused the Khmer Rouge of trying to seize Phu Quoc Island and of making forays into several Vietnamese border provinces. Ironically, some analysts believe that the Khmer Rouge would have made more noise about their offshore claims had it not been for the destruction by the United States of their air force and much of their navy during the *Mayaguez* incident. On May 12, 1975, a Khmer Rouge sector commander, zealously asserting Cambodia's territorial rights in the Gulf of Thailand, boarded and captured the American container ship S.S. *Mayaguez*, which carried a crew of forty, near the island of Wai (which later fell under Vietnamese jurisdiction). Failing to receive a timely response to demands for return of the ship, Washington notified the UN and invoked the right to self-defense under Article 51 of the UN Charter. The ensuing four-day engagement involved U.S. bombing raids on the airfield at Ream and on the port of Kampong Saom, as well as naval barrages and a Marine assault on the nearby island of Kaoh Tang. On orders from the Khmer Rouge leadership, the *Mayaguez* crew was released unharmed and was returned to United States custody.

Deteriorating relations between Cambodia and Vietnam reached a crescendo of recrimination when, on December 31, 1977, Radio Phnom Penh, citing "ferocious and barbarous aggression launched by the Vietnamese aggressor forces against Democratic Kampuchea," denounced the "so-called Socialist Republic of Vietnam" and announced the "temporary severance" of diplomatic relations. Rhetorical exchanges between the two sides became more acrimonious, and border skirmishes involving Cambodian and Vietnamese units erupted into pitched battles in the summer and the fall of 1978. Major engagements were reported in the Parrot's Beak (part of Svay Rieng Province), in the Fishhook (part of Kampong Cham Province), and in Rotanokiri Province. In an effort to court world public opinion, in September 1978 the Ministry of Foreign Affairs of Democratic Kampuchea published its so-called "Black Book," the *Black Paper: Facts and Evidence of Aggression and Annexation Against Kampuchea.* The tract denounced Vietnam's "true nature" as that of "aggressor, annexationist and swallower of other countries' territories."

In November 1978, rhetoric was succeeded by full-scale action: Vietnamese forces launched a sustained operation on Cambodian soil in the area of Snuol and Memot (both in Kracheh Province). This action cleared a liberated zone where anti-Khmer Rouge Cambodians could launch a broad-based political movement that would offer an alternative to the odious Pol Pot regime. Proclamation of this movement, the Kampuchean (or Khmer) National United

Front for National Salvation (KNUFNS—see Appendix B), took place in a rubber-plantation clearing on December 2, 1978, amid rigid security provided by heavily armed Vietnamese units reinforced with air-defense weapons.

Vietnamese Invasion of Cambodia

The public unveiling of the KNUFNS dashed any remaining expectations that Cambodian-Vietnamese disagreements could be solved without further armed conflict, because the Hanoi-backed front openly called for the ouster of the "reactionary Pol Pot-Ieng Sary clique." Because the KNUFNS was far too weak to topple the regime of Democratic Kampuchea, virtually the entire combat burden would fall on Vietnamese forces, which, for this purpose, had been steadily building up troop strength on the border during the preceding months.

Nervous Khmer Rouge leaders in Phnom Penh did not have long to wait after the KNUFNS announcement, for, on December 25, 1978, Hanoi launched its offensive with twelve to fourteen divisions and three Khmer regiments (that later would form the nucleus of the KPRAF), a total invasion force comprising some 100,000 people. Vietnamese units struck across the Cambodian frontier in five spearheads that thrust initially into northeastern Cambodia. One task force drove west from Buon Me Thuot (in Dac Lac Province, Vietnam) along Route 13 and Route 14 to capture Kracheh City (the capital of Kracheh Province). A second column attacked west from Pleiku (in Gia Lai-Cong Tum Province, Vietnam), and followed the circuitous Route 19 to capture Stoeng Treng City (the capital of Stoeng Treng Province). In thus concentrating its initial thrusts in the northeast, Hanoi may have had several objectives. One of these may have been to capture quickly substantial expanses of the Cambodian territory that had been an early spawning ground for the Khmer Rouge and its fledgling RAK in the late 1960s. The remoteness of this region would have rendered it difficult to dislodge Vietnamese forces, no matter what the outcome of the war. An early occupation also would have preempted Khmer Rouge units, if they were pressed harder elsewhere, from falling back to this area where they might have enjoyed a measure of public support. The attacks in the northeast also may have been intended to confuse the leadership of Democratic Kampuchea about where the full brunt of the Vietnamese offensive would fall.

Khmer Rouge commanders were not deceived by the Vietnamese thrusts toward Kracheh and Stoeng Treng, however, and made no attempt to reinforce the northeast. Instead, they erected their main defense line in an arc across the flat, rice-growing plains of

KPNLAF insurgents cross a stream in northwestern Cambodia
Courtesy Frank Tatu

southeastern Cambodia, astride the most probable Vietnamese axes of advance. Their calculation of Vietnamese intentions proved correct, as Hanoi's forces unleashed the full weight of their offensive in this area. From Vietnam's Tay Ninh Province, heavily armed Vietnamese units drove along the axis of Route 7 toward their objective, the river port of Kampong Cham. Farther south, Vietnamese units with air support attacked along Route 1, in the direction of Phumi Prek Khsay (also known as Neak Luong), the Mekong River gateway to Phnom Penh. The fifth and final Vietnamese spearhead drove west from Ha Tien, Vietnam, to capture the ports of Kampot and Kampong Saom, and thus to prevent the resupply by sea of retreating Khmer Rouge forces.

Resistance to the invading Vietnamese units by the RAK could have been suicidal, given the disregard for human life previously displayed by the forces of Democratic Kampuchea. Instead, heavy fighting was localized. Major engagements were fought before Kampong Cham and Phumi Prek Khsay and at Tani, inland from the coast of Kampot Province. RAK units, already deprived of experienced commanders by party purges, withered under sustained pounding by Vietnamese artillery and airstrikes, and many of them simply scattered before the Vietnamese offensive, some to regroup later in western Cambodia.

265

By January 5, 1979, the main Vietnamese spearheads had driven to the eastern banks of the Mekong River. Incomplete evidence hints that the Vietnamese offensive originally may have intended to go no farther.

The way to Phnom Penh lay open, however, because the Khmer Rouge units were falling back. Vietnamese forces paused briefly, perhaps to wait for bridging and ferrying equipment and the latest orders from Hanoi, then proceeded to carry out the final assault on Phnom Penh. Khmer Rouge leaders elected not to defend the city, and it fell on January 7.

After the fall of the capital, Vietnamese units continued their advance in two columns into western Cambodia, capturing Batdambang and Siemreab. The columns met at Sisophon and drove on to the Thai border, where there was heavy fighting in March and in April. In the meantime, some remaining Khmer Rouge units offered scattered resistance before they melted away into less accessible areas. There the Khmer Rouge leaders soon rekindled an insurgency against the new government in power, just as they had in the late 1960s, and insecurity persisted in the countryside in spite of the continued Vietnamese presence.

On the diplomatic front, Vietnam, maintaining it had no troops in Cambodia and attributing the lightning-like victory to the KNUFNS, at first denied responsibility for the invasion. When called before the UN Security Council, however, Hanoi's representative, tacitly admitting the presence of Vietnam and citing numerous Western press reports of Pol Pot's genocidal actions, implied that his country had overthrown the Pol Pot regime in the name of humanitarian and human rights.

The Vietnamese sweep through Cambodia produced an unprecedented level of turmoil on the Thai border, as disorganized and bypassed Khmer Rouge units and civilian refugees fled before their advancing enemy. Amid this chaos, in 1979, two anti-Vietnamese insurgent movements, besides the Khmer Rouge, came into being. The first of these was the Khmer People's National Liberation Armed Forces (KPNLAF—see Appendix B), the armed wing of the Khmer People's National Liberation Front (KPNLF—see Appendix B), which gave allegiance to Son Sann, a noncommunist, perennial cabinet minister in successive Sihanouk administrations. The other was the Sihanouk National Army (Armée Nationale Sihanoukiste—ANS—see Appendix B), the armed wing of the National United Front for an Independent, Neutral, Peaceful, and Cooperative Cambodia (Front Uni National pour un Cambodge Indépendant, Neutre, Pacifique, et Coopératif—FUNCINPEC—see Appendix B), which owed allegiance to

Sihanouk. Fighting independently, these noncommunist guerrilla movements and the Khmer Rouge fomented continuous rebellion in the early 1980s that could not be quelled, despite a substantial Vietnamese military commitment to this purpose. Operating from refugee camps on the Thai frontier, the insurgents made forays into the Cambodian border provinces and kept the countryside in a permanent state of insecurity.

In the 1984 to 1985 dry season, the Vietnamese military command in Cambodia, frustrated because of depredations by the guerrillas, undertook a sustained offensive to dislodge them from their sanctuaries in the refugee camps. These installations were pounded by artillery and were overrun by Vietnamese tactical units. The operation, which was intended to cripple the Khmer guerrillas, had the opposite effect, however. It drove them away from the border, and they undertook prolonged forays deeper into the Cambodian interior.

To restrict guerrilla activity, the Vietnamese erected a physical barrier on the Thai-Cambodian border. Code-named Project K–5, the effort consisted of clearing jungle growth; of erecting obstacles, such as ditches, barbed wire, and minefields; and of building a road parallel to the border. Construction of the project, which began in 1985, was performed by forced labor. All districts in Cambodia were tasked to provide able-bodied males for tours of duty on the project that ranged from three to six months. Living conditions were primitive in the construction camps, and the diet was inadequate; the area was malarial, and unexploded ordnance from past conflicts was a constant threat. The barrier was completed in 1987 at an unrecorded cost in Cambodian lives. Preliminary indications shortly thereafter revealed that it was having little effect on guerrilla movements to and from the Cambodian interior.

Military Developments in Postwar Cambodia
Tenuous Security

In the late 1980s, a Vietnamese military contingent of 140,000 troops, and a Khmer force—a surrogate for the Vietnamese—of 30,000 to 35,000 troops, which comprised the KPRAF of the new government in Phnom Penh, maintained tenuous control over the heartland of Cambodia. This territory included the population centers, the fertile rice-growing area around the Tonle Sap, and the main arteries of communication (see Population, ch. 2; Agriculture, and Transportation and Communications, ch. 3). The combined Vietnamese-KPRAF military effort was opposed by disunited and factious but persistent insurgent forces belonging to each of the three components of the tripartite Coalition Government of Democratic Kampuchea (CGDK—see Coalition Government of Democratic Kampuchea, ch. 4). The insurgents had the capability to conduct long-range combat or reconnaissance patrols with as many as 100 troops. They could engage in small-scale propaganda missions, raids, and ambushes against poorly armed targets, such as militia outposts, and in sabotage against stationary, infrastructural objectives, such as bridges and railroad tracks. They lacked sufficient troop strength, heavy weapons, trained leadership, and dependable logistical support, however, for sustained combat operations. From their jungle havens deep within the country and from their bases near the Thai border, the insurgents were reputed to range widely throughout Cambodia. Verifiable guerrilla actions, however, were confined to the northwestern provinces of Batdambang and Siemreab-Otdar Meanchey (the two provinces were combined into one by the government of the People's Republic of Kampuchea prior to 1980), which continued to be the centers of insurgent activity. Most foreign observers in the late 1980s assessed the military situation as being at a stalemate. The rebels lacked the capability, actual or potential, to drive out the Vietnamese occupation force, while the combined Vietnamese-KPRAF armies, at foreseeable force and equipment levels, were incapable of destroying the CGDK guerrilla units.

Coalition Government Resistance Forces

The tripartite CGDK opposed both the Vietnamese military presence in Cambodia and the government of the People's Republic of Kampuchea that had been installed in Phnom Penh by Hanoi. Each component of the coalition maintained its own force of armed combatants (see fig. 13). Divided by deep-seated animosities among their leaders, these three distinctive and autonomous military forces were brought into a reluctant and uneasy coalition as a result of diplomatic activity by the Association of Southeast Asian Nations (ASEAN). The common goal of contesting the Vietnamese occupation, however, could not bridge the noncommunist coalition partners' deep suspicion toward the renascent Khmer Rouge. Throughout the 1980s, the three combatant forces remained unintegrated, and each maintained separate bases, command structures, and operational planning. An effort by ASEAN to unite the three resistance forces on the Thai border resulted, in May 1984, in the creation on paper of the Permanent Military Coordinating Committee, which apparently never functioned.

Limited tactical cooperation, however, occasionally was reported among the various coalition partners. In one rare example, the three forces participated jointly in a major operation in Batdambang Province in early 1986. Usually, Khmer Rouge units, under their shadowy zonal commanders, remained aloof from their coalition partners and, on occasion, even attacked their military forces and inflicted casualties. Such interfactional clashes were the subject of several complaints by Sihanouk, who charged over the years that Khmer Rouge guerrillas had "repeatedly ambushed and killed [his] troops." These allegations were the principal reason why he chose to step down from the presidency of the CGDK on a leave of absence in May 1987.

National Army of Democratic Kampuchea

The National Army of Democratic Kampuchea (NADK—see Appendix B) was the successor to the RAK of the Khmer Rouge, the name change having gone into effect in December 1979, in an apparent public relations effort that later saw the dissolution of the Kampuchean (or Khmer) Communist Party (KCP—see Appendix B), (replaced by the Party of Democratic Kampuchea, or PDK—see Appendix B) and the purported retirement of Pol Pot to an advisory role in 1985. NADK forces consisted of former RAK troops—large numbers of whom had escaped the 1978 to 1979 Vietnamese invasion of Cambodia—as well as conscripts coerced into submission during the Khmer Rouge retreat and new volunteers or recruits either pressed into service during in-country raids or drawn from among refugee groups. The *New York Times* reported in June 1987 that "the Khmer Rouge army is believed to be having some success in its recruitment, not only among the refugees in its camps but within Vietnamese-controlled Cambodia." The NADK did not make personnel figures public, but estimates by military observers and by journalists generally ranged between 40,000 and 50,000 combatants.

In 1987 the opinion that the NADK was "the only effective fighting force" opposing the Vietnamese was more often expressed by foreign observers. In an interview published in the United States in May 1987, Sihanouk reportedly said, "without the Khmer Rouge, we have no credibility on the battlefield . . . [they are] . . . the only credible military force."

During the 1980s, the Khmer Rouge leadership, composed of party cadres who doubled as military commanders, remained fairly constant. Pol Pot retained an ambiguous but presumably prominent position in the hierarchy, although he was nominally replaced as commander in chief of the NADK by Son Sen, who had also been a student in Paris, and who had gone underground with him in 1963. There were reports of factions in the NADK, such as one

269

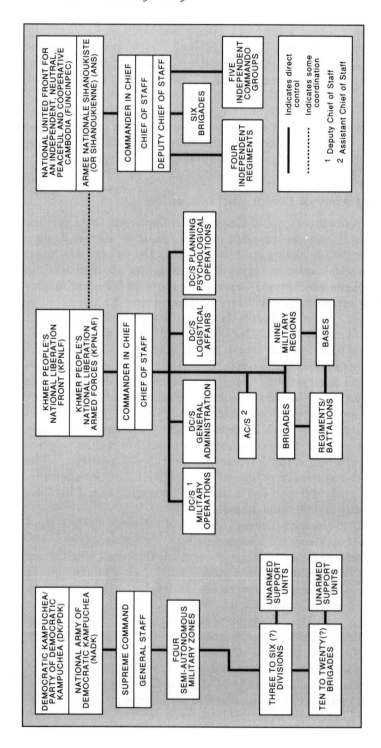

Figure 13. Armed Forces of the Coalition Government of Democratic Kampuchea, 1987

loyal to Khieu Samphan, prime minister of the defunct regime of Democratic Kampuchea, and his deputy Ieng Sary, and another identified with Pol Pot and Ta Mok (the Southwestern Zone commander who conducted extensive purges of party ranks in Cambodia in 1977 to 1978). Although led by party and military veterans, the NADK combatants were reportedly "less experienced, less motivated, and younger" than those the Vietnamese had faced in previous encounters. Nevertheless, the new Khmer Rouge recruits still were "hardy and lower class," and tougher than the noncommunist combatants.

During forays into Cambodia, NADK units employed terror tactics against Khmer civilians, including murder and destruction of economic resources. Such success as they achieved in recruiting was apparently owed to traditional Cambodian hatred of the Vietnamese invader, although there were reports that some of the peasantry would have preferred to endure a continued Vietnamese occupation rather than to suffer a return to Khmer Rouge rule.

The Khmer Rouge divided the country into four military zones that functioned virtually autonomously under their respective commanders. Within these four zones, three areas—the provinces around the Tonle Sap, the western border of Cambodia, and the remainder of the country—were sites of NADK tactical operations. It was the first area, the heartland of Cambodia, that the NADK viewed as the "Achilles' heel of the Vietnamese enemy," where NADK military efforts were concentrated.

NADK units managed to keep the main routes linking Phnom Penh to western Cambodia "in a permanent state of insecurity," according to a senior Vietnamese military observer; traffic to and from the seaport of Kampong Saom was obliged to move in convoys. Both highways and railroads from the capital were interdicted intermittently because of guerrilla activity. Officials in Phnom Penh told a Western correspondent in 1987 that the Khmer Rouge were then operating in small insurgent groups inside Cambodia in a battle for the villages, rather than fighting from the Thai border area, as had been the case prior to the 1984 to 1985 Vietnamese dry-season offensive. In carrying the war to the countryside, the NADK demonstrated that it had gone on the strategic defensive, that is, that it would adhere to a doctrine of guerrilla warfare until the balance of forces was about equal. If this parity were to be achieved, NADK strategists presumably would then switch to offensive operations.

In carrying on its protracted insurgency, the NADK received the bulk of its military equipment and financing from China, which had supported the previous regime of Democratic Kampuchea. One pro-Beijing source put the level of Chinese aid to the NADK at US$1 million a month. Another source, although it did not give a breakdown, set the total level of Chinese assistance, to all the resistance factions, at somewhere between US$60 million and US$100 million a year.

The Chinese weaponry observed in the possession of NADK combatants included AK–47 (Automatic Kalashnikov) assault rifles, RPD light machine guns, RPG (rocket-propelled grenade) launchers, recoilless rifles, and antipersonnel mines. NADK guerrillas usually were seen garbed in dark green Chinese fatigues and soft "Mao caps" without insignia. No markings or patches were evident on guerrilla uniforms, although the NADK had promulgated a hierarchy of ranks with distinctive insignias in 1981.

To keep troops and supplies moving into the combat zone, the NADK, according to Vietnamese sources, followed two infiltration routes. One of them ran south from Thailand through the Dangrek Escarpment into Cambodia. The second ran north from Tra, a minor Thai seaport that may have been an unloading point for Chinese supplies for the Khmer Rouge. In spite of substantial Chinese material assistance, however, the NADK could not maintain the logistical supply line needed to conduct a sustained military campaign.

Khmer People's National Liberation Armed Forces

The Khmer People's National Liberation Armed Forces (KPNLAF), the military component of the Khmer People's National Liberation Front (KPNLF), was formed in March 1979 from various anticommunist groups concentrated near the Thai border with Cambodia, which were opposed to Pol Pot's Democratic Kampuchea. Many had become essentially warlord bands, engaging more in trade and in internecine fighting than in combat operations. They were brought together by General Dien Del, a former career officer of the Khmer Republic, who became chief of the KPNLAF General Staff.

The KPNLAF was loyal to Son Sann, a former Sihanouk minister and the founder of the KPNLF political movement. Because of Son Sann's noncommunist credentials, the KPNLAF offered an alternative to those Cambodians who could support neither Hanoi nor the Khmer Rouge, and it quickly became the second largest guerrilla force in the country. By mid-1981, with about 7,000 personnel under arms, it was able to protect its refugee camps and occasionally to conduct forays into Cambodia.

Two developments in the mid-1980s, however, greatly diminished KPNLAF capabilities as a fighting force. The first of these

*KPNLAF insurgents
in northwestern Cambodia
Courtesy Frank Tatu*

*Two combatants of the
KPNLAF pause
near a stupa in
northwestern Cambodia
Courtesy Frank Tatu*

was the Vietnamese dry-season offensive of 1984 to 1985, which dislodged these guerrillas from their havens on the Thai-Cambodian border. All three insurgent forces were affected by this setback, but the KPNLAF proved less able than the others to sustain the reversal and less flexible in adapting to new conditions. Critical sources noted that the KPNLAF had ''made no significant contribution to the [1984–85] dry season fighting against the Vietnamese'' and that its combatants had been ''virtually immobilized by the loss of their camps.'' The second development, equally harmful to the KPNLAF cause, was the dispute that broke out among the top leaders. Following the loss of the border camps, contemporary reports noted that ''open revolt'' had broken out among guerrilla commanders over the ''dictatorial ways'' of Son Sann, who had continued as president of the KPNLF, and his ''interference in military matters.'' The crisis resulted in the virtual paralysis of the KPNLAF, and the Thai military, presumably on a temporary ad hoc basis, took over the overall management of the insurgent force.

Observers also reported that, as a result of the KPNLAF leadership dispute, members of guerrilla units had returned to the Thai border from the Cambodian interior to await the outcome of the controversy. There were desertions, and discipline became an increasingly serious problem. KPNLAF soldiers became suspect when it was reported that gangs of Khmer bandits had attacked Thai vehicles and buses, and had sometimes abducted or abused passengers. There had long been allegations that Khmer insurgents on the border engaged in black marketing and in other criminal activity.

In 1987 estimates of KPNLAF strength varied widely. At the upper limit, a widely quoted total was 14,000 personnel. In view of the leadership dispute that debilitated the movement in 1985 and in 1986 and prevented its subsequent growth, this figure probably was a considerable exaggeration. A more realistic total was about 8,000 combatants, and KPNLAF leaders expressed the hope that an earnest recruitment drive then beginning might increase the movement's strength to 18,000 by the end of the year.

In accordance with its recruitment and reorganization plans, the KPNLAF divided Cambodia into nine military regions, or operational zones. The force's chain of command was headed by a general officer (in 1987, by General Sak Sutsakhan) who functioned as commander in chief. Reporting to him was a chief of staff, who exercised responsibility over four deputy chiefs of staff. Each of these latter officers was in charge of one of four sections dealing respectively with military operations, general administration, logistical affairs, and planning/psychological operations. At the next subordinate echelon were two or three assistant chiefs of staff, whose functions were undefined. Military units of the KPNLAF were described as battalions, regiments, and brigades, operating presumably from semi-permanent camps in inaccessible areas. Combat elements reportedly, were operating in three provinces of western Cambodia: Batdambang, Siemreab-Otdar Meanchey, and Pouthisat. Actual deployment in the latter province, long a Khmer Rouge stronghold, however, was in question.

The KPNLAF, like the NADK, received most of its military assistance from China. Some aid and training was granted by ASEAN nations, however, especially by Singapore and by Malaysia. In late 1986, the Chinese reportedly delivered a shipment of rocket launchers; this was the first time the KPNLAF was equipped with effective antitank weapons.

KPNLAF combatants sometimes were garbed in camouflage fatigues and combat boots, both probably of noncommunist origin. At other times, they were observed, while on operations, to be wearing merely odds and ends of clothing, gleaned in refugee camps, rather than uniforms. No rank or branch insignia were discernible, but KPNLAF troops frequently wore plastic-laminated chest pocket badges with a photo of Son Sann and the noncommunist Cambodian flag.

Armée Nationale Sihanoukiste

The smaller of the two noncommunist resistance groups, the Armée Nationale Sihanoukiste (ANS) owed allegiance to Sihanouk. It was the armed adjunct of FUNCINPEC, which rallied Sihanouk supporters clustered on the Thai border. The force was formed in June 1981, by consolidating the Movement for the National Liberation of Kampuchea (Mouvement pour la Libération Nationale du Kampuchea—MOULINAKA—see Appendix B) and at least two other armed groups of Sihanouk supporters grouped on the Thai border. These groups existed at first in conditions of near penury, their members poorly armed and equipped as well as half starved. Following the proclamation of the Coalition Government of Democratic Kampuchea, international support consisting of armaments, supplies, and other nonlethal aid, principally from the ASEAN countries and from China, began to transform the ANS into a more effective movement. In about 1986 to 1987, it became the principal noncommunist insurgent force by default when the KPNLAF slipped from that position because of its internal leadership dispute.

No authoritative figures for the personnel strength of the ANS were available in the late 1980s. The most frequently cited totals ranged from a low of 7,000 to a high of 11,000 combatants. The former figure was quoted by Sihanouk, the latter by Sihanouk's son, Prince Norodom Ranariddh, some time afterward. In late 1987, Sihanouk also declared that the ANS maintained "8,500 fighters permanently inside Cambodia." (This number would not necessarily include headquarters, staff, and support elements on the Thai border.)

The ANS was organized into a command structure and maneuver elements. The command structure was headed by the commander in chief of the ANS, who was assisted by both a chief and a deputy chief of staff. In 1987 the positions of commander and of chief of staff were held concurrently by Prince Norodom Ranariddh, and that of deputy chief of staff by Major General Prince Norodom Chakrapong, both middle-aged sons of Sihanouk. Maneuver elements consisted of battalions, grouped under the first through the sixth brigades. There were, in addition, four independent regiments, at least one reportedly composed of Khmer Rouge deserters who had rallied to Sihanouk's cause, and five independent commando groups, each composed of about seventy personnel.

Following the Vietnamese dry-season offensive of 1984 to 1985, the ANS made a major effort to deploy its fighters away from the border camps and more deeply into Cambodia. In 1987 according to Sihanouk, ANS combatants were deployed in five Cambodian provinces, including Batdambang and Siemreab-Otdar Meanchey on the western border with Thailand. Limited deployments also were reported as far east as Kampong Thum.

Photographic evidence indicated that the ANS, like the KPNLAF, was equipped principally with Chinese weapons. This included AK assault rifles, light machine guns, RPG (rocket-propelled grenade) launchers, and recoilless rifles. ANS combatants were dressed in a panoply of uniforms, some of them of ASEAN origin. These included camouflage fatigues and (T-shirts), visored caps, and combat boots. Indications of rank were not evident on uniforms; however, ANS members sometimes wore plastic-laminated chest pocket badges bearing a photograph of Sihanouk and a noncommunist Cambodian flag.

Kampuchean (or Khmer) People's Revolutionary Armed Forces

The Kampuchean (or Khmer) People's Revolutionary Armed Forces (KPRAF) constituted the regular forces of the pro-Hanoi People's Republic of Kampuchea (PRK). Soon after the downfall of the Khmer Rouge, two reasons for the necessity of such forces became apparent to the PRK's Vietnamese mentors when they installed the new Cambodian government in early 1979. First, if the

KPNLAF insurgents assist peasants with their rice planting along the Thai-Cambodian border
Courtesy Frank Tatu

new administration in Phnom Penh was to project internationally the image of being a legitimate sovereign state, it would need a national army of its own apart from the Vietnamese forces. Second, if the Vietnamese army was not to have to shoulder indefinitely its internal security mission in Cambodia, it would need to develop a Khmer military force that could be put in place as a surrogate for Vietnamese troops. Raising such an indigenous force presented no insurmountable obstacle for Hanoi at the time because several precedents already had been established. In Laos, the Vietnamese armed forces maintained a close training and coordinating relationship with their Laotian counterparts as a result of Hanoi's military presence in the country. In Cambodia, Vietnam had been a mainstay for Khmer communist factions since 1954. The Vietnamese army also had helped train Pol Pot's RAK and its successor, the CPNLAF, following the coup that deposed Sihanouk in 1970. More recently, Hanoi had helped raise and train a few, probably battalion-sized, regiments of Khmer troops that had fought alongside the Vietnamese during the invasion of Cambodia. With further Vietnamese tutelage, these Khmer units became the nucleus of a national army. From such ad hoc beginnings, the KPRAF grew as a military force and eventually gained its position as an instrument of both the party and the state. This development, however, was carefully shielded from the scrutiny of outsiders, and much that could be concluded about the armed forces of the PRK was based on analysis rather than incontrovertible hard data.

Threats and Capabilities

The major impetus for the establishment of the KPRAF was the security threat faced by the government in Phnom Penh. Internally this threat consisted of the armed insurgents belonging to the three CGDK components. The total strength of the three forces was impossible to gauge with any precision; it may possibly have reached between 55,000 and 75,000 combatants, but it could have been considerably less than that figure. The insurgent forces were incapable of mounting a sustained offensive and of massing for any tactical operation beyond sporadic patrols in companies, because they could not overcome their destructive factional rivalries. Least of all were they able to bring down the Phnom Penh government. They were capable, however, of keeping Cambodia in a permanent state of insecurity; they raised the cost to Hanoi of its large military presence in the country; and, backed by China, they offered a persistent obstacle to the coalescence of an Hanoi-dominated Indochinese federation.

In addition to the Khmer insurgents in Cambodia itself, the KPRAF and the Phnom Penh government felt that they faced a substantial external menace as well that consisted of the numerically superior Royal Thai Army, supplied by China, the United States, and Thailand, which played host to legions of Khmer guerrillas who crossed the border to prey on KPRAF units and on PRK assets at will. To what extent this perception was realistic was a disputable point. Bangkok did acquiesce to the presence on Thai soil of Khmer refugee camps, which the insurgents used for rest and recuperation. The Thai Army, however, was neither massed nor deployed in an especially threatening posture along the border with Cambodia; moreover, the resistance that the Thai could have offered to a hypothetical Vietnamese offensive into Thailand was the subject of legitimate speculation. Phnom Penh's denunciations of alleged Thai bellicosity were made with such regularity, however, that it was possible that the KPRAF (and the PRK) stood in some danger of being the victims of their own propaganda concerning Bangkok's aggressive intentions.

A lesser, but nevertheless real, threat was posed by the possibility of unauthorized landings along Cambodia's irregular and unprotected coastline. Chinese vessels could exploit this vulnerability by putting in at secluded coves and inlets uncontrolled by the KPRAF, and there they could unload arms and supplies for the insurgents. In 1987 this threat was not decisive, but it had the potential to become so, if the network of obstacles and minefields emplaced on the Cambodian border proved to be an unexpectedly effective barrier in impeding the flow of Chinese supplies to the Khmer guerrillas.

Along its northeastern and eastern borders with Laos and with Vietnam, Cambodia faced no noteworthy external security threat. As long as friendly communist governments remained in power in Vientiane, Phnom Penh, and Hanoi, their interests in protecting the inviolability of their common frontiers converged. In spite of this, however, government control in the upland border areas of all three states probably was tenuous, and insurgent (or bandit) groups, if not too large, could pass back and forth unhindered. The security threat posed by such bands was vexatious but minor, and, in the case of Cambodia, it could probably be contained by the provincial units without requiring the intervention of the KPRAF or of Vietnamese main forces.

The capability of the KPRAF to meet the threats, real or perceived, arrayed against it in 1987 was open to question. Western observers, in consensus, rated the forces of the Phnom Penh government as generally ineffectual, possessed of only a limited capability for any combat mission. In their view, the KPRAF was overstretched and understaffed and could neither cope with the sustained guerrilla activity of the CGDK insurgents, nor prevent their infiltration into Cambodia from Thailand, nor patrol the country's extended coastline. In the face of such limitations, it was necessary to acknowledge, nevertheless, that the KPRAF had been built literally from nothing in a war-torn and devastated country, the population of which had been decimated previously by a brutal dictatorship. The establishment, in the space of a few years, of a credible force under such circumstances would have been a daunting task for any government, let alone one so deprived of resources and of leadership and so dependent upon external support. The most conclusive analysis that could be made about the KPRAF was that Hanoi had laid the foundation for an indigenous Cambodian military force and, by its recurrent insistence that Vietnamese units would be withdrawn by 1990, may have imparted to its clients in the Phnom Penh government a certain degree of urgency in regard to developing an effective force.

Organization and Control

The establishment of a legal and a bureaucratic structure for the armed forces was concurrent with the founding of the KPRAF. The legal basis was found in the Constitution of the PRK, which went through several versions before being adopted by the National Assembly in 1981 (see The Constitution, ch. 4). Article 9 of the Constitution acknowledges the existence of the KPRAF and notes that its obligation is "to defend the fatherland and the revolutionary power, safeguard the revolutionary gains and the peaceful life of the people and join with the latter in national construction." The Constitution also imposes a reciprocal obligation on the people, declaring that it is their "supreme duty and honor" to "build and defend the fatherland," and that all citizens without respect to gender "must serve in the armed forces as prescribed by law."

In an early draft, the Constitution had specified that the chairman of the Council of State was concurrently the supreme commander of the armed forces and the chairman of the National Defense Council. In a curious deviation from the initial draft, however, the definitive version of the Constitution omitted this key passage. Its omission provoked speculation about the true locus of authority over the KPRAF and fueled suspicions that the deletion could have been related to the relief, under murky circumstances, of then-chairman and armed forces head Pen Sovan. In 1987, however, supreme command of the KPRAF was vested once again in the chairmanship of the Council of State (see Government Structure, ch. 4).

The KPRAF was answerable to two organizations below the Council of State, namely, the Ministry of National Defense and the General Staff. The minister of national defense, a position established sometime in 1979, was a member of the Council of Ministers, the executive body empowered by the Constitution "to consolidate and develop the national defense forces; to carry out the mobilization of the armed forces; to order curfews and take other necessary measures for national defense." To carry out his duties, the minister of national defense was assisted by four deputies who oversaw, in 1987, the work of at least nine departments (see fig. 14). The incomplete evidence available in 1987 suggested that functions such as administration, operations, and logistics, normally reserved for general staff sections in some armed forces, were carried out at the Ministry of National Defense level.

Below the Ministry of National Defense, the General Staff was the second echelon concerned with defense and security matters in the PRK. It was one of the earliest KPRAF organs to be established and was already in place by mid-1979. In 1986 it was headed by a chief of general staff, with a secretariat and four deputies, all of whose responsibilities remained obscure. The General Staff exercised jurisdiction over the three components of the KPRAF: the ground force (army), the embryonic coastal/riverine naval force, and the air force. It probably oversaw administratively the country's military regions and certain specialized commands, such as the Signals and Special Warfare Command. It may have exercised operational control over some KPRAF tactical formations as well, especially those operating autonomously, apart from Vietnamese forces. The lines of authority delimiting General Staff responsibilities from Ministry of National Defense responsibilities appeared to be more blurred than in some contemporary armies. This may not have caused jurisdictional disputes, however, because, with the paucity of military leadership, key officers sometimes served concurrently in both bodies.

Control of the KPRAF military establishment and its adherence to the political orthodoxy of the Kampuchean (or Khmer) People's Revolutionary Party (KPRP—see Appendix B) were ensured by a party network, superimposed upon the national defense structure, that extended downward to units at all echelons. Party control of the armed forces also was exercised by the assignment of senior officers to top-echelon military and party positions with, for example, key Ministry of National Defense or General Staff officers also serving on the KPRP Central Committee. At the national level, supervision of party work in the armed forces was entrusted to the General Political Department of the Ministry of National Defense. Incomplete evidence suggested the presence, among the country's regional military commands, of political officers with small staffs or commissions at their disposal. Logically, such officers would have kept in close contact and would have coordinated party activities in their military jurisdictions with their counterparts in KPRAF tactical units and on party provincial committees.

During the 1980s, party activity in the KPRAF focused on building support for the "socialist revolution" in Cambodia, and on increasing membership in all military units. In late 1984, party goals were to establish a committee in each regiment of the provincial forces, as well as a party cell or chapter in each battalion and in each company at the district level. This endeavor reportedly had achieved partial success by mid-1985. In a relentless effort to build party membership in the KPRAF, cadres at all echelons over the years have been urged to spot capable military personnel with potential and to induct them quickly into the party. Such appeals hinted, that for KPRAF members, the trial or waiting period for party acceptance was waived, and that even the act of joining may not have been completely voluntary. KPRP officials also sought to expand membership by junior officers and by KPRAF rank and file in the People's Revolutionary Youth Union of Kampuchea (PRYUK—see Appendix B). As the party's mass organization to

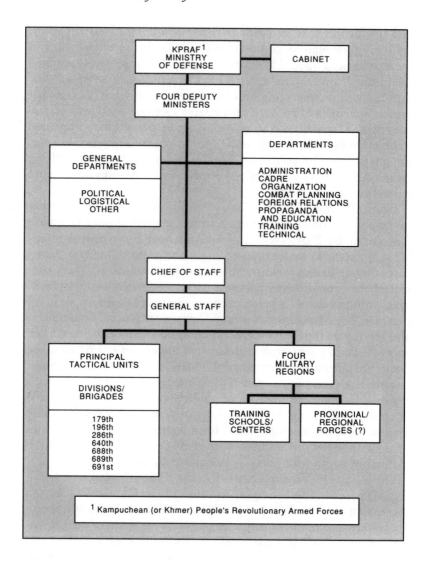

Figure 14. Organization of the Kampuchean (or Khmer) People's Revolutionary Armed Forces, 1986–87

which all young people could belong, the PRYUK was in a strong institutional position to accept all applicants, and it could make deeper inroads into the KPRAF than the more elitist party. In an exhortatory message in early 1987, defense officials proudly noted the existence of PRYUK "structures" in more than 80 percent of the armed forces, and they acknowledged a debt of gratitude to the mass organization for occupying the forefront of a national effort to induce Khmer youth to serve in the KPRAF.

When considering the dynamics of the KPRAF, the possibility of factionalism should at least be considered. In some armies, this factionalism may take the form of interservice rivalry, of the coalescence of groups around certain leaders, or of shared commonalities, such as military schooling, unit affiliation, or combat experience. In the case of the KPRAF, it is unlikely that such factionalism existed. Vietnamese advisers, for example, present at all KPRAF echelons, would have detected such activity at an early stage and would have suppressed it promptly, because it would have detracted from the building of an effective Khmer fighting force, which it was the Vietnamese army's mission to develop.

Interservice rivalry also could be dismissed as a cause of factionalism in the KPRAF for the time being. The ground forces clearly were the dominant service both by size and by seniority. The coastal/riverine naval force and the air force were newly established; very small in numbers, they were not in a position to challenge the primacy of the larger service, despite the possibility of some elitism engendered by their more technical orientation.

The composition of the KPRAF officer corps also militated against the rise of factionalism. As members of a comparatively small armed force, the officers were relatively few in number and were subject to a system of rotational assignments, which bred familiarity with a variety duties. The consequent personnel interchangeability presumably prevented the creation of warlord fiefs and the development of inordinate personal loyalties within the military establishment. As is true of the military elite in other small, undeveloped countries, KPRAF officers were personally known to one another, and they were thoroughly acquainted with one another's family and political antecedents. This network of personal and family relationships, always important in Asia, may have fostered a spirit of cooperation rather than competitiveness; moreover, the ubiquity—the perhaps even suffocating presence—of Vietnamese military advisers also may have been sufficient inducement for Khmer personnel to submerge whatever differences existed among them.

The final factor that may have inhibited the rise of factions within the KPRAF was the range of options available to its dissident officers and to its enlisted troops. Unlike the armed forces in other Third World countries, where disaffected military personnel had little choice but to plot coups or to swallow their resentments, KPRAF personnel could (and many did) simply walk away from their military commitments and join the anti-Vietnamese insurgents, which had policies of welcoming KPRAF defectors. If they exercised this option, they had an additional choice: they could join the communist NADK, the nationalist KPNLAF, or the royalist ANS. For the armed forces of the Phnom Penh government, this range of options meant that those personnel who remained in the KPRAF did so voluntarily because of common purpose and loyalty to the institution or the regime. Although in the short term this dynamic may have had a purgative effect on the KPRAF, ensuring its ideological purity, it was based on Khmer acquiescence to the continued Vietnamese domination of the PRK and of its armed forces. Whether or not continued acceptance of this domination would long prevail in the face of Khmer nationalism among military personnel remained debatable.

Although logic might argue against the existence of factions in the KPRAF, the case is not entirely one-sided. It could be noted, after all, that Cambodia since 1970 has been subjected to cataclysmic events that have produced deep cleavages within Khmer society and that may well have been reflected in the armed forces themselves. In the KPRAF, even among personnel who had chosen not to join the insurgents, it was possible to note a variety of backgrounds; there were ex-Khmer Rouge turncoats, Vietnamese supporters, former royalists, and a younger generation of junior officers and of men without political antecedents. Although it could not be proved by outside observers, it could be inferred that factions in the KPRAF might have coalesced around such shared former political loyalties, affiliations, or backgrounds. If this were the case, such coalescence could take several forms in the future: either there could be a hardening of factional lines as the KPRAF itself becomes more entrenched as an institution of the PRK, or as stated at the outset, Vietnam, in its role of mentor to the armed forces of the Phnom Penh government, could keep a tight rein on the KPRAF and could forcibly prevent its polarization around internal factions.

Mission and Doctrine

In the late 1980s, the KPRAF had several missions. Some were implicit in Cambodia's situation; others were prescribed in the Constitution. Foremost were the duties to defend the nation from foreign aggression, to safeguard the gains of the Marxist revolution in Cambodia, and to ensure domestic security by engaging in combat against insurgents and against domestic foes as determined by the government and the party. In addition to the combat role that was part of their internal security responsibilities, the KPRAF also engaged in propaganda activity on behalf of the government, performed various civic action tasks, and participated in economic production. Because of the poverty of the country, and because the defense budget was not sufficient to meet KPRAF's needs, the KPRAF had to help pay its own way by generating income. In the 1980s, its efforts were limited to growing vegetables and raising poultry and livestock for military use, but, in the future, they could include manufacturing commodities and processing raw materials in military-owned factories.

To accomplish its combat missions, the KPRAF developed its own military doctrine. Although not available in written form to Western observers, this doctrine could be inferred from the Constitution, from the circumstances in Cambodia, and from the dynamics of the Vietnamese military establishment which had acted as mentor and as role model for the KPRAF from its inception. In both the KPRAF and the Vietnamese army there was no doctrinal dichotomy between civilian society and the military establishment as there is in most Western nations. Everyone was potentially a member of the armed forces; in Cambodia as in Vietnam, there were total mobilization of the population and total dedication of whatever resources the nation could muster in order to achieve the military goals the government or the party wished to formulate. The total involvement of the Cambodian population in warfare was enshrined doctrinally in the constitutional statement that "the people as a whole participate in national defense." Because of the security imperatives faced by the Phnom Penh government in fighting a persistent insurgency, virtually the entire able-bodied population was organized into various military and paramilitary bodies. This doctrinal concept worked well defensively when patriotism could be invoked to rally a population against a foreign invader or against a real or fancied, but easily understood, external threat. It worked less well when used to rally indigenous support for a foreign occupier, as the Phnom Penh regime had to do for Vietnam. Hanoi, therefore, incessantly evoked the specter of the return of Pol Pot and the Khmer Rouge to induce the Cambodian population to join the KPRAF, and through active personal involvement, to render unflinching support to the PRK.

The KPRAF probably was also subject to other doctrinal influences from the military establishments of Vietnam and, ultimately, the Soviet Union, which maintained a substantial advisory presence with the Vietnamese armed forces and a smaller one with the KPRAF. The relevance of the military doctrine of the large armies of the Soviet Union and of Vietnam to the small, questionably trained and equipped KPRAF remained speculative, however, especially in the counterinsurgency environment of Cambodia. Soviet advisers, directly or through Vietnamese counterparts, may have relayed their experiences in Afghanistan and they may have advised on measures for countering Chinese or Western equipment and weapons, on methods of controlling or suborning the population, and on means of employing weapons and weapons systems—such as artillery, helicopters, and land mines. Vietnamese advisers, focusing on their army's neutralization of insurgent base camps on the Thai border—through large-scale operations supported by indirect fire—in the dry season offensive of 1984 and 1985, may have unwittingly imparted to their Cambodian understudies a predilection for this tactical doctrine.

Composition and Deployment

Cambodia was divided geographically into four KPRAF military regions (see fig. 15). These regions originally bore numbers assigned by the Vietnamese to conform to the system used by the People's Army of Vietnam (PAVN—see Appendix B). In the mid-1980s they were renumbered to present, at least, the illusion, of their autonomy from the Vietnamese armed forces. Little was known conclusively about the functions of the military regions, especially about the operational control exercised by their headquarters over KPRAF tactical units and missions. It was possible that their responsibilities were restricted to administrative tasks, such as conscription, training, economic production, and coordination with Vietnamese military units and advisers.

Below the level of military region headquarters, the KPRAF was composed of three types of units: main or regular forces, provincial or regional forces, and village militia or local forces. Official strength figures were lacking in 1987, but the main and provincial forces together may have numbered more than 40,000 troops. It was the intention of the KPRAF's Vietnamese mentors to build a reliable Khmer force of between 30,000 and 50,000 personnel, presumably by about 1990, by which date Vietnamese units were to be withdrawn.

In the mid-to-late 1980s, KPRAF regular or main force units consisted of seven understrength infantry divisions, several independent infantry brigades and regiments, as many as four tank battalions, and combat support formations, such as engineer battalions. The forerunners of all these units were several Khmer battalions raised by Hanoi in 1978 as it prepared for the invasion of Cambodia. In approximately 1980, the battalions were reorganized into four brigades, each one posted to one of the four Cambodian provinces of Batdambang, Siemreab-Otdar Meanchey, Kampong Spoe, and Kampong Cham. In these areas, the brigades performed static defense tasks, and they occasionally participated with Vietnamese forces in joint operations against the insurgents. As conscription and voluntary enlistments brought more personnel into the KPRAF, the four brigades were upgraded to infantry divisions, and two additional divisions were founded. In spite of such apparent progress in force development, however, all units remained chronically understrength, according to Western observers. In the mid-to-late-1980s, KPRAF authorities deployed much of their main force strength semipermanently in western Cambodia, and division headquarters were reported to have been established in Batdambang City, in Treng, and in Sisophon in Batdambang Province. There was little agreement among observers on unit designations or on the movements of main force units below division level within Cambodia, or on the extent to which such Khmer units were able to operate independently of Vietnamese forces.

Equipment for the main force units was furnished by Vietnam and by the Soviet Union. Armaments consisted of small arms of Soviet origin, including the AKM (updated version of the AK–47) assault rifle and various crew-served weapons, including towed medium howitzers, and air-defense weapons in several calibers. Tanks in the KPRAF armored battalions included the T–54/55, an old, but capable, main battle tank of Soviet origin; the obsolescent PT–76 light amphibious tank; and the Type-59, an older Chinese main battle tank, probably handed down from Vietnamese stocks. Armored fighting vehicles in the main force inventory consisted of the Soviet BTR series of wheeled vehicles, and some aging American equipment—such as V–100 armored cars and M–113 armored personnel carriers—either bequeathed by Vietnam or left behind from the days of the Khmer Republic (see table 16, Appendix A).

The provincial/regional forces were second echelon troops, ranked below main force regulars in capability, in sustainability, and in equipment. The forerunners of the provincial forces were Khmer units that were raised hastily in 1979. They were composed of defectors or refugees who were pressed into service by the Vietnamese in their invasion of Cambodia. The units numbered perhaps 100 personnel each, and they were allocated, one per province, to accompany officials of the newly proclaimed government in Phnom Penh as they filled the places left vacant by the Khmer Rouge and set up provincial administrations. To extend the government presence to the districts, some provincial units were broken down into platoons or squads and were dispatched to accompany newly appointed district officials. At this time, the provincial forces were merely adjuncts of the Vietnamese occupation forces; they were

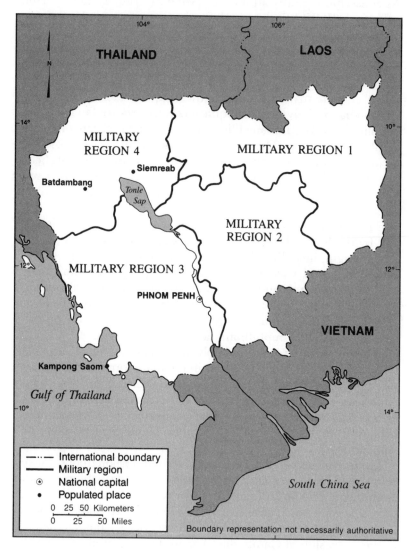

Source: Based on information from "The Military Occupation of Kampuchea," *Indochina Report*, Singapore, No. 3, July–September 1985.

Figure 15. Military Regions, 1987

untrained, and they had few capabilities beyond those needed to provide rudimentary passive defense to their provincial or district administrations.

In 1987 little authoritative information was available on the deployment and the total strength of the Cambodian provincial forces. If the KPRAF followed the examples of its Vietnamese and Laotian counterparts, however, troops for provincial units were raised from among local residents and were deployed exclusively in their home provinces. Such practices may have given these forces an edge, in recruitment and in morale, over their main force counterparts because village youths generally preferred to serve their military obligation closer to home. In a counterinsurgency like the one in Cambodia, provincial forces also could have had an advantage because of their greater knowledge of the area of operations and of local conditions, both friendly and hostile.

An early goal of the government in Phnom Penh was to raise two battalions of provincial forces per province. Given the manpower limitations of the nation, a more realistic goal would have been a single battalion per province. In 1987 Western analysts believed that the latter goal had been achieved and had even been exceeded in some provinces on the Thai border, where the insurgent threat was greatest. It continued to be impossible to gauge the overall strength of the provincial forces with any accuracy, but based on an estimate of 1 battalion per province in general, with 2 to 4 battalions per border province, a figure of 10,000 personnel may have been realistic.

The connections among the provincial forces and the Ministry of National Defense and the KPRAF General Staff were unclear. At subordinate echelons, however, provincial units were responsible to a local military committee. This committee was composed of the chairman, the military commander and his deputy, and a small staff headed by a chief of staff. The military committee reported to the provincial committee of the mass organization of the KPRP, the Kampuchean (or Khmer) United Front for National Construction and Defense (KUFNCD—see Appendix B). The KUFNCD coordinated military affairs with the corresponding party and government committees at each organizational level. It was assumed, although unproved, that the provincial forces, irrespective of intervening committees, kept in close touch with KPRAF main force units and headquarters, and with Vietnamese military garrisons in the vicinity.

The provincial forces had two missions, military and political. In the performance of the former, some Western analysts hypothesized that the provincial units at last might have broken their dependency on their Vietnamese military mentors and have learned to operate by themselves. This premise might hold true if the provincial forces were deployed only in their home provinces, as suspected, and if the insurgents continued to be unable to mass large units.

In the performance of their political mission, the provincial forces were expected by the government to play an important role because they were closer to the people than were the regular forces. This role included both propaganda work and psychological warfare. Propaganda work involved building the loyalty of provincial residents both to government and to party as well as indoctrination in KPRP orthodoxy and in Marxist-Leninist ideology. Psychological warfare involved measures taken against the enemy, such as inducements to defect, arousal of hatred against them, and neutralization of their propaganda appeals.

The third echelon in the KPRAF consisted of the village militia, or local forces. This armed force originated in the 1979 to 1980 period, when directives by the party and the newly proclaimed government mandated the raising of a militia in each village and subdistrict. This objective coincided with the desire of the Vietnamese military authorities to create small local force units in the rural communities along the Thai-Cambodian border, thereby transforming these frontier settlements into combat hamlets that would help to keep the insurgents at bay. According to instructions relayed to village authorities, former officials and soldiers of the defunct Democratic Kampuchea regime were to be excluded from the militia, and preference was to be given to recruiting former Khmer Rouge victims. This recruitment policy initially was quite successful, as there was no dearth of Cambodians who had either grievances against the previous regime or the simple desire to protect their homes and their villages from attack by Khmer Rouge guerrillas. In some localities, former soldiers of the Khmer Republic who had escaped the purges of Democratic Kampuchea were able to dominate the militia. In others, local peasants without political antecedents were in the majority. Villages were able eventually to raise militia forces of ten to twenty personnel each, while subdistricts mustered fifteen to thirty personnel. In virtually all cases, militia members were ill-trained and ill-equipped, possessing only Soviet small arms from Vietnam, or hand-me-down United States weapons provided years before to the Khmer Republic.

In the mid-to-late 1980s, party and military authorities were attempting to consolidate the militia. Indirect evidence suggested that, among the Cambodian citizenry, enthusiasm for joining the local forces had waned considerably since the early years of the decade. Militia units were formed throughout the country, nevertheless, even in the hamlets, in the individual factories, and in the solidarity groups working in the rice fields, in some cases. Some units had offensive missions to search out guerrilla bands in their localities and to destroy them, or at least to report their movement to higher military authorities. On the Thai border, the militia participated in Project K-5. The militia also had the duties of patrolling and protecting this barrier. Away from the frontier, however, the local forces generally were oriented defensively and, according to official Cambodian sources, were "entrusted with the duty of defending production, communication lines, production sites, rubber plantations, fishing grounds, forest exploitation areas, and so on." In all of their duties, the militia units reported to local party and government committees, which in turn were responsible for the recruitment, indoctrination, and training of militia members. Some financial support from the central government, however, may have been available to local authorities to raise militia units within their jurisdictions. In addition to their military and security duties, militia members were expected to participate in economically productive activities and to make their units as self-sufficient as possible.

Aside from the three levels of the KPRAF that were essentially ground forces, the military establishment included a small riverine and coastal navy. This latter force consisted of one battalion, of undisclosed strength, which had the mission of patrolling the Tonle Sap (Great Lake) and the Tonle Sab—a river emanating from the Tonle Sap—between the lake and Phnom Penh. To accomplish its mission, the riverine navy was equipped with at least three patrol craft, each armed with turret-mounted 75mm guns and with twin open-mounted 20mm guns. The force possessed at least one landing craft with a modest lift capability of about one platoon at a time. The commander of the riverine navy served concurrently on the KPRAF General Staff, where he may have performed the functions of a naval chief of staff.

An embryonic air defense corps or air force was being reconstituted in the mid-to-late 1980s, after having been defunct since the days of the Khmer Republic. Cambodian pilots and technicians were in training in the Soviet Union; some already had returned home. Thai sources reported that about forty MiG-21/FISHBED fighter aircraft were either on order or already in the inventory. The delivery or order of Mi-8/HIP transport helicopters was also reported, but not verified, as of late 1987.

Conditions of Service

Military service was compulsory in the People's Republic of Kampuchea. Cambodian males between the ages of eighteen and thirty-five faced an obligation to serve in the armed forces for five years, an increase from three years was made in 1985 because of personnel shortages in the country. Recruitment councils made up of party and government officials existed at all administrative levels;

they may have performed functions, principally the selection of eligible youths to be inducted into the military services, similar to those of local United States Selective Service Boards. The establishment of these recruitment councils may have supplanted the earlier press-gang tactics of KPRAF units who, according to refugee accounts, had forcibly rounded up Khmer youths and had inducted them en masse into the armed forces. In spite of this bureaucratic innovation, however, draft dodging was reported to be widespread, a situation that was acknowledged obliquely by the government and party media in their unrelenting emphasis on recruitment and on the patriotic duty of serving in the armed forces. It was not known whether or not Khmer youths themselves could elect to serve in the main, provincial, or local force, or whether or not a quota system prevailed.

Women as well as men were eligible for military service. A party organ reported authoritatively in the early 1980s that the KPRAF was composed of ''cadres and male and female combatants,'' and ''our people's sons and daughters.'' Women were heavily represented in the local forces, according to official disclosures, which stated that in 1987 more than 28,000 were enrolled in militia units and that more than 1,200 had participated in the construction of frontier fortifications on the Thai-Cambodian border. The presence of women in the provincial and in the main forces, however, could not be verified.

The KPRAF, with the aid of its Vietnamese and Soviet advisers, made a considerable effort to establish a network of military schools and training centers for its personnel. In the early 1980s, about thirteen such institutions were reported to be already in existence. Two of the better known schools in Phnom Penh were the Engineering School and the Technical School. Each of these schools enrolled about 300 students, in curricula lasting one year. The Engineering School, located in the former Cambodian military academy, offered courses in radio, telecommunications, topography, map reading, mechanics, and civil and military engineering. Successful completion of courses at the Engineering School qualified graduates for the Technical School (not to be confused with the civilian Kampuchean—USSR Friendship Technical Institute). The Technical School offered military science subjects, such as weapons and tactics, a higher level than those given by the Engineering School. Both institutions offered language instruction in Vietnamese and in Russian as well as heavy doses of ideology. In Phnom Penh, there also was an Infantry School, presumably for junior officers in the KPRAF; a Political School to train party cadre for the armed forces; a military medical school; and a school for logistics.

Promising graduates of the KPRAF school system had the chance to go abroad for further military education. In the mid-1980s, about 1,000 KPRAF officers had been sent to schools and to training centers in Vietnam, and an additional 500 were being trained in the Soviet Union. This international military education and training program, as well as the entire network of service schools, was believed to be administered by the Training Department of the KPRAF General Staff, which issued specialized training directives in the name of the Ministry of National Defense to subordinate echelons down to the local force level.

Below national level, each KPRAF military region had its own training schools, and Cambodian youths who joined the armed forces were believed to receive their initial military training in such institutions. Instruction reportedly covered political, military, tactical, and vocational subjects. According to a training directive issued in 1984, provincial and local forces were ordered to stress unit training and to vary these instructions with actual combat patrols and operations. Local commanders also were directed to conduct drills for cadres and combatants, to arrange for training areas and materials, to select qualified training officers, to develop training schedules, and to select personnel for course enrollment.

Recent data on pay and allowances in the KPRAF were lacking. In the early 1980s, military salaries for common soldiers amounted to the riel (for the value of the riel—see Glossary) equivalent of three to four dollars a month. This was supplemented by a rice ration of sixteen to twenty-two kilograms a month, supplied at the concessionary rate of one riel per kilogram. Local commanders at all echelons were enjoined to ensure the timely distribution of pay and of rations to all personnel under their jurisdiction. Soldiers in permanent garrisons were expected to supplement their meager salaries by planting individual or unit vegetable gardens and by raising poultry or livestock wherever possible. On the home front, the care of veterans and of military dependents whose sponsors were away on active service was decentralized and entrusted to the solidarity groups (*krom samaki*) and to various party and government committees at the local level.

A system of military justice existed in the KPRAF, but its functional details were unknown. The Constitution provides for military tribunals, and the KPRAF maintained a network of military prisons. At the national level, the principal military prison was T-1, located in the Tuol Sleng area of Phnom Penh. Administrators of T-1 reported to the Ministry of National Defense. Other military prisons existed in the four military regions of the KPRAF, and

Table B. *Branch Insignia of the Kampuchean, or Khmer,*
People's Revolutionary Armed Forces, 1987

Branch	Insignia
Air Force	Wing on a star
Armored	Tank
Artillery	Crossed cannon barrels
Chemical	Chemistry sign (retort?)
Cultural	Musical notes
Engineer	Half a geared wheel, crossed shovel and pick
Infantry	AK assault rifle on a star
Judge Advocate	Shield with stars and crossed swords
Medical	Red cross on a white disk
Military Band	Trumpet
Navy	Anchor
Quartermaster	AK assault rifle with star and rice sheaves
Radar	Radar mounted on a truck
Transportation	Steering wheel over spring shock absorber

Source: Based on information from *Kangtap Padevat* (Revolutionary Army), 1 July 1987.

possibly at the provincial level as well. Military police of the KPRAF served as guards and as administrators of the military penal system.

Military uniforms in the KPRAF were worn by the main and by the provincial forces, although apparently not by the militia. In general, these uniforms resembled those of Vietnam and the Soviet Union. Battle dress for the soldiers consisted of green or khaki fatigues, with Soviet-style soft campaign hats (such as the Soviet Army wore in Afghanistan), or visored caps with a cloth chin strap. Although not part of the uniform, soldiers on an operation widely wore the *krama*, a checkered scarf knotted loosely about the neck. Junior officers serving on staff duty or attending service schools in Phnom Penh wore khaki shirts with ties, brown trousers, and the round service cap. The cap device for all ranks consisted of a five-towered, stylized rendition of Angkor Wat on a red field, surrounded by a wreath. The device for senior ranks showed more elaborate gold ornamentation around the wreath. The KPRAF owned a garment factory in Phnom Penh, and it may have produced at least some of the uniforms it needed at this facility. The KPRAF also authorized a system of rank and branch insignia in July 1987. Although photographic evidence was lacking, these insignia were believed to resemble closely those of the Vietnamese army; they were worn on collar tabs of varying colors: scarlet for the army, dark blue for the navy, and sky blue for the air force (see table B). These branch insignia were worn by personnel up to the rank of deputy platoon commander. Platoon commanders to deputy regimental commanders wore rank insignia on collar tabs with silver borders; regimental commanders to deputy chiefs of military regions wore similar insignia with golden borders. Senior officers from military region commander to deputy defense minister wore collar tabs with a golden dragon surrounded by an ornate border on a maroon background.

After coming to power, the PRK instituted an array of awards and decorations for individuals, military units, and other organizations which performed noteworthy services for the party and the state. Identified awards or decorations included the Order of Angkor, the Fatherland Defense Order (first and second class), the Victory Medal (first, second, and third class), the National Defense Medal (first, second, and third class), and the Labor Medal. In addition to these medals, a number of citations, banners, and streamers were awarded by various government ministries, including the Ministry of National Defense, to both individuals and organizations for meritorious or distinguished performance of duty.

Foreign Troops and Advisers

In the late 1980s, Vietnamese units stationed in Cambodia represented a military force that had broken away from its revolutionary tradition and had become an army of occupation, a dramatic role change in view of the fact that its most formidable adversaries, the Khmer Rouge, were fellow communists and former allies. Consistently designated by Hanoi as "the Vietnamese volunteer army in Kampuchea," the Vietnamese force, comprising some ten to twelve divisions, was made up of conscripts who supported a "regime of military administration."

Military units totalling as many as 200,000 troops invaded Cambodia at the end of 1978 to eradicate the Khmer Rouge regime of Democratic Kampuchea and to install a more pliant government in Phnom Penh. After several years, Vietnam ostensibly began to decrease the size of its military contingent in Cambodia. The first recorded, but unannounced, withdrawal occurred in June 1981, when Vietnam's 137th Division returned home. In July 1982, Hanoi announced publicly that as an "act of goodwill" it would withdraw an unspecified number of troops from Cambodia. These withdrawals became annual occurrences. In 1986 Vietnamese sources announced a pullout of 12,000 troops. In November 1987, an additional 20,000 Vietnamese military personnel were withdrawn. These retrenchments were conducted with considerable publicity and fanfare, including departure ceremonies in Phnom Penh and featuring medals for commanders and citations for units. Skeptics, however, contended that these movements were merely troop rotations. A 1987 study conducted by Chulalongkorn University in Bangkok reached the same conclusion, after its researchers interviewed groups of Vietnamese defectors.

Hanoi publicly committed itself to withdraw its occupation forces by 1990. It first announced this decision following an August 1985 meeting of Vietnamese, Laotian, and Cambodian foreign ministers. The commitment to a pullout engendered continuing discussion, both by foreign observers and by Indochinese participants. What emerged was the clarifying qualification that a total Vietnamese military withdrawal was contingent upon the progress of pacification in Cambodia and upon the ability of the KPRAF to contain the insurgent threat without Vietnamese assistance. Prime Minister Hun Sen declared in a May 1987 interview that ''if the situation evolves as is, we are hopeful that by 1990 all Vietnamese troops will be withdrawn . . . [but] if the troop withdrawal will be taken advantage of, we will have to negotiate to take appropriate measures. . . .'' Shortly thereafter, a KPRAF battalion commander told a Phnom Penh press conference that ''Vietnamese forces could remain in Cambodia beyond 1990, if the Khmer Rouge resistance continues to pose a threat.'' In an interview with a Western correspondent, Vietnamese Foreign Minister Nguyen Co Thach repeated the 1990 withdrawal pledge, insisting that only foreign military intervention could convince Hanoi to change its plans. Some ASEAN and Western observers greeted declarations of a total pullout by 1990 with incredulity. Departing Vietnamese units reportedly left equipment behind in Cambodia, and it was suggested that they easily could return if it looked as though a province might be lost.

As Hanoi's military presence in Cambodia approached its ninth year, it appeared that the Vietnamese troops stationed there were not frontline veterans. Most of Vietnam's main force units and its best troops were deployed in the Red River Delta or on Vietnam's northern border to contain any armed threat from China. Units in Cambodia were composed of conscripts from the southern provinces of Vietnam, or, according to refugee accounts, of military misfits and ''troublemakers.'' Some Vietnamese defectors in Thailand declared that they had volunteered for military service to get out of Vietnam and to have an opportunity for resettlement in third countries.

Vietnam's presence in Cambodia reportedly consumed 40 to 50 percent of Hanoi's military budget. Although substantial portions of the cost had been underwritten by Soviet grant aid, Vietnamese troops in Cambodia apparently were on short rations. Radio Hanoi reportedly commented on troops ''dressed in rags, puritanically fed, and mostly disease ridden.'' The parlous state of Vietnamese

International solidarity: a Cambodian repairman fixes the motorbike of a Vietnamese soldier at a Phnom Penh curbside.
Courtesy Bill Herod

forces in Cambodia also was the subject of a report by the director of an Hanoi military medical institute. According to media accounts, the report acknowledged that Vietnamese troops in the country suffered from widespread and serious malnutrition and that beriberi occurred in epidemic proportions.

The Vietnamese military headquarters in Cambodia was located at Chamka Morn in Phnom Penh. In the mid-1980s, it was responsible to the Vietnamese Fourth Corps commander, at that time General Le Duc Anh (subsequently promoted to minister of national defense). Vietnamese military authorities divided Cambodia into four military regions. These areas probably coincided with KPRAF regions. Each of these regions, in turn, corresponded to a Vietnamese military front that exercised tactical responsibility over it. The four Vietnamese military fronts were Front 479, headquartered at Barai Toek Thla Airport, Siemreab-Otdar Meanchey Province; Front 579, at Stoeng Treng City, Stoeng Treng Province; Front 779, at the Chhupp rubber plantation, Kampong Cham Province; and Front 979, at Somrong Tong, Kampong Spoe Province. Front 479 was considered the most critical because of heavy insurgent activity in the area. A Special Military Administrative Zone was also created, comprising the vital heartland of the country around the Tonle Sap and the alluvial plain to the

297

southeast. The relationship of the zone to the military regions and to the fronts was undetermined. Along the Cambodian coast, the Vietnamese established another type of military jurisdiction. Naval Zone Five comprised the shore lines of Kaoh Kong and Kampot provinces and their contiguous territorial waters. The headquarters of the naval zone was at Kampong Saom.

Vietnamese military advisers also were detached to serve with KPRAF main and provincial forces down to the battalion, and perhaps even the company, level. The functions and the chain of command of these advisers remained unknown, except that it could be assumed that they reported to the Vietnamese military region or front headquarters.

Law Enforcement and Countersubversion

People's Security Service

Law enforcement was the responsibility of the minister of interior, who, as a member of the Council of Ministers, was charged by the Constitution "to protect the interests of the people, preserve security and public order and protect the legal rights and interests of the citizens." To carry out these functions, the ministry exercised control over its own corps of plainclothes police and over the People's Security Service. In the late 1980s, nothing was known publicly about the ministry's agents, except that they fulfilled countersubversion responsibilities and that they may have been advised by Vietnamese and by German Democratic Republic (East German) personnel. In 1987 the People's Security Service consisted of a plainclothes branch and a uniformed police force called the Nokorbal (civil police). Total personnel strength was undisclosed. Day-to-day administration of the entire organization was carried out by the deputy minister of interior, under whom People's Security Service staff functions were carried out by fifteen departments or bureaus. Some of these subministerial offices, such as the traffic and the criminal police bureaus, performed routine law-enforcement functions. Others rendered support services, such as internal administration and supply, and still others fulfilled countersubversion responsibilities. Among the latter were the political ideology bureau, which performed loyalty checks on party cadres; the political security bureau, which arrested persons suspected of political offenses; and an internal defense bureau, or unit, which investigated government ministries and offices.

In Phnom Penh itself, police were organized into seven precinct or ward offices, with an additional thirteen precincts in the greater capital area. In the mid-1980s, the chief of the Phnom Penh police served concurrently as the deputy minister of interior. The organizational functions of the capital police staff approximately replicated those of the Ministry of Interior at the national level. Observers identified fourteen different bureaus, dealing with political security, interrogation, political ideology, internal defense, clandestine investigations, case analysis, organization/appointments, supply, forensics/polytechnics, administration, statistical, defense police (embassy and government building security guards), firefighting, and traffic control. A defecting police official estimated that arrests in the capital for both political and criminal offenses averaged about 100 per month in the 1980s.

At the provincial level, police authority was vested in a chief of the People's Security Service who was responsible to the KUFNCD provincial committee and, through channels, to the Ministry of Interior. The police sought to maintain a physical presence at least as far down as the district level and, where possible, as far down as the commune level. Police officials in the countryside were responsible both to their local party and government committees and to law-enforcement authorities at the next higher echelon. In areas without a police presence, law-enforcement responsibilities devolved upon local party or government officials.

Police control of the population outside the cities was assisted by a pass system. Such passes were issued by local committees and were required for travel among villages, districts, and provinces. Frequent checkpoints by police and by military personnel along principal routes ensured compliance by travelers. Violators of the pass system were subjected to brief incarceration upon being apprehended and to heightened surveillance upon returning home. According to defectors, however, checkpoint personnel were susceptible to bribery.

Protection under the Law

The protection of all Cambodians by the law is guaranteed by the 1981 Constitution, which declares that the state "recognizes and respects human rights" and that it protects "the honor, dignity and life of its citizens" (see The Constitution, ch. 4). In the mid-1980s, lawyers in the Ministry of Justice had published some legal texts and statutes, but by late 1987, it was not possible to verify the existence of a comprehensive criminal and civil code. Decree-laws promulgated in 1980 paid considerable attention to political offenses, and they prescribed five levels of punishment for such crimes. A first-level offense, such as aiding or abetting an individual known to be "a traitor to the revolution," was punishable by two to seven years' imprisonment. A second-level offense, such as subversion or economic sabotage, was punishable by imprisonment for between five and ten years. Third-level offenses, which included the crime of taking up arms against the state, were punishable by five to fifteen years' imprisonment. A fourth-level offense, defined as plotting to overthrow the state or committing "treason against the revolution," and punishable by ten to twenty years' imprisonment. Fifth-level offenses, which included compounded acts of sedition by individuals in positions of authority, acts of rebellion by insurgent leaders, and acts of spying by operatives who maintained espionage networks carried sentences of twenty years to life imprisonment and even the death penalty. A further decree-law, promulgated around 1983, also addressed crimes against the state, such as treason, but included common-law offenses, such as murder, rape, and theft. Penalties for political crimes generally remained the same as they were in the earlier law. For common-law crimes such as murder, however, offenders were subject to ten to twenty years' imprisonment; for aggravated assault, six months to ten years; for rape, two to five years; for rape followed by murder, twenty years to life with the possibility of a death sentence. People convicted of theft were subject to confinement for a period of six months to fifteen years. Former Khmer Rouge cadres who were convicted of outrageous crimes against humanity faced the death sentence. Such sentences, however, had to be approved by the Council of State (see Government Structure, ch. 4).

The first courts in the PRK were the people's revolutionary courts set up almost on an ad hoc basis by the Kampuchean People's Revolutionary Council in 1979. Establishment of a more institutionalized system took place in approximately 1983. At this time, a network of courts was extended to each province and municipality. Officers of each court included a president, one or two vice presidents, and a judge. A reporting channel presumably connected these local courts to the Ministry of Justice, but, as of late 1987, its existence had not been confirmed. Similarly, a People's Supreme Court, evidently under the Ministry of Justice, was established in the early 1980s, but its functions continued to be obscure.

The independence of the judiciary at all levels remained in question. According to a 1982 decree-law, the purpose of the courts was to uphold the policies of the government. Officers of the court were appointed by local party and government committees with the apparent concurrence of the Ministry of Justice. Court officials thus were responsible to the committees that recruited them.

The power to arrest and to detain for political or for criminal offenses was quite widespread among government bodies. It extended from the agents of the Ministry of Interior to the People's

Divided loyalties:
A Phnom Penh policeman
minds his child while
guarding a hotel.
Courtesy Bill Herod

Security Service and to the military units of the main, provincial, and local forces. Refugee and defector accounts indicate that suspicion rather than evidence frequently sufficed to cause the arrest of a suspect. A 1987 Amnesty International report stated that arrested individuals were denied information about the charges against them and were frequently imprisoned without trial. Detention routinely was followed by interrogation, accompanied by repeated beatings and by torture. In an effort to correct the most flagrant of these abuses, the government promulgated its decree-law of March 12, 1986. According to Amnesty International, this statute "codifies and modifies non-legislative instructions against torture, rules on search procedures and regulations concerning powers of arrest and length of detention for interrogation." Amnesty International further observed that this was "the first PRK law to address issues directly related to human rights in these areas."

Accused persons were accorded relatively few constitutional safeguards. They had the right to a defense counsel, but they could represent themselves. Fragmentary information reaching Amnesty International demonstrated that individual guilt or innocence—especially that relating to political crimes—was not decided on the basis of judicial proceedings, but was determined beforehand by the arresting authorities following interrogation. Guilty persons then were sentenced administratively without due process. In the few cases brought to trial, the court confined itself to ratifying the

301

sentence already decided upon behind the scenes. Defendants who were dissatisfied with a court ruling theoretically had the right to appeal, but the procedures remained unclarified, and the role of the People's Supreme Court as the final arbiter of judicial decisions was unknown.

Penal System

Individuals sentenced to imprisonment, as a result of administrative or judicial proceedings, were incarcerated in one of a nationwide network of about 200 prisons. These installations were administered by the Prison Directorate of the Ministry of Interior and by the People's Security Service. They constituted a many-tiered system extending from the national level to the local level. At the national level, the principal prison was T-3, located in Phnom Penh. This institution was built in the early twentieth century, and it has served as a prison for every successive regime to hold power in Cambodia. The facilities were enlarged when the present government was installed in 1979. In the mid-1980s, it held about 1,000 prisoners. Administration of T-3 was shared by the Ministry of Interior and by the Phnom Penh People's Security Service, which used the facility to confine some its own prisoners apprehended in the capital area. In addition to the T-3 central prison, two other national penal institutions, code-named T-4 and T-5, were reported. Both functioned as labor camps, and they appeared not to be maximum security prisons. T-4, located on the outskirts of the capital, was administered by the Phnom Penh People's Security Service; T-5, in Kampong Cham, administered by the provincial People's Security Service. Overall responsibility for T-4 and for T-5 may have rested with the Bureau of Reform Offices of the Prison Directorate.

Each of Phnom Penh's twenty wards or precincts had its own short-term confinement facility. The precincts, however, had to transfer their prisoners after three days to the central People's Security Service headquarters for confinement in T-3. Away from the capital, independent municipalities (such as Kampong Saom), provinces, and districts all had their own jails and prisons. These facilities usually were administered by the People's Security Service at the provincial level, and at lower lower echelons. One of the better known provincial prisons was TK-1 in Batdambang city; the installation was taxed to the utmost in its role as a detention facility for captured guerrillas, smugglers, border-crossers, and insurgent sympathizers, because of its location in an area of heavy resistance activity. The capacity and status of other provincial prisons could not be verified. Given the regime's lack of resources, conditions in all of them must have been spartan, if not appalling. In some of them, inmates were taken out on work details to perform manual labor, such as brush-clearing, ditchdigging, or dike-construction; however, this may have been on an ad hoc, rather than on an institutionalized, basis. Prisoners who had served their sentences were freed by a release order signed by People's Security Service or Ministry of Interior officials and were permitted to return to their home areas. Former detainees kept their release papers on their persons or near at hand, as a safeguard against rearrest.

The law-enforcement apparatus in the PRK, like the armed forces, became more institutionalized as the decade of the 1980s progressed, but how well the two establishments coordinated to insure national security at all levels remained open to question. These establishments did represent, however, the institutional foundations laid down by the regime and by the ruling party in order to retain power, ensure ideological orthodoxy, and impart a measure of internal stability. In the turmoil of a war-ravaged country, the fact that these institutions had been created represented an accomplishment—human rights issues aside—for the government and for its Vietnamese mentors. In a broader sense, these institutions were part of the sovereign nationhood that Cambodia was striving to regain while deferring uneasily, but pragmatically, to Vietnam.

* * *

No published monographs address, either comprehensively or specifically, the armed forces or law-enforcement bodies of Cambodia. Fragmentary accounts are given in the works described below. The reference for Khmer warfare in ancient times is Horace Geoffrey Quaritch Wales's, *Ancient South-east Asian Warfare*. The Japanese occupation period is briefly covered in Joyce C. Lebra's *Japanese-Trained Armies in Southeast Asia*. For the French colonial period and for the early part of the Sihanouk era, up to 1953, useful information is found in Maurice Laurent's *L'Armée au Cambodge et dans les pays en voie de developpement du Sud-est asiatique*. The most concise reference on the Cambodian armed forces of the Khmer Republic is Sak Sutsakhan's *The Khmer Republic at War and the Final Collapse*. For information on United States security assistance to the Cambodian armed forces and on its associated problems, an authoritative source is by the General Accounting Office of the United States, *U.S. Assistance to the Khmer Republic (Cambodia), Report to the Congress*. The armed forces under the Khmer Rouge are discussed in two essential sources: Craig Etcheson's, *The Rise and Demise of Democratic Kampuchea* and Ben Kiernan's *How Pol Pot Came to Power.* Authoritative accounts of the Vietnamese invasion and of the reconstitution of the Cambodian armed forces, are given in Nayan Chanda's *Brother Enemy, The War After the War* and in Elizabeth Becker's *When the War Was Over.* Timothy Carney's ''Heng Samrin's Armed Forces and the Military Balance in Cambodia,'' *International Journal of Politics,* Fall 1986, continues to be a seminal piece indispensable to a discussion of the KPRAF, although by the late 1980s some of the information was dated. Other treatments of the KPRAF and the insurgency in Cambodia are given in *Defense and Foreign Affairs Handbook.* This publication is issued annually, and its discussion of Cambodian affairs from a defense point of view has become more comprehensive over the years. Personnel and military equipment figures for Cambodia are given in *The Military Balance.*

Law-enforcement and security agencies, discussed from a human rights perspective rather than as government institutions, are dealt with in Floyd Abram's and Diane Orentlicher's *Kampuchea: After the Worst* and *Kampuchea: Political Imprisonment and Torture* by Amnesty International. (For further information and complete citations, see Bibliography).

Appendix A

Table 1. Metric Conversion Coefficients and Factors

When you know	Multiply by	To find
Millimeters	0.04	inches
Centimeters	0.39	inches
Meters	3.3	feet
Kilometers	0.62	miles
Hectares (10,000 m²)	2.47	acres
Square kilometers	0.39	square miles
Cubic meters	35.3	cubic feet
Liters	0.26	gallons
Kilograms	2.2	pounds
Metric tons	0.98	long tons
	1.1	short tons
	2,204	pounds
Degrees Celsius	9	degrees Fahrenheit
(Centigrade)	divide by 5 and add 32	

Table 2. Population, Selected Years

Province	1950	1968 (est.)	1981 [1]
Batdambang	371,000	685,000	719,000
Kampong Cham	570,711	977,000	1,070,000
Kampong Chhnang	196,000	331,000	221,000
Kampong Spoe	176,469	361,000	340,000
Kampong Thum	211,500	379,000	379,000
Kampot	252,968	414,000	354,000
Kandal	527,993	805,000	720,000
Kaoh Kong	Kampot [2]	45,000	25,000
Kracheh	79,439	162,000	157,000
Mondol Kiri	Kracheh [2]	17,000	16,000
Otdar Meanchey	Siemreab [2]	50,000	Siemreab [2]
Pouthisat	129,653	223,000	175,000
Preah Vihear	Kampong Thum [2]	45,000	70,000
Prey Veng	361,029	558,000	672,000
Rotanokiri	Stoeng Treng [2]	56,000	45,000
Siemreab	215,000	371,000	477,000
Svay Rieng	207,050	346,000	292,000
Stoeng Treng	47,000	44,000	39,000
Takev	364,295	541,000	531,000
TOTAL	3,710,107	6,410,000	6,302,000

[1] The last census taken by the People's Republic of Kampuchea was in 1981.
[2] Indicates population included in the province the name of which follows.

Source: Based on information from David J. Steinberg, *Cambodia: Its People, Its Society, Its Culture*, New Haven, 1959, 291; Jacques Migozzi, *Cambodge: faits et problèmes de population*, Paris, 1973, np; and Kimmo Kiljunen, ed., *Kampuchea: Decade of the Genocide—Report of a Finnish Inquiry Commission*, London, 1984, 31.

Table 3. *Population Distribution, 1987*
(in thousands)

Categories	Population	Percent of total population
Male	3,231,000	50.0
Female	3,232,000	50.0
TOTAL	6,463,000	100.0
Urban	724,000	11.2
Rural	5,739,000	88.8
TOTAL	6,463,000	100.0
Age 0–14	2,227,000	34.5
Age 15–64	4,040,000	62.5
Age 65 + ...	196,000	3.0
TOTAL	6,463,000	100.0

Source: Based on information from United States, Bureau of the Census, unpublished computerized data on world population, Washington, 1987.

Table 4. *Growth of Schools and of Student Enrollment in the People's Republic of Kampuchea, 1979–84*

Grade	1979–80	1980–81	1981–82	1983–84
Grades 1–4 (Level I)				
Schools	5,290	4,334 [1]	3,521 [1]	3,005 [1]
Pupils	947,317	1,328,053	1,508,985	1,542,825
Teachers	21,605	30,316	37,000 [2]	33,479
Grades 5–7 (Level II)				
Schools	14	62	108	200
Pupils	5,104	17,331	39,434	146,865
Teachers	206	671	1,600 [2]	4,329
Grades 8–10 (Level III)				
Schools	1	2	5	13
Pupils	301	555	1,521	6,969
Teachers	20	28	78 [2]	277

[1] Reflects regrouping and consolidation of schools.
[2] Planned figures.

Source: Based on information from Michael Vickery, *Kampuchea: Politics, Economics, and Society,* London and Boulder, Colorado, 1986, 155; and Kimmo Kiljunen, ed., *Kampuchea: Decade of the Genocide—Report of a Finnish Inquiry Commission,* London, 1984, 40.

Table 5. Land Use, 1980–85
(in thousands of hectares)

Land Use	1980	1985
Arable land/Permanent crops	3,046	3,056
Irrigated land	89	90
Unirrigated land	2,957	2,966
Meadows/Pastures	580	580
Forest/Woodlands	13,372	13,372
Other (Urban/Swamps)	654	644

Source: Based on information from United Nations, Economic and Social Commission for Asia and the Pacific, *Statistical Yearbook for Asia and the Pacific, 1986–87,* Bangkok, 1987, 107.

Table 6. Production of Wood and Lumber, Selected Years
(in thousands of cubic meters)

Type	1979	1981	1983	1985
Fuel wood (including charcoal)	4,189	4,271	4,498	4,736
Industrial wood (sawn logs, veneer, etc.)	567	567	567	567
TOTAL	4,756	4,838	5,065	5,303

Source: Based on information from United Nations, Economic and Social Commission for Asia and the Pacific, *Statistical Yearbook for Asia and the Pacific, 1986–87,* Bangkok, 1987, 108.

Table 7. Area under Principal Food Crops, Selected Years
(in thousands of hectares)

Crop	1980	1982	1984	1986
Rice	1,356	1,680	1,700	1,700
Maize	99	30	33	31
Cassavas	25	10	13	15
Sweet potatoes	2	2	3	3
Groundnuts	5	5	9	10
Soybeans	1	1	1	1
Sesame seeds	8	10	12	13
Dry beans	28	37	40	41

Source: Based on information from United Nations, Economic and Social Commission for Asia and the Pacific, *Statistical Yearbook for Asia and the Pacific, 1986–87,* Bangkok, 1987, 108.

Table 8. Rice Production, Selected Years
(in thousands of tons)

	1980	1982	1984	1986
Paddy rice	1,470	1,400	1,970	2,140
Milled rice *	911	868	1,221	1,327

* Milled rice is computed as 62 percent of the paddy crop.

Source: Based on information from United Nations, Economic and Social Commission for
Asia and the Pacific, *Statistical Yearbook for Asia and the Pacific, 1986-87,* Bangkok,
1987, 108, and Asian Development Bank, Economic Office, *Key Indicators of Developing Member Countries of the Asian Development Bank,* xviii, New York, 1987, 15.

Table 9. Rice Production by Harvest Season, Selected Years
(in thousands of tons)

	1980-81	1982-83	1984-85	1986-87
Paddy rice	1,300	1,563	1,113	2,000 [1]
Milled rice [2]	806	969	690	1,240 [2]

[1] Estimate.
[2] Milled rice is computed as 62 percent of the paddy crop.

Source: Based on information from Peter Schier, ''Kampuchea in 1985—Between Crocodiles and Tigers,'' in *Southeast Asian Affairs, 1986,* Singapore, 1987, 157, and
Economist Intelligence Unit, *Country Profile, 1987-88, Indochina: Vietnam, Laos, Cambodia,* London, December 1987, 46.

Table 10. Production of Principal Secondary Crops, Selected Years
(in thousands of tons)

Crops	1980	1982	1984	1986
Maize	100	46	90	92
Cassavas	150	61	95	100
Sweet potatoes	15	17	30	34
Groundnuts	3	5	8	10
Soybeans	1	1	1	2
Sesame seeds	3	3	6	6
Dry beans	17	26	30	37
Rubber	6	8	13	24.5

Table 11. Index Number of Agricultural Production, Selected Years*

	1980	1982	1984	1986
All commodities	113	117	154	165
Food	113	118	154	163
Cereals	130	117	173	176
Per capita food production	115	113	140	142
Per capita cereal production	132	112	157	152

*1979–81 = 100   '

Source: Based on information from United Nations, Economic and Social Commission for Asia and the Pacific, *Statistical Yearbook for Asia and the Pacific, 1986–87*, Bangkok, 1987, 107.

Table 12. Seafood Catch, Selected Years
(in thousands of tons)

Source	1980	1982	1984	1986
Inland waters	20.0	68.7	57.0	62.2
Deep sea/Coastal waters	7.0	5.5	5.5	n.a.
TOTAL	27.0	74.2	62.5	62.2

n.a.—not available

Table 13. Long-Term External Debt, 1980–84
(in millions of United States dollars)

Year	Amount
1980	251
1981	244
1982	368
1983	426
1984	491

Source: Based on information from Asian Development Bank, Economic Office, *Key Indicators of Developing Member Countries of the Asian Development Bank*, xviii, New York, 1987, 55.

311

Table 14. Trade with the Soviet Union, 1982–87
(in millions of rubles [1])

	1982 [2]	1983	1984	1985	1986	1987
Imports (from the Soviet Union)	53.4	67.8	76.2	91.2	114.0	112.0
Exports (to the Soviet Union)	2.3	4.0	5.2	9.1	8.7	11.2
TOTAL	55.7	71.8	81.4	100.3	122.7	123.2

[1] For value of the ruble—see Glossary.
[2] No trade is recorded prior to 1982.

Source: Based on information from Union of Soviet Socialist Republics, Ministry of Foreign Trade, *Vneshniaia Torgovlia* (Foreign Trade) Moscow, various issues, 1983-87.

Table 15. Net Flows of Resources of Cambodia, Selected Years
(in millions of United States dollars)

	1979	1981	1983	1985
Official development assistance	108.1	130.0	36.7	12.9
Net official flow	108.2	130.0	36.7	12.9
Net private flow	0.0	0.0	0.0	0.0

Source: Based on information from Asian Development Bank, Economic Office, *Key Indicators of Developing Member Countries of the Asian Development Bank,* xviii, New York, 1987, 66–69.

Table 16. *Major Weapons of the Kampuchean, or Khmer,*
People's Revolutionary Armed Forces, 1987

Equipment	Quantity	Model	Origin
Ground Forces			
Main battle tanks	60	T-54/55	Soviet Union
		Type-59	China
Light amphibious tanks	10	PT-76	China
Armored personnel carriers	150-175	BTR-40/BTR-60	Soviet Union
		BTR-152/M-113	United States,
			pre-1975
Artillery	350-380		
76mm gun (towed)		M-1942	Soviet Union
122mm gun (towed)		M-1938	–do–
130mm gun (towed)		Type-59	China
122mm howitzer (towed)		D-30	Soviet Union
105mm howitzer (SP [1])		M-108	United States,
			pre-1975
155mm howitzer (SP [1])		M-109	–do–
107mm MRL [2]		Type-63	China
132mm MRL [2]		BM 13-16	Soviet Union
140mm MRL [2]		BM 14-16	–do–
14.7mm AA/AD [3] gun		ZPU-1/-2/-4	–do–
37mm AA/AD [3] gun		M-1939	–do–
57mm AA/AD [3] gun		S-60	–do–
Mortars			
82mm mortar		M-37	–do–
120mm mortar		M-43	–do–
Antitank weapons			
82mm recoilless gun		B-10	–do–
107mm recoilless gun		B-11	–do–
Portable rocket launcher		RPG-2	Soviet Union
			and China
		RPG-7	–do–
Small arms			
7.62mm assault rifle		AK-47	–do–
7.62mm assault rifle		AKM	–do–
5.56mm rifle		M-16	United States,
			pre-1975
7.62mm light machine gun . . .		RPD	Soviet Union
Naval Forces			
Patrol craft	82 [4]	SWIFT/PBR classes	United States,
			pre-1975
Landing craft	6 [4]	LCU	–do–
Air Forces			
Tactical fighters	12 [4]	MiG-21/FISHBED	Soviet Union
Transport helicopter	6 [4]	Mi-8 HIP	–do–

[1] SP = Self propelled.
[2] MRL = Multiple rocket launcher.
[3] AA/AD = Anti-aircraft air-defense.
[4] Estimated.

Source: Based on information from *Pacific Defense Reporter 1988 Annual Reference Edition,*
Kunyung, Australia, 14, 6-7, December 1987-January 1988, 156, and *The Mili-*
tary Balance, 1987-1988, xii, London, 1987, 161-62.

Appendix B

Major Political and Military Organizations

ANS—Armée Nationale Sihanoukiste, or Sihanouk National Army: Umbrella organization of the military forces (including MOULINAKA (*q.v.*) loyal to Sihanouk, founded in 1981 as armed wing of FUNCINPEC (*q.v.*).

CGDK—Coalition Government of Democratic Kampuchea (*See also* KPRP). Recognized by the United Nations as the official government of Cambodia, the ruling coalition in Democratic Kampuchea, a loose political and military coalition of the three resistance groups—Democratic Kampuchea, the KPNLF (*q.v.*), and FUNCINPEC (*q.v.*).

CPNLAF—Cambodian People's National Liberation Armed Forces. New name given to the RAK (*q.v.*) in the early 1970s.

FANK (formerly FARK)—Forces Armées Nationales Khmères, or Khmer National Armed Forces. Military component of Lon Nol's Khmer Republic (*q.v.*).

FARK—Forces Armées Royales Khmères, or Royal Khmer Armed Forces. Armed forces in the newly independent Cambodia in 1953, replaced by FANK (*q.v.*).

FUNCINPEC—Front Uni National pour un Cambodge Indépendant, Neutre, Pacifique, et Coopératif, or National United Front for an Independent, Neutral, Peaceful, and Cooperative Cambodia. Sihanouk's main political organization, formed in 1981. An autonomous part of the CGDK (*q.v.*).

FUNK—Front Uni National du Kampuchéa, or National United Front of Kampuchea. Established by Sihanouk in Beijing in 1970, shortly after the Lon Nol coup ousted him from power; a political and military coalition committed to destroying the Lon Nol regime.

GRUNK—Gouvernement Royal d'Union Nationale du Kampuchéa or Royal Government of National Union of Kampuchea. Government-in-exile formed by Sihanouk after his ouster in 1970.

ICP—Indochinese Communist Party; founded by Ho Chi Minh in 1930 and dismantled in 1951 into its component parties, i.e., the Vietnam Workers' Party, the KPRP (*q.v.*), and the Lao Itsala.

KCP—Kampuchean (or Khmer) Communist Party. Formerly called the WPK (*q.v.*); renamed in 1966. The CPK dominated

315

the Khmer Republic (*q.v.*) resisting forces from 1970 to 1975 and ruled Cambodia from 1975 to 1978. Succeeded by the KPRP (*q.v.*).

Khmer Bleu (Blue Khmer)—Sihanouk's domestic opponents on the right, whom he so named to distinguish them from his domestic opponents on the left, the Khmer Rouge (*q.v.*).

Khmer Issarak (Free Khmer)—Anti-French, nationalist movement organized with Thai backing in 1945 from elements spanning the political spectrum; within a year split into factions, and by independence all but one of them were incorporated into Sihanouk's political structure. Located in western Cambodia, they were on the wane after 1954. The only dissident group, under Son Ngoc Thanh, they became known as the Khmer Serei (*q.v.*), a heterogeneous left-wing guerrilla movement operating in border areas, in the 1970s.

Khmer Krom—Members of a Cambodian minority who lived in Cochinchina; early nationalists. Several major nationalist leaders came from this group.

Khmer Loeu (Highland Khmer)—Hill tribes comprising several ethnolinguistically diverse groups living in Cambodia, mainly along the northeastern and the eastern frontiers; upland- and forest-dwelling ethnic minorities, especially from Rotanokiri Province, an early RAK (*q.v.*) stronghold.

Khmer Republic—Established in 1970 by Lon Nol.

Khmer Rouge (Red Khmer)—The name given to the Cambodian communists by Sihanouk in the 1960s. Later (although a misnomer) it was applied to the insurgents of varying ideological backgrounds who opposed the Khmer Republic (*q.v.*) regime of Lon Nol. Between 1975 and 1978 it denoted the Democratic Kampuchea regime led by the radical Pol Pot faction of the Kampuchean (or Khmer) Communist Party. After being driven from Phnom Penh by Vietnam's invasion of Cambodia in December 1978, the Khmer Rouge went back to guerrilla warfare, and it joined forces with two noncommunist insurgent movements to form the CGDK (*q.v.*). Also known as the NADK (*q.v.*).

Khmer Rumdo (Liberation Khmer)—Sihanoukists; pro-Sihanouk Cambodians recruited from the country's eastern provinces, trained and armed by Hanoi.

Khmer Serei—(Free Khmer). An anti-Sihanouk group under Son Ngoc Thanh's leadership emanating from the anti-French resistance movement called the Khmer Issarak (*q.v.*), located in southeastern Cambodia; in armed opposition to the Sihanouk regime from 1959 on, but dissolved itself shortly after the deposition of Sihanouk in March 1970. Right wing, anti-monarchical nationalists.

Khmer Viet Minh—Cambodian communists; the 3,000 to 5,000 Cambodian communist cadres who had repatriated to North Vietnam after the Geneva Conference; derogatory term used by Sihanouk to refer to Cambodian leftists organizing pro-independence agitation in alliance with the Vietnamese.

KNUFNS—Kampuchean (or Khmer) National United Front for National Salvation; also known as the Kampuchean United Front for National Salvation and the Salvation Front. It was founded in 1978 by anti-Khmer Rouge (*q.v.*) Cambodians in Vietnam as an alternative to the Pol Pot regime, as a Cambo-dian structure to help legitimize the Vietnamese invasion and the ouster of Democratic Kampuchea. As the first incarnation of what has remained the main political organization in the PRK (*q.v.*) besides the KPRP (*q.v.*), the front had numerous noncommunists, including Buddhist clergy, in its leadership, although it was largely controlled by communists. Name changed in 1981 to KUFNCD (*q.v.*).

KPNLAF—Khmer People's National Liberation Armed Forces, also known as the Khmer People's National Liberation Army (not to be confused with the Khmer People's Liberation Army, the opposition forces organized by the Vietnamese Viet Minh at the end of World War II). Military component of KPNLF (*q.v.*), formed in March 1979 under Son Sann.

KPNLF—Khmer People's National Liberation Front. An autono-mous part of the CGDK (*q.v.*), the KPNLF is a political and military organization, founded and led by former prime minister Son Sann, for the purpose of resisting the Vietnamese.

KPRAF—Kampuchean (or Khmer) People's Revolutionary Armed Forces. Military component of PRK (*q.v.*).

KPRP—Kampuchean (or Khmer) People's Revolutionary Party. The original party was founded in September 1951, when the ICP (*q.v.*) dissolved into three national parties (the leadership and policies of which were aligned with the Vietnamese com-munist movement). The name of the party was changed to the WPK (*q.v.*) in 1960 and then to the KCP (*q.v.*) in 1966. Today this designation applies to the communist party that functions in the PRK (*q.v.*). In one sense it is a new organization; in another sense it is the continuation of the communist parties that preceded it. The date of its founding is uncertain, although the First Party Congress held publicly was convened in May 1981; the party may have come into existence after mid-1978.

KUFNCD—Kampuchean (or Khmer) United Front for National Construction and Defense. Umbrella organization of the KPRP (*q.v.*). (Formerly KNUFNS (*q.v.*).

MOULINAKA—Mouvement pour la Libération Nationale du Kampuchéa, or Movement for the National Liberation of Kampuchea; a pro-Sihanouk group formed in August 1979 by Kong Sileah after he broke ranks with General Dien Del; military organization based among the civilian camps on the Cambodian-Thai border.

NADK—National Army of Democratic Kampuchea. The successor to the RAK (*q.v.*—name change effective December 1979), as the armed forces of the Khmer Rouge (*q.v.*).

NFLSVN—National Front for the Liberation of South Vietnam. Called the Viet Cong by opponents, it led the struggle against the United States.

PAVN—People's Army of Vietnam. The military forces of North Vietnam (until 1976) and, after unification, of the Socialist Republic of Vietnam. During the Second Indochina War (1954–75), PAVN bore the brunt of the fighting against United States military forces in Vietnam.

PDFGNUK—Patriotic and Democratic Front of the Great National Union of Kampuchea. A mass organization established by the exiled KCP (*q.v.*) in September 1979 and headed by Khieu Samphan with the aim of ousting the Vietnamese from Cambodia.

PDK—Party of Democratic Kampuchea. New name given to the communist party in Cambodia in December 1981, when the party allegedly dissolved itself, probably to distance itself from the brutality of Pol Pot's regime.

PRK—People's Republic of Kampuchea. The Vietnamese-sponsored Phnom Penh regime established in 1979.

PRYUK—People's Revolutionary Youth Union of Kampuchea. Mass organization for young people that was less elitist than the communist party.

RAK—Revolutionary Army of Kampuchea. Founded by Pol Pot in 1968, this force was renamed the Cambodian People's National Liberation Armed Forces (CPNLAF (*q.v.*)) in the early 1970s. Also known as the People's National Liberation Armed Forces of Kampuchea (PNLAFK). In 1979 it became the NADK (*q.v.*).

Viet Cong—Contraction of the term Viet Nam Cong San (Vietnamese Communists), the name applied by the governments of the United States and of South Vietnam to the communist insurgents in rebellion against the latter government, beginning around 1957. As used in the Khmer Republic (*q.v.*) the term applied to South Vietnamese communist troops operating in South Vietnam and in Cambodian territory as well.

Viet Minh—Contraction of the term Viet Nam Doc Lap Dong Minh Hoi (League for the Independence of Vietnam), a coalition of nationalist elements dominated by the communists and led by veteran Vietnamese revolutionary Ho Chi Minh. Originally a broadly based Vietnamese nationalist organization in armed opposition to both the French and the Japanese; by 1951 taken over by communists. As used in the Khmer Republic (*q.v.*), the term applies to Vietnamese communists, North Vietnamese in particular.

Bibliography

Chapter 1

Abrams, Floyd, and Diane Orentlicher. *Kampuchea, After the Worst: A Report on Current Violations of Human Rights.* New York: Lawyers Committee for Human Rights, 1985.

Antoshin, Y. "Democratic Kampuchea: Two Years Later," *International Affairs* [Moscow], May 1977, 64-69.

Barnett, Anthony. "Democratic Kampuchea: A Highly Centralized Dictatorship." Pages 212-29 in David P. Chandler and Ben Kiernan (eds.), *Revolution and Its Aftermath in Kampuchea: Eight Essays.* New Haven: Yale University Southeast Asia Studies, 1983.

Becker, Elizabeth. *When the War Was Over, The Voices of Cambodia's Revolution and Its People.* New York: Simon and Schuster, 1986.

Cady, John F. *Southeast Asia: Its Historical Development.* New York: McGraw Hill, 1964.

Caldwell, Malcolm, and Lek Tan. *Cambodia in the Southeast Asian War.* New York: Monthly Review Press, 1973.

Carney, Timothy Michael. *Communist Party Power in Kampuchea (Cambodia): Documents and Discussion.* (Data Paper, 106.) Ithaca, New York: Department of Asian Studies, Cornell University, 1977.

Chanda, Nayan. *Brother Enemy: The War after the War.* New York: Harcourt Brace Jovanovich, 1986.

_____. "The Pieces Begin To Fit," *Far Eastern Economic Review* [Hong Kong], 98, October 21, 1977, 20-24.

Chandler, David P. "The Constitution of Democratic Kampuchea (Cambodia): The Semantics of Revolutionary Change," *Pacific Affairs* [Vancouver], 49, No. 3, Fall 1976, 506-15.

_____. *A History of Cambodia.* Boulder, Colorado: Westview Press, 1983.

_____. "Revising the Past in Democratic Kampuchea: When Was the Birthday of the Party?" *Pacific Affairs* [Vancouver], 56, No. 2, Summer 1983, 288-300.

_____. "A Revolution in Full Spate: Communist Party Policy in Democratic Kampuchea, December 1976," *International Journal of Politics,* 16, No. 3, Fall 1986, 131-49.

_____. "Seeing Red: Perceptions of Cambodian History in Democratic Kampuchea." Pages 34-56 in David P. Chandler and Ben Kiernan (eds.), *Revolution and Its Aftermath in Kampuchea: Eight Essays.* New Haven: Yale University Southeast Asia Studies, 1983.

Chandler, David P., and Ben Kiernan (eds.). *Revolution and Its Aftermath in Kampuchea: Eight Essays.* New Haven: Yale University Southeast Asia Studies, 1983.

Coedès, George. *Angkor: An Introduction.* Hong Kong: Oxford University Press, 1969.

————. *The Making of South East Asia.* (Trans., H. M. Wright.) Berkeley: University of California Press, 1966.

Delvert, Jean. *Le Cambodge.* Paris: Presses Universitaires de France, 1983.

Elliott, David W. P. (ed.). *The Third Indochina Conflict.* Boulder, Colorado: Westview Press, 1981.

Etcheson, Craig. *The Rise and Demise of Democratic Kampuchea.* Boulder, Colorado: Westview Press, 1984.

Hall, D. G. E. *A History of South-East Asia.* London: Macmillan, 1964.

Hawk, David. "International Human Rights Law and Democratic Kampuchea," *International Journal of Politics,* 16, No. 3, Fall 1986, 3-38.

Heder, Stephen R. "Kampuchea 1980: Anatomy of a Crisis," *Southeast Asia Chronicle,* No. 77, February 1981, 3-11.

————. "Democratic Kampuchea: The Regime's Post-Mortem," *Indochina Issues,* No. 13, January 1981.

Herz, Martin F. *A Short History of Cambodia from the Days of Angkor to the Present.* New York: Praeger, 1958.

Hildebrand, George, and Gareth Porter. *Cambodia: Starvation and Revolution.* New York: Monthly Review Press, 1976.

"I Spent a Year Growing Cabbages at the Khmer Rouge Foreign Affairs Ministry," *Le Monde* [Paris], October 27, 1980. Joint Publications Research Service, *Southeast Asia Report,* JPRS-76701, September 20, 1980, 26-30.

International Documentation and Information Centre (INTERDOC). "Cambodia: Problems of Neutrality and Independence." The Hague: May 1970.

Ith Sarin. *Sranaoh Pralungkhmer* (Regrets for the Khmer Soul). (Trans., Chanthou Boua.) unpublished.

Khieu, Samphan. *Cambodia's Economy and Industrial Development.* (Trans., Laura Summers.) Ithaca, New York: Department of Asian Studies, Cornell University, 1979.

Kiernan, Ben. *How Pol Pot Came to Power.* London: Verso, 1984.

————. "Introduction." Pages 1-28 in Ben Kiernan and Chanthou Boua (eds.), *Peasants and Politics in Kampuchea, 1942-81.* London: Zed Press, 1982.

_____. "The 1970 Peasant Uprisings Against Lon Nol." Pages 206–23 in Ben Kiernan and Chanthou Boua (eds.), *Peasants and Politics in Kampuchea, 1942–81.* London: Zed Press, 1982.

_____. "Pol Pot and the Kampuchean Communist Movement." Pages 227–317 in Ben Kiernan and Chanthou Boua (eds.), *Peasants and Politics in Kampuchea, 1942–81.* London: Zed Press, 1982.

_____. "The Samlaut Rebellion, 1967–68." Pages 166–205 in Ben Kiernan and Chanthou Boua (eds.), *Peasants and Politics in Kampuchea, 1942–81.* London: Zed Press, 1982.

_____. "Wild Chickens, Farm Chickens and Cormorants: Kampuchea's Eastern Zone Under Pol Pot." Pages 136–211 in David P. Chandler and Ben Kiernan (eds.), *Revolution and Its Aftermath in Kampuchea: Eight Essays.* New Haven: Yale University Southeast Asia Studies, 1983.

Kiernan, Ben, and Chanthou Boua (eds.). *Peasants and Politics in Kampuchea, 1942–81.* London: Zed Press, 1982.

Kiernan, Ben, and Stephen R. Heder. "Why Pol Pot? Roots of the Cambodian Tragedy," *Indochina Issues,* No. 52, December 1984.

Kiljunen, Kimmo, ed. *Kampuchea: Decade of the Genocide—Report of a Finnish Inquiry Commission.* London: Zed Books, 1984.

Kissinger, Henry. *White House Years.* Boston: Little, Brown, 1979.

_____. *Years of Upheaval.* Boston: Little, Brown, 1982.

Lacouture, Jean. *Ho Chi Minh: A Political Biography.* New York: Random House, 1968.

Le Bar, Frank M. (ed. and comp.). *Ethnic Groups of Insular Southeast Asia.* New Haven: Human Relations Area Files Press, 1964.

Leifer, Michael. "Kampuchea 1979: From Dry Season to Dry Season," *Asian Survey,* 20, No. 1, January 1980, 33–41.

Leighton, Marian Kirsch. "Perspectives on the Vietnam-Cambodia Border Conflict," *Asian Survey,* 18, No. 5, May 1978, 448–57.

Men Xom On. "Major Landmarks of the Kampuchean Revolution," *Vietnam Courier* [Hanoi], 20, No. 11, November 1984, 10–12.

Myrdal, Jan. "When the Peasant War Triumphed," *Southeast Asia Chronicle,* No. 77, February 1981, 12–15.

_____. "Why is There Famine in Kampuchea?" *Southeast Asia Chronicle,* No. 77, February 1981, 16–18.

Osborne, Milton E. *Before Kampuchea: Preludes to Tragedy.* London: George Allen and Unwin, 1979.

_____. "Norodom Sihanouk: A Leader of the Left?" New Haven: Department of History, Yale University, 1974.

Ponchaud, François. *Cambodia: Year Zero.* (Trans., Nancy Amphoux.) New York: Holt, Rinehart and Winston, 1978.

_____. "Le Kampuchéa démocratique: Une révolution radicale," *Mondes Asiatiques* [Paris], No. 6, Summer 1976, 153–80.

Quinn, Kenneth M. "Cambodia 1976: Internal Consolidation and External Expansion," *Asian Survey*, 17, No. 1, January 1977, 43–54.

Schanberg, Sydney H. *The Death and Life of Dith Pran.* New York: Penguin, 1980.

Shawcross, William. "Cambodia: Some Perceptions of a Disaster." Pages 230–58 in David P. Chandler, and Ben Kiernan (eds.), *Revolution and Its Aftermath in Kampuchea: Eight Essays.* New Haven: Yale University Southeast Asia Studies, 1983.

_____. *The Quality of Mercy: Cambodia, Holocaust, and Modern Conscience.* New York: Simon and Schuster, 1984.

_____. *Sideshow: Kissinger, Nixon, and the Destruction of Cambodia.* New York: Simon and Schuster, 1979.

Sihanouk, Prince Norodom. (Trans., Mary Feeney.) *War and Hope: The Case for Cambodia.* New York: Pantheon Books, 1980.

Sisowath, Prince Thomico. "Norodom Sihanouk and the Khmer Factions," *Indochina Report* [Singapore], No. 9, October–December 1986.

Szymusiak, Molyda. *The Stones Cry Out: A Cambodian Childhood, 1975–80.* New York: Hill and Wang, 1986.

"Testimonies: Life Under the Khmer Rouge." Pages 318–62 in Ben Kiernan and Chanthou Boua (eds.), *Peasants and Politics in Kampuchea, 1942–81.* London: Zed Press, 1982.

Thion, Serge. "The Cambodian Idea of Revolution." Pages 10–33 in David P. Chandler and Ben Kiernan (eds.), *Revolution and Its Aftermath in Kampuchea: Eight Essays.* New Haven: Yale University Southeast Asia Studies, 1983.

_____. "Chronology of Khmer Communism, 1940–82." Pages 291–319 in David P. Chandler and Ben Kiernan (eds.), *Revolution and Its Aftermath in Kampuchea: Eight Essays.* New Haven: Yale University Southeast Asia Studies, 1983.

_____. "The Pattern of Cambodian Politics," *International Journal of Politics,* 16, No. 3, Fall 1986, 110–30.

Vickery, Michael. *Cambodia, 1975–82.* Boston: South End Press, 1984.

_____. "Democratic Kampuchea: Themes and Variations." Pages 99–135 in David P. Chandler and Ben Kiernan (eds.), *Revolution and Its Aftermath in Kampuchea: Eight Essays.* New Haven: Yale University Southeast Asia Studies, 1983.

Bibliography

———. *Kampuchea: Politics, Economics, and Society.* (Marxist Regimes series.) London: Frances Pinter, 1986.
———. "Looking Back at Cambodia, 1942–76." Pages 89–113 in Ben Kiernan and Chanthou Boua (eds.), *Peasants and Politics in Kampuchea, 1942–81.* London: Zed Press, 1982.
"Two Views on the Vietnam-Kampuchea War." *Southeast Asia Chronicle,* No. 64, September–October 1978, 1–40.
White, Peter T. "Ancient Glory in Stone," *National Geographic,* 161, No. 5, May 1982, 552–89.
———. "Kampuchea Wakens From a Nightmare," *National Geographic,* 161, No. 5, May 1982, 590–623.
Willmott, W. E. "The Chinese in Kampuchea," *Journal of Southeast Asian Studies* [Singapore], 12, No. 1, March 1981, 38–45.

Chapter 2

Ang, Choulean. "Grossesse et accouchement au Cambodia: aspects rituels," *ASEMI* [Paris], 13, Nos. 1–4, 1982.
———. "Les apparitions de fantômes au Cambodge," *ASEMI* [Paris], 11, 1980, 437–43.
Apsara. "Les enfants du Kampuchéa Démocratique," *ASEMI* [Paris], 13, No. 1–4, 1982, 183–92.
Bartu, Friedemann. "Cambodian Refugees: Tomorrow's 'Palestinians'?" *Swiss Review of World Affairs* [Zurich], 38, No. 1, April 1987, 8–9.
Berberg, Toine. "Life in Kampuchea's Refugee Camps . . . Will They Ever Go Back Home?," *Daily News* [Colombo], July 16, 1987, 6.
———. "Life in Kampuchea's Refugee Camps . . . Dim Hopes of a Viet Pullout," *Daily News* [Colombo], July 17, 1987, 4.
———. "Life in Kampuchea's Refugee Camps . . . Pol Pot's Shadow Still Haunts Kampuchea," *Daily News* [Colombo], July 18, 1987, 8.
Bhikkhu Oung Mean Candavanna. "A Seminar on Khmer Buddhism," *Vatt Khmer,* No. 5, March 1985, 5–8.
———. "A Seminar on Khmer Buddhism," *Vatt Khmer,* No. 6, January 1986, 4–7.
"A Border-Line Existence," *Refugees* [Geneva], No. 45, September 1987, 33.
Bruk, S.I. *Naselenie Mira* [World Population]. Moscow: Nauka, 1981.
Cambodia. Ministry of Information. *Le Bouddhisme au Cambodge.* Phnom Penh: Royal Cambodian Government, 1962.

———. *Cambodia.* Ministry of Information. Phnom Penh: Royal Cambodian Government, 1962.

Chanthou, Boua. "La femme dans la République Populaire du Kampuchéa," *ASEMI,* 13, Nos. 1-4, 1982, 287-314.

Crisp, Jeff. "Refugees in Thailand: The Long Wait For A Solution," *Refugees* [Geneva], No. 45, September 1987, 18-22.

———. "Shattered Past; Uncertain Future," *Refugees* [Geneva], No. 45, September 1987, 30-32.

Delvert, Jean. *Le Cambodge.* Paris: Presses Universitaires de France, 1983.

Dutt, Ashok K. (ed.). *Southeast Asia: Realm of Contrasts.* Dubuque: Kendall Hunt Publishing Company, 1974.

Dy Phan, Pauline. "Facteurs Ecologiques et Végétation du Cambodge," *Seksa Khmer* [Paris], 3-4, 1980, 5.

Ea, Meng-Try. "Kampuchea: A Country Adrift," *Population and Development Review,* 7, No. 2, June 1981, 209-28.

Ebihara, May Mayko. *Svay: A Khmer Village in Cambodia.* Ann Arbor: University Microfilms, 1971.

Goulin, Christian. "Phnom-Penh notes de géographie urbaine," *Les Cahiers d'Outre-Mer* [Bordeaux], January-March 1967, 5-36.

Khin, Sok. "Essai d'Interpretation de formules magiques des Cambodgiens," *ASEMI* [Paris], 13, Nos. 1-4, 1982, 111-19.

Kiernan, Ben. "Kampuchea's Ethnic Chinese under Pol Pot: A Case of Systematic Social Discrimination," *Journal of Contemporary Asia* [Stockholm], 16, No. 1, 1986, 18-29.

———. *Social Cohesion in Revolutionary Cambodia.* Sydney: Australian Institute of International Affairs, 1976.

Kiernan, Ben, and Chanthou Boua (eds.). *Peasants and Politics in Kampuchea, 1942-81.* London: Zed Press, 1982.

Kiljunen, Kimmo (ed.). *Kampuchea: Decade of the Genocide—Report of a Finnish Inquiry Commission.* London: Zed Books, 1984.

Le Bar, Frank M., Gerald C. Hickey, and John K. Musgrave (eds.). *Ethnic Groups of Mainland Southeast Asia.* New Haven: Human Relations Area Files Press, 1964.

Martel, Gabrielle. *Lovea, village des environs d'Angkor* (Bulletin de l'Ecole Francaise d'Extrême Orient). Paris: 1975.

Martin, Marie Alexandrine. "Vietnamized Cambodia: A Silent Ethnocide," *Indochina Report* [Singapore], No. 7, July-September 1986, 2-30.

Migozzi, Jacques. *Cambodge: faits et problèmes de population* (Cambodia: Population Facts and Problems). Paris: Editions du Centre National de la Recherche Scientifique, 1973.

Montagu, John. "Kampuchea." Pages 202-204 in *Asia and Pacific Review 1985.* Middle East Review Company, 1984.

Nepote, Jacques. "Cartographie de l'ethnie Khmère en 1970," *Seksa Khmer* [Paris], 1-2, 1980, 11-18.

Panaritis, Andrea. "Cambodia: The Rough Road To Recovery," *Indochina Issues*, No. 56, April 1985.

Philippides, Daniel. "Medical and Sanitary Situation in Cambodia (1979-1984)," *ASEMI* [Paris], 15, Nos. 1-4, 1984, 235-76.

Po, Dharma. "Notes sur les cam du Cambodge," *Seksa Khmer* [Paris], 3-4, 1981, 161-83.

Pourtier, Roland. "Les Chinois du Cambodge littoral," *Les Cahiers d'Outre-Mer* [Bordeaux], 24, No. 1, January 1971, 45-72.

Steinberg, David J. *Cambodia: Its People, Its Society, Its Culture.* (Survey of World Cultures.) New Haven: Human Relations Area Files Press, 1959.

Thierry, Solange. *Le Cambodge des Contes.* Paris: Editions L'Harmattan, 1985.

Thomas, David, and Robert Headley. "More on Mon-Khmer Subgroupings," *Lingua* [Amsterdam], 25, No. 4, 1970, 398-418.

United Kingdom. Foreign and Commonwealth Office. "Human Rights Violations in Democratic Kampuchea: A Report Prepared by the United Kingdom Government, 14 July 1978." (Foreign Policy Documents, No. 25.) London: 1978.

United States. Bureau of Census. Unpublished, computerized data on world population, Washington, 1987.

Vickery, Michael. *Cambodia 1975-82.* Boston: South End Press, 1984.

_____. "Cambodia's Tenuous Progress," *Indochina Issues*, No. 63, January 1986.

_____. *Kampuchea: Politics, Economics, and Society.* (Marxist Regimes series.) London: Frances Pinter, 1986.

Willmott, W.E. "The Chinese in Kampuchea," *Journal of Southeast Asian Studies* [Singapore], 12, No. 1, March 1981, 38-45.

Chapter 3

Asian Development Bank. Economic Office. *Key Indicators of Developing Member Countries of the Asian Development Bank, XVII.* New York: New York University Press, 1986.

_____. *Key Indicators of Developing Member Countries of the Asian Development Bank, XVIII.* New York: New York University Press, 1987.

Asian Economic Handbook. London: Euromonitor Publications, 1987.

Chanda, Nayan. "A Qualified Recovery," *Far Eastern Economic Review* [Hong Kong], 132, No. 20, May 15, 1986, 25-28.

_____. *Brother Enemy: The War after the War.* New York: Harcourt Brace Jovanovich, 1986.

Ea, Meng-Try. "Kampuchea: A Country Adrift," *Population and Development Review,* 7, No. 2, June 1981, 209–25.

Economic and Social Commission for Asia and the Pacific. *Statistical Yearbook for Asia and the Pacific, 1986–87,* Bangkok: 1987.

Economist Intelligence Unit. *Country Profile: 1987–88, Indochina: Vietnam, Laos, Cambodia.* London: Economist Publications Limited, December 1987.

The Far East and Australasia. London: Europa Publications, 1986.

FAO Production Yearbook. Rome: Food and Agriculture Organization of the United Nations, 1986.

FAO Production Yearbook. Rome: Food and Agriculture Organization of the United Nations, 1987.

Hiebert, Murray. "Cambodia and Vietnam: Costs of the Alliance," *Indochina Issues,* No. 46, May 1984.

_____. "Market Forces Flourish," *Far Eastern Economic Review* [Hong Kong], 136, No. 19, May 7, 1987, 38.

_____. "The Shadow of War," *Far Eastern Economic Review* [Hong Kong], 136, No. 19, May 7, 1987, 36–37.

Jenkins, David. "Destructive Elements Decimate the Harvest," *Far Eastern Economic Review* [Hong Kong], 126, No. 48, November 29, 1984, 26–27.

"Kampuchea." Pages 1617–25 in *The Far East and Australasia, 1987.* London: Europa Publications, 1987.

Khieu Samphan. "Cambodia's Economy and Industrial Development." (Trans., Laura Summers.) Ithaca, New York: Department of Asian Studies, Cornell University, 1979.

Kiernan, Ben. "Kampuchea, 1979–81: National Rehabilitation in the Eye of an International Storm." Pages 167–95 in Huynh Kim Khanh (ed.), *Southeast Asian Affairs, 1982.* Singapore: Heinemann Educational Books (Asia), 1982.

Kirk, Donald. *Wider War.* New York: Praeger, 1971.

Le Thi Tuyet. *Regional Cooperation in Southeast Asia: The Mekong Project, 1973.* (Unpublished Ph. D. dissertation.) New York: City University of New York.

Martin, Marie Alexandrine. "La riziculture et la maitrise de l'eau dans le Kampuchéa Démocratique," *Etudes Rurales* [Paris], No. 83, July–September 1981, 7–44.

Mosyakov, D. "Solving the Food Problem in Kampuchea," *Far Eastern Affairs* [Moscow], No. 4, 1986, 43–51.

Ponchaud, François. "Sous la conduite de l'Angkar: Aperçus sur la révolution cambodgienne," *Etudes* [Paris], February 1977, 167–80, 346.

Quinn-Judge, Paul. "A Crisis Unrelieved," *Far Eastern Economic Review* [Hong Kong], 123, No. 5, February 2, 1984, 47–48.
_____. "The Meagre Harvest," *Far Eastern Economic Review* [Hong Kong], 127, No. 3, January 24, 1985, 66.
Richardson, Michael. "Unity in Adversity," *Far Eastern Economic Review* [Hong Kong], 124, No. 14, April 5, 1984, 56–58.
Schier, Peter. "Kampuchea in 1985—Between Crocodiles and Tigers." Pages 139–61 in *Southeast Asian Affairs, 1986.* Singapore: Institute of Southeast Asian Studies, 1987.
Shawcross, William. *The Quality of Mercy: Cambodia, Holocaust, and Modern Conscience.* New York: Simon and Schuster, 1984.
Sihanouk, Prince Norodom. (as related to Wilfred Burchett). *My War with the CIA: The Memoirs of Prince Norodom Sihanouk.* New York: Pantheon Books, 1973.
Ukraintsev, M. "The Soviet Union's Growing Cooperation with Asian Socialist Nations and Kampuchea," *Far Eastern Affairs,* [Moscow], 47, No. 1, 1986, 51–63.
United States Central Intelligence Agency. *The World Fact Book, 1987.* Washington: GPO, 1987.
_____. Department of State. Bureau of Public Affairs. *Background Notes: Kampuchea (Cambodia).* Washington: GPO, May 1984.
Vickery, Michael. "Cambodia's Tenuous Progress," *Indochina Issues,* No. 63, January 1986.
_____. *Kampuchea: Politics, Economics, and Society.* Boulder, Colorado: Lynne Rienner, 1986.

(Various issues of the following periodicals were also used in the preparation of this chapter: *Cham Ethnic Minority Incorporated Newsletter;* Economist Intelligence Unit, *Country Report: Indochina: Vietnam, Laos, Cambodia* [London]; Far Eastern Economic Review, *Asia Yearbook;* *Far Eastern Economic Review* [Hong Kong]; Foreign Broadcast Information Service, *Daily Report: Asia and Pacific;* and *Daily Report: East Asia; Keesing's Record of World Events* [Harlow, Essex, United Kingdom]; Joint Publications Research Service, *South Asia Report; Vneshniaia Torgovlia* (Foreign Trade) [Moscow].)

Chapter 4

Ablin, David A., and Marlowe Hood (eds.). "Cambodia: Politics and International Relations," *International Journal of Politics,* 16, No. 3, Fall 1986, 3–185.
Barron, John and Anthony Paul. *Murder of a Gentle Land: The Untold Story of Communist Genocide in Cambodia.* New York: Thomas Y. Crowell, 1977.

Becker, Elizabeth. "Stalemate in Cambodia," *Current History*, 86, No. 519, April 1987, 156–59.

Bekaert, Jacques. "Cambodge: Des graves incidents ont opposé des Khmers rouges et des Sihanoukistes," *Le Monde* [Paris], July 31, 1985, 4.

"Cambodia: Vietnam's 1990 Question," *Asiaweek* [Hong Kong], 12, No. 31, August 3, 1986, 20–21.

Central Committee. National United Front for the Salvation of Kampuchea. "Kampuchea's Eight Immediate Policies for Liberated Areas," *Vietnam Courier* [Hanoi], 15, No. 2, February 1979, 3–4.

_____. "Kampuchea's Foreign Policy," *Vietnam Courier* [Hanoi], 15, No. 2, February 1979, 4–5.

Chanda, Nayan. "Communist Compromise? Moscow, Hanoi, and Peking Signal Movement," *Far Eastern Economic Review* [Hong Kong], 134, No. 52, December 25, 1986, 14–15.

_____. "A Qualified Recovery," *Far Eastern Economic Review* [Hong Kong], 132, No. 20, May 15, 1986, 25–28.

_____. "Stop-go Train of Peace," *Far Eastern Economic Review* [Hong Kong], 138, No. 52, December 24, 1987, 10.

_____. "Straw in the Wind: Soviet Hint of Flexibility over Elections," *Far Eastern Economic Review* [Hong Kong], 131, No. 3, January 16, 1986, 21–22.

Chandler, David P. "Cambodia in 1984: Historical Patterns Reasserted." Pages 177–86 in *Southeast Asian Affairs, 1985*. Singapore: Institute of Southeast Asian Studies, 1985.

_____. "Kampuchea: End Game or Stalemate?" *Current History*, 83, No. 497, December 1984, 413–17.

_____. "Revising the Past in Democratic Kampuchea: When was the Birthday of the Party?" *Pacific Affairs* [Vancouver], 56, No. 2, Summer 1983, 288–300.

_____. "The Tragedy of Cambodian History," *Pacific Affairs* [Vancouver], 52, No. 3, Fall 1979, 410–15.

Chandler, David P., and Ben Kiernan (eds.). *Revolution and Its Aftermath in Kampuchea: Eight Essays*. New Haven: Yale University Southeast Asia Studies, 1983.

Chang, Pao-min. "Beijing Versus Hanoi: The Diplomacy over Kampuchea," *Asian Survey*, 23, No. 5, May 1983, 598–618.

_____. *Kampuchea Between China and Vietnam*. Singapore: Singapore University Press, 1985.

Chufrin, Gennady I. "Five Years of the People's Revolutionary Power in Kampuchea: Results and Conclusions," *Asian Survey*, 24, No. 11, November 1984, 1143–50.

Conboy, Kenneth J. (ed.). *The U.S. and Vietnam: Twelve Years After the War.* (The Heritage Lecture Series.) Washington: The Heritage Foundation, 1987.

Eiland, Michael. "Kampuchea in 1985: From Stalemate to Ambiguity," *Asian Survey,* 26, No. 1, January 1986, 118–25.

Elliott, David W. P. (ed.). *The Third Indochina Conflict.* Boulder, Colorado: Westview Press, 1981.

Etcheson, Craig. *The Rise and Demise of Democratic Kampuchea.* Boulder, Colorado: Westview Press, 1984.

Fenton, James (ed.). *Cambodia Witness: The Autobiography of Someth May.* New York: Random House, 1986.

Greenhouse, Steven. "Sihanouk Cancels His Plans to Meet Cambodian Again," *New York Times,* December 11, 1987, A7.

Heder, Stephen P. "The Kampuchean-Vietnamese Conflict." Pages 157–86 in *Southeast Asian Affairs, 1979.* Singapore: Heinemann Educational Books (Asia), 1979.

Hiebert, Murray. "Peace or Propaganda?" *Far Eastern Economic Review* [Hong Kong], 138, No. 43, October 22, 1987, 35.

_____. "That Annual Exercise," *Far Eastern Economic Review* [Hong Kong], 138, No. 50, December 10, 1987, 23.

_____. "The Shadow of War," *Far Eastern Economic Review* [Hong Kong], 136, No. 19, May 7, 1987, 36–37.

Huxley, Tim. "ASEAN and Cambodia: The Hazards of Stalemate," *Asia Pacific Community* [Tokyo], 30, Fall 1985, 30–47.

"Is Pol Pot Dying?" *Asiaweek* [Hong Kong], 12, No. 50, December 14, 1986, 39–41.

Kershaw, Roger. "Multipolarity and Cambodia's Crisis of Survival: A Preliminary Perspective on 1979." Pages 161–88 in *Southeast Asian Affairs, 1979.* Singapore: Heinemann Educational Books (Asia), 1979.

Khien, Theeravit. "Thai-Kampuchean Relations: Problems and Prospects," *Asian Survey,* 22, 6, June 1982, 561–76.

Kiernan, Ben. *How Pol Pot Came to Power.* London: Verso, 1984.

_____. "Kampuchea 1979–81: National Rehabilitation in the Eye of an International Storm." Pages 167–95 in Huynh Kim Khanh (ed.), *Southeast Asian Affairs, 1982.* Singapore: Heinemann Educational Books (Asia), 1982.

_____. "Origins of Khmer Communism." Pages 161–80 in Leo Suryadinata (ed.), *Southeast Asian Affairs, 1981.* Singapore: Heinemann Educational Books (Asia), 1981.

Kiernan, Ben and Chanthou Boua (eds.). *Peasants and Politics in Kampuchea, 1942–81.* London: Zed Press, 1982.

Kiljunen, Kimmo (ed.). *Kampuchea: Decade of the Genocide—Report of a Finnish Inquiry Commission.* London: Zed Books, 1984.

Kissinger, Henry. *White House Years.* Boston: Little, Brown, 1979.
_____. *Years of Upheaval.* Boston: Little, Brown, 1982.
Lao, Mong Hay. "Kampuchea: A Stalemate?" Pages 153-61 in Pushpa Thambipillai (ed.), in *Southeast Asian Affairs, 1984,* Singapore: Heinemann Educational Books (Asia), 1984.
Leighton, Marian Kirsch. "Perspectives on the Vietnam-Cambodia Border Conflict," *Asian Survey,* 28, No. 5, May 1978, 448-57.
Lichenstein, Charles M. "China in the U.N.: The Case of Kampuchea," *World Affairs,* 149, No. 1, Summer 1986, 21-24.
Ma Shengrong. "Kampuchea: Vietnamese Troop Pullout Key to Peace," *Beijing Review* [Beijing], 30, No. 49, December 7, 1987, 14.
Mahbubani, Kishore. "The Kampuchean Problem: A Southeast Asian Perception," *Foreign Affairs,* 62, Winter 1983-84, 407-25.
McBeth, John. "Forced Human Bondage," *Far Eastern Economic Review* [Hong Kong], 129, No. 33, August 22, 1985, 38-39.
McMullen, Greerson G. "New Policy Initiatives for the U.S. in Kampuchea," *Asian Wall Street Journal* [Hong Kong], May 18-19, 1984, 8.
Mean, Sang Khim. "Democratic Kampuchea: An Updated View." Pages 95-106 in *Southeast Asian Affairs, 1977.* Singapore: International Institute of Southeast Asian Studies, 1977.
"Mochtar Kusumaatmadja: ASEAN Will Not Accept Five Articles Proposed by Nguyen Co Thach," *Indonesian Observer* [Jakarta], April 8, 1985, 4.
"Mokhtar Comments on Sihanouk, Cambodia Crisis." *Jakarta Post* [Jakarta], June 23, 1987, 1.
Osborne, Milton E. *Before Kampuchea: Preludes to Tragedy.* London: George Allen and Unwin, 1979.
Ponchaud, François. *Cambodia: Year Zero.* (Trans., Nancy Amphoux.) New York: Holt, Rinehart and Winston, 1978.
Pospelov, D., and Y. Ryakin. "Imperialist and Reactionary Intrigues Against People's Kampuchea," *Far Eastern Affairs* [Moscow], No. 3, 1984, 97-109.
"The PRK's Great National Solidarity Policy," *Nhan Dan* [Hanoi], August 29, 1987, 34-35.
Quinn-Judge, Paul. "Coalition Coalescent," *Far Eastern Economic Review* [Hong Kong], 123, No. 1, January 5, 1984, 14-15.
_____. "Too Few Communists," *Far Eastern Economic Review* [Hong Kong], 123, No. 7, February 16, 1984, 20-22.
Richburg, Keith B. "Sihanouk's Peace Search Splits Cambodia Viewers," *Washington Post,* November 21, 1987, A18.
Schier, Peter. "Kampuchea in 1985: Between Crocodiles and Tigers." Pages 139-61 in *Southeast Asian Affairs, 1986.* Singapore: Institute of Southeast Asian Studies, 1986.

Shawcross, William. *Sideshow: Kissinger, Nixon, and the Destruction of Cambodia.* London: Fontana Paperbacks, 1980.

————. *The Quality of Mercy: Cambodia, Holocaust, and Modern Conscience.* New York: Simon and Schuster, 1984.

Simon, Sheldon W. "Cambodia and Regional Diplomacy." Pages 196–207 in Huynh Kim Khanh (ed.), *Southeast Asian Affairs, 1982.* Singapore: Heinemann Educational Books (Asia), 1982.

Smith, R. B. "Cambodia in the Context of Sino-Vietnamese Relations," *Asian Affairs* (London), 16, October 1985, 273–87.

Spragens, John. "Interview with Hun Sen: Solution Cambodian Style," *Far Eastern Economic Review* [Hong Kong], 123, No. 1, January 5, 1984, 14–15.

Stuart-Fox, Martin. *The Murderous Revolution: Life and Death in Pol Pot's Kampuchea (Based on the Personal Experience of Bungheang Ung).* Chippendale, Australia: Alternative Publishing Cooperative, 1985.

Sukhumbhand, Paribatra, M. R. "Can ASEAN Break the Stalemate?" *World Policy Journal,* 3, No. 1, Winter 1985–86, 85–106.

Sutter, Robert G. "The Fighting in Cambodia: Issues for U.S. Policy," (Library of Congress Congressional Research Service, Report No. 85–43F.) February 1, 1985.

Tasker, Rodney. "Divided on Peace: Thai and Indonesian Differences Persist over Cambodian Solution," *Far Eastern Economic Review* [Hong Kong], 132, No. 17, April 24, 1986, 47.

United States. Central Intelligence Agency. Directorate of Intelligence. *Who's Who in Cambodia: A Reference Aid.* (No. CR85-10626.) Washington: March 1985.

United States. Congress. 97th. 2d Session. House. Committee on Foreign Affairs. Subcommittees on Asian and Pacific Affairs and Human Rights and International Organizations. *The Democratic Kampuchea Seat at the United Nations and American Interests.* (Hearings September 15, 1982.) Washington: GPO, 1983.

Van der Kroef, Justus M. "ASEAN, Hanoi, and the Kampuchean Conflict: Between 'Kuantan' and a 'Third Alternative'," *Asian Survey,* 21, No. 5, May 1981, 515–35.

————. "Cambodia: From 'Democratic Kampuchea' to 'Peoples' Republic'," *Asian Survey,* 19, No. 8, August 1979, 731–50.

————. "Kampuchea: The Diplomatic Labyrinth," *Asian Survey,* 22, No. 10, October 1982, 1009–1033.

————. "Kampuchea: Protracted Conflict, Suspended Compromise," *Asian Survey,* 24, No. 3, March 1984, 314–34.

————. " 'Proximity Cocktails' and 'Provisional Salvation': Cambodia's Tortuous Course," *Issues & Studies* [Taipei], 22, No. 4, April 1986, 120–39.

Vickery, Michael. *Cambodia: 1975-82.* Boston: South End Press, 1984.

_____. *Kampuchea: Politics, Economics, and Society.* (Marxist Regimes series). London: Frances Pinter, 1986.

Wedel, Paul. "Cambodian Communists Build Party from the Top Down," *Korea Herald* [Seoul], October 10, 1987, 8.

Wheeler, Jack. "Cambodian Foes of Hanoi's Imperialism Cry Out for U.S. Aid," *Wall Street Journal,* January 14, 1985, 17.

Willmott, W. E. "Analytical Errors of the Kampuchean Communist Party," *Pacific Affairs,* 54, No. 2, Summer 1981, 209-27.

World Policy Institute. "Special Report on Indochina: The Prospects for Peace," *World Policy Journal,* 3, No. 1, Winter 1985-86, 83-155.

Yearbook on International Communist Affairs. Stanford: Hoover Institution for War, Revolution and Peace, 1987.

(Various issues of the following periodicals were also used in the preparation of this chapter: *Bangkok Post* [Bangkok]; *Far Eastern Economic Review* [Hong Kong]; Far Eastern Economic Review, *Asia Yearbook;* Foreign Broadcast Information Service, *Daily Report: East Asia;* and *Daily Report: Soviet Union;* Joint Publications Research Service, *East Asia Report; Southeast Asia Report; Vietnam Courier* [Hanoi]; *New York Times;* and *Washington Post.*

Chapter 5

Abrams, Floyd, and Diane Orentlicher. *Kampuchea, After the Worst: A Report on Current Violations of Human Rights.* New York: Lawyers Committee for Human Rights, 1985.

Amnesty International. *Kampuchea Political Imprisonment and Torture.* London: 1987.

"Asia and Australia." *Pacific Defense Reporter: 1988 Annual Reference Edition* [Kunyung, Australia] 14, Nos. 6-7, December 1987-January 1988, 144-162.

Asia 1987 Yearbook. Hong Kong: Far Eastern Economic Review, 1986.

Becker, Elizabeth. *When the War Was Over: The Voices of Cambodia's Revolution and Its People.* New York: Simon and Schuster, 1986.

Bekaert, Jacques. "Cambodia: The Last Dry Season," *Asian Defence Journal* [Kuala Lumpur], No. 6, June 1987, 44-51.

_____. "War in Cambodia, 1979-86," *Asian Defence Journal* [Kuala Lumpur], No. 8, August 1986, 17-19.

Bell, Sir Hesketh. *Foreign Colonial Administration in the Far East.* London: Edward Arnold, 1928.

Burchett, W.G. *Mekong Upstream: A Visit to Laos and Cambodia.* Berlin: Seven Seas Publishers, 1959.

Cambodia. Ministry of Foreign Affairs. *Black Paper: Facts and Evidence of Aggression and Annexation Against Kampuchea.* Phnom Penh: September, 1978.

_____. "The Revolutionary Army of Kampuchea," *Democratic Kampuchea Is Moving Forward* [Phnom Penh], August 1977.

Cambodian Documentation Commission. *The Case Against the Khmer Rouge.* New York: Columbia University, 1986.

Cambodian Information Office. *Cambodia Update,* May 1987, 1–4.

"Cambodia to Have MiGs?," *Armed Forces* [London], 6, No. 5, May 1987.

Carney, Timothy. "Heng Samrin's Armed Forces and the Military Balance in Cambodia," *International Journal of Politics,* 16, No. 3, Fall 1986, 150–85.

Center for Defense Information. "Soviet Geopolitical Momentum: Myth or Menace? Trends of Soviet Influence Around the World from 1945," *Defense Monitor,* 15, No. 5, 1986.

Chanda, Nayan. *Brother Enemy: The War After the War.* San Diego: Harcourt Brace Jovanovich, 1986.

_____. "Cambodia in 1986: Beginning to Tire," *Asian Survey,* 27, No. 1, January 1987, 115–24.

Chandler, David P. *A History of Cambodia.* Boulder, Colorado: Westview Press, 1983.

Colbert, Evelyn. "Standing Pat," *Foreign Policy,* Spring 1984, 139–55.

Defense and Foreign Affairs Handbook. Washington: Perth, 1987.

Delvert, Jean. *Le Paysan Cambodgien.* Paris and The Hague: Mouton, 1961.

Duiker, William J. "Applying the Lessons of Vietnam: The View from Hanoi," *Indochina Issues,* No. 68, August 1986.

Economist Intelligence Unit. *Country Report, Indochina: Vietnam, Laos, Cambodia, No. 1* [London], 1986.

Elliott, David W.P. (ed.). *The Third Indochina Conflict.* Boulder, Colorado: Westview Press, 1981.

Etcheson, Craig. *The Rise and Demise of Democratic Kampuchea.* Boulder, Colorado: Westview Press, 1984.

Fall, Bernard B. *The Two Viet-Nams: A Political and Military Analysis.* New York: Frederick A. Praeger, 1963.

Golub, Stephen. *Seeking Shelter: Cambodians in Thailand.* New York: Lawyers Committee for Human Rights, 1986.

Gordon, Bernard K. *The Dimensions of Conflict in Southeast Asia.* Englewood Cliffs, New Jersey: Prentice-Hall, 1966.

––––––. "The Third Indochina Conflict," *Foreign Affairs,* 65, No. 1, Fall 1986, 66–85.

Gordon, Bernard K., and Anne V. Cyr. *Cambodia and Southeast Asian Regionalism.* Washington: Research Analysis Corporation, 1969.

Grant, Jonathan S. (ed.). *Cambodia: The Widening War in Indochina.* New York: Washington Square Press, 1971.

Haing Ngor (with Roger Warner). *A Cambodian Odyssey.* New York: Macmillan, 1987.

Hammer, Ellen J. *The Struggle for Indochina.* Stanford, California: Stanford University Press, 1954.

"Hanoi Deploys More Troops to Kampuchean Border," *Asian Defence Journal* [Kuala Lumpur], 3, March 1986, 128.

International Documentation and Information Center (INTERDOC). *Cambodia: Problems of Neutrality and Independence.* The Hague: May 1970.

Kangtap Padevat [Phnom Penh], July 1, 1987, 7.

Khmer Nationalist Joint Office of Information. "K.P.N.L.F. Bulletin," [Tokyo], 1986–87.

Kiernan, Ben. *How Pol Pot Came to Power.* London: Verso, 1984.

Kiljunen, Kimmo (ed.). *Kampuchea: Decade of the Genocide—Report of a Finnish Inquiry Commission.* London: Zed Books, 1984.

Kobelev, Yevgeny (ed.). *Kampuchea: From Tragedy to Rebirth.* (Trans., Patricia Beriozkina and Galina Glagoleva.) Moscow: Progress Publishers, 1985.

"The K.P.N.L.F. and ANS to Coordinate Military Activities," *Asian Defence Journal* [Kuala Lumpur], No. 8, August 1985, 112–13.

Laurent, Maurice. *L'Armee au Cambodge et dans les pays envoie de developpement du Sud-est asiatique.* Paris: Presses universitaires de France, 1968.

Lawyers Committee for Human Rights. *Kampuchea: After the Worst.* New York: 1985.

Lebra, Joyce C. *Japanese-Trained Armies in Southeast Asia: Independence and Volunteer Forces in World War II.* New York: Columbia University Press, 1977.

Leifer, Michael. *Cambodia, The Search for Security.* New York: Frederick A. Praeger, 1967.

The Military Balance, 1986–1987. London: International Institute for Strategic Studies, 1986.

The Military Balance, 1987–1988. London: International Institute for Strategic Studies, 1987.

"The Military Occupation of Kampuchea," *Indochina Report* [Singapore], No. 3, July–September 1985.

Morris, Stephen J. "Vietnam's Vietnam," *Atlantic Monthly*, January 1983, 71–82.

"Mutiny in the Khmer Viet Army," *Asian Defence Journal* [Kuala Lumpur], No. 7, July 1986, 96.

Nixon, Richard. *U.S. Foreign Policy for the 1970s: A New Strategy for Peace.* (A Report to the Congress.) Washington: GPO, 1970.

_____. *U.S. Foreign Policy for the 1970s: Building for Peace.* (A Report to the Congress.) Washington: GPO, 1971.

_____. *U.S. Foreign Policy for the 1970s: The Emerging Structure of Peace.* (A Report to the Congress.) Washington: GPO, 1972.

Poole, Peter A. *Expansion of the Vietnam War into Cambodia.* (Southeast Asia series.) Athens, Ohio: Ohio University Center for International Studies, 1970.

Pym, Christopher. *The Ancient Civilization of Angkor.* New York and Toronto: New American Library, Mentor Books, 1968.

Quinn, Kenneth. "Cambodian Secret Police." Pages 195–232 in Jonathan R. Adelman (ed.), *Terror and Communist Politics: The Role of the Secret Police in Communist States.* Boulder, Colorado: Westview Press, 1984.

Quinn-Judge, Paul. "The Khmer Resistance: State of the Union," *Indochina Issues*, No. 40, September 1983.

Rogers, William P. *United States Foreign Policy, 1969–1970: A Report of the Secretary of State.* (General Foreign Policy Series 254, Publication 8575.) Washington: GPO, 1971.

_____. *United States Foreign Policy, 1971: A Report of the Secretary of State.* (General Foreign Policy Series 260, Publication 8634.) Washington: GPO, 1972.

_____. *United States Foreign Policy, 1972: A Report of the Secretary of State.* (General Foreign Policy Series 274, Publication 8699.) Washington: GPO, 1973.

Rowan, Roy. *The Four Days of Mayaguez.* New York: W.W. Norton and Company, 1975.

Shawcross, William. *The Quality of Mercy: Cambodia, Holocaust, and Modern Conscience.* New York: Simon and Schuster, 1984.

_____. *Sideshow: Kissinger, Nixon and the Destruction of Cambodia.* New York: Simon and Schuster, 1979.

Sihanouk, Prince Norodom. *Ombre Sur Angkor.* Phnom Penh: Sangkum Reastr Niyum, 1968.

_____. *War and Hope: The Case for Cambodia.* (Trans., Mary Feeney.) New York: Pantheon Books, 1980.

Sihanouk, Prince Norodom (as related to Wilfred Burchett). *My War with the CIA: Cambodia's Fight for Survival.* London: Penguin Books, 1973.

Sisowath, Prince Thomico. "Norodom Sihanouk and the Khmer Factions," *Indochina Report* [Singapore], No. 9, October–December 1986.

Smith, Roger M. *Cambodia's Foreign Policy.* Ithaca, New York: Cornell University Press, 1965.

Solarz, Stephen J. "When to Intervene," *Foreign Policy,* No. 63, Summer 1986, 20–39.

Sutsakhan, Sak. *The Khmer Republic at War and the Final Collapse.* Washington: U.S. Army Center of Military History, 1980.

Swaan, Wim. *Lost Cities of Asia: Ceylon, Pagan, and Angkor.* London: Elek Books, 1966.

Teston, Eugéne, and Maurice Percheron (eds.). *L'Indochine Moderne.* Paris: Librairie de France, 1931.

Thach Bunroeun. *The Kampuchea-Krom Geopolitical Issue.* New York: The National Association of Khmer Kampuchea-Krom, 1986.

Thayer, Carlyle A. "The Vietnam People's Army Today," *Indochina Issues,* No. 72, January 1987.

United Kingdom. Central Office of Information. *Vietnam, Laos and Cambodia: Chronology of Events 1945–68.* London: British Information Services, 1968.

United Kingdom. "Human Rights Violations in Democratic Kampuchea," *Foreign Policy Documents,* No. 25, July 14, 1978.

United States. Congress. 93d, 1st Session. Senate. Committee on Foreign Relations. Subcommittee on U.S. Security Agreements and Commitments Abroad. *Thailand, Laos, Cambodia, and Vietnam, April 1973: A Staff Report.* Washington: GPO, 1973.

_____. Congress. 97th. 2d Session. House. Committee on Foreign Affairs. Subcommittees on Asian and Pacific Affairs and Human Rights and International Organizations. *The Democratic Kampuchea Seat at the United Nations and American Interests.* (Hearings September 15, 1982.) Washington: GPO, 1983.

_____. Congress. 100th, 1st Session. Senate and House. Committees on Foreign Relations and Foreign Affairs of the Senate and the House of Representatives. *Country Reports on Human Rights Practices for 1986.* Washington: GPO, 1987.

_____. Department of State. Bureau of Public Affairs. *Background Notes: Kampuchea* (Cambodia). Washington: GPO, May 1984.

_____. Department of State. "Chronology of Developments Affecting Cambodia, AD 200–1969," Bangkok, February 7, 1975.

_____. Department of State. "Chronology of Developments Affecting Cambodia, June 1969–May 1970," Bangkok, February 7, 1975.

_____. Department of State. "Chronology of Developments Affecting Cambodia, May 1970–December 1974," Bangkok, February 7, 1975.

United States. General Accounting Office. *U.S. Assistance to the Khmer Republic (Cambodia)* (Report to the Congress.) Washington: GPO, 1973.

Van der Kroef, Justus M. "Dynamics of the Cambodian Conflict," *Conflict Studies* [London], No. 183, 1985.

_____. "A New Phase in the Cambodian Conflict," *Issues & Studies* [Taipei], 21, No. 7, July 1985, 109–29.

Vo Dong Giang. "The View from Hanoi," *World Policy Journal,* 3, No. 1, Winter 1985–86, 107–26.

Wales, Horace Geoffrey Quaritch. *Ancient South-east Asian Warfare.* London: B. Quaritch, 1952.

White, Peter T. "Kampuchea Awakens from a Nightmare," *National Geographic,* 161, No. 5, May 1982, 590–621.

_____. "The Temples of Angkor, Ancient Glory in Stone," *National Geographic,* 161, No. 5, May 1982, 552–89.

Willenson, Kim, et al. *The Bad War: An Oral History of the Vietnam War.* New York and Scarborough, Ontario: New American Library, 1987.

Wood, W.A.R. *A History of Siam.* Bangkok: The Siam Barnakich Press, 1926.

Glossary

bodhisattva—One destined to become a buddha (enlightened one); a person who has achieved enlightenment, but who defers achieving nirvana in order to help others achieve it.

Cham—Also known as Chams, as Khmer Islam, and as Cham-Malay; a Muslim minority people.

fiscal year (FY)—Calendar year.

Gross domestic product (GDP)—The value of domestic goods and services produced by an economy over a certain period, such as a year. Only output of goods for final consumption and for investment are included because the values of primary and of intermediate production are assumed to be included in final prices. GDP sometimes is aggregated and shown in market prices, meaning that indirect taxes and subsidies are included; when these have been eliminated, the reductions for depreciation of physical assets have not been made. *See also* gross national product.

Gross national product (GNP)—gross domestic product (GDP) adjusted by net income (such as return on investments), or loss (such as debt service payments), arising from transactions with foreign countries. GNP is the broadest measure of the output of goods and of services by an economy. It can be calculated at market prices, which include indirect taxes and subsidies. GNP is often calculated at factor cost by removing indirect taxes and subsidies because these are only transfer payments. *See also* gross domestic product.

International Monetary Fund (IMF)—Established along with the World Bank (*q.v.*) in 1945, the IMF is a specialized agency affiliated with the United Nations; it is responsible for stabilizing international exchange rates and payments. The main business of the IMF is the provision of loans to its members (including industrialized and developing countries) when they experience balance of payments difficulties. These loans frequently carry conditions that require substantial internal economic adjustments by the recipients, most of which are developing countries.

Phumphaek—Six areas into which Cambodia was divided in 1973.

riel—The Khmer Republic's currency unit, divided into 100 sen. Since October 29, 1971, its exchange rate has been adjusted by the National Bank of Cambodia according to market fluctuations; the initial rate, set on October 29, 1971, was 140 riels

341

to US$1. Past exchange rates have been 35 riels to US$1 (January 1955 to August 1969) and 55.4 riels to US$1 (August 1969 to October 1971, following devaluation).

ruble—The Soviet Union's currency unit. In June 1987, its value was approximately 0.64 rubles to US$1.

sangha—Ascetic community within which a man can improve his karma; brotherhood of Buddhist monks; the Theravada Buddhist clergy.

World Bank—Informal name used to designate a group of three affiliated international institutions: the International Bank for Reconstruction and Development (IBRD), the International Development Association (IDA), and the International Finance Corporation (IFC). The IBRD, established in 1945, has the primary purpose of providing loans to developing countries for productive projects. The IDA, a legally separate loan fund, administered, however, by the staff of the IBRD, was set up in 1960 to furnish credits to the poorest developing countries on much easier terms than those of conventional IBRD loans. The IFC, founded in 1956, supplements the activities of the IBRD through loans and through assistance designed specifically to encourage the growth of productive private enterprises in the less developed countries. The president and certain senior officers of the IBRD hold the same positions in the IFC. The three institutions are owned by the governments of the countries that subscribe their capital. To participate in the World Bank group, member states must first belong to the International Monetary Fund (*q.v.*).

Index

Abdul Gaffar Peangmeth, 206
achar (ritualist), 96, 97, 121
Acquired Immune Deficiency Syndrome (AIDS), 135
administrative divisions (*see also* Naval Zone Five; provincial divisions; Special Military Administrative Zone), 81; Khmer Rouge, 60–61; PRK, xxi, 214, 261–62
agriculture sector (*see also* irrigation system), 141, 145, 148; collectivization of, xvii, xxxii, 90, 151, 153–54, 157, 160–62; commercial crops of, 164–65; development under Vietnamese-directed regime, 158; under Khmer Rouge regime, 58–59, 152–53; livestock production of, 165; principal food crops of, xvii–xviii, 162–64; slash-and-burn, 76, 85, 101; taxation of, 177
air force: KPRAF, 181, 267, 291, 292
Air Kampuchea, xix, 181–82
airlifts, 48, 260
airports/airfields, xix, 181–82
airspace violations, 33, 41 (*see also* Menu series)
air strikes (*see also* Arclight missions; Menu series), connected with Second Indochina War, xxix; against North Vietnam and Khmer Rouge, 5, 45; by United States, 45–46, 68, 255, 260, 263; by Vietnam, 68
Alliance of Communist Youth of Kampuchea, 57
Alliance of Democratic Khmer Youth, 57
American Catholic Relief Services, 174
American Friends Service Committee, 174
Amnesty International, 51, 301, 302
Ang Chan (Khmer king), 13
Ang Duong (Khmer king), 15, 16, 243
Ang Eng (Khmer king), 15
Angkar (Angkar Loeu), 47, 51–55, 61–62
Angkor, xxvi–xxvii, 3, 12, 16, 25
Angkorian period, xxvi, 9, 11, 36, 87, 242
Angkor Thom, xxvi, 3, 11, 12
Angkor Wat, 10–11, 44, 242
Ang Snuol, 47
animism, 57, 124–25

Annam, 18, 36
ANS. *See* Sihanouk National Army (ANS)
arak (spirits), 121
Aranyaprathet (Thailand), 68, 86
Arclight missions, 45–46
armed forces: of CGDK, xxi; development and expansion of, 247, 257; of Vietnam occupation, 276–95; of PRK, xxii
Army of the Republic of Vietnam (ARVN), 33
ASEAN. *See* Association of Southeast Asian Nations (ASEAN)
Asian Development Bank, xx, 150, 169
assimilation, xxix, 103, 104, 108
Association of Democratic Khmer Women, 54–55
Association of Southeast Asian Nations (ASEAN), 187, 224–25; assistance to and support for CGDK by, xxiii, xxxiv–xxxv; position on PRK of, 191, 196; role in coalition government (CGDK) creation, 268, 275; role in conflict resolution in Cambodia of, xxxiv, 225
Association of Vietnamese in Cambodia, 136
atrocities: by Khmer Rouge, 47, 68, 190–92
Australia, 149
Austroasiatic origin, 6, 110
Austronesian languages/groups (*see also* Cham; Jarai; Rade; Malay), 14, 15, 101, 112
autonomous zone, xxviii, 25
Ayutthaya, 105

Bahnaric language (Mon-Khmer), 111
Ba Kev, 143
balance of payments (*see also* trade deficit), xvii, xviii
Bandung Conference (1955), 31
bang classification, 107
Bangkok, 25, 79
Bangkok Plot, 252
banking system, 176
Bantay Meanchey province, xiv

Published Country Studies

(Area Handbook Series)

550-65	Afghanistan		550-153	Ghana
550-98	Albania		550-87	Greece
550-44	Algeria		550-78	Guatemala
550-59	Angola		550-174	Guinea
550-73	Argentina		550-82	Guyana
550-169	Australia		550-151	Honduras
550-176	Austria		550-165	Hungary
550-175	Bangladesh		550-21	India
550-170	Belgium		550-154	Indian Ocean
550-66	Bolivia		550-39	Indonesia
550-20	Brazil		550-68	Iran
550-168	Bulgaria		550-31	Iraq
550-61	Burma		550-25	Israel
550-37	Burundi/Rwanda		550-182	Italy
550-50	Cambodia		550-30	Japan
550-166	Cameroon		550-34	Jordan
550-159	Chad		550-56	Kenya
550-77	Chile		550-81	Korea, North
550-60	China		550-41	Korea, South
550-26	Colombia		550-58	Laos
550-33	Commonwealth Caribbean, Islands of the		550-24	Lebanon
550-91	Congo		550-38	Liberia
550-90	Costa Rica		550-85	Libya
550-69	Côte d'Ivoire (Ivory Coast)		550-172	Malawi
550-152	Cuba		550-45	Malaysia
550-22	Cyprus		550-161	Mauritania
550-158	Czechoslovakia		550-79	Mexico
550-36	Dominican Republic/Haiti		550-76	Mongolia
550-52	Ecuador		550-49	Morocco
550-43	Egypt		550-64	Mozambique
550-150	El Salvador		550-88	Nicaragua
550-28	Ethiopia		550-157	Nigeria
550-167	Finland		550-94	Oceania
550-155	Germany, East		550-48	Pakistan
550-173	Germany, Fed. Rep. of		550-46	Panama